HARCOURT HORIZONS

About My Community

TEACHER'S EDITION

VOLUME 2

Harcourt
SCHOOL PUBLISHERS

Orlando Austin New York San Diego Toronto London

Visit *The Learning Site!*
www.harcourtschool.com

HARCOURT HORIZONS

ABOUT MY COMMUNITY

Video segments are provided by **Reading Rainbow**.
For a catalog of all **Reading Rainbow** videos, CD-ROMs, and DVDs, contact:

Reading Rainbow
C/O GPN/University of Nebraska
P.O. Box 80669
Lincoln, NE 68501-0669
Call: 1-800-228-4630
E-mail: gpn@unl.edu
Internet: gpn.unl.edu

For permission to reprint copyrighted material, grateful acknowledgment is made to the following sources:

Atheneum Books for Young Readers, an imprint of Simon & Schuster Children's Publishing Division: "Someday Someone Will Bet You That You Can't Name All Fifty States" from *Sad Underwear and Other Complications* by Judith Viorst. Text copyright © 1995 by Judith Viorst.

Doubleday, a division of Random House, Inc.: "Celebration" by Alonzo Lopez from *Whispering Wind*, edited by Terry Allen. Text copyright © 1972 by the Institute of American Indian Arts.

Elizabeth M. Hauser: "Fourth of July" from *Around and About* by Marchette Chute. Text copyright 1957 by E. P. Dutton & Co.; text copyright renewed 1985 by Marchette Chute.

Margaret Hillert: "Just Me" by Margaret Hillert.

Henry Holt and Company, LLC: "At the Store" from *Is Somewhere Always Far Away? Poems About Places* by Leland B. Jacobs. Text © 1993 by Allan D. Jacobs.

Marian Reiner: "Martin Luther King" from *No Way of Knowing: Dallas Poems* by Myra Cohn Livingston. Text copyright © 1980 by Myra Cohn Livingston. Published by Margaret K. McElderry Books.

S©ott Treimel NY: "Rules" from *Alexander Soames: His Poems* by Karla Kuskin. Text copyright © 1962, 1980 by Karla Kuskin.

Printed in the United States of America.
ISBN 0-15-339627-X

3 4 5 6 7 8 9 10 032 13 12 11 10 09 08 07 06 05

Contents

About My Community

TABBED SECTION

Harcourt Horizons

Components

For content updates and additional information for teaching Harcourt Horizons, see The Learning Site: Social Studies Center at www.harcourtschool.com.

STUDENT SUPPORT MATERIALS	K	1	2	3	4	5	6
Pupil Editions*		•	•	•	•	•	•
Big Book*	•						
Unit Big Books*		•	•				
Activity Books*	•	•	•	•	•	•	•
Time for Kids Readers*	•	•	•	•	•	•	•

TEACHER SUPPORT MATERIALS	K	1	2	3	4	5	6
Teacher's Editions*	•	•	•	•	•	•	•
Activity Books, Teacher's Editions*				•	•	•	•
Assessment Programs*		•	•	•	•	•	•
Skills Transparencies*		•	•	•	•	•	•
Reading and Vocabulary Transparencies*		•	•	•	•	•	•
Audiotext Collections*	•	•	•	•	•	•	•

The Learning Site

TECHNOLOGY	K	1	2	3	4	5	6
The Learning Site: Social Studies Center	•	•	•	•	•	•	•
GeoSkills CD-ROM*		•	•	•	•	•	•
Field Trip Videos*		•	•	•	•	•	•

* Available in Spanish

HARCOURT HORIZONS

About My Community

Harcourt
SCHOOL PUBLISHERS

Orlando Austin New York San Diego Toronto London

Visit *The Learning Site!*
www.harcourtschool.com

HARCOURT HORIZONS

ABOUT MY COMMUNITY

General Editor

Dr. Michael J. Berson
Associate Professor
Social Science Education
University of South Florida
Tampa, Florida

Contributing Authors

Dr. Sherry Field
Associate Professor
The University of Texas at Austin
Austin, Texas

Dr. Tyrone Howard
Assistant Professor
UCLA Graduate School of Education & Information Studies
University of California at Los Angeles
Los Angeles, California

Dr. Bruce E. Larson
Associate Professor of Teacher Education and Social Studies
Western Washington University
Bellingham, Washington

Series Consultants

Dr. Robert Bednarz
Professor
Department of Geography
Texas A&M University
College Station, Texas

Dr. Robert P. Green, Jr.
Professor
School of Education
Clemson University
Clemson, South Carolina

Dr. Asa Grant Hilliard III
Fuller E. Callaway Professor of Urban Education
Georgia State University
Atlanta, Georgia

Dr. Thomas M. McGowan
Chairperson and Professor
Center for Curriculum and Instruction
University of Nebraska
Lincoln, Nebraska

Dr. John J. Patrick
Professor of Education
Indiana University
Bloomington, Indiana

Dr. Cinthia Salinas
Assistant Professor
Department of Curriculum and Instruction
University of Texas at Austin
Austin, Texas

Dr. Philip VanFossen
Associate Professor, Social Studies Education, and Associate Director, Purdue Center for Economic Education
Purdue University
West Lafayette, Indiana

Dr. Hallie Kay Yopp
Professor
Department of Elementary, Bilingual, and Reading Education
California State University, Fullerton
Fullerton, California

Classroom Reviewers

Dr. Linda Bennett
Assistant Professor
Social Studies Education
Early Childhood and Elementary Education Department
University of Missouri–Columbia
Columbia, Missouri

Rhonda Inzer
Teacher
Vegas Verdes Elementary School
Las Vegas, Nevada

Margaret Massengale
District Social Studies Supervisor
Cleveland Municipal School District
Cleveland, Ohio

Beverly McNair
Teacher
Hollis Hand Elementary School
La Grange, Georgia

Cathy Nelson
Elementary Social Studies Coordinator
Columbus City School District—Northgate Center
Columbus, Ohio

Nancy Pendergrass
Teacher
Jason Lee Elementary School
Portland, Oregan

Karen Ann Ricketts
Teacher
Central Elementary School
Flushing, Michigan

Linda Stephenson
Teacher
Bear Road Elementary School
North Syracuse, New York

Mable Thompson
Reading Coach
F. S. Ervin Elementary School
Pine Hill, Alabama

Sidonia Todd
Teacher
Tanglewood Elementary School
Fort Myers, Florida

Amy Walker
Teacher
Bascomb Elementary School
Woodstock, Georgia

Maps
researched and prepared by

Readers
written and designed by

Take a Field Trip
video tour segments provided by

School Permissions and Copyrights
Harcourt, Inc.
6277 Sea Harbor Drive
Orlando, Florida 32887-6777
Fax: 407-345-2418

Acknowledgments appear in the back of this book.

Printed in the United States of America

ISBN 0-15-339616-4

1 2 3 4 5 6 7 8 9 10 032 13 12 11 10 09 08 07 06 05 04

Contents

· UNIT ·

Our Government

Prior Knowledge

v

· UNIT ·

3

Looking at the Earth

Categorize

VI

· UNIT ·

4

Learn About People

Generalize

VII

· UNIT ·

5

Past and Present

Sequence

VIII

· UNIT ·

6

People at Work

Summarize

Reference

Features You Can Use

Skills

Chart and Graph Skills

Citizenship Skills

Map and Globe Skills

Reading Skills

Music and Literature

Primary Sources

Examine Primary Sources

American Documents

x

Biography

Geography

Heritage

Science and Technology

Charts, Graphs, and Diagrams

XI

Maps

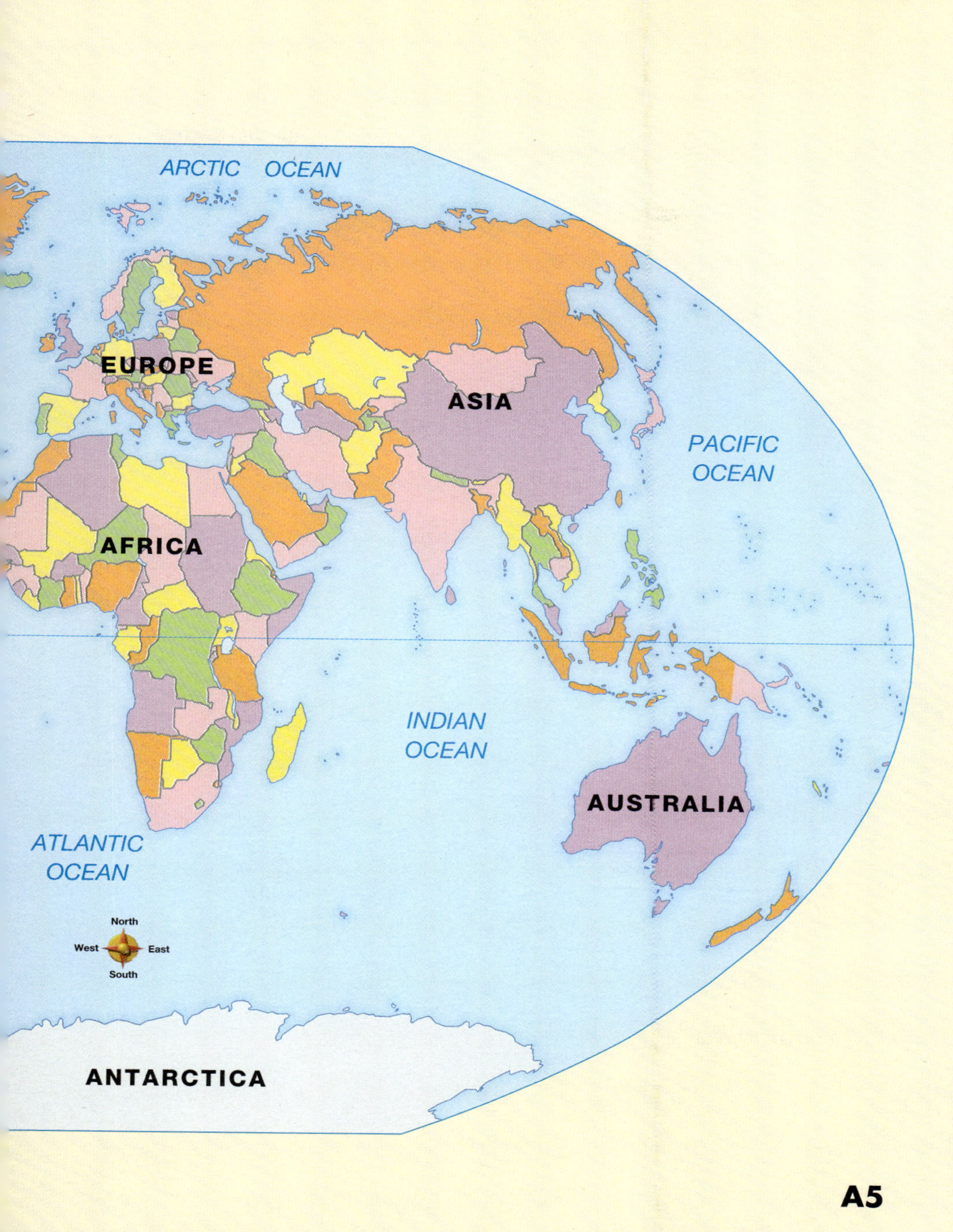

Map Study

Geography Point out that the map on these pages shows country borders as well as the continents. Remind children that a border or boundary is where one place begins and another ends.

Q Which continent do you think has the most countries? Why?

A Africa; there are more country borders shown on the map for this continent than for any other.

Visual Learning

Map Direct attention to the continent of North America and help children locate the boundary lines of the continent.

Q Can you name any of the countries of North America from memory?

A Answers may include: the United States, Canada, Mexico, Guatemala, Belize, Honduras, El Salvador, Nicaragua, Costa Rica, Panama

Make sure children understand the countries of Central America are part of the North American continent.

CD-ROM

Explore GEOSKILLS CD-ROM to give children additional practice using map and globe skills.

INTEGRATE ART

Illustrate a Continent Have children each choose one continent and draw the outline of it on a large sheet of paper. Ask them to research something about the continent, such as the land and water found there. Have them draw or cut out magazine pictures and write phrases on their outlines to tell about the continent. Tell children to write the name and location of the continent in the world, such as *Australia is south of Asia and north of Antarctica. It is bordered by the Indian and Pacific Oceans.*

EXTEND AND ENRICH

Play a Game Invite small groups of children to play Which Continent Am I? Have group members write several clues about each continent—for example, *I am mostly south of the equator; one of my borders is the Pacific Ocean; I have more than ten countries.* Have group members read the clues one by one to another group until someone names the correct continent. (South America)

INTERNET RESOURCES

Go to **www.harcourtschool.com** for more information about continents.

Atlas

Set the Purpose

Main Idea A map can be used to show a general view, or overview, of a place.

Why It Matters Ask a volunteer to read the title of the map. Explain that knowing how to read an overview map helps you more easily compare places.

Map Study

Geography Explain that the overview map on these pages shows part of North America. It shows the names of the countries and major bodies of water.

Q **What other places are shown on this map?**

A islands in the Atlantic Ocean and Gulf of Mexico; the island of Greenland

Q **Why would these places be shown on a map of North America?**

A They are considered part of the continent of North America.

Sometimes the southern portions of the Pacific, Atlantic, and Indian Oceans are referred to as the world's fifth ocean, or the Southern Ocean. However, this term is not universally used, and many major cartographers do not recognize it.

Visual Learning

Map Ask volunteers to compare the labels used for bodies of water.

Q **How are the labels for the Pacific Ocean and Hudson Bay different?**

A The ocean label is in bigger type.

Q **What does this tell you about the two bodies of water?**

A The ocean is bigger than the bay.

Have children compare the Gulf of Mexico and the Gulf of California and explain what the labels reveal. (The Gulf of California is smaller than the Gulf of Mexico.)

REACH ALL LEARNERS

Tactile Learners Provide children with an unlabeled outline map of North America. Have them color in each country and write the country names and major bodies of water on the maps. Ask children to title their maps.

REACH ALL LEARNERS

Below-Level Learners Invite children to look at the compass rose on the maps in this section and on other maps that you have available. Then invite them to create their own compass roses. Encourage them to be creative, but make sure they include the letter labels for *North*, *South*, *East*, and *West*. Display their compass roses around a large overview map. Have children take turns describing a feature on the map, using a compass rose for reference.

ICELAND
Greenland (DENMARK)
Hudson Bay
CANADA
Lake Superior
Lake Michigan
Lake Huron
Lake Ontario
Lake Erie
UNITED STATES
ATLANTIC OCEAN
California
MEXICO
Gulf of Mexico
BAHAMAS
CUBA
DOMINICAN REPUBLIC
HAITI
Puerto Rico (U.S.)

Map Study

Geography Point out that the map on these pages shows national borders. Ask children to run their fingers along the boundaries.

Q **What countries border the United States?**

A Canada and Mexico

Q **Which is the northernmost country in North America?**

A Canada

Q **Why do you think there is no boundary line along the Gulf of Mexico?**

A The Gulf of Mexico forms the boundary; the dark lines only show national land borders.

Visual Learning

Map Direct attention to the shading of the United States on the map.

Q **Why is the area in the western corner of Canada shaded the same as the United States?**

A It is shaded like the United States because it is part of the United States.

Q **Are there other places that belong to the United States? How can you tell?**

A The islands in the far left corner of the map are part of the United States; they are shaded like the United States.

Have children find the places that are not on the mainland United States but are part of the United States. (Alaska, Hawaii)

EXTEND AND ENRICH

Draw a State Overview Map
Provide children with maps showing the states of the United States. Have them work with partners to locate their state and to draw an overview map of their state. Remind children that an overview map is a general view of a place. Suggest they include any major bodies of water and the names of states that border their state.

INTERNET RESOURCES

Gc to **www.harcourtschool.com** for more information about North America.

CD-ROM

Explore GEOSKILLS CD-ROM to give children additional practice using map and globe skills.

Atlas

Set the Purpose

Main Idea A map can be used to show where land and water exist in our country.

Why It Matters Ask children to look at the map on pages A8–A9 and guess what it shows. Then have a volunteer read the title of the map. Explain that knowing how to identify land and water on a United States map helps you know what places in our country look like.

Map Study

Geography Discuss the features of the land and water map.

Q **What place does this map show?**

A the United States

Q **How can you find mountains on this map?**

A Mountainous areas look more wrinkled.

Q **What are the largest mountain ranges?**

A Rocky Mountains, Appalachian Mountains

Have children turn to the overview map on pages A6–A7 and locate the states of Alaska and Hawaii. Explain that the scale used to draw this map makes it possible to show Alaska and Hawaii in their actual places. Then have children compare that map to the land and water map of the United States on these pages. Point out that the scale used to draw this map makes it necessary to place the states of Alaska and Hawaii as insets.

Visual Learning

Map Direct attention to the insets of Alaska and Hawaii.

Q **What do you notice about the land and water in Alaska and Hawaii?**

A Both have mountains; both are on the ocean—Hawaii is a group of islands in the ocean.

Q **What countries are nearest to Alaska?**

A Canada and Russia

INTEGRATE MATHEMATICS

How Far Across? Ask small groups of children to compare the distance scales on the insets of Alaska and Hawaii. Have them measure to find the longest distance across the largest island in the Hawaiian Islands. (about 100 miles) Then ask them to measure to find the longest distance across the main part of Alaska. (about 750 miles) Encourage them to first mark the distance on a piece of paper and then use their markings to measure against the scale.

REACH ALL LEARNERS

Advanced Learners Invite small groups to play a Land and Water game. Assign each group some specific features from the map on these pages. Have children write several clues about their assigned feature. For example, children might say: *I am one of the longest rivers in the United States; I empty into the Gulf of Mexico; other rivers empty into me. What am I?* Ask group members to read the clues one by one to the class until someone names the correct feature. (Mississippi River)

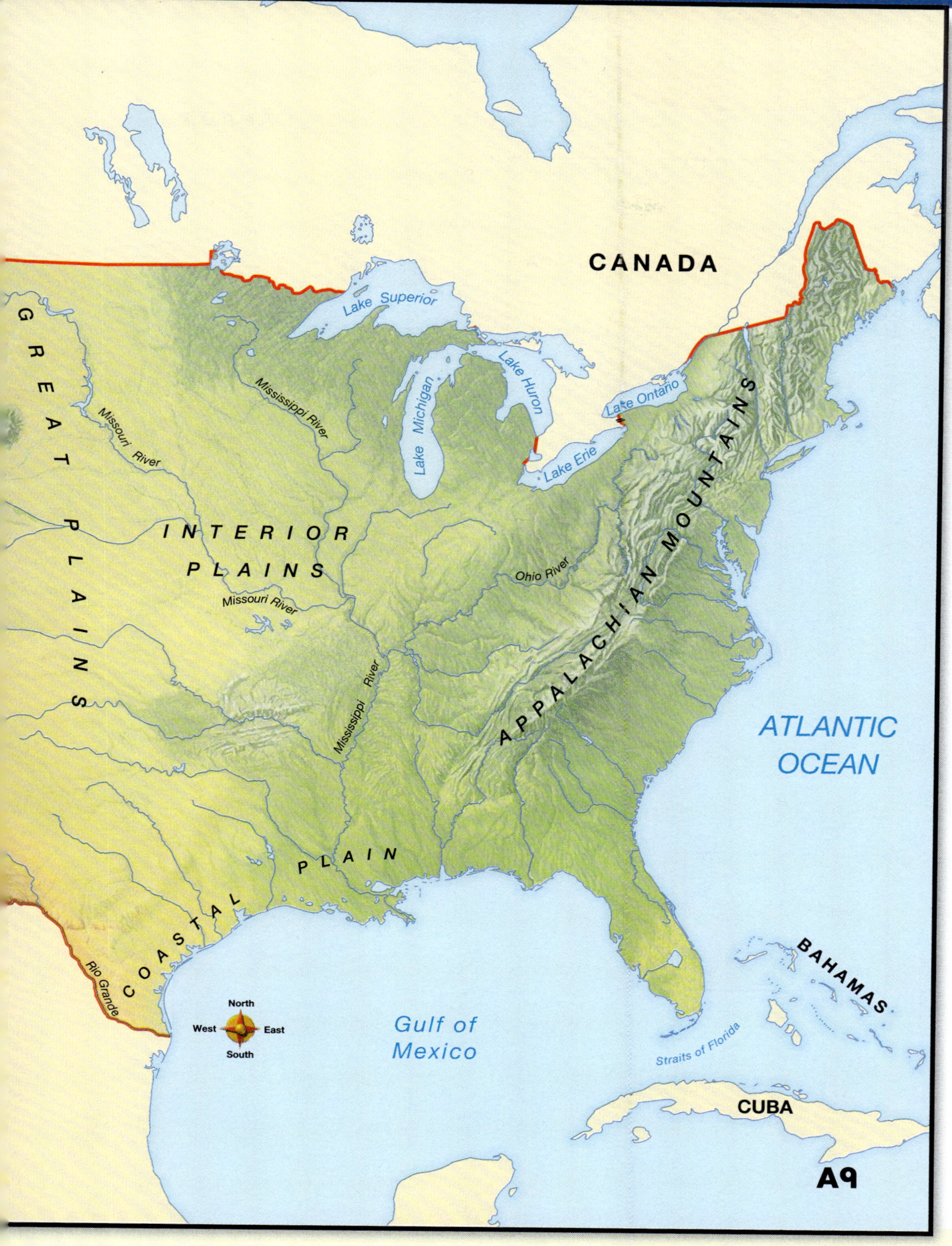

Visual Learning

Map Have children locate the major rivers that flow through the plains on the map.

Q **How can you find rivers on this map?**

A Rivers are blue and are winding and thin.

Q **What are the three long rivers in our country?**

A the Mississippi, Missouri, and Ohio Rivers

Q **Into what large bodies of water do the rivers flow?**

A into the gulfs and oceans

Map Study

Geography Have children compare the land and water map on these pages with the one on pages A2–A3.

Q **How are these maps alike?**

A They both show land and water features.

Q **How are they different?**

A The world map shows the features of all the continents, including North America. The United States map only shows a portion of North America.

CD-ROM

Explore GEOSKILLS CD-ROM to give children additional practice using map and globe skills.

MAKE IT RELEVANT

In Your State Provide children with a land and water map of your state. Have them make a two-column chart to categorize each physical feature of the state as land or water.

EXTEND AND ENRICH

Draw a Land and Water Map
Provide children with an outline map of the United States. Include insets of Alaska and Hawaii. Invite children to draw a box for a map key and use crayons to draw and color symbols in the map key to show the important land and water features. Then have them follow their map key to color the land and water on the map. Have children show mountains, plains, rivers, lakes, and oceans.

Go to **www.harcourtschool.com** for more information about land and water maps.

Atlas

Set the Purpose

Main Idea A map can be used to show where states and their capitals are located in our country.

Why It Matters Point out that the United States is divided into 50 areas of land known as *states*. Invite children to name as many states as they can as you write them on the board. Ask a volunteer to read the title of the map. Explain that knowing how to read a United States map can help you locate states and their capitals.

Map Study

Geography Discuss the features of the map and how the map shows the boundaries between each state. Have children add the names of remaining states to the list they started earlier. Remind children that a state boundary, or border, shows where one state starts and another ends. Have children find their state and outline the boundary with their finger. Point out that a boundary can be land or water.

Q Which states share boundaries with your state?

A Answers depend on the state.

Q Which states have one of the Great Lakes as a boundary?

A Wisconsin, Minnesota, Michigan, Illinois, Indiana, Ohio, New York, Pennsylvania

Visual Learning

Map Have children locate the compass rose on the map.

Q Which states are north, south, east, and west of your state?

A Answers depend on your state.

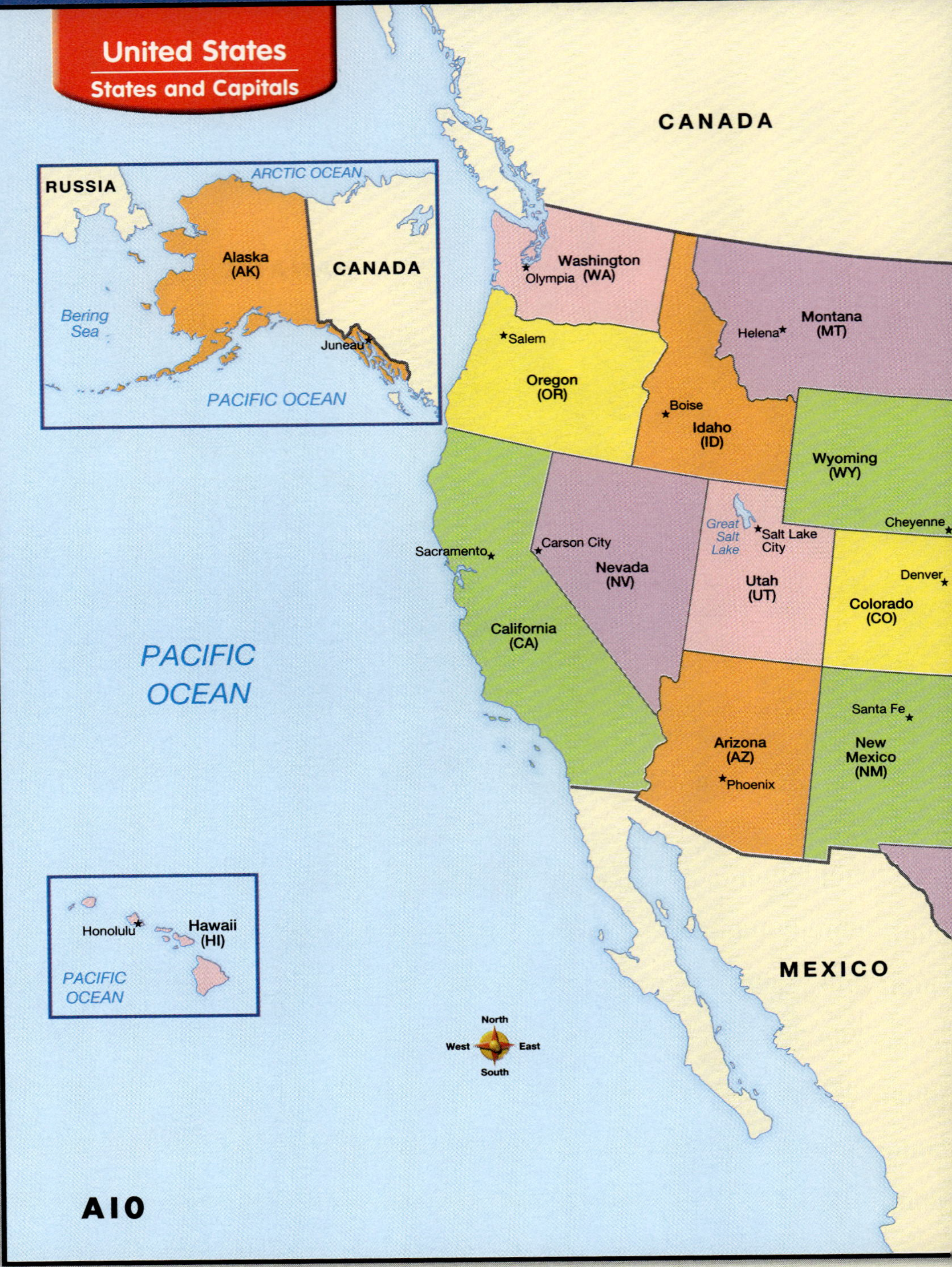

REACH ALL LEARNERS

English as a Second Language Have children make up flash cards that show each state's name and shape on one side and the name of the capital of the state on the other. Invite partners to take turns selecting a card, reading the name of the state, and naming the state's capital.

INTEGRATE LANGUAGE ARTS

Give Directions Invite partners to play What's the Capital City? Have one child silently choose a capital city on the map and guide the partner to it with directions using the compass rose and state names. For example: *Move your finger south from Tennessee to Alabama. Move across Mississippi and Louisiana to the next state. Find the state capital.* Partners follow directions to name the state capital. (Austin) Children switch roles.

CANADA

North Dakota (ND)
Bismarck
Minnesota (MN)
St. Paul
Lake Superior
Michigan (MI)
Lansing
Lake Michigan
Lake Huron
Wisconsin (WI)
Madison
South Dakota (SD)
Pierre
Iowa (IA)
Des Moines
Nebraska (NE)
Lincoln
Illinois (IL)
Springfield
Indiana (IN)
Indianapolis
Ohio (OH)
Columbus
Lake Erie
Lake Ontario
Kansas (KS)
Topeka
Missouri (MO)
Jefferson City
Kentucky (KY)
Frankfort
West Virginia (WV)
Charleston
Oklahoma (OK)
Oklahoma City
Arkansas (AR)
Little Rock
Tennessee (TN)
Nashville
Texas (TX)
Austin
Louisiana (LA)
Baton Rouge
Mississippi (MS)
Jackson
Alabama (AL)
Montgomery
Georgia (GA)
Atlanta
Florida (FL)
Tallahassee
South Carolina (SC)
Columbia
North Carolina (NC)
Raleigh
Virginia (VA)
Richmond
Washington, D.C.
Maryland (MD)
Annapolis
Delaware (DE)
Dover
New Jersey (NJ)
Trenton
Pennsylvania (PA)
Harrisburg
New York (NY)
Albany
Connecticut (CT)
Hartford
Rhode Island (RI)
Providence
Massachusetts (MA)
Boston
Vermont (VT)
Montpelier
New Hampshire (NH)
Concord
Maine (ME)
Augusta
ATLANTIC OCEAN
Gulf of Mexico
BAHAMAS
CUBA
A11

Map Study

Geography Point out the two-letter form of abbreviations for state names on the map. Have children identify the abbreviation for their state. Explain that the abbreviations were introduced by the United States government for use with ZIP codes in mailing addresses, but are now common for other uses. Ask children to share experiences with the abbreviations and ZIP codes.

Visual Learning

Map Direct attention to the symbol that stands for a capital city on the map. Explain that each state has a capital city for its own government. Tell children that our country's capital is Washington, D.C. This capital city does not belong in any state but belongs to the whole nation.

Q What is the name of our state's capital city? How do you know?

A Answer depends on your state; children should recognize that they can find a capital city by first locating the symbol that stands for a capital city on the map.

Q What is the capital city of Pennsylvania? of Arizona?

A Harrisburg; Phoenix

CD-ROM

Explore GEOSKILLS CD-ROM to give children additional practice using map and globe skills.

BACKGROUND

State Capitals Many state capitals are located in the center of a state so that they are easily accessible to as many citizens as possible. However, not all state capitals are located at or near the center of the state. Some of the reasons for this may be that land or water barriers make it hard to travel to the center of the state; the capital may have been chosen before the state's boundaries were determined; or the capital's location may have been the result of a compromise.

EXTEND AND ENRICH

Prepare an Oral Report Invite small groups to research why the capital of your state was chosen. Provide children with appropriate references or access to reference sources on the Internet or a computer. Have groups prepare and give oral reports of their findings.

THE LEARNING SITE

Go to **www.harcourtschool.com** for more maps of the United States.

Atlas

Set the Purpose

Main Idea Geography terms can be used to describe landforms and bodies of water.

Why It Matters Tell children that the geographic dictionary and diagram can be used to help them learn to identify and remember different landforms and bodies of water.

Visual Learning

Diagram Point out that the picture on page A12 is a diagram. Ask children what the diagram shows. (geography terms for landforms and bodies of water) Direct attention to the boldfaced terms and meanings at the bottom of the page. Ask volunteers to read each term and its definition. Then have children locate each body of water or landform in the diagram.

Ask children to share experiences they have had with any of the landforms or bodies of water pictured. Have children identify the larger landforms and bodies of water labeled in the diagram.

Q What bodies of water are shown in the diagram?

A lake, ocean, river, gulf

Q What kinds of land are shown in the diagram?

A desert, forest, hill, island, mountain, plain, valley, peninsula

Map Study

Geography Suggest that children compare the diagram and definitions on this page with the maps on pages A2–A3 and A8–A9. Help children relate the landforms and bodies of water in the dictionary and on the diagram to the areas shown on the maps.

CD-ROM

Explore GEOSKILLS CD-ROM to give children additional practice using map and globe skills.

desert a large, dry area of land
forest a large area of trees
gulf a large body of ocean water that is partly surrounded by land
hill land that rises above the land around it
island a landform with water all around it
lake a body of water with land on all sides
mountain highest kind of land
ocean a body of salt water that covers a large area
peninsula a landform that is surrounded on only three sides by water
plain flat land
river a large stream of water that flows across the land
valley low land between hills or mountains

A12

EXTEND AND ENRICH

Make a Model Invite small groups of children to make a model showing four geographic terms from the diagram. Provide each group with a large piece of cardboard, modeling clay, toothpicks, and small strips of paper to use as labels. Have each group choose two landforms and two bodies of water and make a clay model to show the features. Have group members write the name of each feature on a paper strip, glue the strip to a toothpick, and stick it in the model to label the feature.

INTERNET RESOURCES

Go to **www.harcourtschool.com** for a glossary of geography terms.

Learn About People

A West African djembe

1
2
3
4
5
6

Unit 4 Planning Guide Learn About People

Unit 4 is the story of people. Children will explore the diversity of people in the United States and identify and appreciate examples of various cultures within their own community. They will learn how explorers, pioneers, and immigrants helped make the United States what it is. In addition, children will learn how to follow routes on a map, read a map of world countries, and read a bar graph.

LESSON	PACING	OBJECTIVES	VOCABULARY
Introduce the Unit pp. 161R–161 **Preview the Vocabulary** pp. 162–163A **Start with an Article** pp. 164A–167A	3 Days	■ Use a visual to predict content. ■ Interpret a quotation. ■ Use a main idea chart to prepare for the unit. ■ Use visuals to determine word meanings. ■ Use words and visuals to predict the content of the unit. ■ Obtain information about a topic using a variety of visual sources, such as literature. ■ Identify the Inuit as a Native American culture. ■ Recognize that people of different cultures express themselves in unique ways. ■ Discuss how children and their recreation are alike and different around the world.	**recreation** **Word Work,** pp. 163A, 165
1 Our Country of Many People pp. 168A–169A	2 Days	■ Explore the diversity of the United States. ■ Define *culture*. ■ Compare and contrast people's work, interests, and talents.	**unique** **culture**
READING SKILLS **Find Point of View** pp. 170A–171A	1 Day	■ Recognize that people have different points of view. ■ Relate people's points of view to their culture and environment.	**point of view**
2 People on the Move pp. 172A–175A	3 Days	■ Recognize how explorers led the way for settlement in new places. ■ Discuss the role of pioneers in settling our country. ■ Explain how immigrants bring new ideas when they move.	**explorer** **pioneer** **immigrant**

1 2 3 4 5 6

Time Management

6 WEEKS	WEEK 1	WEEK 2	WEEK 3	WEEK 4	WEEK 5	WEEK 6
	Introduce the Unit / Lessons 1–3	Lessons 1–3	Lessons 1–3	Lessons 4–6	Lessons 4–6	Lessons 4–6 / Wrap Up the Unit

READING	INTEGRATE LEARNING	REACH ALL LEARNERS	RESOURCES
Focus Skill **Generalize,** p. 161 Reading Social Studies: **Make Predictions,** p. 162 Reading Social Studies: **Graphic Organizer,** pp. 164A, 167 Reading Social Studies: **Create Mental Images,** p. 164	**Theme Time,** p. 161I Music **Make a Drum,** p. 161R Language Arts **Write a Biography,** p. 161 Physical Education **Jumping Game,** p. 164 Mathematics **Measure Distance,** p. 166	**English as a Second Language,** pp. 161N, 162 **Below-Level Learners,** pp. 161N, 165 **Advanced Learners,** p. 161N **Kinesthetic Learners,** p. 166 **Extension Activities for Home and School,** p. 167A	**Pupil Book/Unit Big Book,** pp. 161–167 **Audiotext, Unit 4** **Word Cards V47–V48** **Reading and Vocabulary** Transparency 4–1 Internet Resources
Reading Social Studies: **Personal Response,** pp. 168A, 169 Focus Skill **Generalize,** p. 168	Art **Class "Mosaic,"** p. 168	**Extend and Enrich,** p. 168 **Reteach the Lesson,** p. 169 **Extension Activities for Home and School,** p. 169A	**Pupil Book/Unit Big Book,** pp. 168–169 **Word Cards V47–V48** **Activity Book,** p. 40 **Reading and Vocabulary** Transparency 4–2 Internet Resources
	Mathematics **People Graph,** p. 170	**Extend and Enrich,** p. 170 **Auditory Learners,** p. 170 **Reteach the Skill,** p. 171 **Extension Activities for Home and School,** p. 171A	**Pupil Book/Unit Big Book,** pp. 170–171 **Word Cards V47–V48** **Activity Book,** p. 41 **Skill Transparency 4–1**
Reading Social Studies: **Graphic Organizer,** pp. 172A, 175		**Advanced Learners,** p. 173 **Extend and Enrich,** p. 174 **Reteach the Lesson,** p. 175 **Extension Activities for Home and School,** p. 175A	**Pupil Book/Unit Big Book,** pp. 172–175 **Word Cards V49–V50** **Activity Book,** p. 42 **Reading and Vocabulary** Transparency 4–3 Internet Resources

1 2 3 4 5 6

Unit 4 Planning Guide

LESSON	PACING	OBJECTIVES	VOCABULARY
MAP AND GLOBE SKILLS **Follow Routes on a Map** pp. 176A – 177A	1 Day	▪ Find locations on maps. ▪ Determine directions on maps. ▪ Draw maps to show places and routes.	**route**
3 **Family Heritage** pp. 178A–183A	4 Days	▪ Recognize that every family has its own heritage. ▪ Give examples of family traditions. ▪ Appreciate the value of learning from family members.	**heritage** **religion** **tradition** **ancestor**
CHART AND GRAPH SKILLS **Read a Bar Graph** pp. 184A–185A	1 Day	▪ Identify the parts of a bar graph. ▪ Use a bar graph to interpret information.	**bar graph**
4 **Community Celebrations** pp. 186A–189A	3 Days	▪ Identify cultural holidays celebrated in the community. ▪ Describe customs associated with cultural holidays. ▪ Explain the origins of holiday traditions.	**holiday** **custom** **Word Work,** p. 188
5 **Expressions of Culture** pp. 190A–195A	3 Days	▪ Identify and explain expressions of culture in the community. ▪ Identify stories from different cultures. ▪ Identify and explain art forms in different cultures.	**language**

READING	INTEGRATE LEARNING	REACH ALL LEARNERS	RESOURCES
	Reading **Immigration,** p. 173 **Share a Book,** p. 176A	**Tactile Learners,** p. 176 **Extend and Enrich,** p. 176 **Reteach the Skill,** p. 177 **Extension Activities for Home and School,** p. 177A	**Pupil Book/Unit Big Book,** pp. 176–177 **Word Cards V49-V50** **Activity Book,** p. 43 **Skill Transparency 4–2** **GeoSkills CD-ROM**
Reading Social Studies: **Make a Prediction,** pp. 178A, 183 Focus Skill **Generalize,** p. 179	**Languages** **Adobe,** p. 178 **Art** **Houses in Our Town,** p. 178 **Music** **Guitar Music,** p. 179 **Reading** **Family Traditions,** p. 179	**English as a Second Language,** p. 181 **Extend and Enrich,** p. 182 **Reteach the Lesson,** p. 183 **Extension Activities for Home and School,** p. 183A	**Pupil Book/Unit Big Book,** pp. 178–183 **Word Cards V51-V52** **Activity Book,** p. 44 **Activity Pattern P7** **Reading and Vocabulary** Transparency 4–4
		Auditory Learners, p. 184A **Visual Learners,** p. 184 **Extend and Enrich,** p. 184 **Reteach the Skill,** p. 185 **Extension Activities for Home and School,** p. 185A	**Pupil Book/Unit Big Book,** pp. 184–185 **Word Cards V53-V54** **Activity Book,** p. 45 **Skill Transparency 4–3**
Reading Social Studies: **Study Questions,** pp. 186A, 189	**Mathematics** **Chinese Years,** p. 186	**Below-Level Learners,** p. 187 **Extend and Enrich,** p. 188 **Reteach the Lesson,** p. 189 **Extension Activities for Home and School,** p. 189A	**Pupil Book/Unit Big Book,** pp. 186–189 **Word Cards V53-V54** **Activity Book,** p. 46 **Activity Pattern P8** **Reading and Vocabulary** Transparency 4–5 Internet Resources
Reading Social Studies: **Personal Response,** pp. 190A, 195	**Reading** **Cinderella,** p. 191 **Language Arts** **Descriptive Writing,** p. 193 **Music** **Music from Around the World,** p. 194	**English as a Second Language,** p. 190 **Kinesthetic Learners,** p. 194 **Extend and Enrich,** p. 194 **Reteach the Lesson,** p. 195 **Extension Activities for Home and School,** p. 195A	**Pupil Book/Unit Big Book,** pp. 190–195 **Word Cards V53-V54** **Activity Book,** p. 47 **Reading and Vocabulary** Transparency 4–6 Internet Resources

1 2 3 4 5 6

Unit 4 Planning Guide

LESSON	PACING	OBJECTIVES	VOCABULARY
6 **Spreading Culture** pp. 196A–199A	3 Days	■ Explain how ideas and culture spread from one place to another. ■ Describe how science and technology have changed communication. ■ Compare old and new forms of communication.	**communication** **Word Work,** p. 198
MAP AND GLOBE SKILLS **Read a Map of World Countries** pp. 200A–201A	1 Day	■ Identify a map by its title. ■ Locate the United States and other countries on a map. ■ Use a map key to identify regions on a map.	
Visit a Crafts School pp. 202A–203	1 Day	■ Identify examples of the local cultural heritage. ■ Explain the significance of the local cultural heritage. ■ Obtain information about a topic using a variety of visual sources.	
Unit 4 Review and Test Preparation pp. 204–208	3 Days		

READING	INTEGRATE LEARNING	REACH ALL LEARNERS	RESOURCES
Reading Social Studies: Study Questions, pp. 196A, 199	**Language Arts** **Write a Letter,** p. 196 **Technology** **Search,** p. 197	**Below-Level Learners,** p. 196 **Extend and Enrich,** p. 198 **Reteach the Lesson,** p. 199 **Extension Activities for Home and School,** p. 199A	**Pupil Book/Unit Big Book,** pp. 196–199 **Word Cards V55–V56** **Activity Book,** p. 48 **Reading and Vocabulary** Transparency 4–7 Internet Resources
		Tactile Learners, p. 200 **Extend and Enrich,** p. 200 **Reteach the Skill,** p. 201 **Extension Activities for Home and School,** p. 201A	**Pupil Book/Unit Big Book,** pp. 200–201 **Activity Book,** p. 49 **Skill Transparency 4–4** **GeoSkills CD-ROM** Internet Resources
	Art **Make a Branch Loom,** p. 202 **Language Arts** **Write and Make a Book,** p. 203	**Extend and Enrich,** p. 203	**Pupil Book/Unit Big Book,** pp. 202–203 Internet Resources **Take a Field Trip Video**
Focus Skill **Generalize,** p. 204			**Pupil Book/Unit Big Book,** pp. 204–208 **Reading and Vocabulary** Transparency 4–8 **Activity Book,** pp. 50–51 **Assessment Program, Unit 4 Test,** pp. 13–16

1 2 3 4 5 6

Unit 4 Skills Path

Unit 4 features the reading skills of generalizing and finding point of view. It also highlights the social studies skills of following routes on a map, reading a map of world countries, and reading a bar graph.

FOCUS SKILLS

UNIT 4 READING SKILL

GENERALIZE

- INTRODUCE p. 161
- APPLY pp. 168, 179, 204

READING SOCIAL STUDIES

- Make a Prediction, pp. 162, 178A, 183
- Graphic Organizer, pp. 164A, 167, 172A, 175
- Create Mental Images, p. 164
- Personal Response, pp. 168A, 169, 190A, 195
- Study Questions, pp. 186A, 189, 196A, 199

READING SKILLS

FIND POINT OF VIEW

- INTRODUCE pp. 170A–171A

MAP AND GLOBE SKILLS

FOLLOW ROUTES ON A MAP

- INTRODUCE pp. 176A–177A
- APPLY p. 207

READ A MAP OF WORLD COUNTRIES

- INTRODUCE pp. 200A–201A

CHART AND GRAPH SKILLS

READ A BAR GRAPH

- INTRODUCE pp. 184A–185A
- APPLY p. 206

STUDY AND RESEARCH SKILLS

- Using a Dictionary, p. 172
- Look for Questions/Answers, p. 181

Theme Time: Culture Connections

MATH CENTER

Making Sets Game

Teach children to play a game from Africa. Explain that one child is the caller who calls out a number between one and five. The other players gather in groups of that number. Any leftover players group together and call out the number of people in their group. Have children take turns being the caller. After the game, have children tell how many players they had and which numbers allowed them to form even groups with no leftovers. To vary the game, teach children the names of numbers from *one* to *five* in another language and have them call out the numbers in that language as they play.

Swahili Numbers
1=moja,
2=mbili,
3=tatu,
4=mme,
5=tano

READING/LANGUAGE ARTS CENTER

Celebration Comparison

Provide books that contain information about a variety of cultural celebrations. Have children read about one celebration from another country or cultural group and write a short description of the event. Then have children write a sentence telling at least one way the celebration is similar to a tradition of their own.

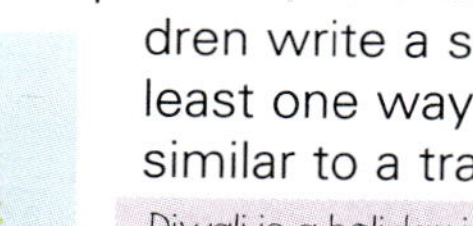

Diwali is a holiday in India. The people have feasts and eat candies. They decorate their houses and towns with lots of lights. We put lights on our house at Christmas.

SCIENCE CENTER

The Language of Scientists

Explain that scientists all over the world use a language called Latin to name plants, animals, parts of the body, and diseases. Tell children that this enables scientists who speak different languages to share information without getting confused. Provide pictures of animals labeled with their Latin names and a cassette recording of the common and Latin names. Encourage children to study the pictures and listen to the recording to learn as many Latin names as they can.

BULLETIN BOARD: CULTURE APPRECIATION

Thank You, World!

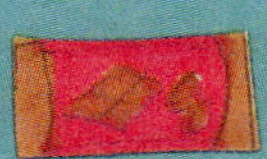

Dear Mexico,
Thank you so much for giving us chocolate. I would be sad if I could never drink hot chocolate!
Sincerely, Dennis G.

Dear Italy,
Thank you so much for pizza. It is my favorite food. I love it with pepperoni. My teacher says that it is from Italy, too.
Your friend, Ana T.

Dear China,
Thank you for giving us paper. We couldn't read and write without paper. I love to draw on paper, too.
Yours truly, Lateisha R.

Dear England,
I would like to thank you for nursery rhymes. I still remember the ones I learned when I was little. I tell them to my baby brother.
Sincerely, Teresa M.

Have children help create a bulletin board about things they like that come from other cultures. Discuss specific examples such as paper, kites, and fireworks from China; chocolate, music, and dance from Mexico; nursery rhymes from England; spices from India; and pizza from Italy. Ask children to write and illustrate a note thanking a country for one of the items. Display children's work below the title "Thank You, World!"

Multimedia Resources

The Multimedia Resources can be used in a variety of ways. They can supplement core instruction in the classroom or extend and enrich children's learning at home.

Independent Reading

Easy

Auzary-Luton, Sylvie. ***1, 2, 3, Music!*** Orchard, 1999. Annie's family has little patience with her because she is always getting carried away by music and rhythms. Her grandpa helps Annie and others see that she has a gift.

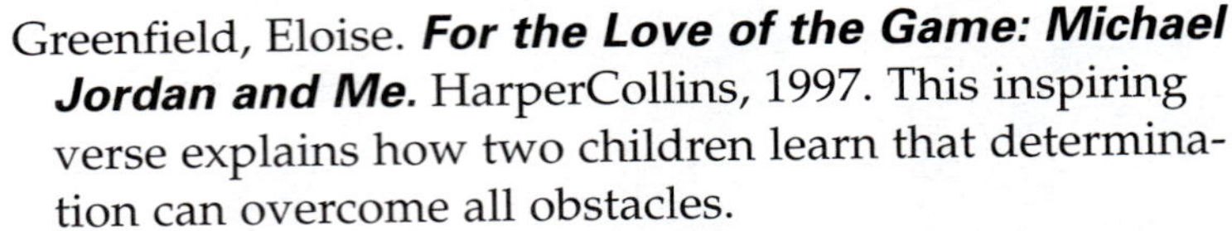

Bruchac, Joseph. ***Many Nations: An Alphabet of Native America.*** BridgeWater Paperbooks, 1998. Through twenty-six beautiful paintings and brief text, this book shows the diversity of Native Americans of the past and present.

Greenfield, Eloise. ***For the Love of the Game: Michael Jordan and Me.*** HarperCollins, 1997. This inspiring verse explains how two children learn that determination can overcome all obstacles.

Johnston, Tony. ***Uncle Rain Cloud.*** Charlesbridge Publishing, 2001. Carlos finds a way to help when he realizes that his uncle's bad moods are caused by his frustration with trying to speak English.

Lin, Grace. ***Dim Sum for Everyone.*** Knopf, 2001. Readers are introduced to the special Chinese tradition of eating "little dishes," or dim sum. Detailed illustrations add to the cultural lesson.

Low, William. ***Chinatown.*** Henry Holt, 1997. A boy and his grandmother take in the sights, smells, and sounds of New York City's Chinatown.

Miller, J. Philip. ***We All Sing with the Same Voice.*** HarperCollins, 2001. This picture book has an upbeat message: children may look different or live differently, but inside they are the same.

Mora, Pat. ***Confetti: Poems for Children.*** Lee & Low Books, 1999. The illustrated poems in this collection show the culture and beauty of the Southwest from the point of view of a Mexican American child.

Oberman, Sheldon. ***The Always Prayer Shawl.*** Viking Penguin, 1997. When Adam must leave Russia to go to America, his grandfather gives him a prayer shawl that has been passed down for generations.

Willey, Margaret. ***Thanksgiving with Me.*** Laura Geringer Books, 1998. This touching story is told as a conversation between a daughter and her mother, who recalls past Thanksgiving gatherings.

Average

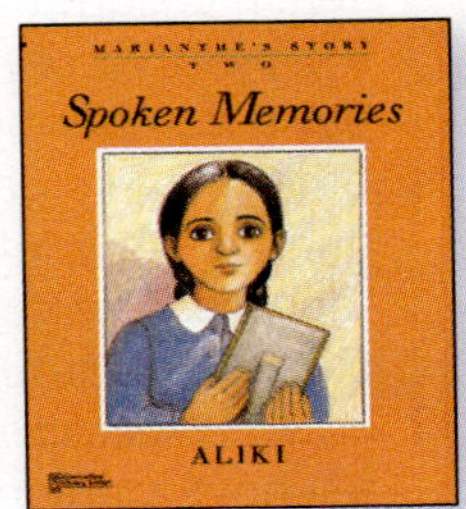

Aliki. ***Marianthe's Story: Painted Words, Spoken Memories.*** Greenwillow, 1998. This book includes two stories that show how a child feels as she struggles to adjust to her new school and home in the United States.

Hearne, Betsy Gould. ***Seven Brave Women.*** Greenwillow, 1997. A young girl tells about the lives of seven brave and remarkable ancestors.

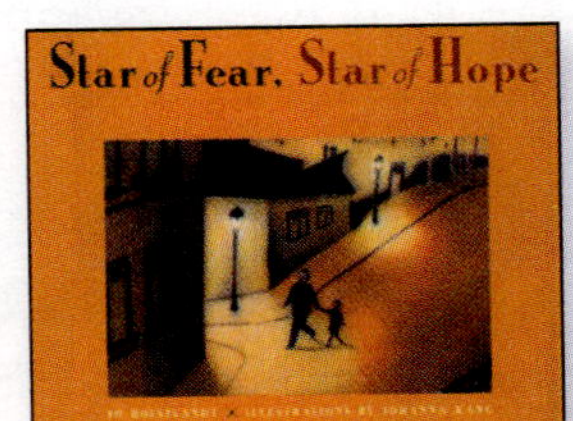

Hoestlandt, Jo. ***Star of Fear, Star of Hope.*** Walker and Co., 2000. On Helen's ninth birthday, Lydia is sleeping over. But Lydia, who is a Jew, must leave to warn her parents that the Nazis are arresting Jews. Helen is hurt and tells her friend, "You're not my friend anymore!" This sensitive story can serve as an introduction to the topic of the Holocaust.

Onyefulu, Ifeoma. ***Chidi Only Likes Blue: An African Book of Colors.*** Cobblehill, 1997. A Nigerian girl tries to help her brother see the colors in their village.

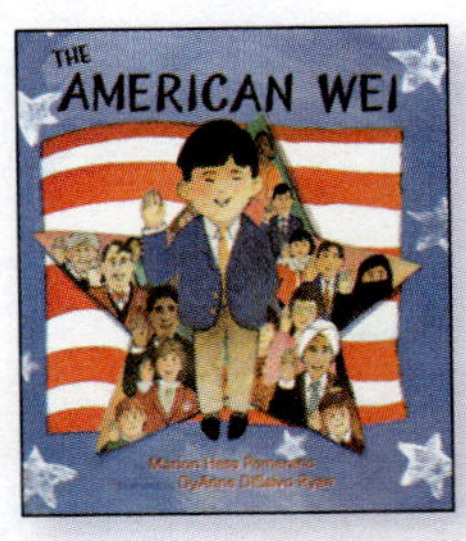

Pomeranc, Marion Hess. ***The American Wei.*** Albert Whitman, 1998. A child loses his first tooth just before he and his family are to become naturalized citizens. People of all backgrounds who are on their way to the same ceremony lend a hand in finding the tooth.

Reid, Margarette S. ***A String of Beads.*** Dutton, 1997. Rich, detailed illustrations support this story of a young girl who enjoys doing beadwork with her grandmother.

Schaefer, Carole Lexa. ***The Copper Tin Cup.*** Candlewick, 2000. This book tells the history of a special family heirloom that has been passed down and used by children for generations.

Watts, Jeri Hanel. ***Keepers.*** Lee & Low Books, 2000. After spending his money on himself instead of buying a birthday gift for his grandmother, a young boy thinks of a gift he can give from his heart.

Challenging

Adler, David A. ***A Picture Book of Sacagawea.*** Holiday House, 2000. In this biography, the author tells how a remarkable Shoshone woman, Sacagawea, joined the expedition of Lewis and Clark.

Bunting, Eve. ***Terrible Things: An Allegory of the Holocaust.*** Jewish Publication Society, 1996. When all animals with feathers are taken away by the Terrible Things, the other animals are just glad it's not them. But the Terrible Things keep returning until all the animals are gone. This allegory of the Holocaust strives to show the importance of sticking together.

Dorros, Arthur. ***Tonight Is Carnaval.*** Penguin Putnam, 1994. The story of a young boy eagerly preparing for Carnaval in Peru is told through informative text and photographs of Peruvian tapestries.

Hest, Amy. ***When Jessie Came Across the Sea.*** Candlewick, 1997. This is the story of a young girl who travels from Europe to the United States and works hard as a lace-maker so she can bring her grand-mother to the United States, too.

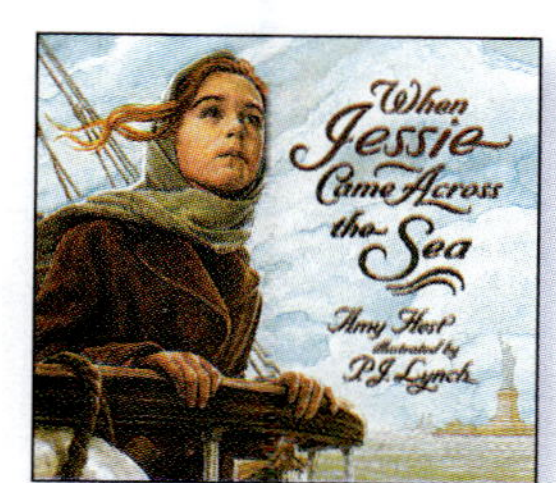

Lopez, Loretta. ***The Birthday Swap.*** Lee & Low Books, 1999. After putting lots of thought into what birthday present to give, Lori is surprised when she becomes the center of the celebration instead of her older sister.

Miller, William. ***Zora Hurston and the Chinaberry Tree.*** Lee & Low Books, 1996. This picture book tells how a well-known African American writer was inspired by her mother's death to follow her dreams.

Mitchell, Lori. ***Different Just Like Me.*** Charlesbridge Publishing, 1999. A young girl finds she has something in common with many different people.

Mochizuki, Ken. ***Passage to Freedom.*** Lee & Low Books Inc., 1997. This true story tells how one man, Chiune Sugihara, saved the lives of thousands of Jews by writing visas for them to leave Lithuania.

Pringle, Laurence P. ***One Room School.*** Boyds Mills Press, 1998. The author tells readers about the last year of World War II and the one room school of his youth.

Rylant, Cynthia. ***When I Was Young in the Mountains.*** Econo-Clad Books, 1999. The author describes her childhood with her grandparents in the Appalachian Mountains.

Zelver, Patricia. ***The Wonderful Towers of Watts.*** William Morrow, 1996. This book describes how an Italian immigrant built three unusual towers in his backyard in the Watts neighborhood of Los Angeles.

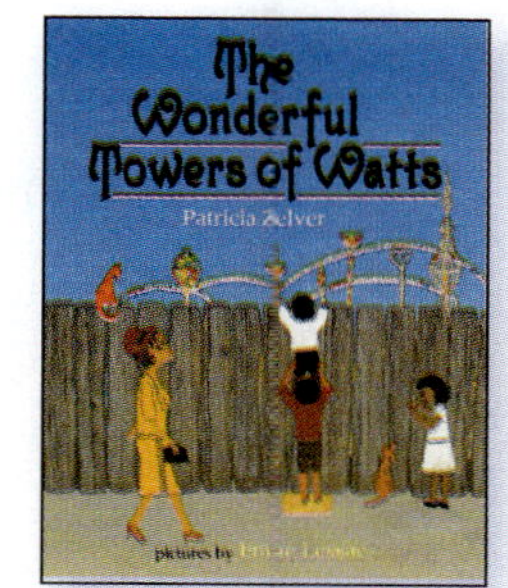

Additional books also are recommended at point of use throughout the unit.

Note that information, while correct at time of publication, is subject to change.

Audiocassettes

Around the World and Back Again. Sony, 1996. Tom Chapin sings about fun and fascinating places and activities around the world.

Too Much Fun! Demasiada Diversion. Educational Activities. Jim Rule makes learning Spanish fun as he teaches manners and customs along with the names of the days, months, and numbers.

Um Hmm. Secrets of the World Audio Series. Library Video, 2000. African American storyteller Ysaye Barnwell sings songs and tells childhood stories, folk-tales, and poems.

Computer Software

Many Places, Friendly Faces. Steck-Vaughn. Mac/Windows. Youngsters from ten different countries introduce their surroundings, customs, and culture. Children use the images and information to create research projects.

Stories and More: Time and Place. Edmark. Mac/Windows. This program is built on three stories in vastly different settings. Through the stories and activities, children learn the importance of time, place, and culture in the way we live.

Thinking Things Collection 2. Edmark, 2000. Mac/Windows. This program helps children develop creativity, problem-solving skills, and critical thinking.

Videos and DVDs

Everybody's Different. Sunburst. Through three school scenarios, children learn that we should accept differences because they are what make people interesting and unique.

Families of the World Series. Library Video. Each of the videos in this series shows the life of an urban family and a rural family living in the same country. Titles include Israel, India, Mexico, Thailand, Sweden, Japan, Brazil, China, Puerto Rico, the United States, and Ghana.

Willy's Worldwide Adventures Collection. Library Video, 1998. In each of the animated videos in this series, the Wuhlmouse family introduces children to four interesting geographic or cultural places in the world.

ISBNs and other publisher information can be found at **www.harcourtschool.com**

The Learning Site: Social Studies Center

The Learning Site at www.harcourtschool.com offers a special Social Studies Center. The center provides a wide variety of activities, Internet links, and online references.

Here are just some of the HARCOURT Internet resources you'll find!

Multimedia Biographies

www.harcourtschool.com

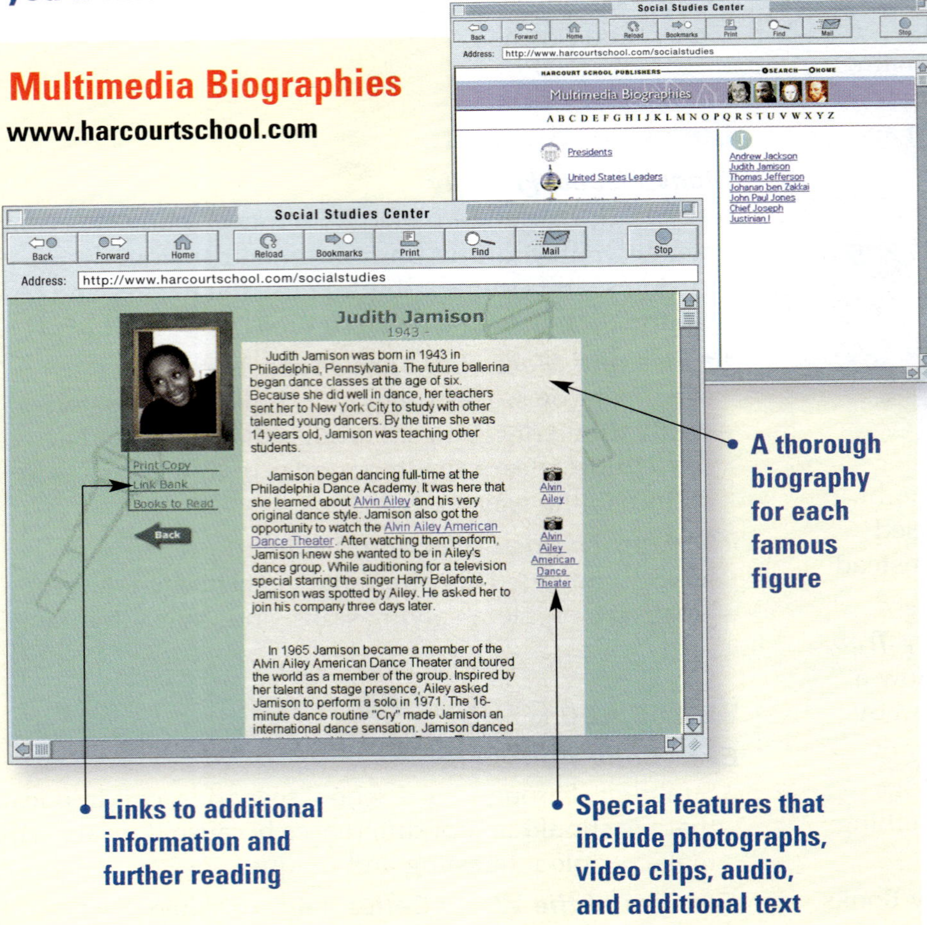

- A thorough biography for each famous figure
- Links to additional information and further reading
- Special features that include photographs, video clips, audio, and additional text

GO ONLINE — INTERNET RESOURCES

Find all this at The Learning Site at www.harcourtschool.com

- Activities and Games
- Content Updates
- Current Events
- Free and Inexpensive Materials
- Multimedia Biographies
- Online Atlas
- Primary Sources
- Video Updates
- Virtual Tours
- Your State

and more!

Free and Inexpensive Materials

- Addresses to write for free and inexpensive products
- Links to unit-related materials
- Internet maps
- Internet references

www.harcourtschool.com

Primary Sources

- Artwork
- Clothing
- Diaries
- Government Documents
- Historical Documents
- Maps
- Tools

and more!

www.harcourtschool.com

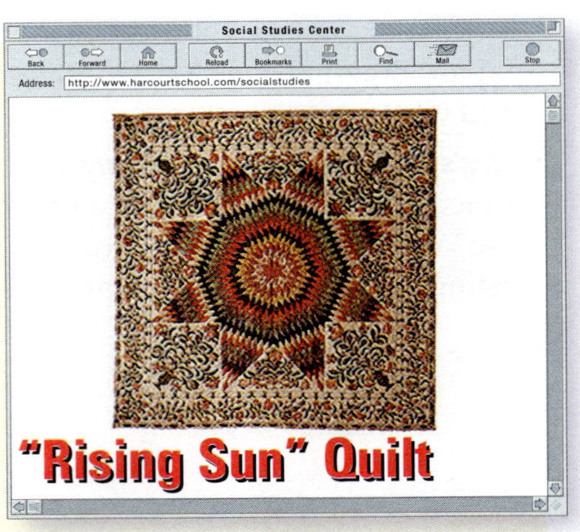

Virtual Tours

- Capitols and Government Buildings
- Cities
- Countries
- Historical Sites
- Museums
- Parks and Scenic Areas

and more!

www.harcourtschool.com

Integrate Learning Across the Curriculum

Use these topics to help you integrate social studies into your daily planning. See the page numbers indicated for more information about each topic.

Social Studies

Art

Class "Mosaic," p. 168
Houses in Our Town, p. 178
Make a Branch Loom, p. 202

Science

The Language of Scientists, p. 161I

Languages

Adobe, p. 178

Language Arts

Celebration Comparison, p. 161I
Write a Biography, p. 161
Descriptive Writing, p. 193
Write a Letter, p. 196
Write and Make a Book, p. 203

Physical Education

Jumping Game, p. 164

Reading/Literature

Ellis Island, p. 167
Pueblo Storyteller, p. 167
World Landmarks, p. 167
As the Crow Flies: A First Book of Maps, p. 176A
The Keeping Quilt, p. 179
The Memory Coat, p. 173
"Together," p. 183A
Cinderella, p. 191
"Papagayo: The Mischief Maker," p. 195A
"Raven: A Trickster Tale from the Pacific Northwest," p. 195A
Chinatown, p. 208
Chidi Only Likes Blue, p. 208
Different Just Like Me, p. 208

Computer/Technology

Search, p. 197
Go Online, pp. 167, 173, 200, 203
GeoSkills CD-ROM, pp. 177, 201
Take a Field Trip Video, p. 203

Mathematics

Making Sets Game, p. 161I
Measure Distance, p. 166
People Graph, p. 170
Chinese Years, p. 186

Music

Make a Drum, p. 161R
Guitar Music, p. 179
Lift Ev'ry Voice, p. 189A
Music from Around the World, p. 194

Reach All Learners

Use these activities to help individualize your instruction. Each activity has been developed to address a different level or type of learner.

English as a Second Language

20 minutes

Materials

- posters or picture word cards for the terms *explorer, pioneer,* and *immigrant*

HISTORY REENACTMENT Suggest historic scenes for children to act out.

- Hold up a word card with a picture for the word *explorer.*
- Say aloud, "We are explorers." Then describe one or more scenes like the following that children can act out: explorers sailing the ocean, clearing trails, making maps, meeting Native Americans, or riding horses across the country.
- Have children repeat the line and act out the scene you described.
- Repeat with different picture word cards and new scenarios for each of the following: "We are pioneers" and "We are immigrants."

Below-Level Learners

30 minutes

Materials

- audiocassette recorder
- blank cassettes

LISTENING MUSEUM Have children interview parents, grandparents, or other adults about celebrations, traditions, songs, or stories that are part of their culture.

- Help children make a list of questions to ask the person they choose to interview.
- Have children record the interviews or make a recording in which they tell about what they learned.
- Set up a Listening Museum where children can listen to the recordings.
- Invite children who listen to the interviews to post comments about what they found to be the most interesting.

I learned that on Chinese New Year, money in a red envelope is good luck. Erin

I think the samba sounds like a fun dance. Mitchell

I would like to taste the bread called dabo. Ari

I found out that in India the coins are called rupees. Eder

Advanced Learners

30 minutes

Materials

- markers
- posterboard
- scissors
- envelopes

EXPLORER PUZZLE Have children create a puzzle about an early explorer or a space explorer.

- List on the board the names of early explorers or space explorers.
- Have children choose one of the people on the list to research. Invite children to make a captioned illustration showing an important event or achievement of that person.
- Have children draw puzzle lines on the back of the drawing and cut the pieces apart.
- Then have children write their explorer's name on an envelope and place their puzzle pieces inside.
- Allow children to take turns putting the different puzzles together.

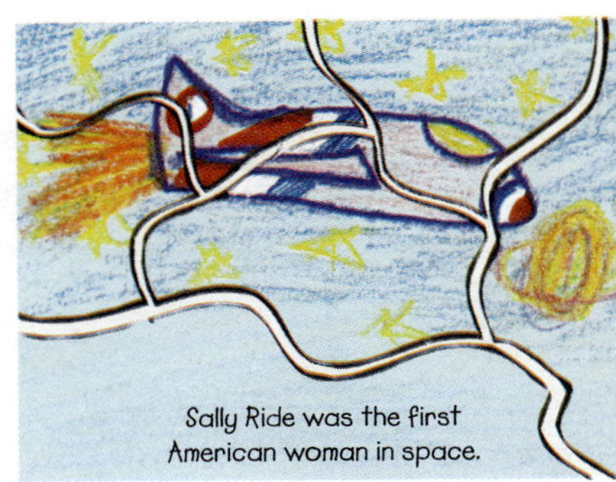

Assessment Options

The assessment program gives all learners many opportunities to show what they know and can do. It also provides ongoing information about each child's understanding of social studies.

Formal Assessment

- **LESSON REVIEWS:** pp. 169, 175, 183, 189, 195, 199
- **UNIT REVIEWS AND TEST PREPARATION,** pp. 204–207
- **UNIT ASSESSMENT**
  Standard Test
  Assessment Program, pp. 13–15
  Individual Performance Task
  Assessment Program, p. 16

Student Self-Evaluation

- **GEOGRAPHY THEME QUESTIONS**
  within lessons of Pupil Book
- **INDIVIDUAL END-OF-PROJECT CHECKLIST**
  Assessment Program, p. viii
- **GROUP END-OF-PROJECT CHECKLIST**
  Assessment Program, p. ix
- **INDIVIDUAL END-OF-UNIT CHECKLIST**
  Assessment Program, p. x

Informal Assessment

- **THINK ABOUT IT,** p. 167
- **SOCIAL STUDIES SKILLS CHECKLIST**
  Assessment Program, pp. vi–vii
- **SKILLS**
  Practice the Skill, pp. 171, 177, 185, 201
  Apply What You Learned, pp. 171, 177, 185, 201

Performance Assessment

- **PERFORMANCE ACTIVITY** in Lesson Reviews
- **UNIT ACTIVITIES,** p. 208
- **COMPLETE THE UNIT PROJECT,** p. 208
- **INDIVIDUAL PERFORMANCE TASK**
  Assessment Program, p. 16

Portfolio Assessment

STUDENT SELECTED ITEMS MAY INCLUDE:

- **THINK AND WRITE,** p. 204
- **UNIT ACTIVITIES,** p. 208
- **COMPLETE THE UNIT PROJECT,** p. 208

TEACHER SELECTED ITEMS MAY INCLUDE:

- **UNIT ASSESSMENT**
  Assessment Program, pp. 13–16
- **PORTFOLIO SUMMARY**
  Assessment Program, p. xv
- **GROUP END-OF-PROJECT CHECKLIST**
  Assessment Program, p. ix
- **INDIVIDUAL END-OF-UNIT CHECKLIST**
  Assessment Program, p. x

1
2
3
4
5
6

Unit 4 Test

STANDARD TEST

Unit 4 Test

Name ______________ Date ________

Vocabulary (5 points each)

Write the word that completes each sentence.

heritage   ancestor   custom   culture   communication

1. Eating with chopsticks is part of my culture.
2. Shaking hands is a custom in the United States.
3. My favorite ancestor is my great-grandmother, who made these pots.
4. Using sign language is a kind of communication.
5. Kevin's family teaches him about his heritage.

Hello!

¡Hola!

STANDARD TEST

Name ______________ Date ________

Main Ideas (5 points each)

6. Which of these can tell about a person's heritage?
   - ○ A weather
   - ● B arts and crafts
   - ○ C number of pets
   - ○ D size of house

7. How do some families pass on their culture?
   - ○ F by learning to use technology
   - ● G by teaching their dances
   - ○ H by going to school meetings
   - ○ J by making new friends

Write the correct letter on each line.

8. b explorers — a. horses, covered wagons, water barrels
9. a pioneers — b. Columbus, Vespucci, Magellan
10. c immigrants — c. suitcases, ships, new neighborhoods

Write the correct holiday celebrations in the table below.

Chinese New Year   Kwanzaa   Mardi Gras   Cinco de mayo

Holiday	What We Do
11 Mardi Gras	eat gumbo, wear costumes, go to parades
12 Chinese New Year	honor grandparents, give gifts, eat rice
13 Kwanzaa	dance, play musical instruments, light *kinara*
14 Cinco de mayo	break open piñatas, sing, see horses in parades

NOTES

STANDARD TEST

Name ______________________ Date ______________

Skills (6 points each)

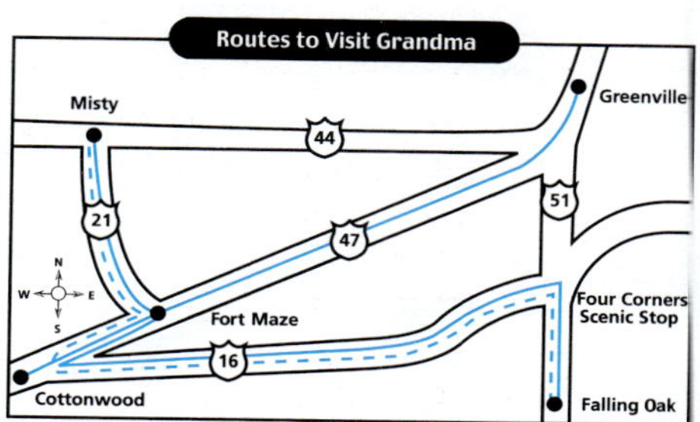

15. Angela is going from Greenville to Cottonwood to visit Grandma. Which highway will her family take? Draw the route in red. 47; Children will trace Highway 47 on map in red.
16. Angela and her family stop to eat in a town where Highways 21 and 47 join. Where do they eat? Fort Maze
17. Angela's cousin Brooke lives in Falling Oak. In what direction is Falling Oak from Greenville? south
18. How would Brooke's family get to Grandma's? Draw that route in blue. Children will draw route from Falling Oak to Cottonwood on map in blue.
19. Where could Brooke and her family stop for a scenic view? Four Corners Scenic Stop

STANDARD TEST

Name ______________________ Date ______________

Performance Task

You have a new pen pal who lives in another country! Tell him or her about your clothes, school subjects, holiday celebrations, and favorite foods. Then draw a picture of yourself. Possible answer:

Dear Sasha,

Do you wear a uniform to school? I don't. I like to wear jeans. My favorite subject is math. We are having a Valentine's Day party soon. We will give cards to our friends. My favorite food is tacos. What do you like to eat? Write soon. I like to get letters.

Your friend,

Denise

Drawings will vary.

RUBRICS FOR SCORING

SCORING RUBRIC The rubric below lists the criteria for evaluating the tasks above. It also describes different levels of success in meeting those criteria.

INDIVIDUAL PERFORMANCE TASK

SCORE 4	SCORE 3	SCORE 2	SCORE 1
▪ Rich description is provided.	▪ Some description is provided.	▪ Little description is provided.	▪ No description is provided.
▪ Letter provides strong details about the child's culture.	▪ Letter provides details about the child's culture.	▪ Letter provides some details about the child's culture.	▪ Letter provides no details about the child's culture.
▪ Illustration provides strong clues about the child's culture.	▪ Illustration provides clues about the child's culture.	▪ Illustration provides few clues about the child's culture.	▪ Illustration provides no clues about the child's culture.

Introduce the Unit

OBJECTIVES

- Use a visual to predict content.
- Interpret a quotation.
- Use a main idea chart to prepare for the unit.

Access Prior Knowledge

Discuss the fact that people who live in the United States come from different places and cultural backgrounds. Point out that a person's last name can sometimes tell something about what country the family is from. For example, names beginning with *Mc* or *Mac* are usually Scottish or Irish; names ending with *-ski* or *-sky* may be Russian or Polish; and names such as *Rodriguez* and *García* may be Mexican or Spanish. Invite volunteers to tell where their families come from. Make a chart of their responses.

Family Name	Country
Riley	Ireland
Sanchez	Mexico
Gretsky	Poland

Visual Learning

Picture Have children examine the photograph of the children on parade. Invite a volunteer to describe what the children are doing. Invite children to tell why they enjoy attending parades.

Children might be interested to know that this marching school band is in Birecik, Turkey. Ask them to predict how they think cultures are alike and different.

BACKGROUND

African Drum Drums made in a variety of shapes and sizes are among the more popular instruments in African music. The *djembe* drum is one type of African drum with a rich heritage. Its origins are tied to the Malinke and Sousou peoples of West Africa. The *djembe* is used to tell a story, like the many other African drums, but in an abstract way, so that the story can mean different things to different people. The Malinke and Sousou peoples usually play the *djembe* during celebrations.

INTEGRATE MUSIC

Make a Drum Have children brainstorm ways to make drums and other percussion instruments from recycled materials such as plastic milk cartons, empty oatmeal containers, and cardboard boxes used for crackers. Invite children to make up rhythms on their instruments and challenge classmates to repeat them.

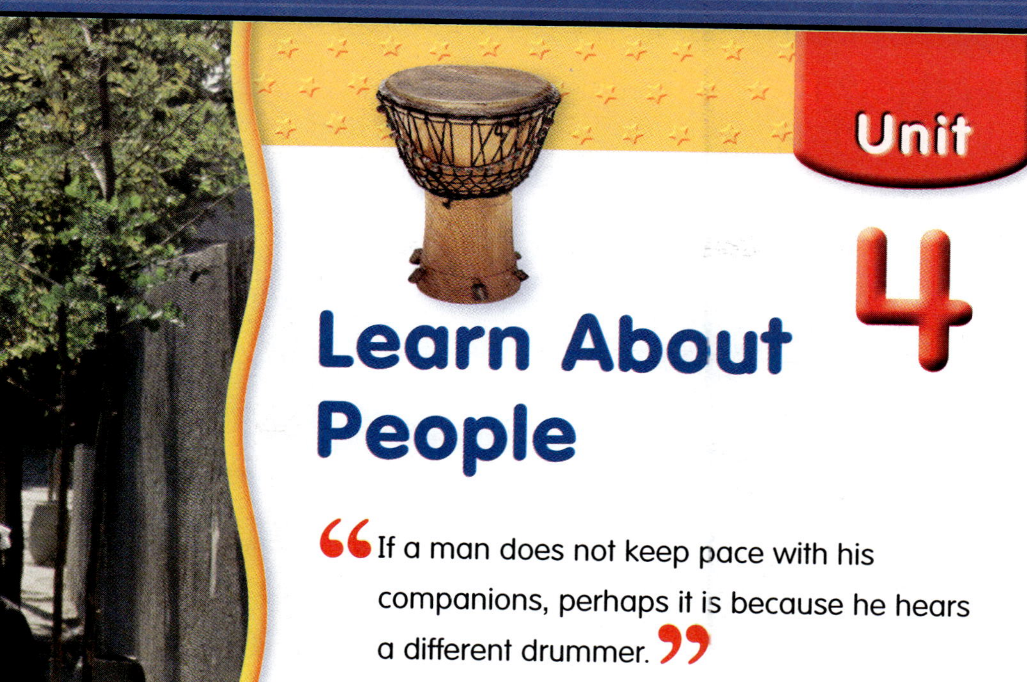

Learn About People

"If a man does not keep pace with his companions, perhaps it is because he hears a different drummer."

—Henry David Thoreau, Walden, 1854

Generalize

As you read this unit, do the following.

- List important facts about different groups of people, such as how they live and what they celebrate.
- Use the facts to write a general statement about how these facts help describe different people.

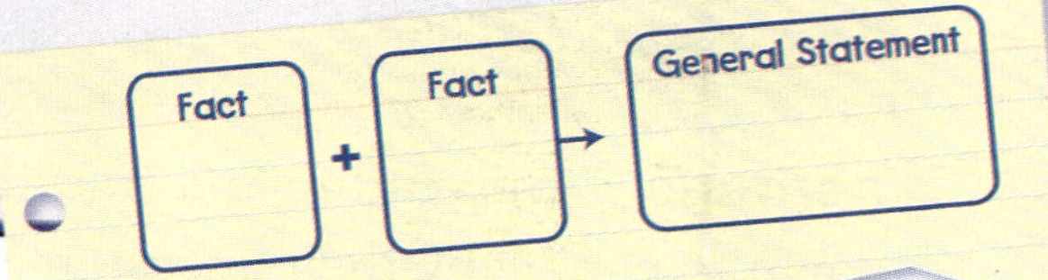

161

Analyze Primary Sources

African Drum Have children identify the artifact at the beginning of the unit as a drum. Explain that this is a drum from Africa called a *djembe*. Invite volunteers to describe and discuss the drum. Have children compare the drum to other drums they have seen.

Quotation Read aloud the quotation, and explain the meanings of the words *pace* and *companions*. Tell children that Henry David Thoreau was a man who believed in living simply. Explain that for two years he lived in a cabin in the woods of Massachusetts and that he wrote the quotation at that time.

Generalize

Explain that when children read social studies books or articles, they should think about ways that the facts they read can be combined into a general statement, or generalization, about the information. Explain that they can use a simple chart to do this. Point out that children should look for factual details as they read and write these facts on the chart. Then they can combine groups of facts into general statements. As children read the first few pages of this unit, help them complete sample charts to demonstrate the skills of finding facts and making generalizations.

- A blank graphic organizer appears on page 50 of the Activity Book.
- A completed graphic organizer can be found on page 204 of this Teacher's Edition.

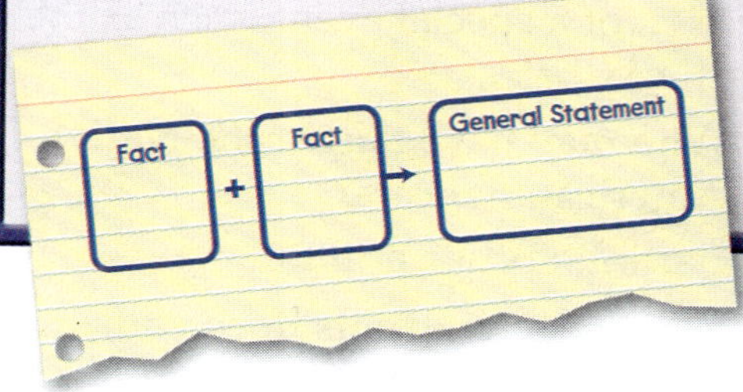

INTEGRATE LANGUAGE ARTS

Write a Biography
Discuss with children that people who make important contributions to society, such as Dr. Martin Luther King, Jr., often "march to the beat of a different drummer." Have children write a brief biography of such a person.

BACKGROUND

Henry David Thoreau (1817–1862) was an essayist, naturalist, and philosopher. A leading transcendentalist, his most well-known writings include "Civil Disobedience" and *Walden*, in which he describes his experiences living in a hand-built cabin in the woods near Walden Pond.

AUDIOTEXT

Use the Unit 4 AUDIOTEXT for a reading of the Unit narrative.

Preview the Vocabulary
PAGES 162–163

OBJECTIVES

- Use visuals to determine word meanings.
- Use words and visuals to predict the content of the unit.

Access Prior Knowledge

Ask children to describe an elderly person and a very young person from their neighborhood. Help them understand that people in our country are different ages and have different talents, jobs, beliefs, and ways of doing things.

Make Connections

Link Pictures and Words Read aloud the word *culture* and its definition. Explain that *way of life* means all the special things people do—the kinds of foods they eat, the kinds of clothes they wear, the languages they speak, and even what they do for fun. Explain that the other words and pictures are related to culture because they show that people live in different ways.

Visual Learning

Pictures Point out the picture of the Asian dancer. Ask children what clues there are to her culture. (her costume, the dance)

Direct attention to the word *heritage* and read its definition. Explain that a powwow is a Native American celebration of a special event, such as the birth of a baby.

Q Who may have taught the Native American dancers?

A parents; other adults

Q What special events does your family celebrate?

A Children may suggest birthdays, christenings or bar mitzvahs, or special days like Cinco de Mayo.

Preview the Vocabulary

culture A people's way of life. (page 169)

heritage The culture and traditions handed down to people by their ancestors. (page 178)

162

READING SOCIAL STUDIES

Make Predictions Remind children that thinking about what they may learn in a lesson can help them when they read the text. Ask them to use the two vocabulary words on the page to predict what this unit will be about. (different kinds of people and why they do special things)

REACH ALL LEARNERS

English as a Second Language As you discuss the words on the pages and ask follow-up questions, allow children who speak the same first language to sit together in small groups and share ideas about the meanings of the words. Then have them relate these ideas in English to other children.

Learn from others.

communication The sharing of ideas and information. (page 196)

ancestor A family member who lived a long time ago. (page 182)

custom A people's way of doing something. (page 186)

163

Visual Learning

Pictures Point out the picture that illustrates *ancestor.* Read aloud the definition. Explain that finding out about one's ancestors can help people understand about their own culture.

Direct attention to the picture of the child lighting a menorah and ask what this picture shows. If children do not know, tell them that the child in the picture is celebrating Hanukkah. Read aloud the definition and discuss how customs such as this religious celebration are passed from generation to generation.

Q What customs do many Americans observe on Thanksgiving?

A They eat a large meal with family members.

Q What customs do many Americans observe on the Fourth of July?

A They watch parades; they eat hot dogs; they watch fireworks.

Ask children what they see in the picture at the top left of the page. Read the word *communication* and its definition.

Q What other ways do people communicate?

A They talk in person, use a cell phone, send e-mail, write letters, and send faxes.

BACKGROUND

Hanukkah Hanukkah is the Jewish Festival of Lights, celebrated for eight days in December, near the winter solstice. The menorah shown on page 163 has eight candles, one for each day, to represent oil that miraculously burned for eight days. The middle candle is the "helper candle," which is used to light the others from right to left. On the first day, one candle is lit; on the second day, two candles; and so on. Hanukkah is a happy holiday, with gift giving.

SCHOOL TO HOME

Use the Unit 4 SCHOOL TO HOME NEWSLETTER on pages S7–S8 to introduce the unit to family members and suggest activities they can do at home.

CITIZENSHIP — DEMOCRATIC VALUES
Individual Rights

Discuss how the United States provides equal opportunities and many freedoms to people who have come to live here. Explain that cultural diversity makes our country unique. Have a volunteer read aloud what Earnest says. Point out that children can learn many things from others. Ask them to name people they learn from. Remind children that they teach people things, too.

Word Work

The following activities may be used to preteach vocabulary. You may also wish to duplicate and distribute the word cards found in the back of this book on pages V47–V56. Children can use them as flash cards to practice saying and defining each word. Remind children to use the glossary at the back of their books to help them define these words.

VOCABULARY TEAM CHALLENGE

Organize the class into teams of four and have each team choose a name. Write the vocabulary words on strips of paper and place them in a basket. Have two members from the first team draw a strip and give the other team members clues about the word. Display the list of words on a chart to help those who are guessing. Each time a team guesses a word, write the team name next to that word on the chart. Continue having teams draw and guess words until all the words on the chart have a team name next to them.

culture	Stars
route	
immigrant	
heritage	
language	Hot Shots
holiday	Champs
pioneer	Stars
ancestor	

CULTURE WEB

Display the vocabulary words on a chart or bulletin board. Draw a graphic organizer like the one shown below and write *Culture* in the main oval. Ask children to make sentences telling how children learn their culture from their family. Encourage them to use words from the vocabulary list. Write in the smaller ovals key words from children's responses.

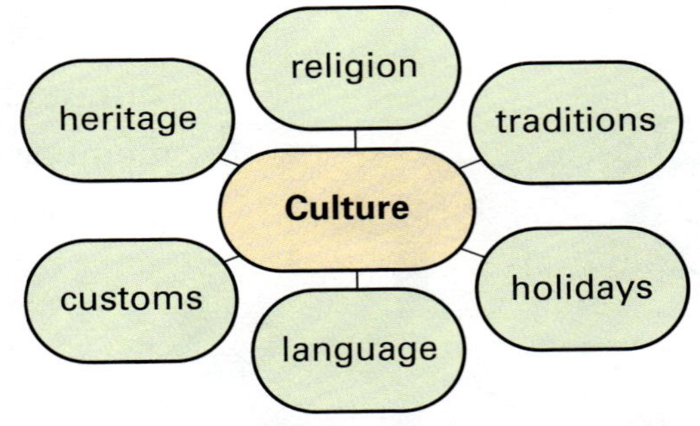

LOOKING FOR LIKENESSES

Display vocabulary words and have children look for words that have something in common. Tell children they may look for similarities in meaning or in spelling. Have a volunteer hold up two word cards while classmates try to guess what similarity that child sees in the two words. If children do not guess, have the volunteer explain the similarity he or she thought of.

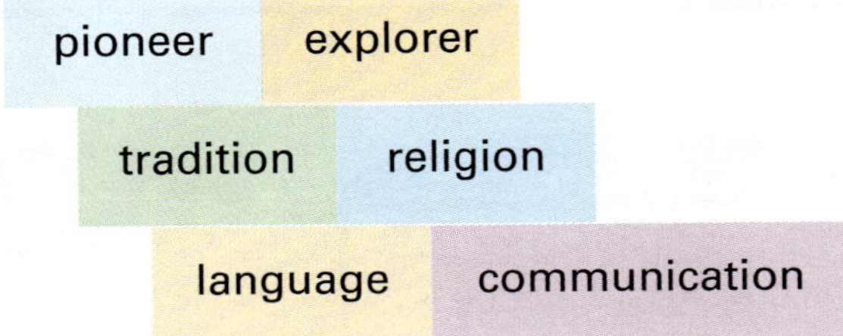

KEYS TO CULTURE

JOURNAL Have children record in their vocabulary journal the words shown here. Then ask them to use as many of the words as possible to write a paragraph about their own family's culture and traditions.

Start with an Article

Eskimo Games

OBJECTIVES

- Obtain information about a topic using a variety of visual sources, such as literature.
- Identify the Inuit as a Native American culture.
- Recognize that people of different cultures express themselves in unique ways.
- Discuss how children and their recreation are alike and different around the world.

RESOURCES

Pupil Book/Unit Big Book, pp. 164–167

Word Cards V47–V48

Reading and Vocabulary Transparency 4–1

Internet Resources

READING SOCIAL STUDIES

Graphic Organizer Invite children to name some of their favorite outdoor games. Then ask children if they think they could play those games where the Eskimos live. Remind them that Eskimos live where it is usually cold and snowy. Then ask children what indoor games they know. Record their ideas.

Outdoor Games	Indoor Games

USE READING AND VOCABULARY TRANSPARENCY 4-1.

4-1 TRANSPARENCY

Vocabulary

recreation p. 164

Summary

This article describes the Native Youth Olympics held in Anchorage, Alaska, each year. The article focuses on the seal hop, an event in which athletes try to see how far they can hop like a seal.

1 Motivate

Set the Purpose

Explain that writers write for different reasons. The usual reasons are to entertain, to make readers agree with the author's opinion, or to explain something. Read aloud the title of the article. Ask children why they think the author wrote "Eskimo Games." Children may guess that the article will teach them how to play Eskimo games. Some may guess that the article will be entertaining. Suggest children read the article to find out.

Access Prior Knowledge

Have children name games that they like to play at home or at school. Encourage children to explain why they like to play those games.

2 Teach

Read and Respond

Geography Read page 164 with children. Remind them that Alaska is a state in the United States. Have a volunteer find Alaska on a class map. Point out that Alaska, a neighbor of Canada, is in the north, in a cold part of the world, and borders the Arctic Ocean.

Understand the Article Write *Native Youth Olympics* on the board. Discuss the meaning of each word. Then explain that the word *competition* comes from the word *compete,* which means to try hard to win a game or contest. Ask if children have ever seen the Olympics on television. Point out that many sports are part of an Olympics. Explain that when people compete in a series of competitions, each individual contest is called an *event*.

Q What games do you play by hopping, jumping, kicking, or tugging?

A Children may mention hopscotch, jump rope, kickball, karate, tug-of-war, leapfrog, and others.

Visual Learning

Pictures Have children look at the pictures. Ask them if these games look like any that they have played.

BACKGROUND

Eskimo The name Eskimo was given to the native peoples of the Arctic and sub-Arctic areas of Greenland, Alaska, Canada, and Siberia in Russia by European people. Today, Canadian Eskimos prefer to be called Inuit, whereas those in Alaska still prefer to call themselves Eskimos.

READING SOCIAL STUDIES

Create Mental Images Explain that when children read about how to do something new, they should try to picture each step in their mind. This strategy might help them understand what they are supposed to do. As practice, explain how to wash a dog (find dog, put squirming dog in tub of water, soak dog, apply doggy shampoo, rinse, towel dry both you and dog). Encourage children to picture in their minds each step of the process.

INTEGRATE PHYSICAL EDUCATION

Jumping Game Explain that another Inuit game involves players jumping as far as they can while holding their toes. Invite children to form relay teams of three or four players. Ask players from each team to stand at marks placed along a course divided into three or four parts, depending on the number of players per team. Have the teams race, relay style, to the finish line while holding their toes. For safety have children play on cushioned floor mats.

The modern Native Youth Olympics have been held every year since 1971 in Anchorage, Alaska. They are open to all kids in Alaska elementary and high schools. The games help people remember Eskimo culture.

Here are rules and tips for one of the events. Challenge yourself and your friends!

SEAL HOP

In water, seals are graceful swimmers, but on land, they bounce and flop. They wriggle on their bellies and pull themselves along with their front flippers. The seal-hop event copies the way a seal moves on land.

Hop like a seal by springing off your hands and toes. How far can you hop?

Warning: The seal hop is really tough to do!

165

Read and Respond

Understand the Article Read aloud the first two paragraphs on page 164. Explain that long ago, Eskimos hunted animals and caught fish for food.

Q How did playing athletic games most likely help the children long ago in their daily lives?

A The games helped them learn how to move, concentrate, and think quickly. These skills helped them when they hunted and fished.

Point out that Eskimo children today can learn about this part of their ancestors' lives by playing the Eskimo games they once played.

Invite volunteers to tell what they know about seals and to demonstrate how seals move and sound. Next, invite a volunteer to read page 165. Ask the class to listen without looking at their book and to try to picture seals in their mind.

Visual Learning

Diagram Have children read the caption under the diagram on page 165. Ask if they would be able to do the seal hop by reading the caption alone. Guide children to conclude that the diagram provides visual instructions that help them picture the written words.

BACKGROUND

In 1971 one hundred students participated in the first Native Youth Olympics organized by Sarah Hanuske, a boarding school coordinator. The games put an emphasis on flexibility, power, balance, concentration, agility, physical strength, and stamina. Sportsmanship is also stressed, and special awards are given for individual and team sportsmanship.

REACH ALL LEARNERS

Below-Level Learners Direct children's attention to the words *jump, kick, hop, tug, bounce,* and *flop* on pages 164–165. Point out that the words describe movements. Invite volunteers to demonstrate each motion. Have children start a word wall of words describing motions. Tell children to add to the wall other words from the article, as well as words they hear and read in other places. Invite children to add both words and illustrations to the wall.

WORD WORK

Contrast Words Write on the board *In water, seals are graceful swimmers, but on land, they bounce and flop.* Underline *In water* and *on land* and discuss that these are opposite ideas. Then draw a circle around the word *but*. Point out that this word sometimes indicates opposite ideas, in this case, that seals are graceful in water *but* awkward on land.

Read and Respond

Understand the Article Read aloud the instructions for doing the seal hop. Remind children to look at the diagram on page 165 and the picture on page 166 to help them understand the steps involved in doing the movement.

Q **What parts of your body should touch the floor when you do the seal hop?**

A hands and feet

Q **What happens if another part of your body touches the floor when you hop?**

A You must stop hopping and stay where you are.

Culture and Society Ask children if they have ever played a game in which they walked like a crab, an elephant, or another animal. Discuss that such games probably began long ago, when young people watched the movements of animals in their environment and imitated them.

3 Close

Summarize the Reading

- Each spring, young athletes compete in the Native Youth Olympics in Alaska.
- Games like the seal hop help people learn about Eskimo culture.

Begin by marking a starting line on the floor. Then get into a push-up position behind the line. Only your toes and hands should be touching the floor. Keep your body straight and your arms bent at the elbows. If you want to make the event easier, keep your arms straight (as shown in the photograph), not bent at the elbows.

When you are ready, hop forward. Do this by springing up and forward with your arms and feet. Land in the push-up position after each hop, and then hop forward again. On each hop, your hands and feet must lift off the ground. Keep your body flat so that your hips do not rise higher than your head.

166

QUESTIONS KIDS ASK

Q **Do Eskimos live in igloos today?**

A No. Today, Eskimos live in the same kinds of houses as everyone else. They go to the same schools, have the same kinds of jobs, wear the same clothes and eat the same kinds of foods as we do. But like all of us, they keep some of their traditions. Igloos are still used sometimes by hunters.

REACH ALL LEARNERS

Kinesthetic Learners Encourage partners to read page 166 together. Have one child read each step, while the other child practices doing it. When they have completed all the steps, have them switch roles.

INTEGRATE MATHEMATICS

Measure Distance Take children to the playground. Remind them that the boys' record for the seal hop is 160 feet 2 1/8 inches, and the girls' record is 136 feet. Help children use a tape measure to measure these distances. If possible, allow volunteers to see how far they can do the seal hop.

You must stop if you touch the floor with any part of your body other than your hands or toes.

In competition, the seal hoppers all start at the same time. The "seal" who hops the farthest wins.

At first, you probably will hop only a couple of times and travel a few feet, but keep practicing. The boys' record is 160 feet 2 1/8 inches. The girls' record is 136 feet.

Think About It

1. Where did the Eskimos get their idea for the seal hop?
2. Find out more about the Eskimos (Inuit). Write a short article telling what you learned.

Read a Book

Start the Unit Project

A Culture Fair Your class will plan a fair to celebrate the cultures in your community. As you read this unit, remember the ways people show their cultural heritage.

Use Technology

Visit The Learning Site at **www.harcourtschool.com** for additional activities, primary sources, and other resources to use in this unit.

READING SOCIAL STUDIES

Graphic Organizer Invite children to make any changes they can think of to the chart they started in Access Prior Knowledge.

Outdoor Games	Indoor Games
baseball	leapfrog
sledding	board games
hockey	seal hop
kickball	jumping game

USE READING AND VOCABULARY TRANSPARENCY 4-1.

Read a Book

Children may enjoy reading these leveled independent Readers. Additional books are listed on pages 161J–161K of this Teacher's Edition.

Easy *Ellis Island* by Susan Ring. Explore the history of Ellis Island.

Average *Pueblo Storyteller Dolls* by Susan Ring. Meet the Native Americans of the Pueblo tribe.

Challenging *World Landmarks* by Susan Ring. This book visits the landmarks that inspire travel.

Start the Unit Project

Hint Suggest children look over Preview the Content on page 161 before they begin the Unit Project. As children work through the unit, encourage them to note the things that make cultures special.

Use Technology

THE LEARNING SITE — Go to **www.harcourtschool.com** to read more about the games and ways of life of other cultures.

TIME FOR KIDS — Go to **www.harcourtschool.com** for the latest news in a student-friendly format.

Think About It

Answers

1. The Eskimos probably got their idea for the seal hop from watching seals move around on land.
2. Encourage children to learn interesting facts about traditional Eskimo culture.

REACH ALL LEARNERS

Tactile Learners Invite children to create a display showing how science and technology have changed recreation. Encourage them to find or draw pictures of games played in the past like hoops, marbles, jump rope, and jacks, and present-day toys and games that have resulted from changes in technology. Children might also show how recreations such as skating or biking have progressed over time.

Extension Activities For Home and School

Tic-Tac-Toe with Eskimo Symbols

Materials: **reference books about Eskimos, construction paper, markers, ruler, two-color counters**

Have children work with a family member to find examples of animal symbols, such as the owl and the polar bear, that have been used in Eskimo artworks. Encourage children to find out why these symbols are important to the culture of the Eskimo people. Ask children to share what they discovered. Then invite children to create tic-tac-toe sets using the symbols.

Have children use a black marker and a ruler to divide a piece of construction paper into nine squares for tic-tac-toe. Ask them to draw a different Eskimo animal symbol in each square. Children can take turns playing tic-tac-toe on each other's game boards, each child using a different side/color of the counter. As children put a counter on a square, they should name the animal. Encourage children to take home their game board to play tic-tac-toe with family members.
(VISUAL/TACTILE)

A Jumping Game

Materials: **string, object such as spoon**

Remind children of the games they play that involve jumping or kicking, such as jump rope or kickball. Explain that an Eskimo game called Aratsiaq involves both jumping and kicking. To play this game, children stand in front of a target, such as a piece of bone or fur, and then try to kick it. The object of the game is to jump in the air, kick the target with one foot, and land on the same foot. Tell children that players play this game in rounds and raise the target as the game progresses.

Help children hang an object, such as a spoon, from the branch of a tree or in another spot. Have children take turns trying to kick the object and then land on one foot. After everyone has had a chance to kick the object, allow children who enjoy the game to play in rounds, raising the object after each round.
(AUDITORY/KINESTHETIC)

Eskimo Mural

Materials: **reference materials, craft paper, tempera paint, paintbrushes, smocks**

Have children research in books and on the Internet to learn more about how the Inuit survived the harsh Arctic winters in early times. Arrange children in small groups and assign each group a topic, such as tools, shelter, or clothing. Have each group plan a scene for a mural based on their topic. Then have children work together to paint a scene showing how the Inuit lived long ago.
(VISUAL/TACTILE)

LESSON 1

Our Country of Many People

OBJECTIVES

- Explore the diversity of the United States.
- Define *culture*.
- Compare and contrast people's work, interests, and talents.

Generalize pp. 161, 168, 204

RESOURCES

Pupil Book/Unit Big Book, pp. 168–169

Word Cards V47–V48

Activity Book, p. 40

Reading and Vocabulary Transparency 4-2

Internet Resources

READING SOCIAL STUDIES

Personal Response To help prepare children for the lessons in this unit, have them think of family members, friends, neighbors, and even people they see on television. Ask the following questions: *How are these people alike? How are they different?* Write their responses on chart paper.

How Are People Alike?	How Are People Different?

USE READING AND VOCABULARY TRANSPARENCY 4-2.

4-2 TRANSPARENCY

Vocabulary

unique p. 168 **culture** p. 169

When Minutes Count

Direct children to examine the pictures in the lesson. Have them predict what the Big Idea of the lesson is. Encourage them to read the lesson to find out if they were correct.

Quick Summary

This lesson emphasizes the diversity in our country. It describes a "mosaic" of people of different ages, colors, interests, jobs, and talents who come from different cultures. It also teaches the importance of respecting differences.

1 Motivate

Set the Purpose

Big Idea Have children read the Big Idea statement before starting the lesson. As they read and discuss the lesson, invite them to tell about people they know who are part of the American "mosaic."

Access Prior Knowledge

Before reading the lesson with children, have children share what makes them unique.

2 Teach

Read and Respond

Culture and Society Show children a picture of a mosaic in an art book. Point out that its design is made up of many tiny tiles. Explain that although the tiles are different sizes, shapes, and colors, together they create a beautiful artwork. Have children read aloud the text on pages 168 and 169. Point out that all the different people and cultures who make up our country are part of what makes it beautiful.

Visual Learning

Pictures Ask children what their neighborhood would be like if everyone looked the same, had the same job, ate the same foods, and wore the same clothing. Direct children's attention to the photographs showing people with different jobs and talents. Guide children to recognize that diversity adds interest to a community.

As children discuss the photographs showing families, ask if they have ever done any of these activities in their community. Have them describe different ways of dressing, different foods, and different customs that people enjoy. Challenge children to use what they see in the pictures to create a definition of *culture*.

Lesson **1**

Big Idea
Many kinds of people live in the United States.

Vocabulary
unique
culture

Our Country of Many People

A mosaic is a picture made from many tiles of different colors. Our country is like a mosaic. It is made up of people of different ages and colors. They speak different languages and do different jobs. Many have **unique**, or special, talents.

168

READING SKILL

Generalize Ask children to name two facts about the people who live in their community. Then help children use the two facts to make a general statement about the people in their community.

INTEGRATE ART

Class "Mosaic" Have children bring in a photograph of themselves, or have them draw a self-portrait. Let them work together to attach the pictures to a large sheet of paper. Under each picture have them write their name and something unique, or special, about themselves. Mount the mosaic on a bulletin board titled "Our Unique Class."

EXTEND AND ENRICH

List Questions Have children imagine that a new classmate has arrived from a different country. Remind them that people in other countries may live in different types of houses, wear different clothes, and eat different foods. Ask them what questions they could ask the new student about his or her culture. List the questions on the board. Discuss that being interested in how others live is one way to respect differences and make friends.

Americans come from many cultures. A **culture** is the way a group of people live. It is what they eat, how they dress, and what they believe.

Americans also share something important. They believe that by respecting one another's ways they can live and work together in peace.

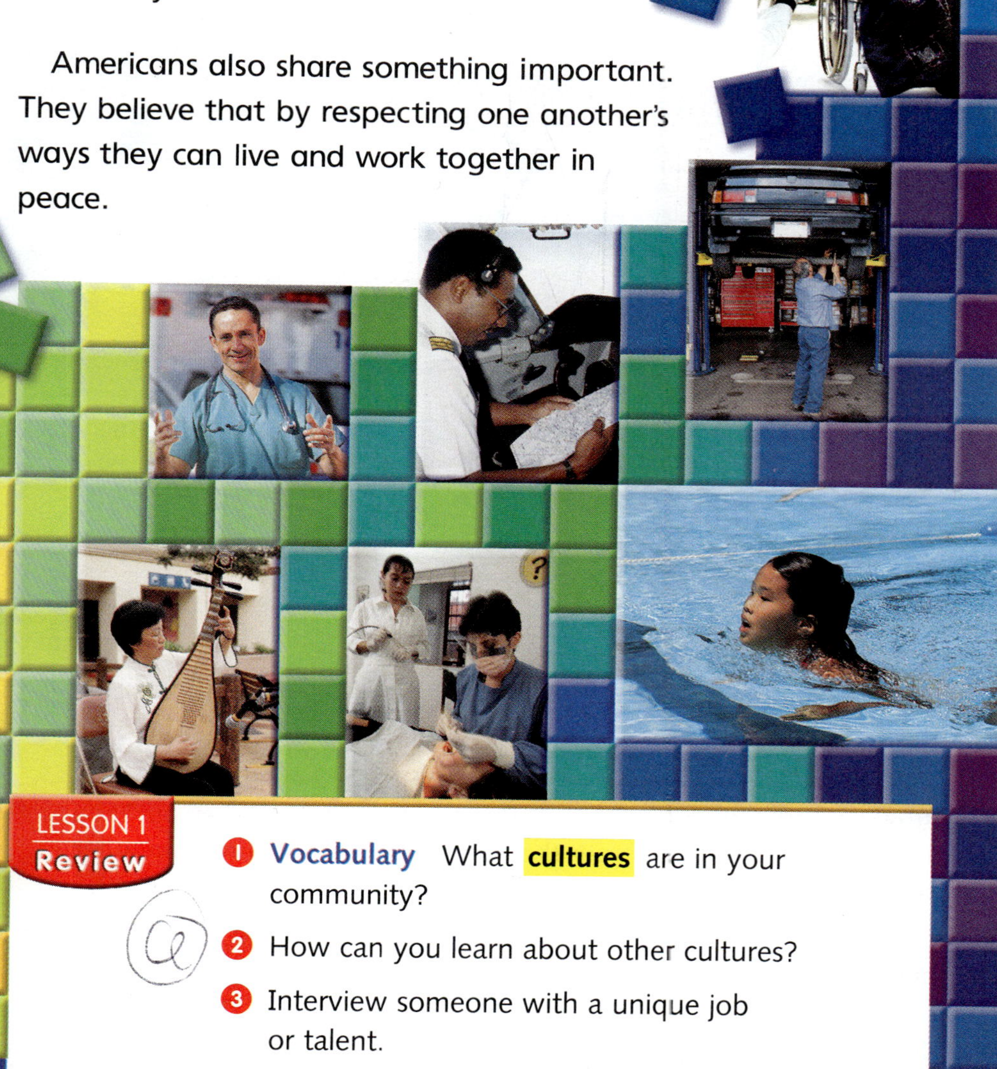

LESSON 1 Review

1. **Vocabulary** What **cultures** are in your community?
2. How can you learn about other cultures?
3. Interview someone with a unique job or talent.

RETEACH THE LESSON

Make an H-Map Create on the board an H-map. Have children look at the photographs on pages 168 and 169 and compare two people at their jobs. Have them tell how these people are different and alike.

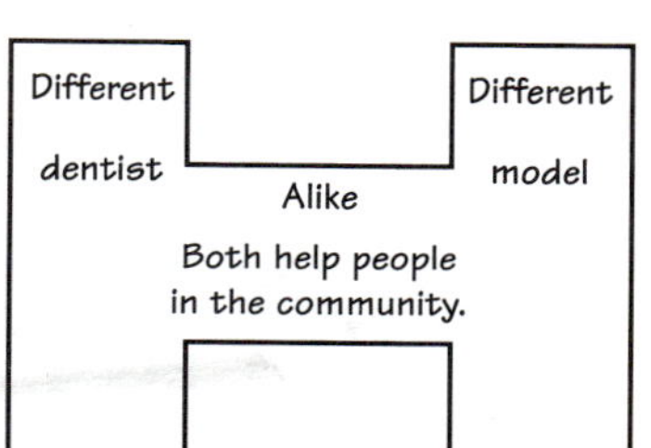

ACTIVITY BOOK

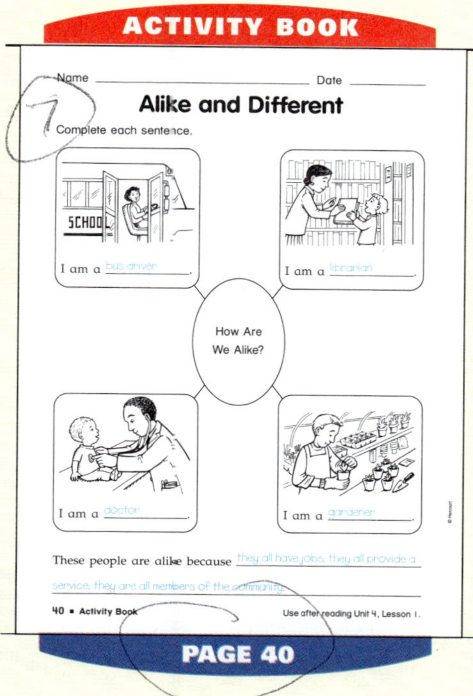

Name ________ Date ________

Alike and Different

Complete each sentence.

I am a bus driver

I am a librarian

How Are We Alike?

I am a doctor

I am a gardener

These people are alike because they all have jobs, they all provide a service, they are all members of the community.

40 ■ Activity Book — Use after reading Unit 4, Lesson 1.

PAGE 40

3 Close

Summarize Key Content

- Many kinds of people live in our country.
- They are different ages and colors, and they have different jobs and unique talents.
- They come from many cultures.
- By respecting these differences, we can keep our country a welcome place to live.

READING SOCIAL STUDIES

Personal Response Ask children to add things they have learned in this lesson to the chart. Then help children summarize how people are alike and different.

How Are People Alike?	How Are People Different?
They like to laugh and have fun. They eat food, wear clothes, and have special talents. They all live in the United States.	They have many jobs and interests, and are different ages. They eat different food, dress in different clothes, and believe different things.

USE READING AND VOCABULARY TRANSPARENCY 4-2.

Assess

Lesson 1 Review—Answers

1. Children may suggest nationalities as well as religions.
2. Children may say that they could ask people about their jobs, talents, and culture to learn more about them. They could also read books.
3.

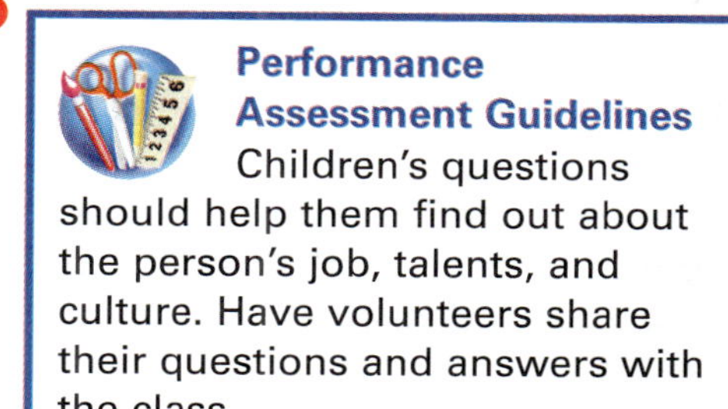

Performance Assessment Guidelines Children's questions should help them find out about the person's job, talents, and culture. Have volunteers share their questions and answers with the class.

Extension Activities For Home and School

Mosaic of Cultures

Materials: **magazines that show different parts of the United States, multicolored drawing or construction paper, scissors, glue**

Invite children to use pages 168 and 169 as a model to create their own "Mosaic of Cultures." Ask them to cut out pictures from magazines that show a variety of people at work and play. Encourage them to choose examples that illustrate diverse cultures in the United States. Have children glue their pictures onto different-sized squares of colored paper. Then help them piece together their "tiles" to make a large mosaic for display.
(VISUAL/TACTILE)

Family Culture

Materials: **drawing paper, crayons or markers**

Have children draw on a large sheet of paper individual portraits of their family members, including extended family, doing something they enjoy that shows their culture. Remind them that culture can relate to a foreign country, but "just plain American" is a culture too. Have them label their drawings with the first name of each family member. Then arrange children in small groups to discuss how the families are alike.

Next, have children "introduce" their family members. Encourage children to pretend that their family members are actually present and to tell about each person's special talents and interests. For example, a child might say, "I'd like you to meet my mother. She likes to go jogging every afternoon."
(VISUAL/AUDITORY)

Sharing Special Memories

Materials: **cultural objects, drawing paper, crayons or markers**

Have children invite family members to share favorite memories by telling a story that relates to their family's culture. For example, a grandmother may tell about a special celebration she enjoyed as a child; an aunt may tell about a special religious ceremony that she remembers; or an uncle may describe learning to prepare a certain food. If possible, have children bring from home an object to share with the class that represents both the culture and the special memory.

Next, create a Memory Corner in your classroom. After children share their memories and objects with the class, have them draw a picture of the memory and write a story to go with it. Instruct children to place their drawing and story in the Memory Corner, along with any objects brought from home. Children can add to the Memory Corner as they learn more about their families and cultures.
(VISUAL/AUDITORY)

SKILLS

Find Point of View

OBJECTIVES

- Recognize that people have different points of view.
- Relate people's points of view to their culture and environment.

RESOURCES

Pupil Book/Unit Big Book, pp. 170–171

Word Cards V47–V48

Activity Book, p. 41

Skill Transparency 4-1

Vocabulary

point of view p. 170

1 Motivate

Ask children to draw a picture of the best pet to have. Then have children show their picture and tell what makes their pet the best pet and why. Point out that everyone drew a different picture; even people who all chose cats drew different cats. Each child has a different opinion, or point of view, about what pet he or she would like best.

Why It Matters

Discuss the fact that people have different favorite things, beliefs, and ways of doing things, based on where they live, what they have been taught, and what their particular interests and talents are. As a result, no two people see the world in exactly the same way. For example, parents and children in a city may want town leaders to spend money on a new playground, while people who were soldiers might want to use the same money for a statue to honor the city's veterans. Neither group is right or wrong—they just have different points of view. Explain that thinking about individual points of view can help people understand and respect each other's differences.

MENTAL MAPPING

Different Perspectives Have half the class imagine that they are birds and half imagine that they are mice. Tell them to think about what the classroom would look like from the point of view of their animal—from up above or on the ground. Then have them draw a bird's-eye or mouse's-eye view of the room. Volunteers can explain what their animal saw and why.

2 Teach

What You Need to Know

Explain that the environment influences what people eat, the types of houses they live in, and the types of clothes they wear. Because of this, the environment influences people's points of view.

Q What might you wear if you lived where it snowed much of the year? What might your house look like? What would you eat?

A Children may suggest that they would wear warm clothes, such as jeans, sweaters, and jackets; live in a house made of bricks, with a large fireplace in the living area; eat soup and other hot foods.

Q What would you wear if you lived where it was very warm much of the year? What would your house look like? What would you eat?

A Children may suggest wearing cool clothes, such as shorts, T-shirts, and sandals; living in a house with many windows to let in cool breezes and with ceiling fans in every room; or eating lots of fruits, salads, and other cool foods.

Skills

Find Point of View

Vocabulary
point of view

Why It Matters

Some people have a **point of view**, or way of looking at things, that is different from yours. What is important to people can tell us something about who they are or where they come from.

What You Need to Know

Everyone has special interests. These interests give clues about the things the person thinks are important.

170

REACH ALL LEARNERS

Auditory Learners Play recordings of different styles of music or music played with instruments from different cultures, such as reggae, salsa, jazz, country western, sitar, and bagpipe. Invite children to discuss which music they find most appealing. Allow them to debate their choices, but remind them to listen to all points of view.

INTEGRATE MATHEMATICS

People Graph Using children's "best pet" pictures, write on a sheet of paper the name of each animal chosen. Attach the papers on the wall as if they were labels for a bar or picture graph. Then have children stand in line next to their chosen pet. Count each line and help children create sentences based on their people graph, such as, *Seven classmates chose cats but only one chose a snake* or *Most of us chose dogs.*

EXTEND AND ENRICH

Write Sentences Ask children to write five sentences each, comparing and contrasting the points of view of two family members, or themselves and a family member. For example, *My mom likes wheat bread, but my dad likes white* or *My brother Hector and I both like to ride our bikes.*

Practice the Skill

Would a person using chopsticks eat rice or mashed potatoes?

Would a person using this bat play cricket or baseball?

Would a person playing bongo drums learn Latin music or opera?

Would a person who wears sandals live in a warm climate or a cold climate?

Apply What You Learned

Bring something from home that represents your point of view and share it with the class.

READING SKILLS

Link Culture and Civics Remind children that Americans enjoy special freedoms guaranteed by the Bill of Rights. Explain that freedom of speech is a longstanding custom in our country.

Q Why can Americans have different points of view?

A Americans are free to be different and to say what they think.

Practice the Skill—Answers

1. rice, because rice is often eaten by people who use chopsticks
2. cricket, because this bat is made for that game
3. Latin music, because a drummer can create a Latin rhythm with bongo drums
4. a warm climate, because sandals keep your feet cool

3 Close

Apply What You Learned

Have children share what they bring from home. Children should describe how the object represents their point of view.

RETEACH THE SKILL

Point of View Questions Use the following questions to prompt children to think about a person's point of view in the statement *Snails are a delicious meal.*

- How does where you live affect your point of view?
- How does your family affect your point of view?

TRANSPARENCY

Use SKILL TRANSPARENCY 4-1.

ACTIVITY BOOK

Name ____________ Date ____________

READING SKILLS

It's a Fire!

Each person below sees the fire but thinks something different about it. Fill in the thought bubbles to show what each person is thinking about the fire.

It is my job to put out fires.

Don't get too close to the fire. You might get burned.

Yum! I love hot dogs cooked over a campfire.

Use after reading Unit 4, Skill Lesson 1.

Activity Book ▪ 41

PAGE 41

QUESTIONS KIDS ASK

Q What if I do not agree with someone else's opinion or point of view?

A You don't have to agree. But you do need to be polite and listen to the other person's opinion. Lots of people—even best friends—don't agree on everything.

Extension Activities For Home and School

Story Characters' Points of View

Materials: storybook

Take children to the school library to choose a book to take home and read with a family member. They can read it aloud to the family member, have the story read to them, or read together. Tell them to stop at several places during the story and tell in their own words what is happening in the scene. Then both should role-play what the characters may be thinking at that moment. For example, after reading the scene in which Little Red Riding Hood finds a wolf in her grandmother's bed, the parent might say, "I'm the wolf, and I'm thinking, 'That little girl looks surprised!' Now you tell me what Little Red Riding Hood is thinking."
(AUDITORY)

Design a Home

Materials: photographs of homes built in tropical climates, shoe boxes, scissors, markers, posterboard, construction paper, clay, glue, other craft materials

Display pictures of homes built in tropical climates. Have children point out palm trees, beaches, and other environmental clues that identify the location. Lead children to realize that the temperatures are usually warm in these places. Then point out features of the homes that are related to the climate, such as large windows and shaded porches. Ask children how these features help keep the homes comfortable.

Discuss how architects, like artists, have a point of view. They design homes and buildings to suit the geography of an area and the needs of people there.

Have children work in small groups to design shoe-box homes suited to different climates and landscapes. Provide materials such as posterboard, construction paper, clay, glue, and other craft materials that children can use to add details to their design. Some children may want to create a setting for their homes by adding scenery. Encourage children to share their designs and discuss their point of view.
(VISUAL/TACTILE)

People on the Move

OBJECTIVES

- Recognize how explorers led the way for settlement in new places.
- Discuss the role of pioneers in settling our country.
- Explain how immigrants bring new ideas when they move.

Generalize pp. 161, 175, 204

RESOURCES

Pupil Book/Unit Big Book, pp. 172–175

Word Cards V49–V50

Activity Book, p. 42

Reading and Vocabulary Transparency 4–3

Internet Resources

READING SOCIAL STUDIES

Graphic Organizer Help children begin a K-W-L chart about explorers such as Christopher Columbus. Save the chart for use at the end of the lesson.

What We Know	What We Want to Know	What We Learned
Christopher Columbus sailed across the Atlantic Ocean.	Who were other explorers? What lands did they explore?	

USE READING AND VOCABULARY TRANSPARENCY 4-3.

Vocabulary

explorer p. 172 **pioneer** p. 173 **immigrant** p. 174

When Minutes Count

Have pairs of children read the lesson together. Then ask them to write a summary sentence for the lesson.

Quick Summary

This lesson explains that after explorers came to this country from Europe, people began to settle along the coasts. Later, pioneers moved inland, and settlements began to spread across the continent. Over the years, immigrants continued to move here, bringing with them their cultures and new ideas.

1 Motivate

Set the Purpose

Big Idea Have children read the Big Idea statement before starting the lesson. As they read, ask them to note how people, cultures, and ideas spread to new places.

Access Prior Knowledge

Before reading the lesson with children, ask children to define the word *explorer*. Have them name any explorers that they know about.

K-W-L chart on explorers

2 Teach

Read and Respond

Link History and Geography Use a globe to demonstrate that, at one time, European explorers believed they could reach Asia if they sailed west across the Atlantic Ocean. Explain that they did not know the Americas existed.

Read aloud page 172. Help children locate the United States, India, Spain, and the West Indies on a globe. Explain that in 1492 Columbus sailed from Spain to the West Indies. Because Columbus believed he had reached India, he called the people he met Indians.

Tell children that Amerigo Vespucci was one of the first people to realize that explorers had sailed to an unknown land. Point out that the Americas are named in his honor. Add that Ferdinand Magellan wondered what lay on the other side of the Americas. His ships left Spain in 1519 and sailed around South America and Africa. Magellan died during the journey, but his men continued, returning to Spain in 1522 after making the first known voyage around the world.

Visual Learning

Map Explain that rulers of European countries paid for the explorers' trips. For example, even though Columbus was Italian, the Spanish king and queen paid for his voyage. Columbus claimed the land he found for Spain.

Q What other countries claimed land in the Americas?

A France, England

CAPTION ANSWER: English

Picture Direct attention to the picture of the sailing ship. Explain that explorers—and later, settlers—sailed on ships like this one.

Q What would you take on a voyage that might last months?

A clothes, food, water, tools

Lesson

2

People on the Move

Big Idea
Many people have moved to our country, bringing their cultures.

Vocabulary
explorer
pioneer
immigrant

People have always been curious about the world. Some of them became **explorers**. They traveled to find and learn more about new places. Long ago, explorers Christopher Columbus, Amerigo Vespucci, and Ferdinand Magellan sailed to North America. After that, people began moving to this continent, bringing their cultures with them.

GEOGRAPHY THEME

Who settled around Hudson Bay?

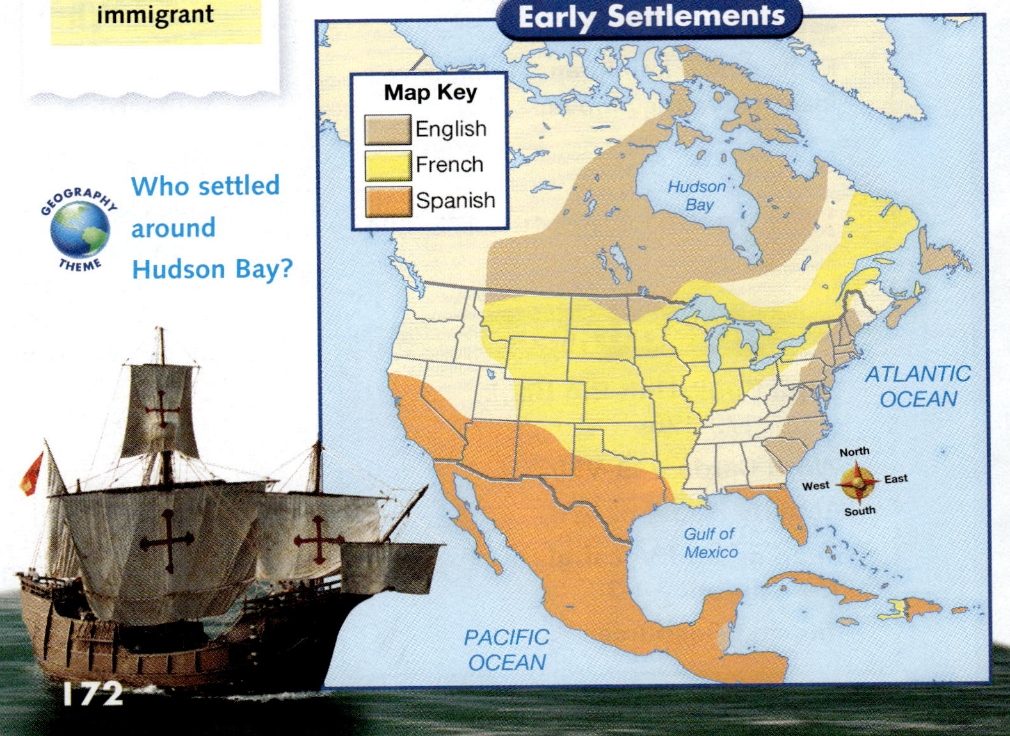

BACKGROUND

Early Explorers Christopher Columbus spent eight years persuading Queen Isabella and King Ferdinand of Spain to fund his trip. On October 12, 1492, his ships reached Watling Island in the Bahamas. Portuguese navigator Ferdinand Magellan discovered the Strait of Magellan when he sailed around South America. Although he was killed in the Philippines, his ships returned to Spain, completing the first circumnavigation of the world. Many people celebrate Columbus Day on the second Monday of October (see page H2 in the back of this book).

STUDY/RESEARCH SKILLS

Using a Dictionary Tell children that sometimes they will read words that have similar—but not exactly the same—meanings, such as *explorer* and *pioneer*. Show children how they can use a dictionary to find out how an explorer is similar to and different from a pioneer. Challenge children to make up their own sentences using each word.

leveled readers tomorrow on explorer

At first most people settled along the coasts of America. Then pioneers began to move across the country. A **pioneer** is a person who first settles in a new place.

The pioneers traveled on foot, on horseback, and in wagons. Later, trains brought more people and goods until farms, ranches, towns, and cities spread across every part of the country.

173

Read and Respond

History Have children read and discuss page 173. Explain that when people learned about the Americas, some decided to start a new life there. They sailed across the ocean and settled near the coasts. They cleared land, built homes, and grew crops. Eventually, farms, towns, and cities grew up along the coast.

Q **Why do you think the Americas were a good place to settle?**

A good land for farming, many trees for houses, lots of animals and fish to eat

Explain that pioneers are people who make the first homes in a new place. Discuss that as the coastal areas became crowded, pioneers began to move into less-settled regions. Tell children that these people had no roads to follow. Settlers who came later followed paths or trails made by pioneers and explorers who went before them. Some pioneers lived in small communities, but many lived miles from anyone else. Remind children that while these lands were new to pioneers, there were many Native Americans living there.

Visual Learning

Picture Direct attention to the picture of the wagon train. Explain that pioneers sometimes traveled in groups. Wagons held everything they owned—their furniture, food, clothing, and tools.

Q **What dangers and difficulties do you think the pioneers might have faced?**

A People could get sick or hurt and not be able to get help; they might run out of food or water; bad weather might occur; wagons might break down.

Children can learn more about early settlements. Have them visit The Learning Site at **www.harcourtschool.com**

INTEGRATE READING

Immigration Share the book *The Memory Coat* by Elvira Woodruff, a story of a family emigrating from Russia to the United States. In Russia, the family had experienced great tragedy and was hoping for a better life in the United States. After reading, discuss how Rachel helped her cousin. Talk about Ellis Island and how the people who were turned away might have felt. Then work together with children to create a sequel for *The Memory Coat*.

REACH ALL LEARNERS

Advanced Learners
Children can ask the school librarian to help them find appropriate books about explorers or pioneers. Encourage children to pick a book that interests them and to take it home to read with a family member. Ask children to write a short report about the person or people in their book. Place the reports in a central area so other children can read them.

Read and Respond

Geography Have children follow along as you read aloud page 174. Tell them that immigrants came to the United States from around the world. Display a world map and a map of the United States. Help children locate Ellis Island in New York Harbor and Angel Island in San Francisco Bay on a map. Explain that many immigrants had to pass through one of these places to enter the United States. Encourage children to choose a place in Europe or Asia and trace a route that immigrants may have traveled.

History Explain that the immigrants' voyages took many weeks. When they arrived, everyone had to answer certain questions and pass a physical exam. Some immigrants were turned away.

Q **Why do you think people went to so much trouble to come here?**

A Children may say they wanted a better life or job; they wanted to live in a country at peace; they believed life would be easier here; they wanted to be free and equal.

Visual Learning

Picture Discuss the photograph of immigrants. Have children describe the people's expressions and belongings. Help them realize that immigrants brought things with them that would help them survive and start a new life.

• BIOGRAPHY •

Sally Ride

Heroic Deeds Point out that explorers are often looked upon by others as heroes. Explain that explorers must have great courage to go into new places and discover new things and that these new discoveries often help people. Ask children to describe how transportation has changed since early explorers and pioneers crossed the country.

Immigrants kept coming from other places around the world to live in the United States. They sailed here on big ships. Many of them landed at Ellis Island in New York Harbor. There they got permission to enter the United States.

WORD WORK

Root Words Point out to children that they can figure out the meaning of many longer words by finding the root word they contain. Prefixes and suffixes can be added to a root word to slightly change the meaning of the word. Ask children to divide the words *immigrant*, *migration*, and *immigration* into their parts. Have children look up what the root word *migrate* means and how the meaning of each word changes with the addition of *im-* and *-ion*

EXTEND AND ENRICH

Make a Map Assign partners an explorer and provide them with a world map. Possible explorers might include Leif Eriksson, John Cabot, Giovanni da Verrazano, La Salle, Sir Francis Drake, Sir Walter Raleigh, Henry Hudson, Samuel de Champlain, Hernando Cortés, Juan Ponce de León, Francisco Pizarro, Francisco de Coronado, or Vasco Nuñez de Balboa. Ask children to find out where the explorer began one of his journeys and where he ended up. Then have them draw on the map the route the explorer took.

Immigrants learned about their new home from their neighbors. In turn, the newcomers shared their cultures.

Immigrants are still finding new homes here. People also move from place to place in our country. New ideas and ways of living spread this way and become part of all our lives.

• BIOGRAPHY •

Sally Ride
born in 1951
Character Trait: Heroic Deeds

Today some explorers are traveling to space. Sally Ride was the first American woman to fly into space. As a scientist, she spent a week on the space shuttle *Challenger* doing experiments. The work astronauts are doing today will help more people live and work in space someday.

MULTIMEDIA BIOGRAPHIES
Visit The Learning Site at **www.harcourtschool.com** to learn about other famous people.

LESSON 2 Review

1. **Generalize** How do immigrants bring changes?
2. **Vocabulary** How do **explorers** and **pioneers** help a country grow?
3. Write a diary entry describing how you would feel about moving to a strange new place.

175

3 Close

Summarize Key Content

- European explorers sailed to the North American continent.
- People began to settle along the coasts, and later, pioneers began moving to areas in the West.
- For years, immigrants have come to this country from all over the world, bringing new ideas and cultures.

READING SOCIAL STUDIES

Graphic Organizer Help children complete the K-W-L chart and use the chart to summarize the lesson.

What We Know	What We Want to Know	What We Learned
Christopher Columbus sailed across the Atlantic Ocean. His ships were called the *Niña*, the *Pinta*, and the *Santa María*.	Who were other explorers? What lands did they explore?	Other explorers were Ferdinand Magellan, Amerigo Vespucci, and Sally Ride. The explorers claimed land in North and South America. Sally Ride went into space.

USE READING AND VOCABULARY TRANSPARENCY 4-3.

RETEACH THE LESSON

Be a Pioneer Have children work in small groups. Encourage each group to choose a place they would all like to move to as pioneers. Ask them to decide what they would take with them, especially things from their culture. Remind them that culture is the special way they live. Have groups write a packing list, then present their destination, reasons for going there, and lists to the class.

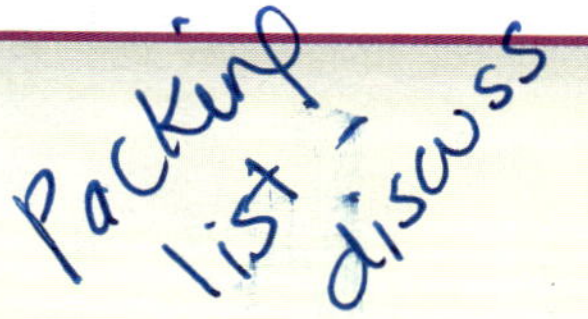

ACTIVITY BOOK

Name ________ Date ________

A Christopher Columbus Poem

Use words from the tree to finish the poem about Christopher Columbus. Write a word on each line to make the poem rhyme.

breeze Spain sun wave

When Columbus was only forty-one,
He sailed toward the setting ___sun___.

He and his crew were very brave.
They were not scared by the biggest ___wave___.

They reached an island with tall palm trees,
And friendly people and a nice cool ___breeze___.

The native people did not complain when
Columbus claimed the land for ___Spain___.

42 • Activity Book Use after reading Unit 4, Lesson 2.

PAGE 42

Assess

Lesson 2 Review—Answers

1. **Generalize** Immigrants bring their culture and new ideas with them.
2. Explorers find new land, and pioneers settle on it.
3. 

Performance Assessment Guidelines Children can describe a real move they experienced, or an imaginary move. Their diary entries should include words that describe feelings.

Extension Activities For Home and School

A Railroad Map

Materials: **copies of a United States map, crayons or colored pencils**

Provide each child with a copy of a United States map. Suggest that children work with a family member to make a map of the transcontinental railroad. Ask children to write the following instructions on the back of their maps and then take the maps home to complete the activity.

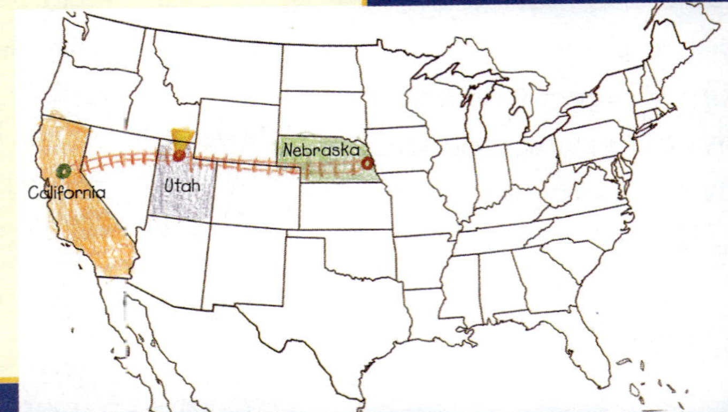

- Locate and color in the states of California, Nebraska, and Utah.
- Draw circles to represent Sacramento, Omaha, and Promontory Point and label the towns.
- Draw tracks from Sacramento to Promontory Point.
- Draw tracks from Omaha to Promontory Point.
- Draw a golden spike at Promontory Point.

(VISUAL/TACTILE)

Old and New Ways

Materials: **feathers or twigs, 2/3 cup fresh or frozen blueberries, 1/2 teaspoon salt, 1/2 teaspoon vinegar, containers with lids, colander, large spoon, heavy writing paper, paint smocks**

Tell children that the settlers wrote with feather quills from large birds such as turkeys and they made ink from berries. Invite children to make their own ink.

Have children use a large spoon to mash the berries in a colander placed over a container. Remove the pulp from the berry juice in the bowl. Then help children stir the vinegar and salt into the juice. Provide feather quills or twigs and heavy writing paper. Tell children to imagine that they are English settlers who have just arrived in this country. Invite them to use the berry ink to write a letter to a friend back in England.

(TACTILE/KINESTHETIC)

Exploring the *Niña*

Materials: **masking tape or chalk**

Discuss that the three ships that Columbus used to sail across the ocean, the *Niña*, the *Pinta*, and the *Santa María*, were actually small trading vessels. Then invite children to learn more about the size of Columbus's favorite ship, the *Niña*. Write the following dimensions on the board:

- Length of ship: 93.6 feet
- Length of deck: 66 feet
- Width of ship: 17.3 feet

Take children to a large open space on the playground or in the gym and help them mark off the dimensions of the ship. If space permits, you may want to use masking tape or chalk to create an outline of the ship. Have groups of children stand on the "deck" of the ship to get an idea of its size. Remind them that the men who sailed on the ship were sailing into unknown seas. Ask what sailing on a ship this size might have been like.

(VISUAL/KINESTHETIC)

Follow Routes on a Map

OBJECTIVES

- Find locations on maps.
- Determine directions on maps.
- Draw maps to show places and routes.

RESOURCES

Pupil Book/Unit Big Book, pp. 176–177
Word Cards V49–V50
Activity Book, p. 43
Skill Transparency 4-2
GeoSkills CD-ROM

Vocabulary

route p. 176

1 Motivate

Create a path on the classroom floor by using masking tape. If possible, create several curves in the path. Give the path specific beginning and ending points, such as from the door to your desk. Invite children to walk along the path. Then ask them to tell where the path begins and ends. Have them describe the places they passed along the way.

Why It Matters

Ask children to think of times when they travel from place to place. For example, they travel from home to school and back again; they travel to stores, the park, the library, and the movie theater. They travel from their home to a friend's home. Sometimes they travel from one town to another to visit relatives. Tell children that people must figure out how to get to places. Explain that people sometimes use maps to learn the routes that they must follow.

INTEGRATE READING

Share a Book Read aloud the book *As the Crow Flies: A First Book of Maps*, written by Gail Hartman and illustrated by Harvey Stevenson. Discuss the different maps used by the animals in the story. After reading the story, show children a map of their state. Pick two cities on the map and have children use the map scale to measure the shortest route between the two cities.

2 Teach

What You Need to Know

Read aloud the sentence that defines the word *route*. Then have children use direction words to describe the following routes: from the classroom to the cafeteria, from the cafeteria to the playground, and from the playground to the library. Encourage children to break down each route into specific steps. For example, they could say, "Turn left at the end of the hall. Then look for the third door on the right. That is the library." Write and number the steps for each route on separate sheets of chart paper. Discuss that the routes describe the directions for getting from place to place. Point out that if you gave these directions to a classroom visitor, he or she would be able to find the routes to the cafeteria, playground, and library.

Next, draw on the board a simple map of the school. Ask volunteers to point out the routes to the cafeteria, playground, and library by tracing them with a finger. Ask children how the listed steps and the routes are similar.

Have children look at the map on page 177.

Q What kind of routes are shown on this map?

A highways; routes from town to town

Point out that this map shows only a few of the highways in the United States. You may wish to show children a road atlas.

Skills

Follow Routes on a Map

Vocabulary
route

Why It Matters

A map can show you not only where places are, but also how to get to them.

What You Need to Know

The path you follow from one place to another is called a **route**. Highways are routes between towns and cities.

176

REACH ALL LEARNERS

Tactile Learners Provide children with a simple map. Discuss the title of the map and ask children to identify its symbols. Also, provide several index cards with questions relating to the map, such as *How do you get from the town center to the bus stop?* Place the cards facedown on a table. Have children take turns choosing a card and demonstrating the designated route by using a finger to trace it on the map.

EXTEND AND ENRICH

Find Our School Use a photocopier to enlarge the section of a city map showing the neighborhood around your school. Have children work in small groups. Give each group a copy of the neighborhood map and have children locate your school. Then have them find a familiar landmark that is near the school. Ask them to write step-by-step directions for the best route between the school and the landmark.

Practice the Skill

1. Which highway goes from Seattle to San Diego?
2. What direction would you travel on Highway 70 to go from St. Louis to Denver?
3. Which highway links many eastern cities?

U.S. Highways

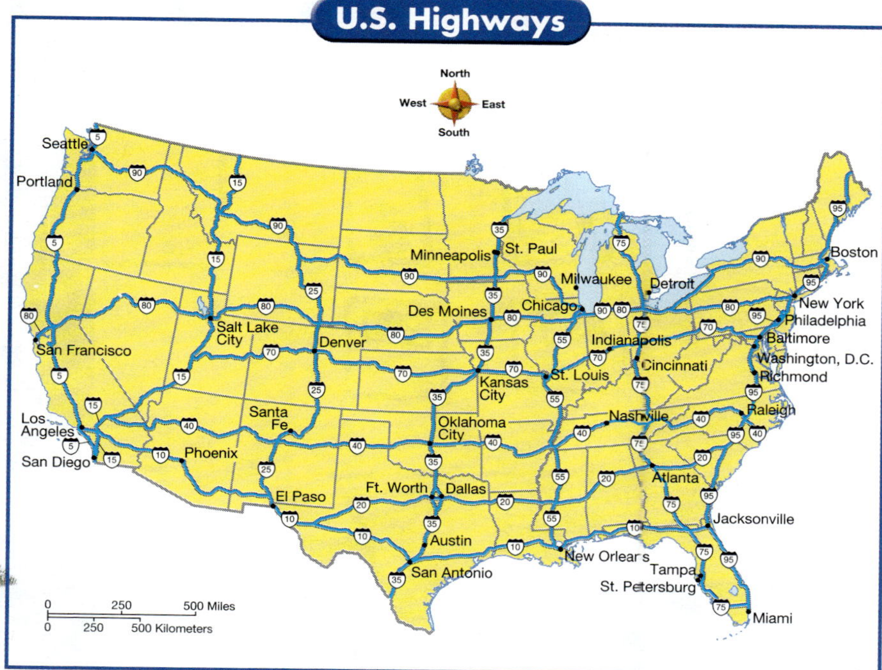

MAP AND GLOBE SKILLS Practice your map and globe skills with the **GeoSkills CD-ROM**.

Apply What You Learned

Draw a map to show your route to school.

MAP AND GLOBE SKILLS

Practice the Skill—Answers

1. 5
2. west
3. 95

3 Close

Apply What You Learned

Encourage children to include important places or landmarks on their map. They may want to use black for the map and a color to show the route.

RETEACH THE SKILL

Follow the Road Have children follow a route on the map on page 177 as you call out directions. For example, *Put your finger on Chicago. Travel south on Highway 55 to St. Louis; turn west. What highway would you take to Kansas City?* (70) Have partners take turns calling out and tracing routes on the map.

ACTIVITY BOOK

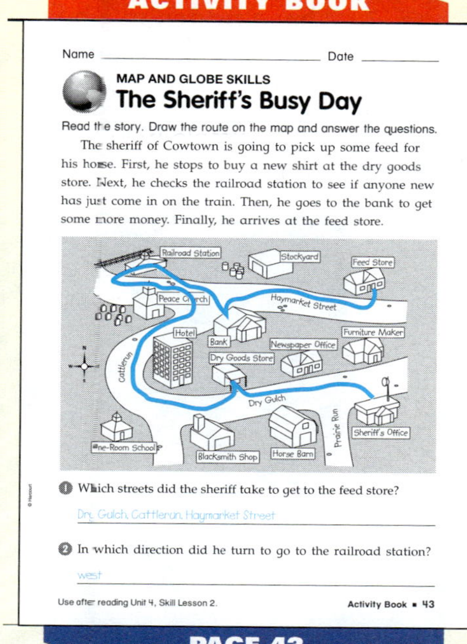

Name ______________________ Date __________

MAP AND GLOBE SKILLS
The Sheriff's Busy Day

Read the story. Draw the route on the map and answer the questions.

The sheriff of Cowtown is going to pick up some feed for his horse. First, he stops to buy a new shirt at the dry goods store. Next, he checks the railroad station to see if anyone new has just come in on the train. Then, he goes to the bank to get some more money. Finally, he arrives at the feed store.

1. Which streets did the sheriff take to get to the feed store?
Dry Gulch, Cattlerun, Haymarket Street

2. In which direction did he turn to go to the railroad station?
west

Use after reading Unit 4, Skill Lesson 2. Activity Book • 43

PAGE 43

TRANSPARENCY

Use SKILL TRANSPARENCY 4-2.

CD-ROM

Explore GEOSKILLS CD-ROM to learn more about map and globe skills.

Extension Activities For Home and School

Map a Shopping Trip

Materials: paper, pencils, crayons or markers, clipboard (optional)

Tell children to pay attention to where things are in the grocery store the next time they go shopping with a family member. If children have a clipboard, suggest they take it with them to draw sketches. Then have children work with the family member to make a map of the store when they get home. Tell them to include all the various areas in the store, such as fruit and vegetables, the meat section, dairy and frozen foods, school supplies, the aisles, and the check-out area. Then, using the family shopping list to refresh their memory, children should use a different color crayon to show the route they followed when shopping. They can draw little pictures to show items in the appropriate places on the map.
(VISUAL/KINESTHETIC)

From Here to There

Materials: paper, crayons or markers, world map

Remind children that in Lesson 2 they talked about immigrants moving to the United States. Tell children to draw a route on a map to show where immigrants traveled. Have children use the world map as a guide to draw their own outline map of the places they wish to show. Then have them draw a beginning point, an ending point, and the possible route. Children may also want to include important places on the map, such as a river on which the immigrant might have ridden in a boat. Under their map, children should write a description of the route, for example: *Juan took a plane from Havana, Cuba, to Miami, Florida. Then he took a train west through Alabama, Mississippi, and Louisiana to Texas. He settled in Beaumont.*
(VISUAL/TACTILE)

Family Heritage

OBJECTIVES

- Recognize that every family has its own heritage.
- Give examples of family traditions.
- Appreciate the value of learning from family members.

Generalize pp. 161, 179, 204

RESOURCES

Pupil Book/Unit Big Book, pp. 178–183

Word Cards V51–V52

Activity Book, p. 44

Reading and Vocabulary Transparency 4-4

Activity Pattern P7

Internet Resources

READING SOCIAL STUDIES

Make a Prediction Tell children that in this lesson they will learn about four children and their families. Have them preview the pictures on pages 178–183. Ask them what they might learn about these children and their families. Create a web to show their responses.

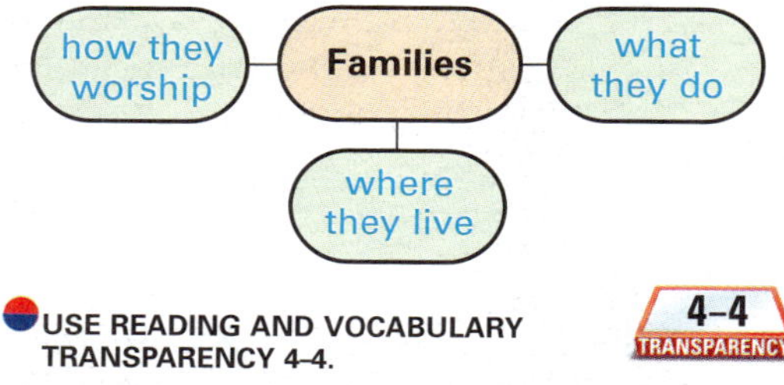

USE READING AND VOCABULARY TRANSPARENCY 4-4.

4-4 TRANSPARENCY

Vocabulary

heritage p. 178 **religion** p. 180 **tradition** p. 181 **ancestor** p. 182

When Minutes Count

Have children read the Big Idea of the lesson. Then have them read the lesson and find at least one sentence that supports the Big Idea.

Quick Summary

In this lesson, readers meet children with different cultural backgrounds. They learn that knowledge and ideas are passed from one generation to another through memories, experiences, and the sharing of special traditions.

1 Motivate

Set the Purpose

Big Idea Have children read the Big Idea statement before starting the lesson. As they read, ask them to note details about how families pass their culture from parents and grandparents to children.

Access Prior Knowledge

Invite volunteers to tell something they have learned about their culture from an older family member.

2 Teach

Read and Respond

Culture and Society Have children read pages 178 and 179 and look at the pictures. Ask children what they learned about María and her family. Point out that many members of the García family have lived on the same land for hundreds of years. This means that María's grandparents, and even her grandparents' parents, may have lived in the same house.

Q **What do you think it would be like to live in the same house where your grandparents once lived?**

A Some may say that it would be interesting, while others may say that they prefer their own houses.

Analyze Primary Sources

Deed Direct children's attention to the image of the land grant deed. Explain that at one time, the government gave away land in certain regions. Deeds were documents showing ownership of the land. Have children suggest how a deed today would look different. (machine printed rather than hand scripted)

Visual Learning

Picture Ask children to describe María's house. Discuss features of the house that show a Spanish influence. (tile roof, shutters, arched doorways and windows, thick walls, balcony)

Q **How is this house like yours? How is it different?**

A Children's answers will vary based on the type of home in which they live.

Lesson 3

Family Heritage

Big Idea
Families pass their culture from parent to child.

Vocabulary
heritage
religion
tradition
ancestor

María García lives in Arizona. Members of the García family have been living there for hundreds of years. They have a long heritage. **Heritage** is culture that is passed down from family to family over the years.

The Garcías live in a Spanish-style home. In the community, many homes like the Garcías' remind people of their history.

Land deed, 1673

178

INTEGRATE LANGUAGES

Adobe Many homes in the Southwest are made of sun-dried mud bricks called adobe. *Adobe* comes from an Arabic word *at-tub*, which was the name of bricks used thousands of years ago. When Arabic and Spanish mixed, the word became *adob*. Then with the meeting of Spanish people and Native Americans, it became *adobe*. Adobe is made from natural resources—sunshine, water, straw, and sand or clay.

INTEGRATE ART

Houses in Our Town Remind children that the older houses and buildings in your town are examples of the town's heritage. Show children pictures of these structures. Have them draw a picture of one structure and write a sentence describing it.

María is learning to play the guitar. She especially likes some of the old Mexican songs she hears on the radio.

Mrs. García has a job at a community history center. She takes schoolchildren through the center. She explains the Spanish and Mexican heritage of Arizona.

179

Visual Learning

Picture Direct children's attention to the picture of María with her guitar. Explain that it is a special type of guitar called a Spanish guitar. Tell children that María probably heard this instrument played in some of the songs that she listened to on the radio. She might also have heard an older family member playing the Spanish guitar.

Q What do you learn about María from this picture?

A She likes music.

Read and Respond

Culture and Society Invite a volunteer to describe the picture of Mrs. García. Explain that the Hispanic culture is based on the cultures of both Spain and Mexico. Explain that a history center is a place where people can learn about the history of a place.

Q What do you think you might see at a history center?

A photographs; objects that people used in earlier times, such as clothes, tools, and toys; historical documents

Geography Explain that, like María, many Hispanic people live in the southwestern states, such as Arizona, California, New Mexico, and Texas. Have children find these states on a map.

INTEGRATE MUSIC

Guitar Music Ask the school music teacher to show children how to hold a guitar and strum the strings. Allow volunteers to try to make different sounds by strumming and plucking different strings (or combinations of strings) and holding the neck in different places.

Bring a recording of Spanish guitar music to class, preferably by a master such as Andrés Segovia. Play different kinds of songs so children can hear the range of this instrument.

READING SKILL

Generalize Ask students to name some traditions that their families have. Then ask students to create a general statement about why traditions are important to their family.

INTEGRATE READING

Family Traditions Share the book *The Keeping Quilt* by Patricia Polacco, a story that describes the traditions of a Russian Jewish family living in the United States during the early part of the twentieth century. After reading, ask children to tell why they think the quilt was so important to the family. Then invite children to work in pairs to draw pictures to show the different ways the quilt in the story was used over the years.

Read and Respond

Geography Have children follow along as you read aloud page 180. Tell them that many immigrants have come to the United States from Russia. Display a world map and help children locate Russia. Invite them to compare the sizes of Russia and nearby countries.

Civics and Government Remind children that the Constitution includes a Bill of Rights that lists the freedoms and individual rights Americans enjoy.

Q **Why did Saul's grandfather bring his family to the United States?**

A So they could be free to follow their religion.

Economics Direct children's attention to the image of the catalog. Ask children if they have ever ordered anything from a catalog. Explain that companies sell a variety of objects such as foods, clothing, tools, and furniture from catalogs. Ask children to explain the freedom Saul's family has to own and run their own business. Explain that Saul's family takes orders over the phone or from a Web site. Then the family packages and mails the selected items. Because Saul's family sells foods, they may send some items in special containers to keep the items cold, or on refrigerated trucks. You may wish to point out that caviar is a popular Russian food and that Jews often serve lox (smoked salmon) with bagels and cream cheese.

Visual Learning

Picture Direct children's attention to the picture of Seder (SAY•dur). Explain that Seder, an important Jewish celebration, is a feast that occurs on the first two days of a religious holiday called Passover. Invite children who have attended a Seder to share their experiences and describe some of the traditional dishes.

Saul Volkoff's great-grandfather moved his family to New York in 1927. They came here because they wanted freedom to follow their **religion**, or belief in God. Saul's family is Jewish. Their religion is one of the oldest in the world.

Saul lives in a neighborhood with other families from Russia. His parents own a restaurant. They also send special foods around the country. The family works together and goes to temple together.

180

BACKGROUND

Seder Jews celebrate Passover for seven or eight days each spring. Jewish families celebrate the beginning of Passover by sharing the Seder meal. Before the feast begins, people say prayers, sing songs, and tell stories describing the Exodus of the Jews from Egypt. Special foods are served at the meal, such as bitter herbs (horseradish), unleavened bread (matzo), and a mix of apples, nuts, wine, and honey. Children play an important part. During the Seder, the youngest child asks four questions about the Passover holiday.

QUESTIONS KIDS ASK

Q **What are Saul and his father wearing on their heads?**

A The headwear is called a yarmulke (YAH•muh•kuh).

Some Jewish men and boys wear their yarmulkes all the time. Others wear them when they celebrate or go to temple.

Aneesa Anwar lives in New Jersey across the river from Saul's family. The Anwars are newcomers from a country in Asia called Pakistan. They are learning English and making friends in their new country.

People often ask Aneesa about the clothes her parents wear. The Anwars are Muslims. They have many **traditions**, or special ways of doing things. Aneesa brought a prayer rug to school. It has belonged to her family for many years. She talked about some of her family's traditions.

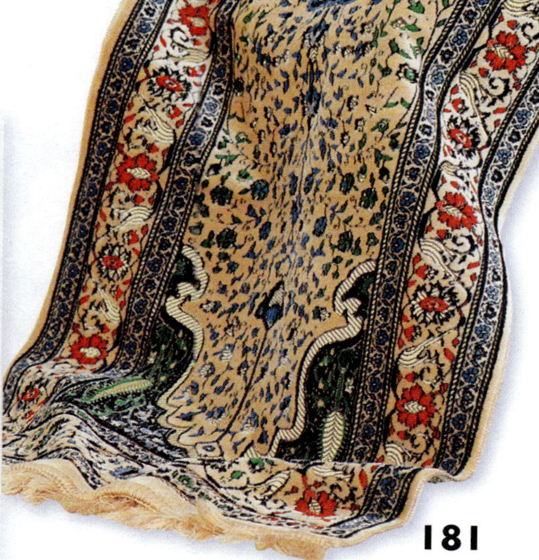

181

Read and Respond

Geography Have children follow along as you read aloud page 181. Display a world map and help children locate Pakistan on the map.

Q What are the two biggest countries located along the border of Pakistan?

A India and China

Culture and Society Direct children's attention to the photograph of the mosque. Tell children that mosques, temples, and churches are all places of worship. Point out that a cross, a Jewish star, and a prayer rug are all symbols of religious beliefs.

Visual Learning

Picture Direct children's attention to the photograph of Aneesa's family. Encourage children to describe the clothing worn by the adults in Aneesa's family. Ask them to compare this clothing with the clothing worn by the children.

Explain to children that families of all cultures have traditions.

Q What traditions is Aneesa learning about from her family?

A She is learning about special clothing and prayer rugs.

STUDY/RESEARCH SKILLS

Look for Questions/Answers Point out that the story says that Saul lives in New York and Aneesa lives across the river in New Jersey. Ask children what question careful readers might ask themselves after reading this information. For example, *What river flows between New York and New Jersey?* Have children write the question on a sheet of paper. Then provide a map and have children record the answer. (the Hudson River)

REACH ALL LEARNERS

English as a Second Language Have children write the proper nouns from page 181 on index cards. (Give them this hint: *Look for capital letters.*) Write the following headings on the board: *Names of People, Names of Places,* and *Names of Religions.* Have children sort the cards by placing them on the chalk ledge under the appropriate heading.

MAKE IT RELEVANT

At Home Have children interview an older family member about the family's heritage. Before the interview, guide children to think of several questions that will help them learn about family traditions and customs. Children may want to tape-record the answers or take notes. Have children present an oral report to the class describing the person and details about the family's heritage.

Read and Respond

Geography Have children follow along as you read aloud page 182. Tell them that many immigrants have come to the United States from Korea. Display a world map and help children locate Korea on the map. Then have them locate Seattle, Washington.

Q Why do you think many Koreans have immigrated to Seattle?

A It is closer to Korea than places in the center of the United States. It is near the water, like many places in Korea.

Visual Learning

Pictures Direct children's attention to the photographs showing Kim and his grandmother and other relatives. Explain that Kim's ancestors are people who lived a long time ago, such as his grandmother's parents.

Point out that the first photo is of Kim's great-grandmother at her wedding. The second photo shows Kim's father on his first birthday. Help children create a family tree to show family relationships.

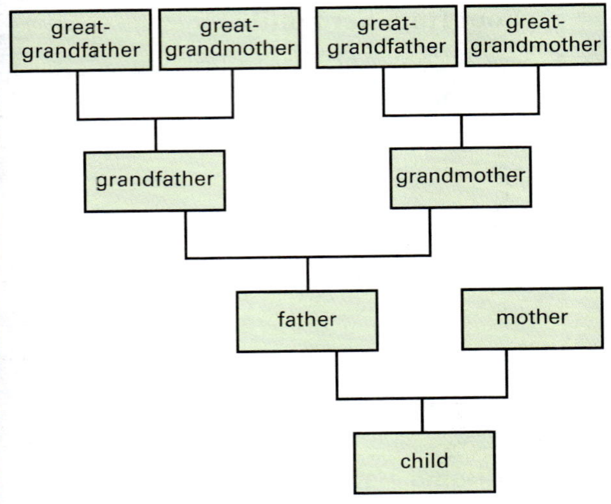

• HERITAGE •

Family Reunion Discuss how family reunions are a good way to share family histories and traditions. Ask children to identify occasions when families might reunite. (an anniversary, a birthday, a graduation, a wedding, or a holiday)

Kim Lee's grandmother helps his family remember their ancestors in Korea. An **ancestor** is a family member who lived long ago. She shows Kim photographs of their family.

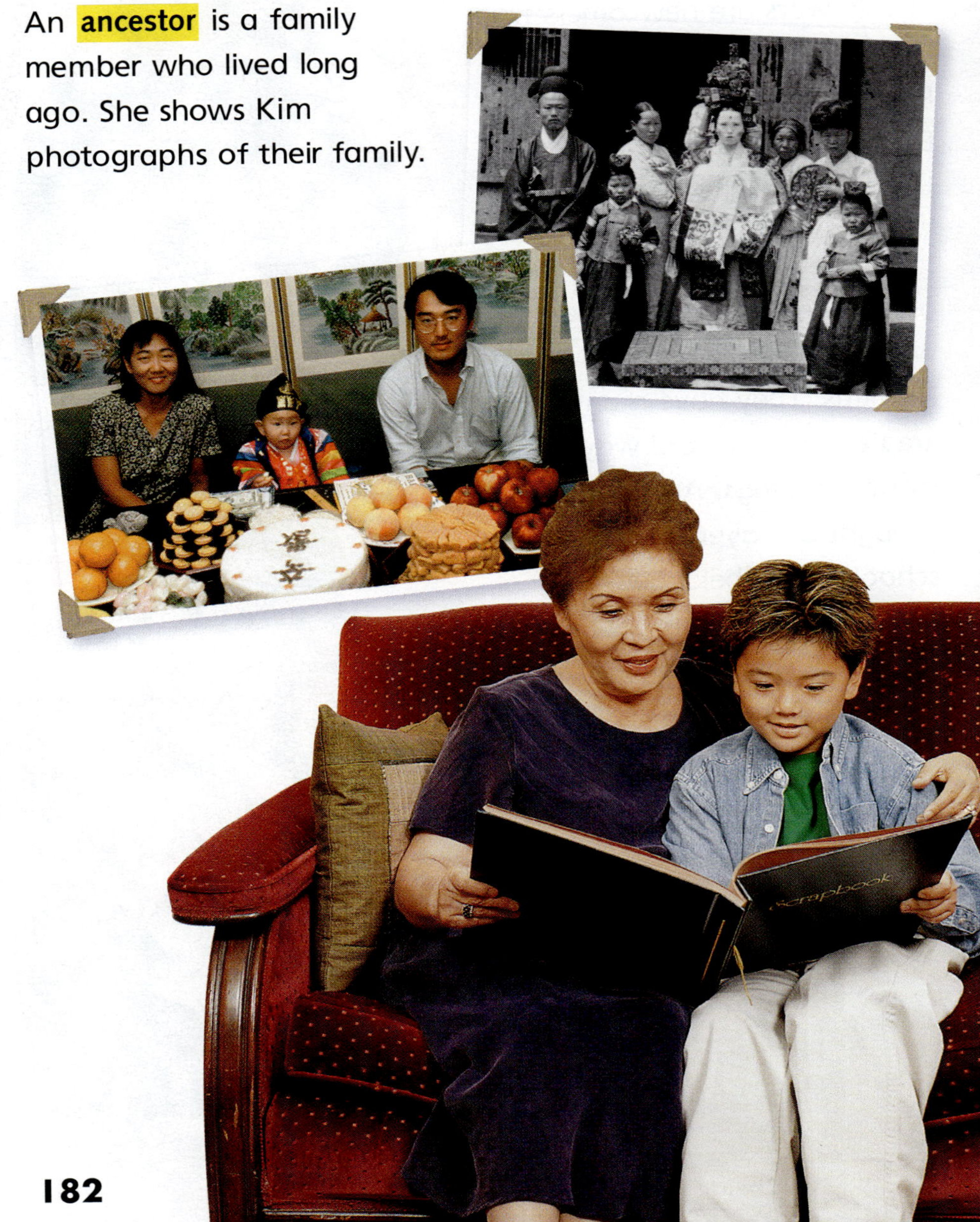

182

BACKGROUND

Koreans Koreans celebrate the family. They have ceremonies called *chesas* to remember their ancestors. They also enjoy birthdays. Families gather for large parties. A child's first birthday and a senior's sixtieth birthday are especially festive. The guest of honor is surrounded by fruit, rice cakes, candies, and cash.

EXTEND AND ENRICH

Make a Scrapbook As a class, choose a country to study in depth. With the help of an adult, have children collect examples of community life in that country. Examples can be photographs, pictures from magazines, or written descriptions. Then have students work in pairs to create pages for a class scrapbook of community life in that country. Have children discuss the similarities and differences between their lives and the lives of the people who live in that country.

There are many Koreans living in Seattle, Washington. Kim's dad designs Web pages for a computer company. Kim wants him to put their family's pictures on a Web page to share with other Koreans.

• HERITAGE •

Family Reunion

As families grow, family members may move far apart. They can write letters and e-mails or phone their relatives. They can also plan family reunions. A reunion is a gathering of the family. Great-grandparents and grandparents, aunts, uncles, and cousins all join together for a fun celebration of their family's heritage.

LESSON 3 Review

1. **Vocabulary** What can you learn from a family's **heritage**?
2. Give an example of a family tradition.
3. Ask a parent or other adult to describe a family ancestor.

3 Close

Summarize Key Content

- Heritage is culture that is passed down from family to family.
- A religion is one's beliefs in God.
- Traditions are special ways of doing things.
- An ancestor is a family member who lived long ago.

READING SOCIAL STUDIES

Make a Prediction Review the topics that children predicted they would learn about in this lesson. Ask them if they would like to make changes or add other topics to the web. Help them summarize the lesson by adding circles to complete the web.

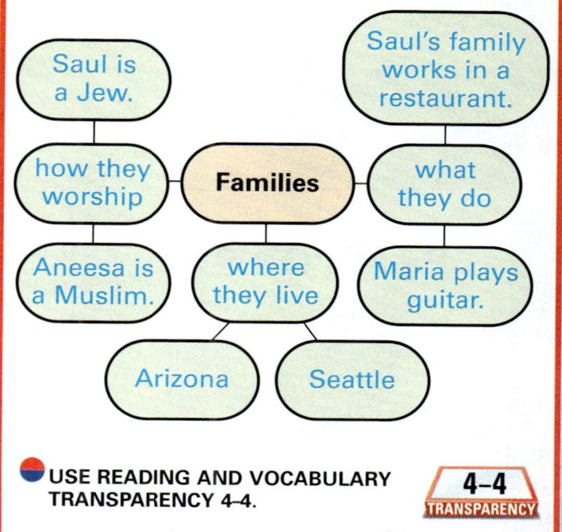

USE READING AND VOCABULARY TRANSPARENCY 4-4.

4-4 TRANSPARENCY

RETEACH THE LESSON

Use Pictures Have children use the photographs to help them review the information and vocabulary words in the lesson. Ask them to point out details in the photographs and explain what is happening. Help children relate the pictures to vocabulary words that are not on the same page.

ACTIVITY BOOK

Name ______________ Date ________

Pass It On!

Draw a picture to show something the person on the left might pass on to the person on the right.

44 • Activity Book — Use after reading Unit 4, Lesson 3.

PAGE 44

Assess

Lesson 3 Review—Answers

1. Children might say they can learn about traditions and culture.
2. Children may describe religious ceremonies or traditional family meals.
3. 

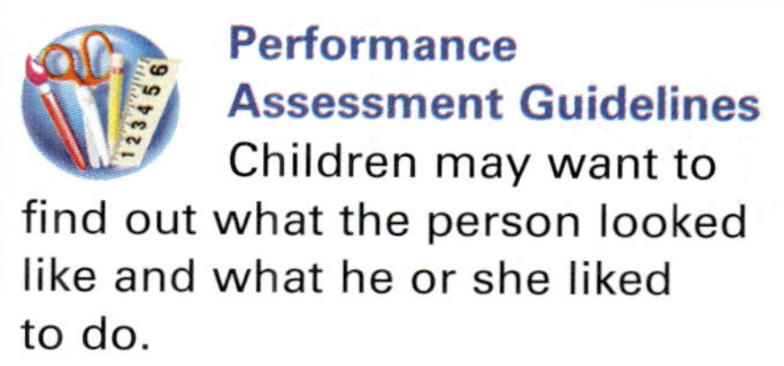

Performance Assessment Guidelines Children may want to find out what the person looked like and what he or she liked to do.

Extension Activities For Home and School

Together

Materials: **copies of the poem "Together," paper, pencil, crayons or markers**

Distribute the poem to each child and read it aloud as children follow along.

Together

Because we do
All things together
All things improve,
Even weather.

Our daily meat
And bread taste better,
Trees are greener,
Rain is wetter.

by Paul Engle

Talk about what the poem means. If you do things with a special person or people, the weather does not really get better. But if the weather is bad, you do not mind it so much because you are—together!

Ask children to think about something they do with a family member that is special or better because they do it together. Then have them draw a picture showing them doing the activity. Help them write a poem that explains the picture.
(AUDITORY/TACTILE)

Take a Trip

Materials: **pencils, crayons, scissors, glue or tape, copies of Activity Pattern P7 (passport)**

Ask children to tell what countries their ancestors came from, if they know. Have children imagine that they are going to take a trip to the country or countries of some of their ancestors. Children who do not know where their ancestors came from can imagine traveling to favorite countries. Point out that when people travel to other countries, each person must have a passport with his or her name, date and place of birth, picture, and signature on it. Provide children with a copy of Activity Pattern P7 and have them fill out their passports. Then have them fold the passports like books, with the word *Passport* on the front cover. Inside they should include a picture of themselves—they can use a real photograph or draw a self-portrait. Then have them write on the inside of their passports the names of the countries they plan to visit. Next to each country they can draw a picture; for instance, if the country is Egypt, they might draw a pyramid.
(TACTILE/KINESTHETIC)

Let's Celebrate!

Materials: **drawing paper, markers or crayons**

Remind children that all families have traditions—something they do year after year on special occasions. Ask children to suggest traditions in their family, such as a christening, a wedding, playing with a piñata at a birthday party, attending a parade on Chinese New Year, or eating spaghetti and meatballs for dinner on Saturday. Have children choose their favorite family tradition and draw a picture of it. Display children's pictures on a "Let's Celebrate!" bulletin board.
(AUDITORY/VISUAL)

Read a Bar Graph

OBJECTIVES

- Identify the parts of a bar graph.
- Use a bar graph to interpret information.

RESOURCES

Pupil Book/Unit Big Book, pp. 184–185
Word Cards V53–V54
Activity Book, p. 45
Skill Transparency 4–3

Family Ancestors

Africa
Asia
North America
South America
Europe
Australia
Not sure

0 1 2 3 4 5 6 7

Vocabulary

bar graph p. 184

1 Motivate

List the names *Maria, Saul, Aneesa,* and *Kim* horizontally at the bottom of the board. Remind children that they met these children in Lesson 3. Maria is the girl who plays Spanish guitar. Saul is the Russian boy whose family owns a restaurant. Aneesa's family is from Pakistan, and they worship in a mosque. Kim is Korean, and his family pictures are on a Web site. Go around the room and ask each child which of the four children on the board they would most like to meet. As each child gives a name, draw a smiley face above that name on the board, to make a bar graph. Then count the votes and write the numbers at the top of each bar.

Why It Matters

Explain that a bar graph makes it easy to see and understand information. You could write the results of the vote in sentences, but if you look at the graph, you can see right away which child got the most votes and which got the fewest. The graph also makes it easy to compare the number of votes.

REACH ALL LEARNERS

Auditory Learners Discuss the information on the bar graph that children helped create. Invite volunteers to describe something about each category. For example, a child may point out that more children would like to meet Kim than Maria.

2 Teach

What You Need to Know

Have children examine each type of bar graph.

Q How do you know which bar represents the most people or things on each graph?

A The longest or the tallest bar means the most people or things.

Q How do you know which bar represents the fewest people or things on each graph?

A The shortest or smallest bar means the least or fewest.

Have children look at the graph on page 185. Ask a volunteer to read the title and the first column. Make sure children realize that this is a horizontal bar graph read from left to right.

Skills

Read a Bar Graph

Vocabulary
bar graph

Why It Matters

Some information can be understood more easily if it is shown on a chart or graph.

What You Need to Know

A **bar graph** is a drawing that uses bars to show the numbers of things. The title of the graph tells you what information it shows. Each bar stands for a different group being counted. Some bar graphs are read from left to right. Some bar graphs are read from bottom to top.

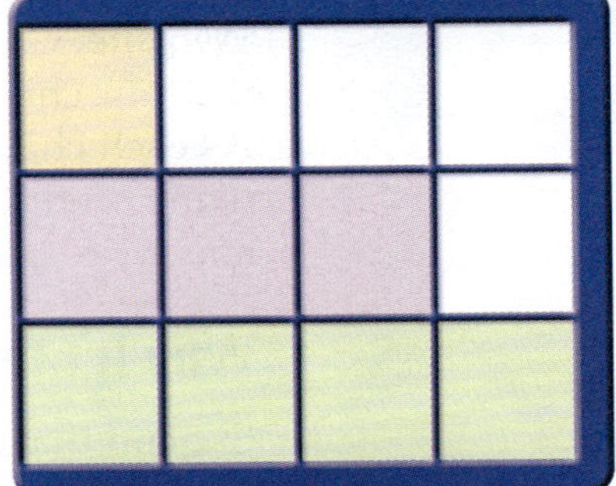

REACH ALL LEARNERS

Visual Learners Discuss children's favorite outdoor activities, such as swimming, swinging, or skating. Record their responses on the board. Place tally marks to show how many children chose each activity. Have children use the information to create a bar graph on chart paper. Ask children questions that help them interpret the graph. For example, *How many more children chose skating than swimming?*

EXTEND AND ENRICH

Create a Graph Have small groups work together to make graphs by themselves. They can choose a topic, poll classmates, and fill in the bars. Let groups display and explain their completed graphs. Warn them not to make their graphs too complicated. If they asked "What is your favorite food?" they might end up with 20 bars. A better question might be, "Which do you like best, spaghetti, tacos, hot dogs, or hamburgers?"

Family Ancestors

Africa
Asia
North America
South America
Europe
Australia
Not sure
0 1 2 3 4 5 6 7

Practice the Skill

1. How many children have ancestors from Europe?
2. Are there fewer children with ancestors from Asia or from Africa?
3. In which rows would you count someone whose ancestors were Native American?
4. Why do you think the bar graph has a row labeled Not sure?

Apply What You Learned

Work with classmates to make a bar graph. Show how many people you know from other continents.

Practice the Skill—Answers

1. 7
2. Asia
3. North or South America
4. Some people may not know where their ancestors came from.

3 Close

Apply What You Learned

Children's bar graphs should include bars, numbers, and a title. They should be easy to read.

RETEACH THE SKILL

Read a Graph Make a simple favorite-pudding graph with only *chocolate, vanilla,* and *banana* as choices. Do not allow any flavor more than 10 votes. Then ask children simple questions such as these: *Does the graph go up and down or across? What is the title? What are the flavor choices? How many people chose vanilla? Is that more or fewer than those who chose banana?*

ACTIVITY BOOK

Name ______________ Date ______

CHART AND GRAPH SKILLS
Use a Bar Graph

This bar graph shows how many families from other countries moved into a neighborhood. Use the graph to answer the questions.

New Neighbors
Number of Families
5
4
3
2
1
0
Japan Mexico Vietnam Russia South Africa
Country

1. How many families came from Mexico? 4
2. Where did the greatest number of families come from? Russia
3. How many more families came from Japan than from South Africa? 2
4. What country might you add for someone who lives in your neighborhood? Answers will vary.

Use after reading Unit 4, Skill Lesson 3. Activity Book ▪ 45

© Harcourt

PAGE 45

TRANSPARENCY

Use SKILL TRANSPARENCY 4–3.

Extension Activities For Home and School

Creepy Crawlies

Materials: **paper, pencils, crayons, reference books about insects**

Tell children that there are more insects—and more different kinds of insects—than any other animal on Earth. Some are tiny, like fleas, and some are bigger, like grasshoppers. Have children work in small groups to research kinds of insects and their sizes, so that they can make a bar graph of insect sizes. They can decide if they want to label the graph *Small, Medium,* and *Large* (as long as they define what these labels mean) or be more specific, such as *Shorter than Half an Inch, Half an Inch to One Inch, Longer Than One Inch.* Tell children to find at least 20 insects, note their sizes, and then fill in their bar graph grid. Children should agree on a title for their graph, and they can decorate it with drawings of some insects. Let groups display and compare their graphs.
(VISUAL/TACTILE)

Many Cultures

Materials: **paper, pencils**

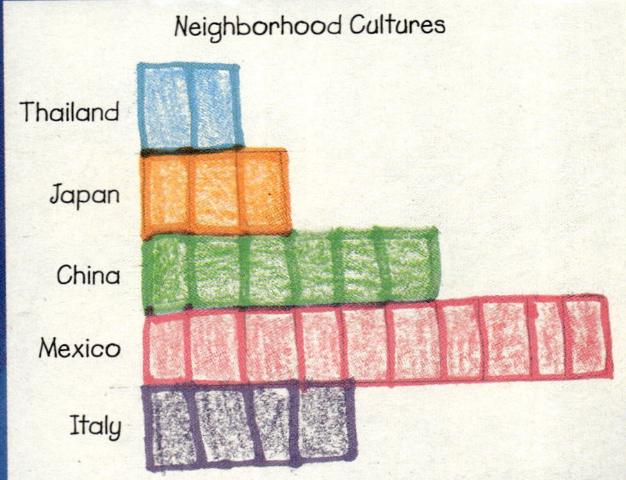

Suggest that children take a walk around their community with a family member. Encourage them to look for stores, restaurants, and other establishments that reflect other cultures, such as a Chinese or Italian restaurant, a Mexican grocery, or a Korean gift shop. Before children take their walk, tell them to make a list of several countries. As children spot places, they can make a tally mark next to the appropriate country or list a new one. Back home, children and their family member can work together to create a bar graph using the information. Afterward, suggest that children look at their graph and discuss what it tells them about their community and the people who live there.
(AUDITORY/VISUAL/TACTILE)

Where in the World?

Materials: **lists of biggest cities, bar graph grids, world map, paper, pencils, crayons or markers**

Provide partners with a list of 10 large cities around the world and a bar graph grid. Have them label four of the bars *Ocean, River, Both,* and *Neither.* Ask them to locate each city on a world map and decide if the city is on (or very near) an ocean, a river, both, or neither, and then color in a box on the graph for each city. (You may want to suggest that they cross out each city on their list as they color it on the graph.) Have children write a title for their graph and, on another sheet of paper, write three sentences based on the information in their graph.
(VISUAL/TACTILE)

World's 10 Largest Cities

Kolkata, India
Delhi, India
Shanghai, China
Tokyo, Japan
Mexico City, Mexico
Mumbai (Bombay), India
New York City, United States
São Paulo, Brazil
Lagos, Nigeria
Los Angeles, United States

Community Celebrations

OBJECTIVES

- Identify cultural holidays celebrated in the community.
- Describe customs associated with cultural holidays.
- Explain the origins of holiday traditions.

 **Generalize** pp. 161, 189, 204

RESOURCES

Pupil Book/Unit Big Book, pp. 186–189
Word Cards V53–V54
Activity Pattern P8
Activity Book, p. 46
Reading and Vocabulary Transparency 4-5
Internet Resources

READING SOCIAL STUDIES

Study Questions Have children discuss the following questions: *What events do holidays celebrate? What activities do people do during each holiday? What do people wear? What do they eat?* Use responses to begin a chart. Revisit the chart at the end of the lesson.

Question	Chinese New Year	Cinco de mayo	Kwanzaa
What events do holidays celebrate?			
What activities do people do during each holiday?			

USE READING AND VOCABULARY TRANSPARENCY 4-5. **4-5 TRANSPARENCY**

Vocabulary

holiday p. 186 **custom** p. 186

When Minutes Count

Have children examine the pictures on pages 186–189. Use the pictures to discuss the Big Idea in the lesson.

Quick Summary

In this lesson, children will learn about holidays celebrated in different communities and by different cultures.

1 Motivate

Set the Purpose

Big Idea Have children read the Big Idea statement before starting the lesson. As they read, ask them to pay attention to how the celebrations are similar and different.

Access Prior Knowledge

Have children think of some of the special days celebrated in their community. Ask volunteers who have seen or been part of these celebrations to share their experiences.

2 Teach

Read and Respond

Geography Read page 186 with children. Explain that many holidays originated in other countries and were brought here by immigrants. Display a globe or world map and have children locate China. Explain that Chinese New Year, which originated in China, is now celebrated in many cities in the United States and all over the world. In some big cities in the United States, such as San Francisco and New York City, there is an area called Chinatown, where many Chinese people live and work. Explain that in these cities the Chinese New Year parade takes place in Chinatown. Point out that this day differs from the New Year's Day many people celebrate on January 1.

Visual Learning

Pictures Explain that a custom is something that is done the same way each time. Direct children's attention to the red *lai-see* envelope. Explain that on the first day of the Chinese New Year, parents give their children gifts of money presented in red envelopes. Point out that this is an example of a custom because it is done the same way every year. Have children name the other customs pictured on this page. Invite children to share some of their family customs related to holidays, such as having a Thanksgiving dinner or hanging a flag from a window on the Fourth of July.

HOLIDAY ACTIVITY

For more information about holidays and their customs, see HOLIDAY ACTIVITIES in the back of this Teacher's Edition.

Lesson

Big Idea
Communities celebrate their cultures.

Vocabulary
holiday
custom

Community Celebrations

Americans celebrate many **holidays**, or special days, that began in other parts of the world. At these times people show everyone how proud they are of their cultures.

Chinese New Year

For Chinese people, the New Year is an important holiday. For two weeks, families follow many popular customs as they celebrate. A **custom** is the way a group of people does something. Chinese New Year has many customs. People give gifts, decorate homes and buildings, parade in costumes, and eat favorite Chinese foods. The Chinese also honor the elderly and remember their ancestors.

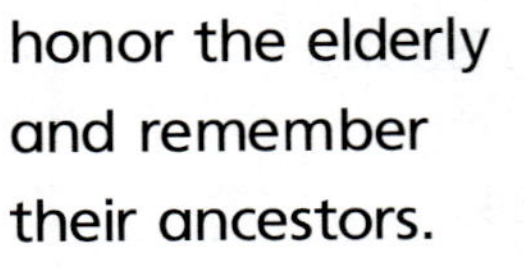

186

INTEGRATE MATHEMATICS

Chinese Years Explain that the years in the Chinese calendar have animal names: rat, ox, tiger, rabbit, dragon, snake, horse, sheep, monkey, rooster, dog, and pig. The year 1995 was the year of the pig, 1996 was the year of the rat, and so on through the cycle. Write the years *1995* through *2015* on the board, along with the animal names. Then ask children math questions such as *What year were you born? What is your animal? When you are nine, what year will it be? What is that year's animal?*

MENTAL MAPPING

Parade Route Have children imagine that a parade celebrating Chinese New Year or Mardi Gras will be marching down the halls of your school. Have them draw a map of the school and show a route that the parade might follow.

Mardi Gras

Mardi Gras means "fat Tuesday" in French. It is the day before Lent, the beginning of a season of the Roman Catholic Church. Lent is a serious time, so before it starts, everyone has fun on Mardi Gras. People like to dress up in costumes and march around the streets or go to parties.

Louisiana has the biggest Mardi Gras celebrations in the United States. The Cajun culture group there has a special custom. People go from door to door asking for food. They combine everything to make a big stew called gumbo for everyone to eat.

Melt 1 tablespoon butter
Stir in and cook until golden:
1/4 cup chopped onion
Stir in until blended:
2 tablespoons flour
Add and stir until smooth:
2 cups strained tomatoes
4 cups stock
1 quart thinly sliced okra
Add in small pieces:
1/2 lb. raw cleaned shrimp
1/2 lb. raw crab meat
Simmer until okra is tender
Add 16 shelled oysters
Serve when oysters are plump

MAKE IT RELEVANT

At Home Have children ask family members about traditional celebrations, foods, customs, sports, games, or music that are part of the culture of their country of origin. Ask them to find out where aspects of that culture can be found today, such as in everyday meals, cultural festivals, and so on. As a class, create a mural so that children can share what they discovered about their culture.

REACH ALL LEARNERS

Below-Level Learners Invite children to look at the pictures in this lesson. Ask them to identify objects and activities they do not know the names of. Use self-stick notes to label these things. After children learn the words, remove the labels and distribute them to children. Ask them to read each label aloud and place it next to the appropriate object or activity. Children can then use the word in a sentence to tell about the picture.

Read and Respond

Geography Have children locate Louisiana and New Orleans on a map. Tell children that the biggest Mardi Gras celebration in the United States occurs in New Orleans. Tourists from all over the world visit New Orleans at that time to share in the celebration.

Culture and Society Explain that the season of Lent lasts for 40 days before Easter. Long ago, people fasted during Lent, eating only one meal a day and spending time preparing for Easter. Fat Tuesday got its name because it was the last day before Lent when people could eat a lot of food—and get fat—before they began their fast. Today, few Catholics fast during Lent, but many of them give up something special, such as chocolate or meat, for those 40 days. Lent ends with Easter, which celebrates the resurrection of Jesus after the Crucifixion.

Q **Why are celebrations important to a community?**

A They help people remember important events; they bring people together; they are fun.

Q **What is a happy celebration you take part in? What is a serious one? Can a celebration be happy and serious at the same time?**

A Jewish children might mention Yom Kippur, the day of atonement. Other children might suggest that Dr. Martin Luther King, Jr., Day is both happy and serious, because we remember the good things he did but are sad that he was killed.

Visual Learning

Picture Have children describe the masks on page 187. Ask children also to describe times when they have worn costumes or masks.

Q **How do you know that the people in the picture are probably having fun?**

A Because we had fun when we wore costumes and masks.

Read and Respond

Culture and Society Have children note similarities in the celebrations of Chinese New Year, Mardi Gras, Cinco de Mayo, and Kwanzaa, such as wearing costumes and sharing special foods. Point out that people all over the world celebrate similar events, such as harvest festivals or end-of-winter festivals.

Q What other events might be celebrated around the world?

A birthdays, the new year, the year that country became independent, the birthday of a national hero

Visual Learning

Picture Direct children's attention to the picture of the piñata. Explain that children take turns trying to break a piñata during a celebration such as a birthday. They are blindfolded and spun around in a circle to make them dizzy. Next, they are given a bat or stick to use to strike the piñata, which is swinging from the branch of a tree. When the piñata is finally broken, candy or small toys fall to the ground, and the children scramble for them.

Culture and Society Tell children that Kwanzaa is both a happy and a serious holiday. Each of the seven days centers on an idea important to African Americans. The seven ideas are unity (being together as a group), self-determination (not letting other people tell you how to live or what to do), collective work and responsibility (helping one another), cooperative economics (helping others succeed in business and helping poor people), purpose (doing things for the right reasons), creativity (having and sharing new ideas), and faith (religion). Each day families light one candle on a kinara.

Q Do you remember another group of people you learned about in this unit who light candles? Do you remember what their candle holder is called?

A Jewish people light a menorah to celebrate Hanukkah.

Cinco de Mayo

Cinco de Mayo is a fiesta, or holiday, celebrated by Mexican Americans. There are many street parties, at which people in beautiful costumes play music and dance with great energy. Parades of riders on horses remind everyone of the freedom Mexicans fought for many years ago.

piñata

Favorite Mexican foods are served. Some are very hot and spicy. Children play games and break open colorful piñatas stuffed with fruits, candies, and toys.

188

WORD WORK

Use Context Clues Remind children that when they are reading and come to a word they do not know, they should look at the words and sentences nearby to help them figure out what the new word means. Have a volunteer read aloud the first sentence about Cinco de Mayo. *What clue in the sentence tells you what* fiesta *means?* (holiday) Ask children to read the fourth sentence in the second paragraph about Kwanzaa. *How can you tell what* karamu *means?* (The sentence says *or feast.*)

EXTEND AND ENRICH

Research and Report Have partners or small groups conduct research about a holiday that they would like to learn more about. They may choose a holiday from the lesson or any other holiday that interests them. Then have them make a chart on posterboard describing the holiday and illustrating it with magazine pictures or their own art. Display the posters on a "Holidays" bulletin board. Have children explain how these holidays are celebrated in the community today.

Kwanzaa

Kwanzaa is a week-long celebration in December. It began in 1966 as a way for African Americans to celebrate African traditions. On each of the seven days, families light a candle on the kinara. They remember their past and what is important to them.

kinara

Each day is special. One day is for thinking about being together. Another day is for music, dancing, and storytelling. On the last day, everyone joins in a karamu, or feast. Children often get books or handmade gifts as a reward for working hard during the year.

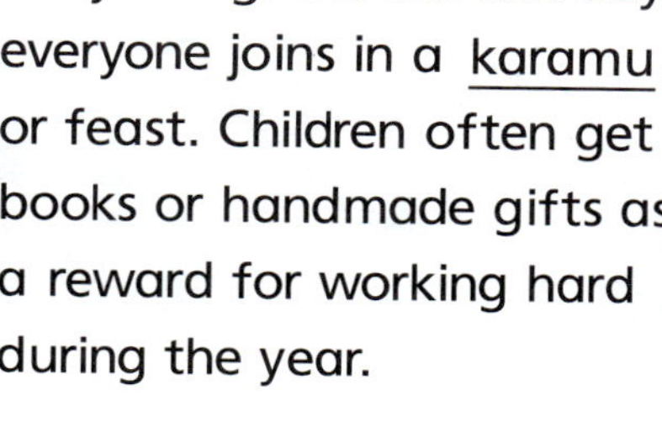

LESSON 4 Review

1. **Generalize** What can you learn about others through their holidays?
2. **Vocabulary** Describe a **custom** from one of the holidays in this lesson.
3. Make a greeting card for a special holiday in your community.

3 Close

Summarize Key Content

- Americans celebrate many holidays.
- A custom is the way people usually do things.
- Celebrations such as Chinese New Year, Mardi Gras, Cinco de Mayo, and Kwanzaa bring the people in a community together.

READING SOCIAL STUDIES

Study Questions Review children's answers to the questions asked at the beginning of the lesson. Ask children if they would like to change or add to their answers.

Question	Chinese New Year	Cinco de Mayo	Kwanzaa
What events do holidays celebrate?	the beginning of a new year	Mexico's independence	traditions of African American people
What activities do people do during each holiday?	costumes, Lion Dance, lai-see	dances, music, wear traditional costumes	lighting of the kinara, sharing a feast, telling stories

USE READING AND VOCABULARY TRANSPARENCY 4-5.

Assess

Lesson 4 Review—Answers

1. **Generalize** The special foods, costumes, songs, and dances can tell you what others think are important.
2. Children might mention eating special foods or wearing traditional costumes.
3. **Performance Assessment Guidelines** Children's cards can tell something about a holiday from the lesson or another holiday they know about. They may want to include words and pictures.

RETEACH THE LESSON

Compare and Contrast Help children create a Venn diagram to compare two of the holidays discussed in this lesson. Have children take turns telling one way that the holidays are alike and one way they are different. Use children's responses to complete the diagram.

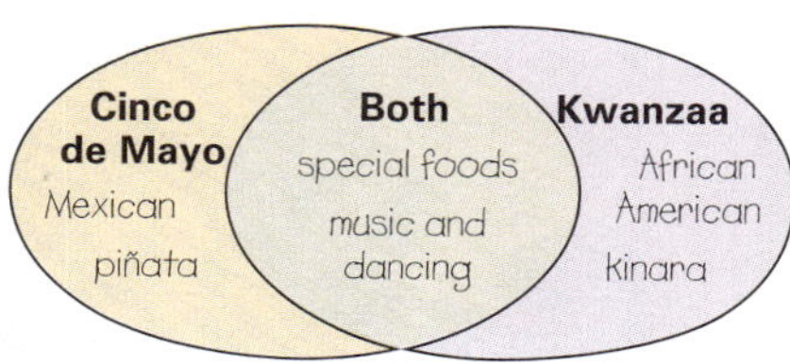

ACTIVITY BOOK

Name ______ Date ______

Happy Kwanzaa!

Read about Kwanzaa and follow the directions to color the kinara. Then write about unity.

The Kwanzaa candleholder is called a kinara. It holds seven candles. The candle in the middle is black. Black stands for the color of African people everywhere. Color the middle candle black. Three red candles are on the left. Red stands for the blood of ancestors. Color those candles red. Three green candles are on the right. Green stands for earth, life, and hope for the future. Color these candles green.

Every night, when families light one of the candles, they talk about an important idea. One of these ideas is unity, which means working together as a group and helping one another. On the lines below, write a way you can work with and help others in your classroom or at home.

Children's answers should reflect an understanding of ways they can work with and help others.

46 • Activity Book — Use after reading Unit 4, Lesson 4.

PAGE 46

Extension Activities For Home and School

Lift Every Voice

Materials: **song lyrics for "Lift Ev'ry Voice and Sing"**

Tell children about the holiday called Juneteenth. Explain that when the Civil War ended in 1865, slavery also ended. African American people were now free. But life was not easy for African Americans. They had not been allowed to go to school or learn trades so that they could earn a living. Many white people hated them. It took many years for African Americans to be really equal. In 1900, a man named James Weldon Johnson wrote a song called "Lift Ev'ry Voice and Sing." This song has been called the African American national anthem because, like America's national anthem, "The Star-Spangled Banner," it tells about the hopes of a group of people. This song is often sung on Juneteenth and during other events. Distribute copies of the excerpt from the song and read the words with children. Explain some of the hard words or ideas. If a recording of the song is available, play it so children can sing along. **(AUDITORY)**

Lift ev'ry voice and sing,
Till earth and heaven ring,
Ring with the harmonies of Liberty;
Let our rejoicing rise
High as the list'ning skies,
Let it resound loud as the rolling sea.
Sing a song full of the faith that the dark
past has taught us,
Sing a song full of the hope that the present
has brought us;
Facing the rising sun of our new day begun,
Let us march on till victory is won.

Children's Day: A Japanese Celebration

Materials: **Activity Pattern P8 (fish pattern); materials to decorate fish, such as crayons or markers, paint, yarn, glitter; scissors; tissue streamers; staples; hole punch; string; glue**

Remind children that in the United States, families celebrate both Mother's Day and Father's Day. Invite volunteers to describe how their families celebrate these days. Then tell children that in Japan, families celebrate Children's Day. On this day, families place paper fish on poles in front of homes where children live.

Give each child two copies of Activity Pattern P8 (fish pattern). Have children decorate their fish with materials such as markers, paint, yarn, and glitter. Also, have them attach tissue paper streamers to the tail of one of the fish. Then help them staple the two shapes together, leaving the mouth and tail of the fish open. Finally, punch a hole near the mouth of the fish and have children thread and tie a string through the hole. Invite children to run with their fish in an open space outdoors and watch while the wind passes through the fish and the streamers fly behind it. **(VISUAL/TACTILE/KINESTHETIC)**

Magnificent Masks

Materials: **variety of craft materials such as construction paper, feathers, glitter, markers, glue, scissors, scraps of fabric and ribbon, buttons, old magazines, string or yarn, hole punch**

Remind children that people wear costumes to celebrate many holidays. Have children name as many holidays as they can, and add some of your own so there is a long list. Have children pick one that interests them and think of a good mask to wear to celebrate it. Then let children use craft materials to make their mask (or a hat, if they prefer). Afterward, invite children to don their masks and tell the class about them. Invite children to march around the classroom in a holiday parade. **(VISUAL/TACTILE/KINESTHETIC)**

Expressions of Culture

OBJECTIVES

- Identify and explain expressions of culture in the community.
- Identify stories from different cultures.
- Identify and explain art forms in different cultures.

 **Generalize** pp. 161, 204

RESOURCES

Pupil Book/Unit Big Book, pp. 190–195
Word Cards V53–V54
Activity Book, p. 47
Reading and Vocabulary Transparency 4-6
Internet Resources

READING SOCIAL STUDIES

Personal Response Have children think of favorite books, paintings, historic buildings, types of music, and types of dance from their community or state. List their responses on the board. You may want to show children photographs from your newspaper or a tourist magazine to begin the activity.

1. Buildings
2. Paintings
3. Dances
4. Gardens
5. Stories
6. Music

USE READING AND VOCABULARY TRANSPARENCY 4-6.

Vocabulary

language p. 190

When Minutes Count

Have children read the Big Idea of the lesson. Then have them read the lesson and find at least one sentence that supports the Big Idea.

Quick Summary

This lesson focuses on ways people express their cultural traditions—through language, art and architecture, music, and dance.

1 Motivate

Set the Purpose

Big Idea Have children read the Big Idea statement of the lesson. Explain that people in different cultures create stories, artworks, and even types of buildings that reflect their culture. As children read, ask them to pay attention to details about what these art forms tell about a culture.

Access Prior Knowledge

Invite children to recall any folktales or fairy tales they may have heard. Ask volunteers to tell what they remember about the characters, locations, or plots of these stories.

2 Teach

Literature

Read and Respond

Culture and Society Read page 190 with children. Explain that the word *language* refers to the words people use to speak and write. You are speaking the English language. Ask children to tell any other languages they speak or hear at home. Then explain that the word *literature* refers to stories, poems, and plays. Literature can be written in any language.

Help children understand that there are different kinds of literature—myth, legend, folktale, and fairy tale.

Q Why do you think people tell stories?

A to have fun, to learn about people, to explain new things

Explain that some of the stories on page 190 are very old, and children like themselves have been enjoying them for hundreds of years. Point out that people in different places and at different times laugh and cry and think about the same kinds of things.

Lesson 5

Big Idea
People express their cultures through stories and the arts.

Vocabulary
language

Expressions of Culture

Literature

People in every culture use **language** as a way to express themselves. People write stories and poems. The myths, legends, folktales, and fairy tales of a culture tell us what the people believe.

190

BACKGROUND

Grimm Brothers German scholars Jakob and Wilhelm Grimm are known for their classic collections of folktales, especially *Grimm's Fairy Tales* (1812–1822). This important collection, which played a role in originating the science of folklore, included material from Scandinavia, Spain, the Netherlands, Ireland, Scotland, England, Serbia, and Finland.

REACH ALL LEARNERS

English as a Second Language Help children read and pronounce the words *myths, legends, folktales,* and *fairy tales.* Explain that these types of stories are made-up stories that were handed down from one generation to the next and were eventually written down. Cultures all around the world have these types of stories. Encourage volunteers to give an example of one of these stories.

MAKE IT RELEVANT

At Home Have children ask an adult family member about his or her favorite folktale when he or she was a child. The adult should tell the story to the child and explain why it was a favorite. Suggest they talk about whether it is still a good story today.

Some stories are told around the world.
They are the same story in different languages.

Read and Respond

Culture and Society Ask children if, after hearing a story, they have ever felt happy or sad, or dreamed of a wonderful experience. Discuss how stories and poetry help people understand their world better. Tell children that there were stories even before people knew how to print books. In those early times, storytellers told stories that were passed along from one generation to the next.

Poetry is also a part of the arts of many cultures. Children might be interested in Japanese poetry called haiku. Read selected examples of haiku and help children identify the familiar pattern of syllables. Ask children to explain what they can learn about people from their poetry. (what they feel and think)

Culture and Society Invite children to tell what they know about the story of Cinderella. Explain that similar stories have traditionally been told in many cultures. Tell children that more than 500 similar stories have been recorded in Europe alone. The earliest known Cinderella story came from China. Explain to children that sometimes legends and folk stories can be based on real people and real stories. Legends and folk stories are passed down orally from generation to generation. As the stories are passed down, they are sometimes changed and added to by the people telling the story. Point out that legends and folk stories are fiction stories, because they are made up. Tell children that nonfiction stories are true stories.

Visual Learning

Pictures Ask children to compare and contrast the different versions of the Cinderella story on the page. Have them find details that are alike and different.

INTEGRATE READING

Cinderella Ask your school or local librarian to find two different Cinderella stories appropriate for second graders. Read them to children and then compare and contrast the settings, characters, and details of the plots.

MAKE IT RELEVANT

In Your Community Invite a local storyteller to visit your class. If possible, request that your visitor tell a folktale or legend that originated in your region and a similar story from another place or time. Prepare children for the visit by helping them generate a list of questions to ask the storyteller and by reminding them to listen quietly to the story. Afterward, have the class send a thank-you note to the storyteller.

Art and Architecture

Read and Respond

Culture and Society Read page 192 aloud as children read along. Then invite volunteers to tell about museums they have visited. Encourage them to tell about the paintings and statues they saw as well as the building itself. Then direct children's attention to the painting on the page.

Q **What do you think paintings can tell about a culture?**

A Some paintings are like a photograph. For example, they can show an important event, what people wear, how people do things, or what cities and towns look like.

Visual Learning

Pictures Help children identify the art on the page. Make sure they understand that *art* describes not only pictures or paintings. Explain that art can also be a sculpture, a vase, a basket, jewelry, a piece of cloth or clothing, a building, and other creative things.

Point out to children that the painting shown on page 192 is an Aboriginal painting from a long time ago. Explain that Aborigines live in Australia. Locate Australia on a world map. Tell children that contemporary Australian paintings are very similar to paintings they might see in a museum in the United States.

Q **When might people enjoy wearing masks or colorful clothing?**

A during holidays or special celebrations

Q **Do you think everyone sees art in the same way?**

A Children's responses may indicate that while all cultures express themselves, they may have different ideas about what is beautiful or artistic.

Art and Architecture

You can visit museums in your community to find out about cultures. Paintings can tell about a group's history. Paintings, masks, and patterns woven in cloth can show you a group's traditions.

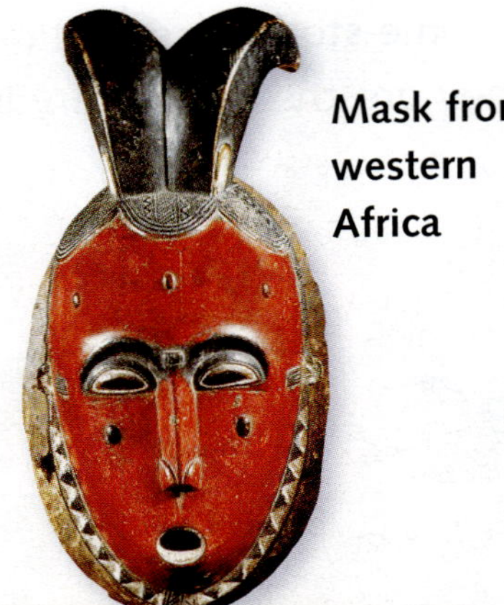

Mask from western Africa

Bark painting from Australia by Banapana

Kente cloth from Ghana

192

BACKGROUND

Kente Cloth Kente cloth, the best-known of all African textiles, is colorful cloth made by the Asante and Ewe peoples of Ghana. The word *kente* comes from the word *kenten*, meaning "basket." Kente cloth is made from woven strips of cloth, usually silk or cotton. Widely recognized as a symbol of the African cultural heritage, the designs of Asante kente cloth often use multicolored patterns of bright colors and geometric shapes. The kente cloth is a ceremonial cloth used for special occasions.

MAKE IT RELEVANT

At School Take children on a walk around the school. Have them discuss displayed artworks created by children in other classes. Ask them questions about the subjects and themes of the artworks in order to help them discover what the artworks show about the school's people and their cultures.

Buildings and gardens often remind us of the cultures in a community. Churches also show what groups of people live in a community.

Russian Orthodox church

English Victorian home

Spanish mission

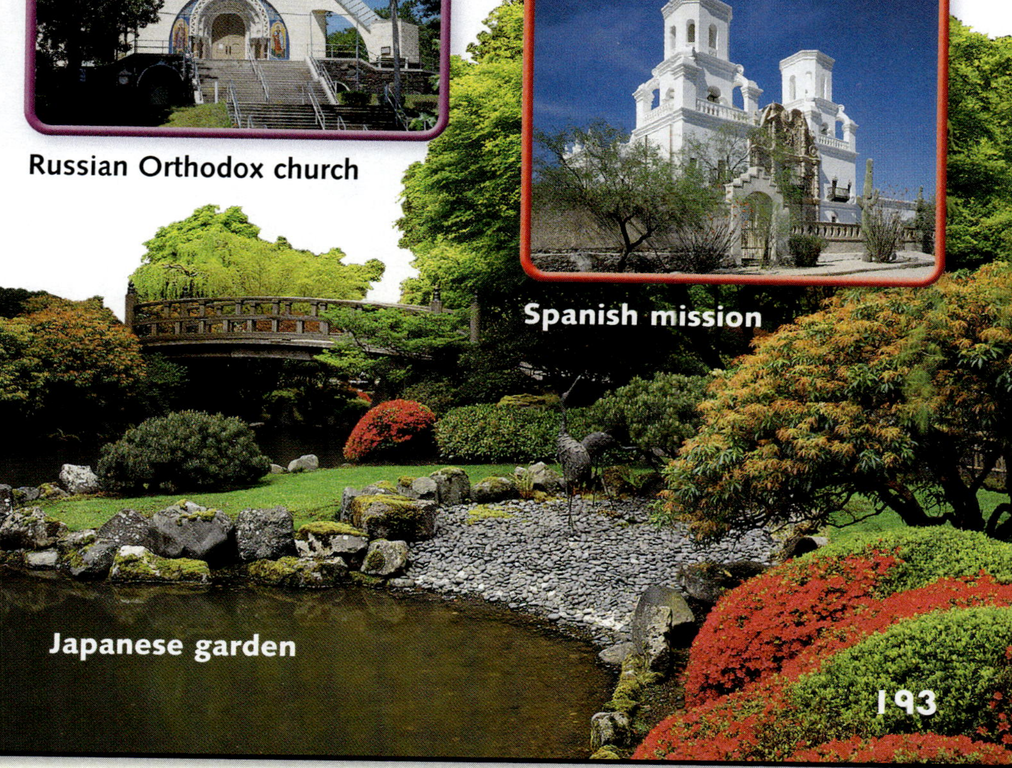

Japanese garden

Read and Respond

Link Culture and Society with Geography Point out to children that buildings are examples of the culture of a country. Explain that sometimes these buildings are so well known that they become landmarks. Show children a picture of Big Ben in England or the Leaning Tower of Pisa in Italy. Then ask volunteers to share what countries their families came from. Compile a list of those countries. Help children locate sites or landmarks from a country on the list. Create a collage showcasing what the children find.

Visual Learning

Pictures Discuss the pictures of buildings on the page, helping children identify the culture of each building. Explain that, just as stories are handed down from generation to generation, so are some building styles. As an example, direct children's attention to the picture of the Orthodox church. Explain that the person who designed this place of worship may have used ideas from earlier churches in the design. For example, the designer may have gotten ideas about where to put doors, windows, and places for people to worship.

Geography Direct children's attention to the picture of the Japanese garden. Tell them that, like stories, paintings, and buildings, gardens reflect the culture of a community. Explain to children that in present-day Japan, gardens are used as an expression of culture and tradition, whereas gardens in the United States are used mainly for beauty and for growing food.

Help children locate Japan on a globe.

Q How might living in a small island country affect how gardens are designed?

A The gardens might be neat and small; they would have plants that grow well in the area.

INTEGRATE LANGUAGE ARTS

Descriptive Writing Show children a photograph of a building that serves as a landmark in your community. Have children describe what it looks like. Discuss how the building reflects the cultural heritage of your community. Then ask children to draw a picture of their favorite building in the community and write a description of it.

MAKE IT RELEVANT

In Your State Share photographs and facts about well-known buildings in your state, such as the state capitol building and large museums. Suggest that children create a booklet about important buildings in the state. Children can do research in a library or on the Internet as well as write letters to local tourist bureaus to find information for the book. Lead a discussion about the importance of the buildings to the people who live in or visit the state.

Music and Dance

Read and Respond

Culture and Society Have children read page 194. Discuss that musicians through the ages have created music to express their feelings and ideas. Ask children to name community festivals they have been to.

Q **What kinds of music have you heard at festivals?**

A Children may mention different types of cultural music or patriotic music.

Visual Learning

Picture Direct children's attention to the picture of the dancers. Have children explain how dance is like other art forms, such as painting and storytelling. (It is a way that people can express themselves and tell stories.) Point out that some types of dances are special to certain cultures and have been passed along from generation to generation. Explain that these types of dances, such as polka and square dancing, are called folk dances.

DEMOCRATIC VALUES
Individual Rights

Ask a volunteer to read what Earnest says. Invite children to comment on what it means to "Look, listen, and learn." Help children understand that when we look at things and listen to people, we learn about others and become better citizens. Invite volunteers to tell about times when they have learned something by listening. Emphasize that freedom of expression allows people the opportunity to get to know one another.

Music and Dance

Many communities celebrate their cultures with festivals. At these community gatherings you can enjoy the costumes, food, music, and dance from places around the world.

Scottish bagpiper

Irish folk dancers

Nigerian drummer

194

INTEGRATE MUSIC

Music from Around the World Play music such as bagpipes, African drums, or a Viennese waltz. Ask children to tell which music they liked best, and why.

REACH ALL LEARNERS

Kinesthetic Learners Have children choose a kind of music and create a dance to go along with it.

EXTEND AND ENRICH

Write a Travel Brochure Form small groups of children. Have each child choose one familiar subject from the list started at the beginning of the lesson and tell the group what they know about it. Discuss with children that the listed subjects tell a story about your community's cultural heritage. Have groups create a travel brochure for visitors to your area. Tell them to include some of the subjects on the list in their brochure.

Dancers from Thailand

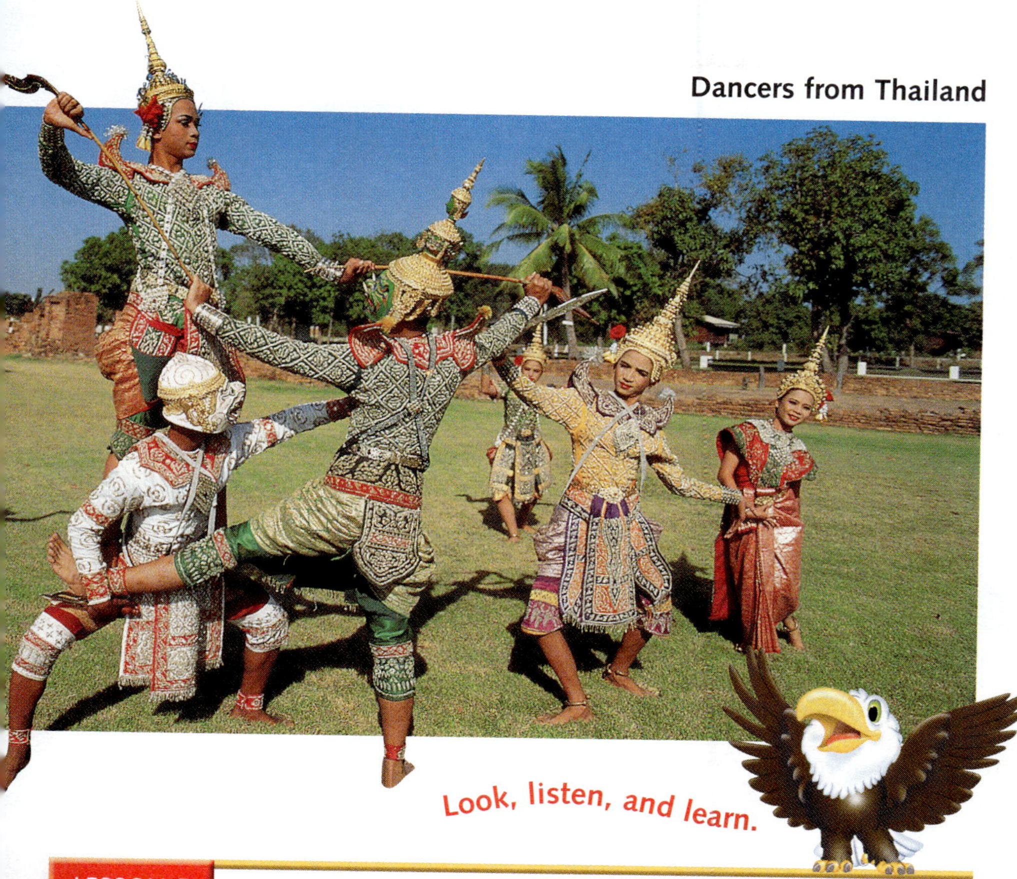

Look, listen, and learn.

LESSON 5 Review

1. **Vocabulary** How do people use **language** to express their culture?
2. What else can express culture?
3. Find out about something in your community that expresses culture.

3 Close

Summarize Key Content

- People use language to tell about their culture through stories.
- Paintings, cloth art, and statues tell about a culture.
- A community's buildings and gardens reflect the local cultural heritage.
- Community festivals celebrate a community's cultures with music and dance.

READING SOCIAL STUDIES

Personal Response Invite children to add to the list started at the beginning of the lesson. Save the list for use in Extend and Enrich.

1. Buildings: Alamo, Mission San Jose
2. Paintings: Mural at HemisFair
3. Dances: Ballet Folklorico, square dancing
4. Gardens: San Antonio Botanical Gardens
5. Stories: "The Legend of the Bluebonnet"
6. Music: Mariachi bands

USE READING AND VOCABULARY TRANSPARENCY 4-6.

4-6 TRANSPARENCY

Assess

Lesson 5 Review—Answers

1. Children may say that people use language to express their ideas and tell stories.
2. Paintings, architecture, music, and dance tell about culture.
3.

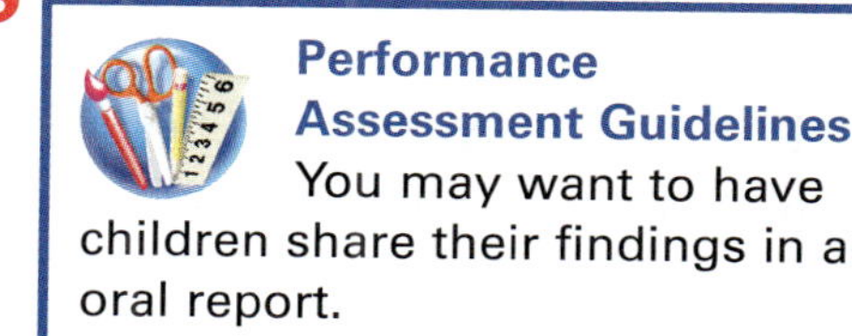

Performance Assessment Guidelines You may want to have children share their findings in an oral report.

RETEACH THE LESSON

Visit a Museum Have children visit a museum online. There are many specialized museums—including children's museums—around the country, and most have Web sites. Have children tour the museum, find something from their own culture or another culture that they especially like, and print out (or draw) a picture of it. Have children share their pictures and tell why they like the object they chose.

ACTIVITY BOOK

Name ____________ Date ________

Write a Haiku

Read about haikus. Then write one of your own.

A haiku is a kind of poem from Japan. It is just three lines long. The first line has five syllables, the second line has seven, and the third line has five. A haiku usually tells about nature—animals, plants, the weather, or the seasons. Read the two examples.

One by one, circling
down to earth, these yellow birds,
these frail, falling leaves

Piles of ragged leaves,
flung together, huddle up
against winter's chill.

Children should write a haiku with the correct number of syllables in each line.

Use after reading Unit 4, Lesson 5. Activity Book ▪ 47

PAGE 47

Extension Activities For Home and School

A Sculpture for Your School

Materials: clay, clay-carving tools, cardboard, smocks

Ask children what public statues they have seen in your community. (Be prepared with suggestions if children cannot think of any.) Discuss what the statues show, such as a war hero or an important person who was born in your community. Invite children to design a statue for your school. Provide clay and a cardboard base for each child. Have children design a statue that would be appropriate for your school. Tell them it does not have to be a person. It could be an animal that would be a good school mascot or it could show something they learn or do in school. Ask children to describe their finished statues, tell what size the statue would be if it were actually made, where in the school or on the grounds it would stand, and what the statue would tell about your school or community. Display the models.
(VISUAL/KINESTHETIC/TACTILE)

My bird is flying away to share what we have learned with children in other schools.

Comparing Folktales

Materials: two folktales that reflect different cultures, story frames

Story Title	
Main Characters	
Setting	
Plot: Beginning of Story Middle of Story End of Story	

Take children to the library to find two folktales from different cultures, such as the following:

- *Papagayo: The Mischief Maker* by Gerald McDermott (Harcourt, 1992.)
- *Raven: A Trickster Tale from the Pacific Northwest* by Gerald McDermott (Harcourt, 1993.)

Have each child borrow a pair of books to read at home with a family member. While they read, suggest they stop now and then to ask questions that help focus on the setting, plot, and characters' actions and motives. After reading the stories, ask children to work with their family member to complete a story frame for each story. Before children return their books to the library, allow time for them to share their books and story frames with the class.
(AUDITORY)

A Quilt of Many Cultures

Materials: art books showing works from all over the world, pictures of quilts, colored construction paper squares (8 1/2 by 8 1/2), crayons or markers, large posterboard square, glue

Display pictures of some quilts. Explain that quilts are made of cloth squares sewn together. Some show a pretty design, and some tell a story. Tell children that they are going to make a class quilt. Instead of sewing together pieces of fabric, each child will design a paper square. After the paper squares have been completed, children should decide how to put all the squares together on the posterboard to make a "quilt." Tell children that their quilt should show ideas and pictures from many different cultures. They can use art books to get ideas. Children may want to make a picture or symbol describing their own family cultures. After the quilt is complete, invite each child to describe his or her square and tell what culture it represents.
(VISUAL/KINESTHETIC/TACTILE)

Spreading Culture

OBJECTIVES

- Explain how ideas and culture spread from one place to another.
- Describe how science and technology have changed communication.
- Compare old and new forms of communication.

Generalize pp. 161, 204

RESOURCES

Pupil Book/Unit Big Book, pp. 196–199

Word Cards V55–V56

Activity Book, p. 48

Reading and Vocabulary Transparency 4-7

Internet Resources

READING SOCIAL STUDIES

Study Questions Invite children to discuss the following questions. Save the questions for children to answer at the end of the lesson.

Question	Answer
How did people send information in the past?	
How do people send information today?	

USE READING AND VOCABULARY TRANSPARENCY 4-7.

Vocabulary

communication p. 196

When Minutes Count

Have children examine the pictures on pages 196–199. Use the pictures to discuss the Big Idea of the lesson.

Quick Summary

This lesson focuses on ways that people have shared ideas through the ages and on the tools they have used to communicate these ideas.

1 Motivate

Set the Purpose

Big Idea Ask children to read the Big Idea statement of the lesson. Tell them they will learn how people shared ideas in the past and how they do this today. As children read, have them compare old and new ways of sharing ideas.

Access Prior Knowledge

Invite two volunteers to stand far apart and imagine that they are on different continents. Give one child a slip of paper with a message written on it. Guide children to discuss ways that the message could be sent from one person to the other.

2 Teach

Read and Respond

Culture and Society Read page 196 with children. Ask children what they do when they have wonderful news to share. Point out that most people tell other people. Explain that the word *communication* refers to all the ways that people talk to one another, whether in person, on the phone, on the computer, or in letters. Review that people also express ideas, or communicate, through art forms such as stories, poems, plays, paintings, dance, and music.

History Direct children's attention to the picture of a monk copying a book. Explain that long ago, people copied books by hand because there were no computers or other machines to copy the pages. Many people who did this work were monks, people who lived together in special religious communities. Explain that monks called scribes copied the words on each page, while others decorated the pages with fancy miniature paintings and borders. Tell children that the monks used real gold and silver in their artworks. These books took a long time to make, so they were very expensive. Because of this, only rich people had books. In fact, most people did not even know how to read. Tell children that some of these early books can be seen in museums around the world.

Q What do you think people can learn from books written in the past?

A They can learn about other people, what they believed, how they felt, how they lived, and what they liked to do.

Q What tools did the monks use to write?

A feathers (quills) and ink

Lesson

Big Idea
Ideas spread from place to place.

Vocabulary
communication

Spreading Culture

You have read that people pass on their culture in their families. You know that holidays celebrate a culture's unique customs. You know, too, that people express their cultures in many ways.

You have read that culture is spread as people move to new places. Culture is also spread through different kinds of communication. **Communication** is the sharing of ideas.

Long ago, people shared ideas through stories told aloud. Most people could not read or write. Books were written by hand, so there were not many of them. Only a few people could afford a book.

quill pen

196

REACH ALL LEARNERS

Below-Level Learners
Help children understand the importance of communication. Point out that the word begins like *community*. Tell them that communication brings people together. Have children write a slogan or a short poem using the word *communication*.

INTEGRATE LANGUAGE ARTS

Write a Letter Tell children that one of the oldest forms of communication is letters. Have children write a letter to a friend or family member who lives in another town, city, or state. Help children recall the parts of a friendly letter—date, greeting, body, closing, and signature—and how to capitalize and punctuate each part. Help children write a mailing address and return address on an envelope. Then allow children to stamp and mail the letters. Discuss how e-mail has changed letter writing.

All this changed when Johannes Gutenberg invented a way to print more copies of books. Soon more people began to read and to write down their ideas.

Today books and newspapers are printed even more quickly and in greater numbers. We can also get information sent through satellites to our television sets.

Read and Respond

History Direct children's attention to the picture of the Gutenberg printing press. Tell them that this machine changed the world forever. Explain that Johannes Gutenberg lived in Germany 600 years ago and that his invention allowed people to print many copies of the same book. Explain that after his invention became known, people began setting up printing presses all over Europe. As a result, more people had books, and ideas and information spread more easily from culture to culture.

Economics Recall that before the invention of the printing press, books were printed by hand. Explain that it took many people a very long time to copy and decorate these early books, and this labor made the books very expensive. In fact, at one time, a hand-printed book might have cost as much as a farm! Explain that it did not cost as much to print a book with a printing press because the machine did the work that many people had done earlier.

Q **How do you think the invention of the printing press changed communication?**

A Books became cheaper to make, so more people could afford to buy and read books.

Visual Learning

Pictures Ask children to describe the painting showing Gutenberg's printing press and the picture of the newspaper press. Guide children to compare the two presses.

Q **How do people use newspapers to spread ideas and culture from one place to another?**

A People learn about people in different places by reading the newspaper.

BACKGROUND

Communications Satellites Satellites are spacecraft in orbit around Earth. Most satellites do not have a crew. A network of satellites provides instant communication around the world. A signal from Earth is sent to a satellite. The satellite amplifies it and transmits it back to another location on Earth.

INTEGRATE TECHNOLOGY

Search Ask children to name keywords they could use on the Internet to find out more information about Gutenberg's invention. (Gutenberg, printing press) Let children try their ideas by using a search engine. Then invite them to share and discuss the information they found. Ask children how computers and the Web have changed book printing.

Read and Respond

History Read pages 198 and 199 aloud. Explain that in the 1800s, two inventions changed communication. The first was the telegraph, which allowed people to send messages over wires. Later, in 1876, Alexander Graham Bell demonstrated the use of the telephone for the first time.

Visual Learning

Artifacts Ask children to describe how the new and old telephones are different. Point out that one has a dial and the other has buttons to push. Tell children that the very first telephones did not even have dials. You asked an operator to connect you to the person you wanted to talk to. Explain that the fax machine lets people send papers with words or pictures over telephone wires to a fax machine in another place. The receiving fax machine prints out a page with the same information.

Economics Explain to children that as technologies are created, new jobs are too. Advances in technology also help people who work in communications jobs by making their jobs faster, easier, and more efficient.

Q **How is the fax machine like the telegraph?**

A It lets people send messages to a distant place.

Geography Discuss how inventions make it easier for people around the world to communicate.

Q **How does communication help make the world a better place?**

A People can talk about ways to solve problems.

Long ago, messages were carried by runners or by messengers on horseback. Over the years, inventions such as the telegraph and telephone made sending messages much easier and faster.

Telegraph, 1922

Telephone, 1922

Cellular phone, 1971

Fax, 1982

FAST FACT In the past, carrier, or homing, pigeons delivered messages. They could fly up to 60 miles an hour for as far as 1,000 miles to find their way home again.

198

WORD WORK

Prefixes Write the words *telegraph* and *telephone* on the board. Ask children what part of the words is the same. Circle *tele-* in each word and explain that this is a prefix that means "distance" or "far off." Discuss that *telegraph* refers to a written message that travels a distance, while *telephone* refers to a spoken message that travels a distance. Ask children what other words they know that begin with the prefix *tele-*, such as *television* or *telescope*.

EXTEND AND ENRICH

Write a Biography Have children write a biography of Alexander Graham Bell, Johannes Gutenberg, Samuel F. B. Morse, or another inventor of some sort of communication device. Instruct them to include information telling about the person's childhood, education, and inventions.

Today you can sit at a computer and find out about anything in the world through the World Wide Web. You can also send and receive messages called e-mail on the Internet.

1. **Vocabulary** How has technology changed **communication**?
2. Name three kinds of communication you use to learn about other cultures.
3. Send an e-mail to a school in another country. Ask questions about the culture there.

3 Close

Summarize Key Content

- Culture is spread through different forms of communication.
- The printing press changed the way people communicated.
- Today, people use inventions such as telephones, fax machines, and computers to communicate.

READING SOCIAL STUDIES

Study Questions Read children's questions from the beginning of the lesson. Discuss their answers and write their responses on the chart.

Question	Answer
How did people send information in the past?	on foot, by horseback, by boat
How do people send information today?	e-mail, telephone, answering machines, fax machines, Internet

USE READING AND VOCABULARY TRANSPARENCY 4-7.

Assess

Lesson 6 Review—Answers

1. Inventions have made communicating easier, faster, and cheaper.
2. Children may suggest newspapers, magazines, television, movies, or the Internet.
3. 

Performance Assessment Guidelines Help children use the Internet to find the name and e-mail address of another school. Children should tell something about themselves and their school before they ask questions. Suggest they invite students in the other school to ask them questions, too.

RETEACH THE LESSON

Make a List Have children work in small groups to write a message on a slip of paper. Challenge the groups to think of at least four ways they could send the message to someone in another country. Have them place a check mark by the listed items that were not available for people who lived long ago.

ACTIVITY BOOK

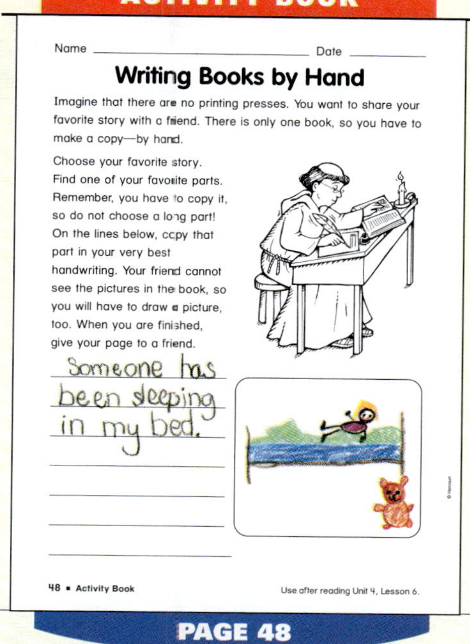

Name ______________ Date ________

Writing Books by Hand

Imagine that there are no printing presses. You want to share your favorite story with a friend. There is only one book, so you have to make a copy—by hand.

Choose your favorite story. Find one of your favorite parts. Remember, you have to copy it, so do not choose a long part! On the lines below, copy that part in your very best handwriting. Your friend cannot see the pictures in the book, so you will have to draw a picture, too. When you are finished, give your page to a friend.

Someone has been sleeping in my bed.

48 ■ Activity Book

Use after reading Unit 4, Lesson 6.

PAGE 48

Extension Activities For Home and School

Communication Time Line

Materials: butcher paper, crayons or markers, reference books or the Internet

Explain to children that they will make a time line showing communications inventions in the order in which they were invented. Work with children to make a list of old and new inventions that people used to communicate (suggest ones that children do not name, to help create a long list). Possible inventions might include paper, pencils, postage stamps, the Pony Express, newspapers, telegraph, telephone, radio, television, typewriter, home computer, fax machine, e-mail. Assign partners one of the inventions and have them use reference books or the Internet to find out when it was first used. Help them write the name of their invention where it belongs and draw a picture of it.
(VISUAL/TACTILE)

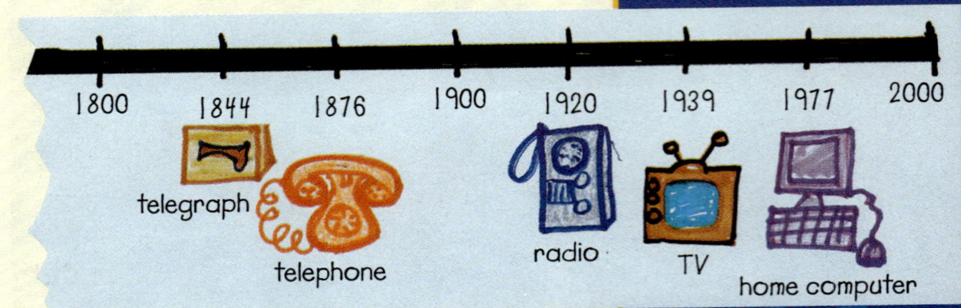

Hello, World!

Materials: drawing paper, crayons or markers

Remind children that when people communicate, they usually begin with a greeting. Write on the board the following words of greeting from around the world and help children learn to pronounce them:

Hola (OH•lah)—Spanish
Aloha (ah•LOH•hah)—Hawaiian
Konnichiwa (koh•NEE•chee•wah)—Japanese
Ti kanis (TEE KAH•nees)—Greek
Nee how ma (NEE HOW MAH)—Mandarin Chinese
Yaytahey (yah•tah•HAY)—Navajo
Shalom (shah•LOHM)—Hebrew
Guten tag (GOO•tin TAHK)—German
Jambo (JAHM•boh)—Swahili
Bonjour (bohn•ZHOOR)—French
Saluto (sah•LOO•toh)—Italian

Have children choose two greetings and draw a picture of two children from those countries saying hello to each other. They should put a speech balloon around each child's greeting.
(VISUAL/KINESTHETIC)

100 Years from Now

Materials: paper, pencil, crayons or markers

Tell children that ideas spread from one place to another and from one time to another. For example, chocolate was used by the Aztec Indians in Mexico more than 500 years ago, and we still enjoy it today. Ask children to brainstorm good ideas they have today that they think children their age should know about 100 years from now. Ideas might include these: share your toys with your friends, puppies make great pets, the Internet, flat-screen television, how to play baseball or soccer. Have each child select an idea and draw a picture to illustrate it. Tell them to also label their illustration of their idea. Then let children show their pictures and tell why the idea will still be good in the future.
(AUDITORY/TACTILE)

Sneakers are a very good idea because they come in lots of colors and let you run fast.

Read a Map of World Countries

OBJECTIVES

- Identify a map by its title.
- Locate the United States and other countries on a map.
- Use a map key to identify regions on a map.

RESOURCES

Pupil Book/Unit Big Book, pp. 200–201

Activity Book, p. 49

Skill Transparency 4-4

GeoSkills CD-ROM

Internet Resources

1 Motivate

Show children several books that have colorful pictures of different countries. Invite them to pass the books around and discuss the pictures. Have them choose two countries that they would like to visit. Ask them what they would need to do to plan a trip to these countries. Elicit that they would have to use a map to plan such a trip.

Why It Matters

The United States is only one country in a big world. It is important to know that other countries exist and where they are located. Because countries share their ideas and cultures, it is important to know which countries are our next-door neighbors and which are farther away.

MENTAL MAPPING

A Memory Test Children have been looking at the classroom United States map for months, but have they been paying attention? Cover up the map and tell children that you are going to test their memory. Have children close their eyes and try to remember the map. Then have them draw an outline of the United States. Encourage them to outline your state in its proper location and put a star approximately where your community is located. Ask children also to locate on their maps our neighbors, Mexico and Canada. Uncover the map and have children compare their own maps to it.

2 Teach

What You Need to Know

Read the text on page 200 with children. Then have them look at the world map on pages 200–201. Have a volunteer read the title of the map. Tell children that the map title gives the main idea of the map. Then have children find the map key. Remind children that the key helps them read the map. Have children use the key to find the continents of Africa and Australia. Then direct children's attention to the names of the countries and the lines that show their borders. Have children find borders that divide countries and borders along the coast. Invite children to locate the countries they would like to visit. Then help children find Russia and China on their maps.

Tell children that *country* and *nation* mean the same thing. Define the word *nation* as a community of people of one or more nationalities in a certain territory.

Remind children that they have learned that people around the world are alike in many ways, but that the people in each culture have their own way of doing things. Help children locate the equator on a globe. Explain that countries located near the equator have very hot weather. Then help children find Kenya and Uganda on the African continent.

Q What are some ways that the countries of Kenya and Uganda are alike?

A They are on the African continent. They have very hot weather. They are near the equator.

Q What are some ways that people in Kenya and Uganda might be different?

A They might speak different languages, eat different foods, or have different religions.

To find more countries shown on maps, visit The Learning Site at **www.harcourtschool.com**

Skills

Read a Map of World Countries

Why It Matters

When you read about other countries, it helps to see where they are on a map. It also helps to know what countries are their neighbors. Countries that are close together are more alike than different.

What You Need to Know

There are more than 190 countries in the world. Russia is the largest country. China has the most people. The country of Australia fills the continent of Australia.

The World

Practice your map and globe skills with the **GeoSkills CD-ROM**.

200

REACH ALL LEARNERS

Tactile Learners Using the map on page 200, have children trace the borders between Canada, the United States, and Mexico. Then provide each child with a copy of a blank outline map of North America. (You can use the copying master T22.) Have children use different colors to identify Canada, the United States, and Mexico.

EXTEND AND ENRICH

Make a Chart Remind children that they have learned that Russia is the largest country in the world. Challenge them to use reference materials to find out about the Republic of San Marino, the smallest country in the world. Help them find San Marino on a map. Then ask them to create a chart that compares the areas and population sizes of Russia, San Marino, and the United States.

Practice the Skill

1. Which continent has more countries, South America or Africa?
2. Which country is farthest north in Asia?
3. What countries are Ecuador's neighbors?

Apply What You Learned

When you read or hear about a country, find it on a map or globe. Keep a list of the countries.

MAP AND GLOBE SKILLS

Practice the Skill—Answers

1. Africa
2. Russia
3. Colombia, Peru

3 Close

Apply What You Learned

Children should correctly spell the name of each country and capitalize the important words. Encourage them to find out the capital of the country and include that on their list.

RETEACH THE SKILL

Use Maps Write *Brazil* and *New Zealand* on the board. Help children locate these countries on the map. Ask which country has no land neighbors. (New Zealand) Then help them find and name Brazil's neighbors. (French Guiana, Suriname, Guyana, Venezuela, Colombia, Peru, Bolivia, Paraguay, Argentina, Uruguay)

ACTIVITY BOOK

Name ____________________ Date ________

MAP AND GLOBE SKILLS

A Map of Central America

The map shows the countries south of Mexico in Central America. Use the map and the compass rose to answer the questions. Then color each country a different color.

Central America

BELIZE
GUATEMALA
HONDURAS
Caribbean Sea
EL SALVADOR
NICARAGUA
PACIFIC OCEAN
COSTA RICA
Panama Canal
PANAMA

1. What country is north of Costa Rica? Nicaragua
2. Find El Salvador. What country is to the east of it? Honduras
3. What country is farthest south? Panama
4. What countries border Honduras? Guatemala, El Salvador, Nicaragua
5. What country is west of Belize? Guatemala

Children should color each country a different color.

Use after reading Unit 4, Skill Lesson 4. Activity Book • 49

PAGE 49

TRANSPARENCY

Use SKILL TRANSPARENCY 4-4.

CD-ROM

Explore GEOSKILLS CD-ROM to learn more about map and globe skills.

Extension Activities For Home and School

A Map of North America

Materials: **outline map of North America, crayons or colored pencils**

Provide children with untitled maps of North America. Then have them do the following:

- What continent does the map show? Write the name of the continent as the title of the map.
- Find the United States, Canada, and Mexico. Write their names where they belong on the map.
- Color each country a different color.

(VISUAL/TACTILE)

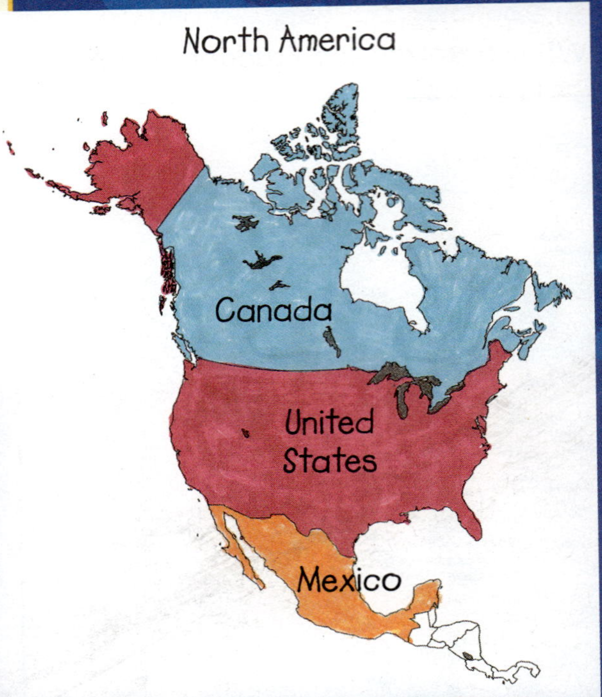

Team Acrostic Puzzle

Materials: **map or globe, paper, pencil**

Write the word *Asia* on the board. Ask children to identify what the word means. Then have them find the continent of Asia on a world map.

Have children work in small groups to complete an acrostic puzzle. Tell them to write the word *ASIA* vertically on a sheet of paper. Then have them find countries in Asia that begin with the letters, *A*, *S*, *I*, and *A*. Have them write the names of the countries, using the first letters in the word *Asia* as the first letters of the country names. You may want to challenge groups to see which one can complete their puzzle in the shortest amount of time.

(VISUAL/TACTILE)

Afghanistan
Sri Lanka
India
Armenia

Name Game

Materials: **world map, drawing paper, crayons or markers**

Challenge children to work with a family member to find as many countries as they can that begin with the same letter as the first letter of their first name. Have children find the countries on a map or globe. Then have them list the names of the countries and the continents where they are located. Invite children to read their lists aloud in class.

(VISUAL/TACTILE/AUDITORY)

Cynthia
China
Chile
Chad
Canada
Colombia
Cuba
Cambodia

VISIT

A Crafts School

OBJECTIVES

- Identify examples of the local cultural heritage.
- Explain the significance of the local cultural heritage.
- Obtain information about a topic using a variety of visual sources.

RESOURCES

Pupil Book/Unit Big Book, pp. 202–203

Take a Field Trip Video

Internet Resources

Summary

In this lesson children will visit the Penland School of Crafts, a national center for craft education in North Carolina's Blue Ridge Mountains, to observe students of all ages learning a variety of traditional crafts.

1 Motivate

Get Ready

Tell children they will be visiting a special school where students can learn traditional crafts by taking classes with artists and craftspeople who know how to do them. Invite children to share what they know about traditional crafts and what they would like to learn on their visit. Record their responses on a K-W-L chart. Save the chart for use at the end of the lesson.

What We Know	What We Want to Know	What We Learned
• Crafts are ways of making things by hand.	• What craft classes can people take at the school?	
• A traditional craft is often passed on in families.	• Why is it important to teach and learn traditional crafts?	
• Weaving and pottery are crafts.		

BACKGROUND

About the Crafts School In 1923 in the Blue Ridge Mountains of North Carolina, Miss Lucy Morgan, a teacher, organized the Penland Weavers. The group invited instructors to teach weaving, provided looms and weaving materials to women in the area, and marketed their handwoven goods. By 1929, interest in learning the craft had spread to many other parts of the country. To meet the requests for instruction, the Penland School of Crafts was founded. Before long the school added other crafts. Penland now has 400 acres and 41 buildings with 1,200 people coming each year to learn a variety of crafts.

2 Teach

What to See

Have children study the photographs on pages 202–203 and read the captions. Explain that silk cloth is made from the fine, soft thread that a silkworm, a moth caterpillar, produces to make its cocoon. Invite children to suggest ways to create designs on fabrics, such as sewing, stitching, drawing, stamping, or tie-dying. Encourage children to share experiences they have had creating designs on fabric. Have them tell how they learned the skill and what materials they used.

As children examine the photograph of students working with the loom, point out that many kinds of materials are used to create textiles, or woven fabrics.

Q What materials do you think the child is using to weave the rug?

A Children may say yarn spun from the wool of sheep or strips of cloth.

Ask children how they think fabric and yarn come to be in different colors. Then point out the picture of the student dyeing the cloth by hand. Explain that parts of many different plants, such as the leaves of the indigo plant, can be used to make natural dyes. Ask children to name other plant parts that might be used to make dyes (berries, stalks, stems, roots, flowers, and seeds).

Have children identify some of the other crafts taught at the school as they examine the remaining pictures (woodcarving, yarn dyeing, and bookmaking). Explain that the crafts school also teaches many other kinds of traditional crafts that use clay, glass, and metals.

Q Why do you think it is important to have crafts schools like the one in North Carolina?

A so people will learn how to make crafts for a long time to come

An older student helps a child create a rug on a loom, a machine used for weaving.

202

INTEGRATE ART

Make a Branch Loom Have pairs of children work together to make a loom using a tree branch with three or four small branches. Instruct them to weave the yarn around the branches, working from the narrow end to the open end. Then have partners gather a variety of natural materials such as leaves, feathers, seed pods, and tall grasses and then weave these materials through the strands of yarn. Hang the completed weavings around the room.

MAKE IT RELEVANT

At Home Suggest that children interview adult family members and relatives to learn about any traditional crafts, such as quilting and weaving, that have been handed down in their family. Encourage them to learn the tradition and share with their classmates what they learned. Children may wish to organize a display with examples of the traditional crafts made in their families.

A student dyes cloth by hand, using the deep blue color of the indigo plant.

Woodcarving

Yarn Dyeing

Bookmaking

A student paints designs on silk cloth.

Take a Field Trip

A VIRTUAL TOUR
Visit The Learning Site at **www.harcourtschool.com** to take virtual tours of other places of interest.

A VIDEO TOUR
Check your media center or classroom library for a video featuring a segment from Reading Rainbow.

203

3 Close

If you started a K-W-L chart at the beginning of the lesson, have children complete it now. Otherwise, invite children to create a radio or television advertisement telling about the crafts school.

Take a Field Trip

A Virtual Tour Depending on the availability of computers, have children work individually, in pairs, or in small groups to view the virtual tour. Suggest they research other traditions that families pass on or traditional crafts of different cultures.

INTERNET RESOURCES

Go to **www.harcourtschool.com** for a listing of Web sites focusing on the traditions and traditional crafts of other cultures.

A Video Tour Have children watch the Reading Rainbow video in small groups. Ask the members of each group to write five questions about information in the video as they watch it. Then have groups exchange and answer each other's questions. You may want to show the video a second time before groups answer the questions.

VIDEO

Use the Reading Rainbow TAKE A FIELD TRIP videotape of a family quilting tradition.

EXTEND AND ENRICH

Traditional Craft Card File Ask children to research and gather instructions for craft activities such as making natural dyes, paint, crayons, and paper; sandpainting; basket weaving; drying flowers; weaving; or making natural clay pots. Create and duplicate a form for children to use to record the name of the activity, necessary materials, and steps in the process. Provide a container in which children can organize the activity cards. Encourage children to refer to the craft card file for activities they might like to try.

INTEGRATE LANGUAGE ARTS

Write and Make a Book As you remind children that bookmaking is a traditional craft taught at the crafts school, encourage them to think of a favorite family story or a story that has been passed down in their family or culture. Invite children to then write and illustrate a book, retelling the story in their own words. Remind children to include a front and back cover and a title page. Help children bind their books when they are complete.

Unit 4 Review and Test Preparation

PAGES 204–208

Generalize

Children's general statements should be supported by their facts. Their charts should demonstrate that they understand the main ideas about culture in the lesson. Children may use the graphic organizer that appears on page 50 of the Activity Book.

ACTIVITY BOOK

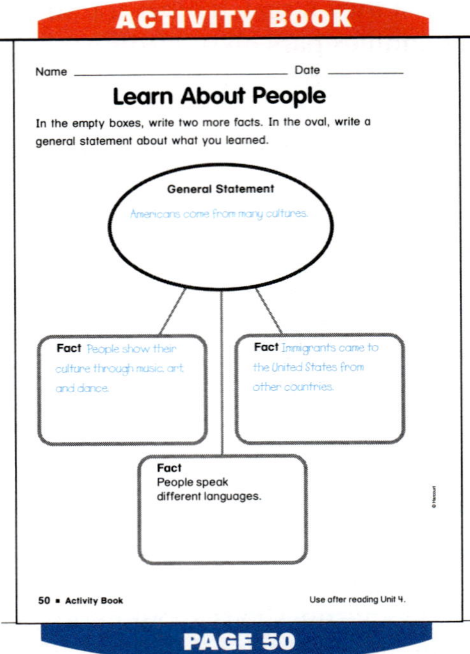

Name ______________ Date ________

Learn About People

In the empty boxes, write two more facts. In the oval, write a general statement about what you learned.

General Statement: Americans come from many cultures.

Fact: People show their culture through music, art, and dance.

Fact: Immigrants came to the United States from other countries.

Fact: People speak different languages.

50 ■ Activity Book — Use after reading Unit 4.

PAGE 50

Think & Write

Children should be able to draw one custom that they have studied in the unit. However, they may also draw customs that they know about personally. The customs shown in children's drawings should be mentioned in their stories. Their stories should have a beginning, middle, and ending. The main character should practice the custom in the drawing.

TRANSPARENCY

This graphic organizer appears on READING AND VOCABULARY TRANSPARENCY 4-8.

Unit 4 Review and Test Preparation

Generalize

Use what you have learned about culture to complete the chart. Add one fact, and then write a general statement.

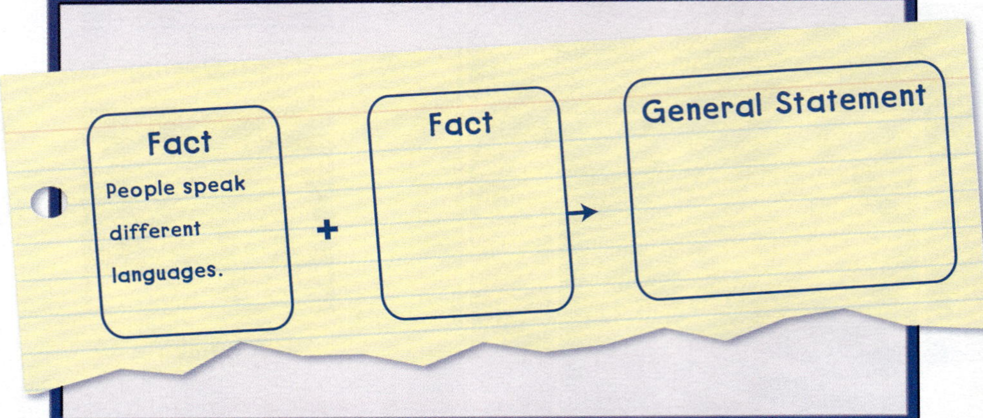

Think & Write

Draw a Custom Draw a picture of people following a custom from another country.

Tell a Story Write a short story about the people in the picture you drew.

204

TEST PREPARATION

Review these tips with children.

- Read the directions before reading the questions.
- Read each question twice, focusing the second time on all the possible answers.
- Take the time to think about all the possible answers before deciding on an answer.
- Move past questions that are giving you trouble, and answer the ones you know. Then return to concentrate on the difficult items.

Use Vocabulary

Choose the word that matches the description.

1. Clara's great-great-grandmother was a pioneer. She raised her family on a farm.
2. During Kwanzaa, Chris lights the candles on the kinara.
3. Every year Gregory, like his father, puts on his kilt and marches in the Highland Parade.
4. We use our computer to learn about people in other countries.

heritage
(p. 178)
ancestor
(p. 182)
custom
(p. 186)
communication
(p. 196)

Recall Facts

5. How are Americans unique?
6. Where did many immigrants stop before entering the United States?
7. Describe a family tradition.
8. Which of these holidays begins a religious time?
   - **A** Chinese New Year
   - **B** Cinco de Mayo
   - **C** Mardi Gras
   - **D** Kwanzaa
9. Which of these is not part of a person's culture?
   - **F** hair color
   - **G** language
   - **H** art
   - **J** music

Use Vocabulary

1. ancestor
2. custom
3. heritage
4. communication

Recall Facts

5. A sample answer is that Americans come from different cultures, and so they each have their own customs and beliefs.
6. Many of them stopped at Ellis Island.
7. A sample answer is that one family tradition is having Thanksgiving dinner at Grandma's house.
8. C—Mardi Gras
9. F—hair color

Think Critically

10. When people communicate, they share their thoughts, feelings, and beliefs.
11. It affects the customs, the beliefs, and the way of life of the community.

Apply Chart and Graph Skills

12. five
13. Australian didgeridoo
14. three
15. Spanish castanets and Moroccan drum

Think Critically

10. How does communication help spread ideas?
11. How does a culture's heritage add to a community?

Apply Chart and Graph Skills

The graph shows instruments from other countries. It tells how many children in a class want to learn to play each one.

Instruments We Want to Play

Indian sitar
Spanish castanets
German fluegelhorn
Moroccan drum
Australian didgeridoo
0 1 2 3 4 5 6

12. How many instruments are shown on the graph?
13. Which instrument did the most children choose?
14. How many children wanted to play the sitar?
15. Which instruments did the same number of children choose?

Apply Map and Globe Skills 

Florida Highways

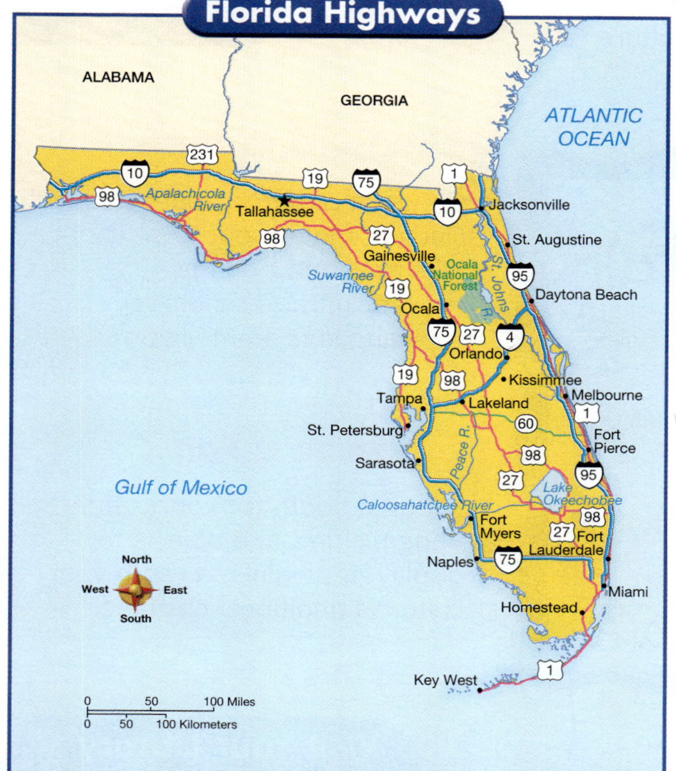

16. Which highway goes from Jacksonville to Tallahassee?

17. If you were traveling on Highway 75 from Tampa to Gainesville, what would you see along the way?

18. What highway takes you to Key West?

19. On which highway could you drive the entire east coast of Florida?

Apply Map and Globe Skills

16. 10
17. Ocala National Forest
18. 1
19. 95 or 1

ACTIVITY BOOK

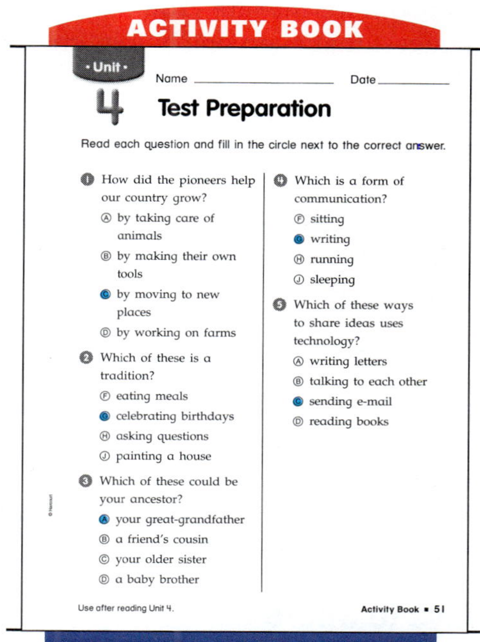

• Unit • 4

Name ______________ Date ________

Test Preparation

Read each question and fill in the circle next to the correct answer.

1. How did the pioneers help our country grow?
   - Ⓐ by taking care of animals
   - Ⓑ by making their own tools
   - Ⓒ by moving to new places
   - Ⓓ by working on farms
2. Which of these is a tradition?
   - Ⓕ eating meals
   - Ⓖ celebrating birthdays
   - Ⓗ asking questions
   - Ⓙ painting a house
3. Which of these could be your ancestor?
   - Ⓐ your great-grandfather
   - Ⓑ a friend's cousin
   - Ⓒ your older sister
   - Ⓓ a baby brother
4. Which is a form of communication?
   - Ⓕ sitting
   - Ⓖ writing
   - Ⓗ running
   - Ⓙ sleeping
5. Which of these ways to share ideas uses technology?
   - Ⓐ writing letters
   - Ⓑ talking to each other
   - Ⓒ sending e-mail
   - Ⓓ reading books

Use after reading Unit 4.

Activity Book • 51

PAGE 51

ASSESSMENT

Use the UNIT 4 TEST on pages 13–16 of the Assessment Program.

Unit Activities

Have children brainstorm a list of cultures. Then arrange children into groups, and assign each group a different culture. Have groups list and divide the tasks involved in setting up a booth for the fair. (You may want to suggest that everyone help with the clean-up.) Then have children research the food, clothing, art, music, dance, language, and religion of their assigned culture. Make available a place in the classroom for children to store materials they bring to class before the fair.

Where to Get Information

Encourage children to use a wide variety of reference sources, including encyclopedias, library books, travel brochures, social studies books, picture atlases, magazines, and the Internet.

Ways to Share

Have children make posters advertising the culture fair and post them around the school. They may also want to create invitations for family members.

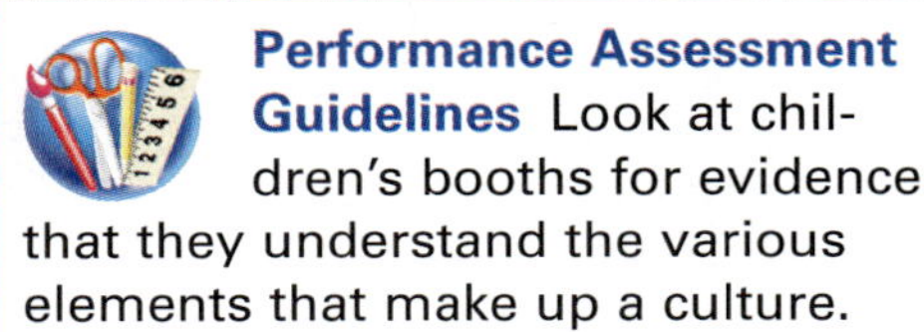

Performance Assessment Guidelines Look at children's booths for evidence that they understand the various elements that make up a culture.

Visit Your Library

Encourage independent reading with these books or others of your choice after children have completed their study of communities. Additional books are listed in the Multimedia Resources on pages 161J–161K of this Teacher's Edition.

Easy *Chinatown* by William Low. Henry Holt, 1997. This story describes a walking tour of Chinatown in New York during the New Year celebration. The tour is conducted by a young Chinese-American boy and his grandmother.

Average *Chidi Only Likes Blue* by Ifeoma Onyefulu. Cobblehill, 1997. A Nigerian girl tries to help her brother see the colors in their village.

Challenging *Different Just Like Me* by Lori Mitchell. Charlesbridge Publishing, 1999. While waiting to go visit her grandmother, April discovers how much people are alike even though they also are unique.

Unit Activities

Complete the Unit Project Work with a group to finish the unit project. Make a poster to advertise your Culture Fair.

GO ONLINE Visit The Learning Site at **www.harcourtschool.com** for additional activities.

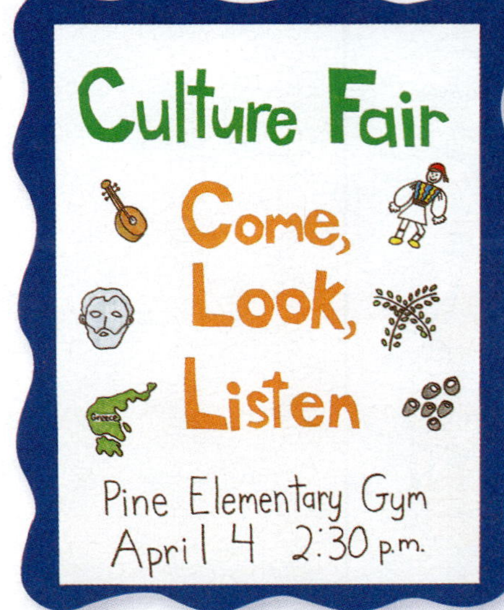

Choose a Culture

Choose a culture in your community. Find out more about these things.

- its food and clothing
- its art, music, and dance
- its language and religion

Organize a Fair

Set up a booth for your culture. Bring pictures and objects to display. If possible, dress in your culture's traditional costume.

Visit Your Library

Chinatown by William Low. A boy and his grandmother enjoy the sights, smells, and sounds of New York City's Chinatown.

Chidi Only Likes Blue by Ifeoma Onyefulu. A rainbow of colors introduces the culture of people in a Nigerian village.

Different Just Like Me by Lori Mitchell. A young girl finds she has something in common with many different people.

208

Past and Present

A "winker" clock, 1865

1

2

3

4

5

6

Unit 5 Planning Guide Past and Present

Unit 5 deals with time: past and present. Children will explore ways of measuring time. They will trace the history of one community and sequence early American history. Children will recognize the contributions made by historical figures, ancient Egyptians, Chinese, and Native Americans. In addition, children will learn how to read a time line, read a history map, read a diagram, predict outcomes, identify causes and effects, and read a map grid.

LESSON	PACING	OBJECTIVES	VOCABULARY
Introduce the Unit pp. 209R–209 **Preview the Vocabulary** pp. 210–211A **Start with a Story** pp. 212A–215A	**3 Days**	■ Use a visual to predict content. ■ Interpret a quotation. ■ Use a sequence chart to prepare for the unit. ■ Use visuals to determine word meanings. ■ Use words and visuals to predict the content of the unit. ■ Obtain information about a topic using a variety of visual sources, such as literature. ■ Describe seasonal changes and their effects. ■ Compare family life today and in the past.	**season** **Word Work,** pp. 211A, 212
1 **Measuring Time** pp. 216A–219A	**3 Days**	■ Identify early uses of calendars and clocks as ways to measure time. ■ Describe the order of events by using designations of time periods such as *ancient times* and *modern times.* ■ Use vocabulary related to chronology, including *past, present,* and *future.*	**ancient** **modern** **Word Work,** p. 216
CHART AND GRAPH SKILLS **Read a Time Line** pp. 220A–221A	**1 Day**	■ Trace the history of space exploration on a time line. ■ Create and interpret time lines. ■ Sequence and categorize information.	**time line**
EXAMINE PRIMARY SOURCES **Learning About the Past** pp. 222A–225A	**2 Days**	■ Name sources of information, such as people, places, and artifacts. ■ Obtain information about a topic using a variety of sources. ■ Compare sources of information about the past.	**history** **source** **artifact**

Time Management

6 WEEKS	WEEK 1	WEEK 2	WEEK 3	WEEK 4	WEEK 5	WEEK 6
	Introduce the Unit	Lessons 1–3		Lessons 4–5		Wrap Up the Unit

READING	INTEGRATE LEARNING	REACH ALL LEARNERS	RESOURCES
Sequence, p. 209 Reading Social Studies: **Outline,** p. 210 Reading Social Studies: **Graphic Organizer,** pp. 212A, 214 Reading Social Studies: **Use Picture Clues,** p. 212	**Theme Time,** p. 209I Art **Decorate a Clock,** p. 209 Science **Grow Potatoes,** p. 213 **Trees in Different Seasons,** p. 215 Health **Nutrition,** p. 214 Mathematics **Feeding a Family,** p. 214	**English as a Second Language,** pp. 209N, 213 **Below-Level Learners,** pp. 209N, 211 **Advanced Learners,** p. 209N **Extension Activities for Home and School,** p. 215A	**Pupil Book/Unit Big Book,** pp. 209–215 **Audiotext, Unit 5** **Word Cards V57-V58** **Reading and Vocabulary** Transparency 5–1 Internet Resources
Reading Social Studies: **Graphic Organizer,** pp. 216A, 219	Language Arts **Poetry,** p. 216	**English as a Second Language,** p. 217 **Extend and Enrich,** p. 218 **Reteach the Lesson,** p. 219 **Extension Activities for Home and School,** p. 219A	**Pupil Book/Unit Big Book,** pp. 216–219 **Word Cards V57-V58** **Activity Book,** p. 52 **Activity Pattern P9** **Reading and Vocabulary** Transparency 5–2 Internet Resources
	Mathematics **Time Intervals,** p. 220A	**Extend and Enrich,** p. 220 **Visual Learners,** p. 220 **Reteach the Skill,** p. 221 **Extension Activities for Home and School,** p. 221A	**Pupil Book/Unit Big Book,** pp. 220–221 **Word Cards V57-V58** **Activity Book,** p. 53 **Skill Transparency 5-1** Internet Resources
	Reading **Share a Book,** p. 222 Language Arts **Write About a Place,** p. 223 **Diary,** p. 224	**English as a Second Language,** p. 222 **Extend and Enrich,** p. 225 **Reteach,** p. 225	**Pupil Book/Unit Big Book,** pp. 222–225 **Word Cards V59-V60** Internet Resources

Unit 5 Planning Guide

LESSON	PACING	OBJECTIVES	VOCABULARY
READING SKILLS **Predict a Likely Outcome** pp. 226A–227A	1 Day	■ Recognize the importance of knowing the past to predict the future. ■ Follow steps for making a prediction.	**predict**
2 **Tracing a Community's History** pp. 228A–233A	3 Days	■ Trace the history of Fort Myers, Florida. ■ Explain how local people and events have influenced local community history. ■ Describe changes in a community over time.	**museum** **settler**
READING SKILLS **Identify Cause and Effect** pp. 234A–235A	1 Day	■ Explain how one event can cause another. ■ Analyze the effects of change. ■ Recognize that history is a series of causes and effects.	**cause** **effect**
3 **Celebrating Our Country's History** pp. 236A–241A	3 Days	■ Explain the significance of various national celebrations. ■ Compare early Native American groups. ■ Sequence early American history. ■ Identify places that remind us of our history.	**colony** **independence** **freedom** **landmark**
MAP AND GLOBE SKILLS **Read a History Map** pp. 242A–243A	1 Day	■ Learn about the past from a history map. ■ Draw maps to show places and routes.	**history map** **region** **settlement**

READING	INTEGRATE LEARNING	REACH ALL LEARNERS	RESOURCES
	Reading **Share a Poem,** p. 226A **Science** **What Will Happen?** p. 226	**Auditory Learners,** p. 226 **Extend and Enrich,** p. 226 **Reteach the Skill,** p. 227 **Extension Activities for Home and School,** p. 227A	**Pupil Book/Unit Big Book,** pp. 226–227 **Word Cards V59–V60** **Activity Book,** p. 54 **Skill Transparency 5-2**
Reading Social Studies: **Study Questions,** pp. 228A, 233 Focus Skill **Sequence,** p. 232	**Mathematics** **Finding Dates,** p. 231	**Extend and Enrich,** p. 232 **Reteach the Lesson,** p. 233 **Extension Activities for Home and School,** p. 233A	**Pupil Book/Unit Big Book,** pp. 228–233 **Word Cards V61–V62** **Activity Book,** p. 55 **Reading and Vocabulary** Transparency 5–3 Internet Resources
	Art **Draw Pictures,** p. 234 **Science** **Changing Water,** p. 234	**Auditory Learners,** p. 234A **Extend and Enrich,** p. 234 **Reteach the Skill,** p. 235 **Extension Activities for Home and School,** p. 235A	**Pupil Book/Unit Big Book,** pp. 234–235 **Word Cards V61–V62** **Activity Book,** p. 56 **Activity Pattern P10** **Skill Transparency 5-3**
Reading Social Studies: **Make a Prediction,** pp. 236A, 241 Focus Skill **Sequence,** p. 240	**Reading** **The Plymouth and Jamestown Settlers,** p. 236 **Read a Book,** p. 237 **Read a Poem,** p. 239 **Music** **Sing a Song,** p. 238 **Language Arts** **American Revolution,** p. 238	**Extend and Enrich,** p. 240 **Reteach the Lesson,** p. 241 **Extension Activities for Home and School,** p. 241A	**Pupil Book/Unit Big Book,** pp. 236–241 **Word Cards V63–V64** **Activity Book,** p. 57 **Reading and Vocabulary** Transparency 5–4 Internet Resources
		Kinesthetic Learners, p. 242 **Extend and Enrich,** p. 242 **Reteach the Skill,** p. 243 **Extension Activities for Home and School,** p. 243A	**Pupil Book/Unit Big Book,** pp. 242–243 **Word Cards V65–V66** **Activity Book,** p. 58 **Skill Transparency 5-4** **GeoSkills CD-ROM**

Unit 5 Planning Guide

LESSON	PACING	OBJECTIVES	VOCABULARY
4 Celebrating Heroes of the Past pp. 244A–249A	3 Days	■ Identify contributions of historical figures who have influenced the community, state, and nation. ■ Describe ways people honor their heroes. ■ Give examples of places in the community where individuals are remembered.	**monument** **memorial** **hero** **Word Work,** p. 247
MAP AND GLOBE SKILLS **Read a Map Grid** pp. 250A–251A	1 Day	■ Read a grid. ■ Use a map grid to locate places on the map. ■ Draw a map grid of a familiar place.	**map grid**
5 Contributions in World History pp. 252A–255A	3 Days	■ Understand that cultures and civilizations existed in ancient times. ■ Identify contributions made by ancient Egyptians, Chinese, and Native Americans. ■ Trace the history of writing.	**scribe** **papyrus** **maize** **Word Work,** p. 252
CHART AND GRAPH SKILLS **Read a Diagram** pp. 256A–257A	1 Day	■ Explain how diagrams are used. ■ Read a cross-section diagram of a pyramid.	**diagram**
Visit Mount Rushmore pp. 258A–259	1 Day	■ Identify and explain the significance of various community, state, and national memorials such as Mount Rushmore. ■ Obtain information about a topic using a variety of visual sources.	
Unit 5 Review and Test Preparation pp. 260–264	3 Days		

READING	INTEGRATE LEARNING	REACH ALL LEARNERS	RESOURCES
Reading Social Studies: **Anticipation Guide,** pp. 244A, 249	Art **Design a Monument,** p. 244 Language Arts **Write a Letter,** p. 246 Reading **Share a Poem,** p. 248	**Advanced Learners,** p. 244 **Extend and Enrich,** p. 248 **Reteach the Lesson,** p. 249 **Extension Activities for Home and School,** p. 249A	**Pupil Book/Unit Big Book,** pp. 244–249 **Word Cards V65–V68** **Activity Book,** p. 59 **Reading and Vocabulary** Transparency 5–5
	Mathematics **Math Problem Grid,** p. 250	**Tactile Learners,** p. 250A **Below-Level Learners,** p. 250 **Extend and Enrich,** p. 250 **Reteach the Skill,** p. 251 **Extension Activities for Home and School,** p. 251A	**Pupil Book/Unit Big Book,** pp. 250–251 **Word Cards V67–V68** **Activity Book,** p. 60 **Skill Transparency 5-5** **GeoSkills CD-ROM**
Reading Social Studies: **Make Word Webs,** pp. 252A, 255	Science **Silkworms,** p. 253	**Extend and Enrich,** p. 254 **Reteach the Lesson,** p. 255 **Extension Activities for Home and School,** p. 255A	**Pupil Book/Unit Big Book,** pp. 252–255 **Word Cards V67–V70** **Activity Book,** p. 61 **Reading and Vocabulary** Transparency 5–6
	Art **Make a Drawing,** p. 256	**English as a Second Language,** p. 256A **Extend and Enrich,** p. 256 **Reteach the Skill,** p. 257 **Extension Activities,** p. 257A	**Pupil Book/Unit Big Book,** pp. 256–257 **Word Cards V69–V70** **Activity Book,** p. 62 **Skill Transparency 5-6**
	Mathematics **Scale,** p. 258	**Extend and Enrich,** p. 259	**Pupil Book/Unit Big Book,** pp. 258–259 Internet Resources **Take a Field Trip Video**
Focus Skill **Sequence,** p. 260			**Pupil Book/Unit Big Book,** pp. 260–264 **Reading and Vocabulary** Transparency 5–7 **Activity Book,** pp. 63–64 **Assessment Program, Unit 5 Test,** pp. 17–20

1 2 3 4 5 6

Unit 5 Skills Path

Unit 5 features the reading skills of sequencing, predicting a likely outcome, and identifying cause and effect. It also highlights the social studies skills of reading a time line, reading a history map, reading a map grid, and reading a diagram.

FOCUS SKILLS

UNIT 5 READING SKILL

SEQUENCE

- INTRODUCE p. 209
- APPLY pp. 232, 240, 260

READING SOCIAL STUDIES

- Outline, p. 210
- Graphic Organizer, pp. 212A, 214, 216A, 219
- Use Picture Clues, p. 212
- Study Questions, pp. 228A, 233
- Make a Prediction, pp. 236A, 241
- Anticipation Guide, pp. 244A, 249
- Make Word Webs, pp. 252A, 255

CHART AND GRAPH SKILLS

READ A TIME LINE

- INTRODUCE pp. 220A–221A

READ A DIAGRAM

- INTRODUCE pp. 256A–257A
- APPLY p. 262

READING SKILLS

PREDICT A LIKELY OUTCOME

- INTRODUCE pp. 226A–227A

IDENTIFY CAUSE AND EFFECT

- INTRODUCE pp. 234A–235A

MAP AND GLOBE SKILLS

READ A HISTORY MAP

- INTRODUCE pp. 242A–243A
- APPLY p. 263

READ A MAP GRID

- INTRODUCE pp. 250A–251A

STUDY AND RESEARCH SKILLS

- Using Reference Sources, p. 229
- Note Taking, p. 246

Theme Time: Moments in Time

MATH CENTER

Time Line Quiz

Display a time line showing events in the life of an important person from history. Show children how to subtract or count years to figure out the person's age at the time of each event on the time line. Provide calculators to help children check their answers.

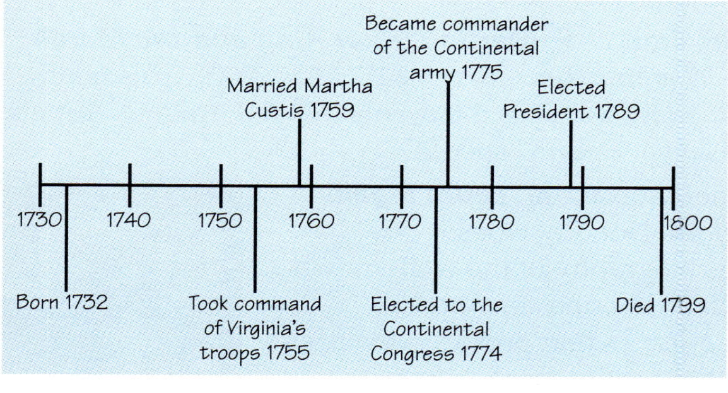

SCIENCE CENTER

Scientists' Hall of Fame

Provide books with information about famous scientists. Have children read about one of the scientists and design a medal or an award that reflects the person's accomplishments. Ask children to write a paragraph telling when the scientist lived and why he or she was important. Display children's writings and awards in a Scientists' Hall of Fame.

READING/LANGUAGE ARTS CENTER

Stories Maps Tell

Display a modern map and a historical map of the same area. Have children study and compare the two maps. Then have them write a description of how the area has changed.

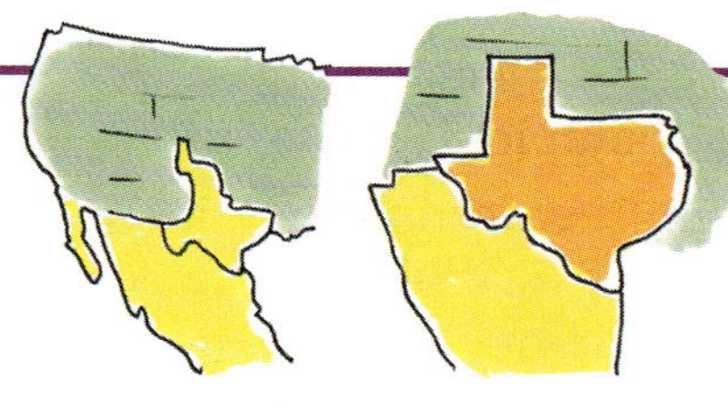

BULLETIN BOARD: PEOPLE IN HISTORY

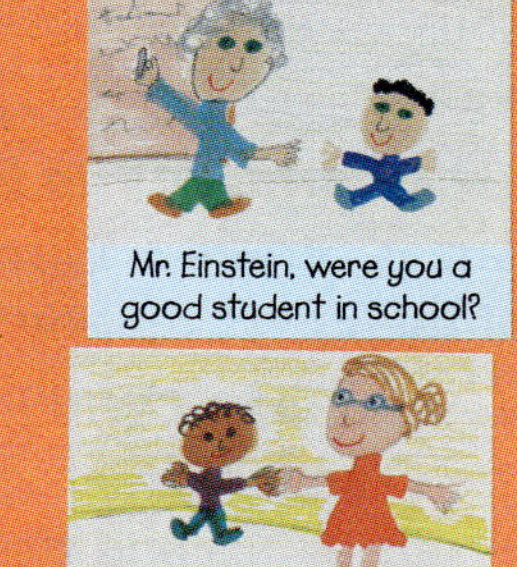

Ms. Anthony, are you surprised to find your face on a coin?

After studying important people in history, invite children to create a bulletin board about them. Have children imagine they could go back in time and meet a famous person. Ask them to draw a picture of the meeting. Encourage them to think of a question that they would like to ask the person. Provide sentence strips and markers and have children write their questions. Display the questions and illustrations with the title "Questions About the Past."

Multimedia Resources

The Multimedia Resources can be used in a variety of ways. They can supplement core instruction in the classroom or extend and enrich children's learning at home.

Independent Reading

Easy

Addy, Sharon Hart. ***Right Here on This Spot.*** Houghton Mifflin, 1999. Objects dug from the ground give clues about what happened in the same place long ago.

Helldorfer, Mary-Claire. ***Hog Music.*** Viking, 2000. When Aunt Liza sends a straw hat to Lucy, it travels by mail coach, handcart, covered wagon, carriage, and peddler's cart. When it arrives, it is full of surprises.

LaMarche, Jim. ***The Raft.*** HarperCollins, 2000. When Nicky spends a summer with his grandmother in her riverside cabin, he discovers a raft floating downstream in the river. His observations about the raft and its drawings help him discover something important about himself.

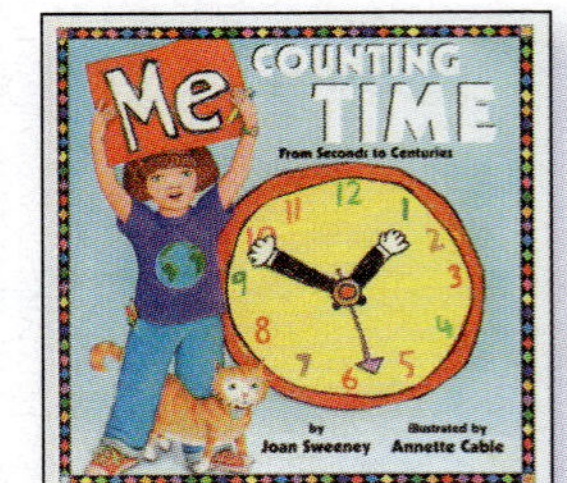

Sweeney, Joan. ***Me Counting Time: From Seconds to Centuries.*** Crown, 2000. A little girl uses concrete examples to illustrate terms of time measurement from seconds to millenniums.

Thornhill, Jan. ***Before and After: A Book of Nature Timescapes.*** National Geographic Society, 1997. Through pairs of "Before" and "After" illustrations, this book shows how the passing of time brings change.

Ziefert, Harriet. ***Hats Off for the Fourth of July!*** Viking, 2000. A small-town parade gets all the local celebrities and community groups involved and ends with a blaze of fireworks.

Average

Brenner, Barbara. ***Wagon Wheels.*** HarperCollins, 1999. An African American family travels west, hoping to get free land after the Civil War.

Howard, Elizabeth. ***Virgie Goes to School with Us Boys.*** Simon & Schuster, 2000. Set in the Reconstruction era, this is the story of a young African American girl who is determined to get an education in spite of the custom of sending only boys to school.

Karim, Roberta. ***Kindle Me a Riddle.*** Greenwillow, 1999. A pioneer father shares riddles with his daughter to explain how old things change into new things.

Quasha, Jennifer. ***The Pony Express: Hands-On Projects About Early Communication.*** Rosen, 2001. This book suggests projects to help children learn about communication in early America.

Ruffin, Frances E. ***Martin Luther King and the March on Washington.*** Grosset & Dunlap, 2001. This nonfiction book describes the events that led up to Dr. King's "I Have a Dream" speech.

Wallner, Alexandra. ***Laura Ingalls Wilder.*** Holiday House, 1997. This biography of the well-known author describes the pioneer experiences that provided the basis for her writing of such books as *The Little House on the Prairie.*

Challenging

Adler, David A. ***A Picture Book of Louis Braille.*** Holiday House, 1998. This easy biography tells about the life of the French child who was blinded and later grew up to invent the Braille system of reading and writing.

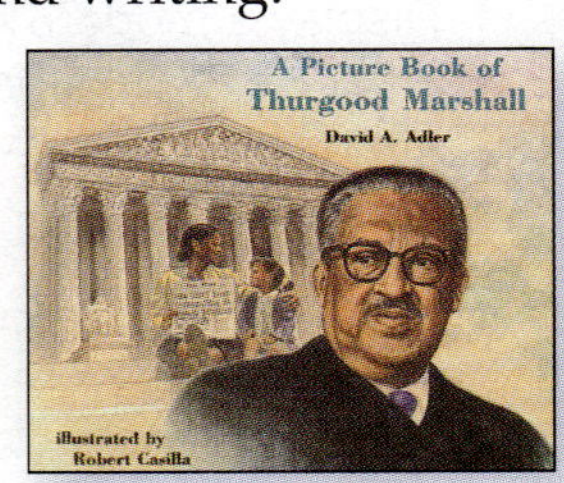

Adler, David A. ***A Picture Book of Thurgood Marshall.*** Holiday House, 1997. This book shows how Marshall's childhood experiences led him to become a great legal mind and civil rights champion.

Ansary, Mir Tamim. ***Veterans Day.*** Heinemann Library, 1998. This nonfiction book gives a brief history of Veterans Day and highlights the contributions of veterans from World Wars I and II.

Dunbar, James. ***Tick-Tock.*** Carolrhoda, 1998. The author shows why it is important to have standard units for measuring time. This book also describes the units we use and discusses the concepts of past, present, future, and the seasons.

Frank, John. ***The Tomb of the Boy King: A True Story in Verse.*** Farrar, Straus & Giroux, 2001. Explore the mysteries of the Egyptian boy king, Tutankhamen.

Hunter, Ryan Ann. ***Take Off!*** Holiday House, 2000. This history of the changes in aeronautics includes pictures of 25 historic airplanes and descriptions of some important flights.

Isaacs, Sally Senzell. ***Life in America's First Cities.*** Heinemann Library, 2000. Through illustrations and photographs of reenactments, this book shows what the homes, occupations, education, clothing, food, and methods of communication were like in early cities.

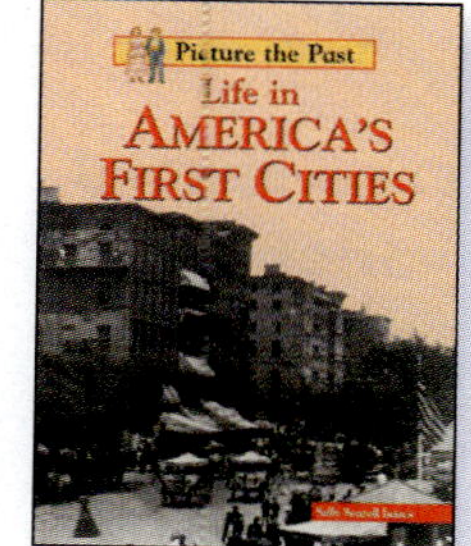

Schaefer, Lola M. ***Henry Ford.*** Capstone Press, 2000. This interesting account of Ford's life describes his boyhood as well as his success after creating the assembly line.

Trottier, Maxine. ***Prairie Willow.*** Stoddard Kids, 1998. A Canadian pioneer family plants a tree on the prairie.

Wroble, Lisa. ***Kids in Colonial Times.*** PowerKids Press, 1997. This nonfiction book shows what everyday life was like for children in the 1600s and 1700s.

Audiocassettes

More American Heroes. 2000. Jonathan Sprout sings about the Wright brothers, Eleanor Roosevelt, Neil Armstrong, Tecumseh, and heroes in general.

The Third Ear. Secrets of the World Audio Series. Library Video, 2000. Johnny Moses tells tales of folk heroes from his Tulalip Native American tradition.

Computer Software

Imagination Express:

Time Trip, USA. Edmark. Mac/Windows. In this program, children create stories set in a New England town. Users choose scenery and characters from different time periods in the town's history.

Invention Studio. Discovery. Mac/Windows. Children can use this program to design, build, and test their own useful or outrageous inventions.

Timeliner 5.0. Tom Snyder Productions. Mac/Windows. This program allows children to create, illustrate, and print time lines.

Videos and DVDs

Liberty and Justice.

American History for Children Video Series. Library Video, 1997. Viewers visit the Statue of Liberty, the Lincoln Memorial, and the Supreme Court to learn about American ideals. Children tell their own ideas about fairness and prejudice.

National Observances. My America: Building a Democracy Series. Schlessinger, 1996. This journey through American history explains the history of voting in America and the reasons we celebrate Veterans Day, Memorial Day, Labor Day, Independence Day, and Election Day.

The Smithsonian and the Presidency. Peanuts: This Is America Series. Library Video, 1995. While visiting the Smithsonian Institution, the Peanuts gang travels back in time to learn about United States Presidents and historic events.

Additional books also are recommended at point of use throughout the unit.
Note that information, while correct at time of publication, is subject to change.

ISBNs and other publisher information can be found at **www.harcourtschool.com**

The Learning Site: Social Studies Center

The Learning Site at www.harcourtschool.com offers a special Social Studies Center. The center provides a wide variety of activities, Internet links, and online references.

GO ONLINE — INTERNET RESOURCES

Find all this at The Learning Site at www.harcourtschool.com

- Activities and Games
- Content Updates
- Current Events
- Free and Inexpensive Materials
- Multimedia Biographies
- Online Atlas
- Primary Sources
- Video Updates
- Virtual Tours
- Your State

and more!

Here are just some of the HARCOURT Internet resources you'll find!

Multimedia Biographies

www.harcourtschool.com

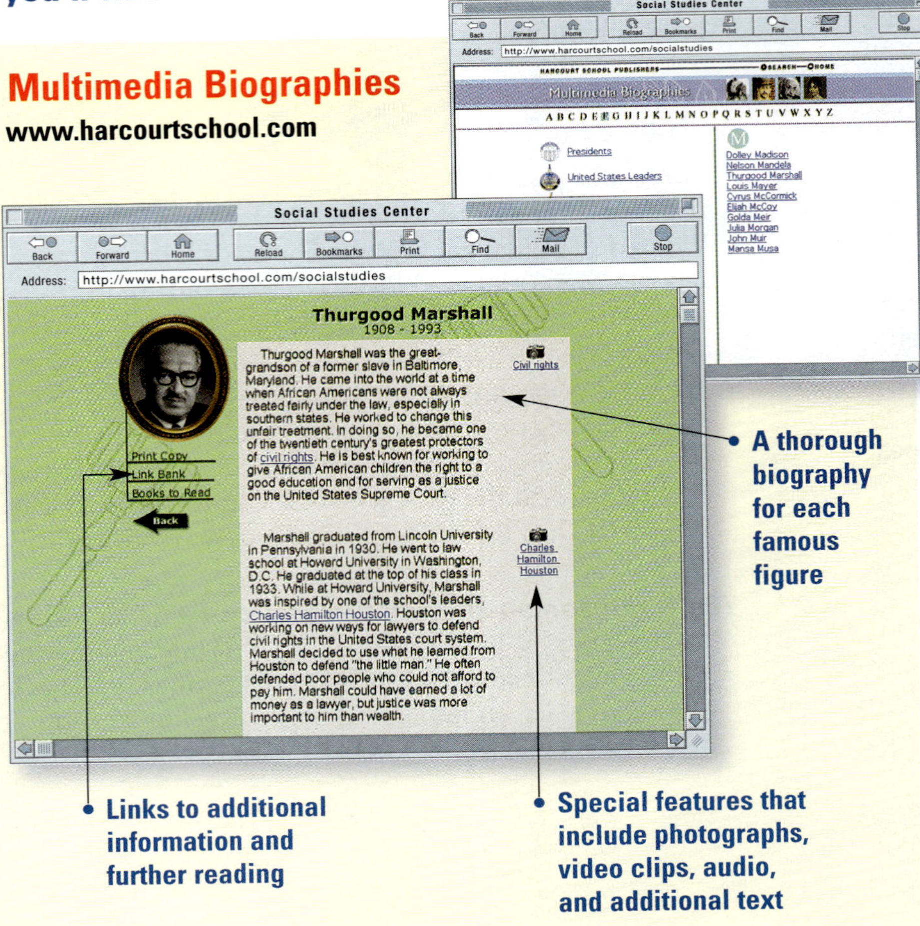

- A thorough biography for each famous figure
- Links to additional information and further reading
- Special features that include photographs, video clips, audio, and additional text

Free and Inexpensive Materials

- Addresses to write for free and inexpensive products
- Links to unit-related materials
- Internet maps
- Internet references

www.harcourtschool.com

Primary Sources

- Artwork
- Clothing
- Diaries
- Government Documents
- Historical Documents
- Maps
- Tools

and more!

www.harcourtschool.com

Virtual Tours

- Capitols and Government Buildings
- Cities
- Countries
- Historical Sites
- Museums
- Parks and Scenic Areas

and more!

www.harcourtschool.com

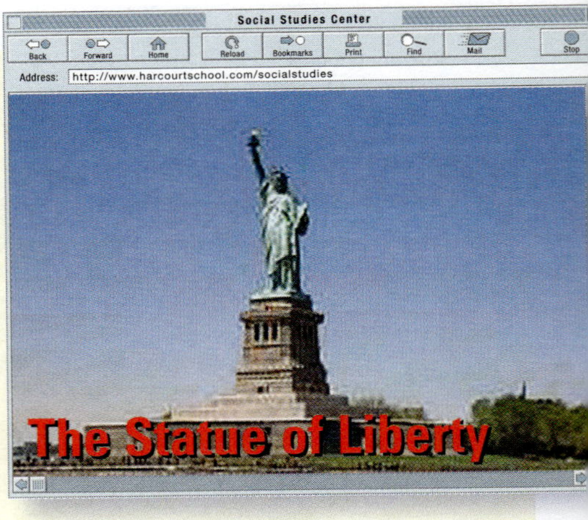

Integrate Learning Across the Curriculum

Use these topics to help you integrate social studies into your daily planning. See the page numbers indicated for more information about each topic.

Social Studies

Computer/Technology

Go Online, pp. 215, 217, 221, 225, 245, 259
GeoSkills CD-ROM, pp. 243, 251
Take a Field Trip Video, p. 259

Health

Nutrition, p. 214

Music

Sing a Song, p. 238

Science

Scientists' Hall of Fame, p. 209I
Grow Potatoes, p. 213
Trees in Different Seasons, p. 215
What Will Happen?, p. 226
Changing Water, p. 234
Silkworms, p. 253

Language Arts

Stories Maps Tell, p. 209I
Poetry, p. 216
Write About a Place, p. 223
Diary, p. 224
American Revolution, p. 238
Write a Letter, p. 246

Mathematics

Time Line Quiz, p. 209I
Feeding a Family, p. 214
Time Intervals, p. 220A
Finding Dates, p. 231
Math Problem Grid, p. 250
Scale, p. 258

Art

Decorate a Clock, p. 209
Draw Pictures, p. 234
Design a Monument, p. 244
Make a Drawing, p. 256

Reading/Literature

Historic St. Augustine, p. 215
Martin Luther King, Jr., p. 215
At the Museum, p. 215
Pearl, p. 222
Meema's Memory Quilt: Treasured Stories of Watauga County History, p. 222
"Surprise Party," p. 226A
James Towne: Struggle for Survival, p. 236
The Pilgrims of Plimoth, p. 236
A Birthday Basket for Tía, p. 237
Itse Selu: Cherokee Harvest Festival, p. 237
Nadia's Hands, p. 237
Sequoyah: Inventor of the Cherokee Written Language, p. 237
"Fourth of July," p. 239
"Martin Luther King," p. 248
Right Here on This Spot, p. 264
Kindle Me a Riddle, p. 264
The Tomb of the Boy King: A True Story in Verse, p. 264

Reach All Learners

Use these activities to help individualize your instruction. Each activity has been developed to address a different level or type of learner.

English as a Second Language

Materials

- craft paper
- markers

Using Time Words **Help children create a time line for the school year.**

- Draw on craft paper and display a time line showing the months of the school year.
- Ask children to name school events that have happened during the year.
- Help children begin by placing some events on the time line.
- As children respond, ask questions about where to place each new event.
- When the time line is complete, continue asking questions about the order of events and have children answer using the words *before* or *after.*

First day of school
Zoo field trip
Read-a-thon
August September October

Below-Level Learners

Materials

- posters, pictures, symbols, or artifacts

History Walk **Create a history walk for children to experience. Use posters, pictures, symbols, and artifacts that represent events in history.**

- Display along one wall of the classroom, in chronological order, items that represent important historic events.
- As children follow you on a history walk, explain each item. Have children strike a pose that matches their idea of the event.
- Invite children to guide others on the walk to show and share what they remember about each event.

Advanced Learners

Materials

- books about historic events
- paper
- pencils

Cause and Effect in History **Have children research a historic event and create a cause-and-effect chart about the event.**

- Have children read about a historic event.
- Ask them to look for causes of the event or effects that happened because of the event.
- Have children draw a two-column chart. Tell them to label the left side *cause* and the right side *effect.*
- Encourage children to record what they learn on the chart.
- Invite children to report on their reading and explain the cause-and-effect relationships they discovered.

Cause	Effect
The Pilgrims wanted freedom.	They came to America.
The first winter was very hard.	Many people got sick or died.
The Indians helped the Pilgrims.	The Pilgrims learned to survive in America.

Assessment Options

The assessment program gives all learners many opportunities to show what they know and can do. It also provides ongoing information about each child's understanding of social studies.

Formal Assessment

- **LESSON REVIEWS:** pp. 219, 233, 241, 249, 255
- **UNIT REVIEWS AND TEST PREPARATION,** pp. 260–263
- **UNIT ASSESSMENT**
  Standard Test
  Assessment Program, pp. 17–19
  Individual Performance Task
  Assessment Program, p. 20

Student Self-Evaluation

- **GEOGRAPHY THEME QUESTIONS**
  within lessons of Pupil Book
- **INDIVIDUAL END-OF-PROJECT CHECKLIST**
  Assessment Program, p. viii
- **GROUP END-OF-PROJECT CHECKLIST**
  Assessment Program, p. ix
- **INDIVIDUAL END-OF-UNIT CHECKLIST**
  Assessment Program, p. x

Informal Assessment

- **THINK ABOUT IT,** p. 215
- **EXAMINE PRIMARY SOURCES,** pp. 222–225
- **SOCIAL STUDIES SKILLS CHECKLIST**
  Assessment Program, pp. vi–vii
- **SKILLS**
  Practice the Skill, pp. 221, 227, 235, 243, 251, 256
  Apply What You Learned, pp. 221, 227, 235, 243, 251, 257

Performance Assessment

- **PERFORMANCE ACTIVITY** in Lesson Reviews
- **UNIT ACTIVITIES,** p. 264
- **COMPLETE THE UNIT PROJECT,** p. 264
- **INDIVIDUAL PERFORMANCE TASK**
  Assessment Program, p. 20

Portfolio Assessment

STUDENT SELECTED ITEMS MAY INCLUDE:

- **THINK AND WRITE,** p. 260
- **UNIT ACTIVITIES,** p. 264
- **COMPLETE THE UNIT PROJECT,** p. 264

TEACHER SELECTED ITEMS MAY INCLUDE:

- **UNIT ASSESSMENT**
  Assessment Program, pp. 17–20
- **PORTFOLIO SUMMARY**
  Assessment Program, p. xv
- **GROUP END-OF-PROJECT CHECKLIST**
  Assessment Program, p. ix
- **INDIVIDUAL END-OF-UNIT CHECKLIST**
  Assessment Program, p. x

Unit 5 Test

STANDARD TEST

Unit 5

Name ______ Date ______

Test

Vocabulary (5 points each)

Draw a picture and write a sentence to describe each word.

1. history
   Possible answer: History tells us about life long ago.
   Possible drawing: a person, place, or event from the past
2. settler
   Possible answer: This settler traveled to the west.
   Possible drawing: a person wearing clothing from the 1800s
3. colony
   Possible answer: This is the colony of Georgia.
   Possible drawing: a simple labeled map of one of the thirteen colonies
4. artifact
   Possible answer: This artifact is from a Spanish colony.
   Possible drawing: a Spanish helmet
5. landmark
   Possible answer: This landmark reminds us of a battle.
   Possible drawing: a cannon

STANDARD TEST

Name ______ Date ______

Main Ideas (5 points each)

6. Which holiday celebrates the beginning of our country?
   - ○ A Thanksgiving
   - ○ B Memorial Day
   - ○ C Presidents' Day
   - ● D Independence Day
7. Which can help you learn about the past?
   - ● F museums
   - ○ G homes
   - ○ H markets
   - ○ J parades

Write Aztecs or Incas.

8. Aztecs built a great city on an island.
9. Incas lived in Peru.
10. Incas built highways in the mountains.
11. Aztecs lived in Mexico.

Match each person with what he or she might say.

12. Thurgood Marshall — "I was a Supreme Court justice."
13. Louis Pasteur — "I discovered a way to kill germs in food."
14. Golda Meir — "I was a leader in Israel."
15. Albert Einstein — "I won the Nobel prize for science."

NOTES

STANDARD TEST

Name ______________________ Date ______________

Skills (5 points each)

The time line shows when each President was elected. Use the time line to answer the questions.

U.S. Presidents

1780	1790	1800	1810	1820
George Washington 1789	John Adams 1797	Thomas Jefferson 1801	James Madison 1809	James Monroe 1817

16. Which President was elected in 1817?
    James Monroe
17. In what year was President Washington elected?
    1789
18. Was Thomas Jefferson elected before or after 1800?
    after
19. Which President was elected first, John Adams or Thomas Jefferson?
    John Adams
20. For how many years was James Madison President?
    8 years

STANDARD TEST

Name ______________________ Date ______________

Performance Task

Pretend that you are a Spanish settler in Mexico or an English settler in the colonies. Write a letter describing your new home, clothes, food, and work and how you feel about them.

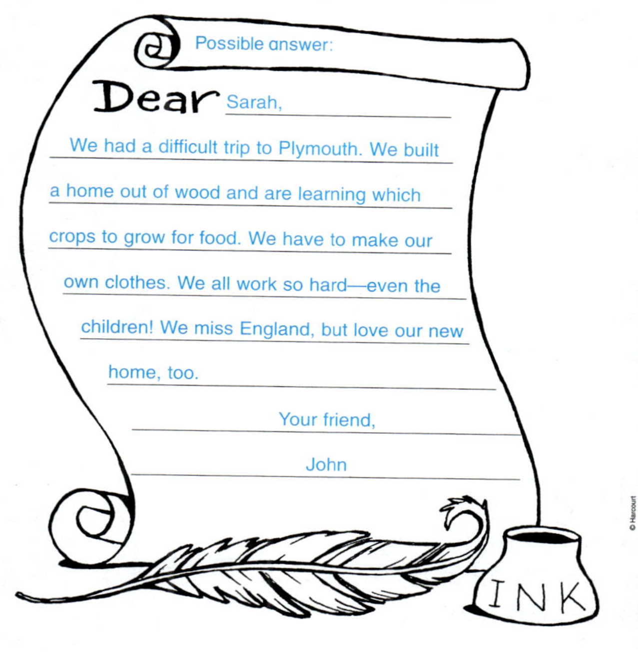

RUBRICS FOR SCORING

SCORING RUBRIC The rubric below lists the criteria for evaluating the tasks above. It also describes different levels of success in meeting those criteria.

INDIVIDUAL PERFORMANCE TASK

SCORE 4	SCORE 3	SCORE 2	SCORE 1
▪ Rich description is provided.	▪ Some description is provided.	▪ Little description is provided.	▪ No description is provided.
▪ Details fit historical period and type of settlement strongly.	▪ Details fit historical period and type of settlement.	▪ Details fit historical period and type of settlement weakly.	▪ Details do not fit historical period and type of settlement.
▪ Letters indicate strong understanding of past and present.	▪ Letters indicate understanding of past and present.	▪ Letters indicate some understanding of past and present.	▪ Letters do not indicate understanding of past and present.
▪ Ideas are well organized and developed.	▪ Ideas are fairly well organized and developed.	▪ Ideas are minimally organized and developed.	▪ Ideas are not organized or developed.

Introduce the Unit

OBJECTIVES

- Use a visual to predict content.
- Interpret a quotation.
- Use a sequence chart to prepare for the unit.

Access Prior Knowledge

Ask children to name activities they do in school every day. Record the activities they mention on separate sentence strips and display the activities on the chalkledge in random order. Then call on volunteers to arrange the activities in time order.

Visual Learning

Picture Have children look at the picture on pages 209R and 209. If your town has a clock tower, discuss it with children.

Q **How can you tell what time it is in the picture?**

A We can look at the clock's hands.

Q **How do you know what season the picture shows?**

A The blossoms show that it is spring.

Q **If you could look at the same scene on a December evening, how might it look different?**

A Children may say that the clock hands might show a different time and the tree branches would be bare.

Q **How would the scene be the same?**

A The clock and tower would still be there, and so would the trees.

Point out that time is always passing. Over time, some things change and some stay the same. Have children predict what changes they might learn about in this unit.

BACKGROUND

Zora Neale Hurston Zora Neale Hurston is best known as a writer, but she was also an anthropologist. As part of her studies, she traveled to Jamaica, Haiti, Bermuda, and Honduras. She put what she had learned as an anthropologist to work when she became one of the famous Harlem Renaissance writers in the 1930s. Hurston collected folktales. She also wrote novels, short stories, plays, and articles whose characters were African Americans. After the 1930s, most of Hurston's work disappeared for a time. When she died in 1960, she was poor and ill, and few people knew about her writing. In the 1970s, readers again began to appreciate the work of Zora Neale Hurston, and today her work is again widely read. One of her most well-known works is the novel *Their Eyes Were Watching God.*

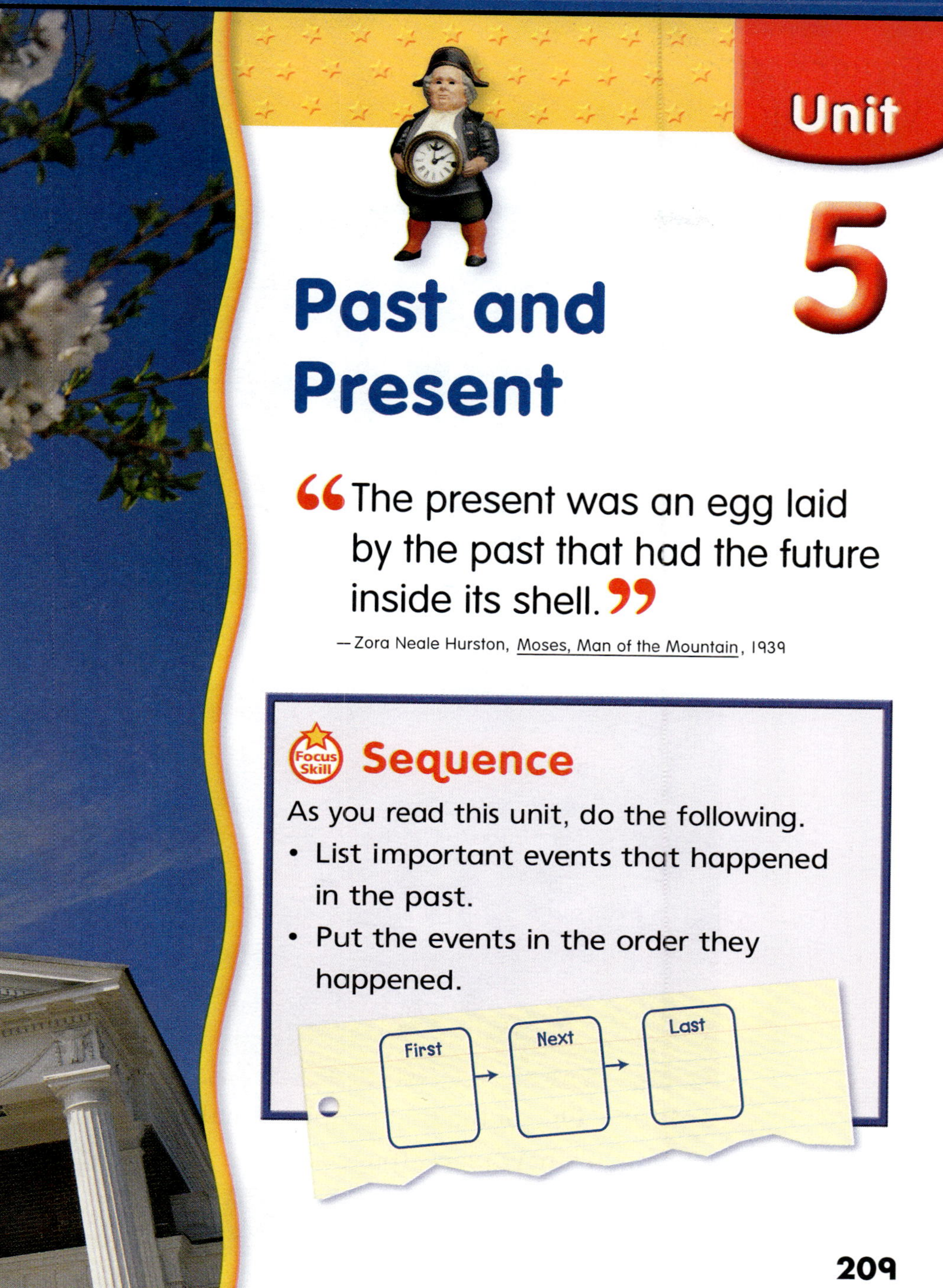

Unit 5

Past and Present

"The present was an egg laid by the past that had the future inside its shell."

—Zora Neale Hurston, Moses, Man of the Mountain, 1939

Focus Skill: Sequence

As you read this unit, do the following.

- List important events that happened in the past.
- Put the events in the order they happened.

209

Analyze Primary Sources

Colonial Figurine Clock Tell children that while clocks are very useful, they can also be decorative.

Q Have you ever seen an interesting clock? What did it look like?

A Children may mention clocks such as cuckoo clocks, cartoon figure clocks, and grandfather clocks.

Quotation Read aloud the quotation. Then invite children to say it with you. Tell children that Zora Neale Hurston was a famous African American writer. Then draw a hen, an egg, and a chick on the board. Explain that when Hurston wrote the quotation, she made a comparison between time, which readers cannot picture, and a simple process that is familiar to most people.

Ask children what part of the picture stands for the past (the hen), what part stands for the present (the egg), and what part stands for the future (the chick).

Explain that the quotation shows that the present, past, and future are all connected.

Focus Skill: Sequence

Tell children that sequence is the order in which events happen. Words such as *before, after, first, next,* and *last* help readers understand sequence. Have children look at the sequence flow charts. Tell them to think about the order of events as they read Unit 5. Explain that when they have completed the unit, they will use sequence charts to help them remember the order of some historical events.

- A blank graphic organizer appears on page 63 of the Activity Book.
- A completed graphic organizer can be found on page 260 of this Teacher's Edition.

INTEGRATE ART

Decorate a Clock
Duplicate and distribute pictures of a clock face with numerals but without hands. Leave space for children's drawings around the outside of the clock. Have children draw and decorate an interesting clock and add hands to show the time. Tell children to share their clocks with a partner and have the partner tell what time the clock face shows.

AUDIOTEXT

Use the Unit 5 AUDIOTEXT for a reading of the Unit narrative.

Preview the Vocabulary

PAGES 210–211

OBJECTIVES

- Use visuals to determine word meanings.
- Use words and visuals to predict the content of the unit.

Access Prior Knowledge

Discuss the idea that one way we learn about the past is by studying objects that give clues about how people lived long ago. Ask children to consider items in their homes that might give clues about the past, such as photographs, old clothing, artworks, antique furniture, or old-fashioned cooking utensils.

Make Connections

Link Pictures and Words Have a volunteer read the word *history* and its definition. Remind children that when they are reading, looking at the pictures can help them understand the words. Ask how the picture helps them understand what *history* means. (The picture shows people from long ago, and *history* means "the past" or "long ago.")

Visual Learning

Pictures Ask children to look at the pictures used to illustrate the words *settler* and *colony*. Have volunteers read the definitions aloud. Ask children what they can tell about the place the people are settling from details in the picture. (There are trees for building.) Discuss how the clothes people wore, the kinds of houses they built, and the kinds of food they ate all depended on the place where they settled.

Preview the Vocabulary

history The study of what happened to people in the past. (page 222)

settler One of the first people to make a home in a new place. (page 229)

210

READING SOCIAL STUDIES

Outline Have children preview the unit by reading the lesson titles and looking at the illustrations. Help them prepare an outline using the lesson titles as major headings. Remind children to leave space between headings so that they can add important ideas as they read. As you complete each lesson, encourage children to return to their outlines and fill in important details.

Past and Present

A. Measuring Time
   1. Long ago, people measured time by the passing seasons.
   2. Later, they invented calendars and clocks.

B. Tracing a Community's History

C. Celebrating Our Country's History

D. Celebrating Heroes of the Past

E. Contributions in World History

Find the "story" in history.

landmark A familiar object at a place. (page 239)

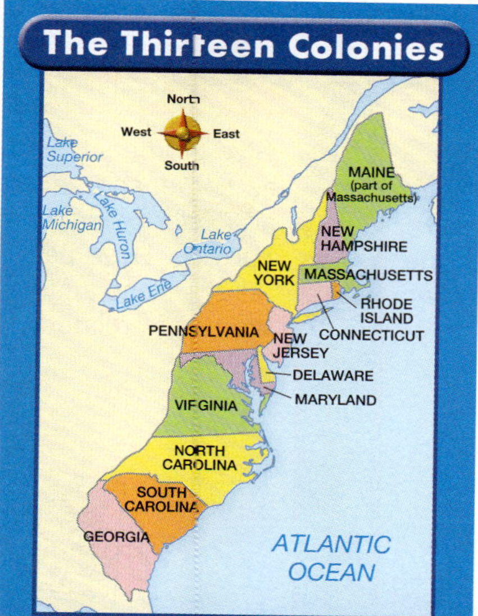

colony A place that is ruled by another country. (page 238)

artifact An object from another time or place. (page 224)

211

Explain that when the Pilgrims and other people came to America, America was a colony of England. Even though the colonists lived here, they were still English citizens and had to obey English laws.

Q How many colonies were there?

A 13

Review the word *artifact* and then discuss the artifact shown in the picture.

Q What might this artifact help us know about the people who used it?

A People wanted their clothes to be neat; they didn't have electricity.

Q If second graders 50 years from now came to this classroom, what artifacts might they find?

A Anything in our classroom now would be considered an artifact.

Have a volunteer read the word *landmark* and the definition. Explain that a landmark is an important place that everyone knows. Give examples in your town, such as a statue, an important building, or a sports stadium.

DEMOCRATIC VALUES

Individual Rights

Have a volunteer read aloud what Earnest says. Then write the word *history* on the board and ask children to point out the word *story*. Explain that history is the story of what happened in the past. Discuss the ways we know about history. Point out that the way the story of history is told depends on the person telling the story. As an example, explain that an American colonist would tell the events of the American Revolution in a very different way from the way a British soldier would. As children read this unit, ask them to identify good citizens who have helped shape our history.

REACH ALL LEARNERS

Below-Level Learners
Reinforce the meanings of the vocabulary words by giving children simple cloze sentences that use the words. For example: *The _______ moved from the city to build a home on the prairie.* (settler) *The scientists found an _______ that told them how people in the colony lived long ago.* (artifact)

SCHOOL TO HOME

Use the Unit 5 SCHOOL TO HOME NEWSLETTER on pages S9–S10 to introduce the unit to family members and suggest activities they can do at home.

Word Work

The following activities may be used to preteach vocabulary. You may also wish to duplicate and distribute the word cards found in the back of this book on pages V57–V70. Children can use them as flash cards to practice saying and defining each word. Remind children to use the glossary at the back of their books to help them define these words.

SPIN AND SORT

Provide a three-part spinner with the sections labeled *Person, Place,* and *Thing.* Have children take turns spinning the pointer, choosing a vocabulary word card that matches that category, and making a sentence with the word. Children receive one point for each word choice that correctly matches the category and another point for each correct sentence.

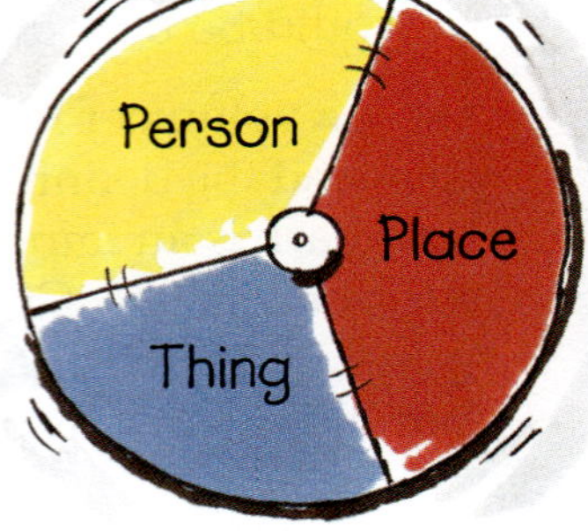

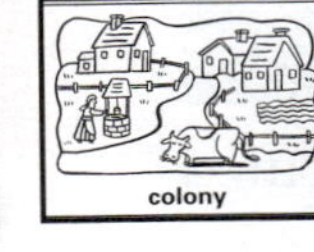

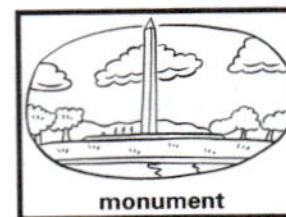

VOCABULARY CONNECTIONS

Give partners pairs of related vocabulary words, such as *settler* and *settlement, ancient* and *modern, cause* and *effect, hero* and *monument,* and *scribe* and *papyrus.* Have partners discuss the words and then tell the class a story to show how they think the two words are related.

RACE THROUGH TIME

Display a time line showing ten decades. For example, the time line would start with 1700 and end with 1800. Tell children they will have ten chances to guess vocabulary words and move through the ten decades of the time line. Give a clue about one of the vocabulary words. If the class guesses the word, place a mark or a self-stick note on the mark for the first decade. Continue giving clues and having the class guess words. After giving the class ten tries, ask children to read the year on the time line where their marker is. Then have a volunteer look in a history book to find out about some things that happened in that year.

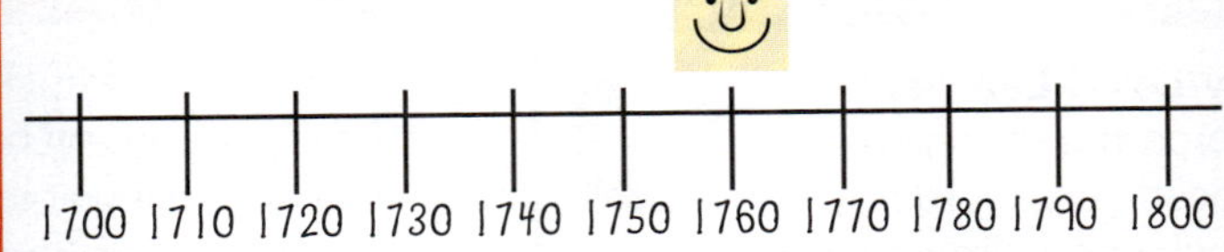

MEMORIES OF THE PAST

JOURNAL Have children record the following words in their vocabulary journal. Ask them to tell how each one helps us understand the past.

Start with a Story

Growing Seasons

OBJECTIVES

- Obtain information about a topic using a variety of visual sources, such as literature.
- Describe seasonal changes and their effects.
- Compare family life today and in the past.

RESOURCES

Pupil Book/Unit Big Book, pp. 212–215

Word Cards V57–V58

Reading and Vocabulary Transparency 5-1

Internet Resources

Audiotext, Unit 5

READING SOCIAL STUDIES

Graphic Organizer At the left side of the board, begin a flow chart. Explain that a flow chart shows what happens in a process in the order in which it happens. Invite children, as they read the story, to use the chart to keep track of the steps in growing potatoes.

Plow and till the soil.

↓

Cut seed potatoes in pieces.

↓

USE READING AND VOCABULARY TRANSPARENCY 5-1.

5-1 TRANSPARENCY

Vocabulary

season p. 212

Summary

This story is about a family that lived 100 years ago. It describes the family's seasonal activities in their potato garden and the resulting potato harvest.

1 Motivate

Set the Purpose

Have children read the story title and look at the pictures. Then ask them what the people in the story are doing. Finally, invite children to read the story to learn what the people are growing in their garden and what they do with the food they grow.

Access Prior Knowledge

Ask children if they have ever grown a plant. Invite them to tell what they did—or forgot to do—and what the result was. Encourage children to name the things a plant needs to grow. If necessary, help children recall that you place a plant in soil and give it water and sun.

2 Teach

Read and Respond

Geography This story is set in Herscher, Illinois. Help children locate Illinois on a map. Explain that the small town of Herscher is about halfway between the cities of Peoria and Chicago, in the northeastern part of the state.

Q What kind of weather do you think Herscher has in the summer? in the winter? Why do you think so?

A It is most likely warm in the summer and cold in the winter. It is located in the northern part of the United States, where winters are cold and summers are warm.

Explain that a year is divided into four seasons: spring, summer, fall, and winter. Discuss aspects of the seasons as you experience them in your area. Emphasize that qualities of seasons vary from place to place; for example, winter weather in southern Texas is very different from winter weather in northern Minnesota.

Q How do seasons affect activities where you live?

A Children's responses should indicate how work and recreation can be affected by changing weather patterns.

START with a STORY

by Elsie Lee Splear
illustrated by Doug Bowles

One hundred years ago, the Lee family lived on a farm near the small town of Herscher, Illinois. They worked hard to grow their own food. Each **season**, or time of year, meant different jobs had to be done.

212

BACKGROUND

About the Author Elsie Lee Splear and her sisters were children of tenant farmers in northeastern Illinois. Growing up in the early twentieth century, Splear helped her family make by hand most of what they needed, such as clothes, soap, butter, and canned goods. In *Growing Seasons*, she writes about her memories of life on a farm at that time in our country's history.

WORD WORK

Multiple-Meaning Words Explain to children that some words have more than one meaning. Illustrate this by writing the following sentences on the board:

Spring is my favorite season.

I like to season my potatoes with salt and pepper.

Discuss the meaning of *season* in each sentence.

READING SOCIAL STUDIES

Use Picture Clues Tell children to look at the illustrations to help them figure out unfamiliar words. For example, if children do not recognize the word *furrow,* they can look at the illustration to see that people are making long rows in the soil.

Planting Potatoes

The whole family helped Mama in her garden when early spring came and it was time to plant potatoes.

First Papa plowed and tilled the soil while my sisters and I helped Mama cut the seed potatoes into pieces. Each piece had to have a sprouting "eye." When the soil was soft, we went out into the garden with Mama and planted the potatoes in the furrows Papa had made. We used a measuring stick to make sure there was just the right distance between each piece of potato. It took the whole day just to plant the potatoes. Then Papa had to spread the soil over them again.

213

Visual Learning

Illustration Direct children's attention to the illustration showing the planting of potatoes.

Q **What is happening in the picture on the bottom of page 213?**

A Papa is plowing and tilling the soil.

Q **What time of year do you think it is?**

A It is probably spring.

Read and Respond

Understand the Story Discuss the way some families work together on farms or in gardens. Explain that the family in this story lived on a farm and they grew much of their food. Discuss the job that each family member did to prepare the spring garden.

Link History and Economics Ask volunteers to share each of their family members' occupations or jobs. Have children compare the current jobs of people in their family to the jobs of the family in the story.

INTEGRATE SCIENCE

Grow Potatoes Children can grow their own potatoes. Find a sunny spot and fill a container about two feet long and one foot tall with soil. Be sure the container has holes in the bottom for drainage, and put something under it to collect extra water. Use fingerling potatoes (smaller potatoes ripen sooner) and some purple potatoes (for fun). Cut the potatoes into approximately two-ounce pieces, each with two eyes. Let the pieces dry out overnight. Then let children plant them several inches apart, with the eyes "looking up." Cover the potato pieces and water the soil. As the stems begin to grow, some of the potato may peek out of the soil. Be sure to add more soil to cover it up. Children can harvest the potatoes as soon as the plants flower. Potatoes will be better, however, if children wait to harvest them until ten days after the tops dry out and die.

REACH ALL LEARNERS

English as a Second Language Write the following words on the board: *plow, plant, measure, spread.* Have children repeat each word as you point to it and say it aloud. Then model acting out each word. Finally, have children pantomime the activity described by the words as you point to each one and say it aloud.

Read and Respond

Understand the Story Explain that the author tells how her family worked through the summer and fall to grow, harvest, and store the potatoes. Then, in the winter, they enjoyed eating the potatoes.

Visual Learning

Illustration Ask children to look at the illustration and to point out details that help them know that there has been a change in the seasons.

3 Close

Summarize the Reading

- In the spring, the Lee family worked together to plant potatoes.
- During summer, they cared for the growing plants.
- In the fall, they harvested and stored the potatoes.
- In winter, the family enjoyed cooked potatoes.

READING SOCIAL STUDIES

Graphic Organizer Ask children to complete the flow chart with the steps needed to grow and eat potatoes. Ask volunteers to retell the story, using the flow chart.

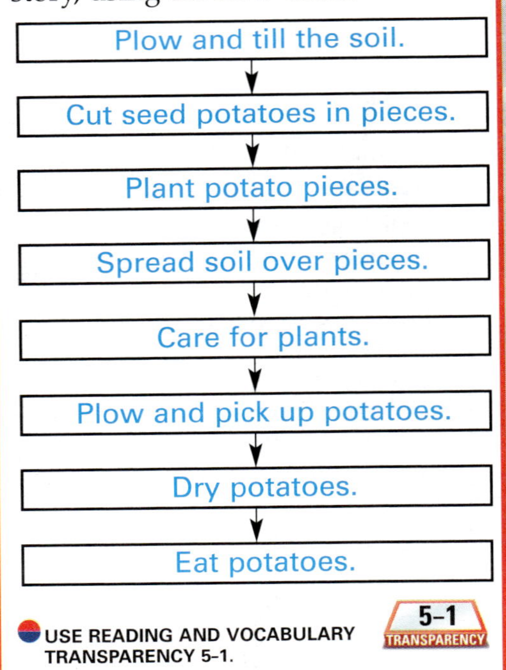

USE READING AND VOCABULARY TRANSPARENCY 5-1.

5-1 TRANSPARENCY

As the potato sprouts grew, Mama showed us how to hoe gently around each plant and how to pick the insects off the leaves. Finally, in the fall, the time came to lift the potatoes. Papa used the plow to bring them to the surface, and we girls picked up the potatoes one at a time, gently brushing off the loose dirt. We carried them by bushel baskets to a lumber wagon where the potatoes dried.

INTEGRATE HEALTH

Nutrition Help children use the Internet to find out about the different kinds of potatoes. Have them find out the names and what kind is best for different dishes (baked potato, potato salad, and so on). Children can print out pictures of the different potatoes or make their own drawings. Then create a bulletin board display of the many kinds of potatoes.

INTEGRATE MATHEMATICS

Feeding a Family Tell children that for mashed potatoes, you need 4 ounces of potatoes for each person. Ask how many ounces of potatoes the six members of the Lee family would need to cook to feed everyone. ($6 \times 4 = 24$) If the Lees invited two guests for dinner, how many ounces of potatoes would they need then? (32) Let children use counters to do the math.

Practice the Skill

In 1961 President John F. Kennedy said, "I believe that this nation should commit itself to achieving the goal, before this decade is out, of landing a man on the moon and returning him safely to Earth." Look at the time line below to see how well we did.

1. When did Neil Armstrong walk on the moon?
2. Did John Glenn make his second space flight before or after the landing on Mars?
3. When is the space station supposed to be finished?

Apply What You Learned

Make a time line of events in your life.

1990 Hubble Space Telescope is launched.

1998 John Glenn becomes oldest space traveler.

2005 International Space Station to be finished.

CHART AND GRAPH SKILLS

Practice the Skill—Answers

1. 1969
2. after the landing on Mars
3. 2005

3 Close

Apply What You Learned

Children should make a time line showing in chronological order meaningful events from their lives. If children are uncomfortable revealing personal information, allow them to create a time line for a fictional character.

RETEACH THE SKILL

Make a Human Time Line Make sentence strips for each event listed on the Space Exploration Time Line. Give the strips in random order to seven volunteers and have them stand in a line at the front of the room. Ask them to read aloud what is written on their strips. Then have children rearrange the volunteers so they are in chronological order, based on their events.

ACTIVITY BOOK

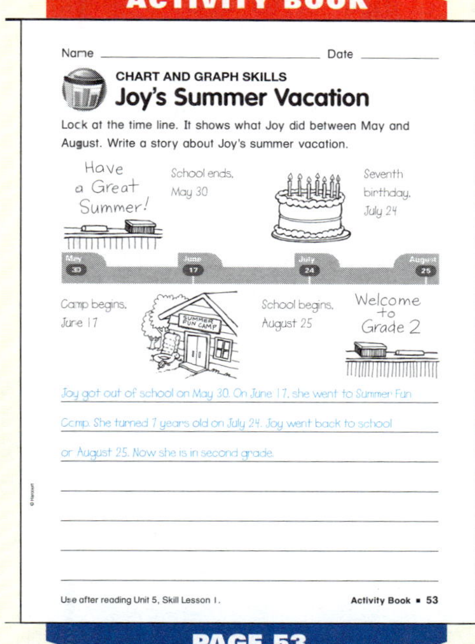

Name ____________ Date ______

CHART AND GRAPH SKILLS

Joy's Summer Vacation

Lock at the time line. It shows what Joy did between May and August. Write a story about Joy's summer vacation.

Joy got out of school on May 30. On June 17, she went to Summer Fun Camp. She turned 7 years old on July 24. Joy went back to school on August 25. Now she is in second grade.

Use after reading Unit 5, Skill Lesson 1. Activity Book ▪ 53

PAGE 53

TRANSPARENCY

Use SKILL TRANSPARENCY 5-1.

GO ONLINE — INTERNET RESOURCES

THE LEARNING SITE

Go to **www.harcourtschool.com** for a tour of the International Space Station.

Extension Activities For Home and School

Apollo Program Time Line

Materials: **craft paper, markers, reference tools**

Arrange children in five groups. Give each group a sheet of craft paper with one of five years—1968 to 1972—written at the top. Tell children that each group will complete a one-year segment of a time line for the Apollo space program. Ask children to find information about the Apollo program using an encyclopedia or the Internet. Have them check **www.harcourtschool.com** to find a link that will help them in their search. Have children create their time lines, marking off spaces for each month in the year noted at the top of their sheet. Then have them identify and show on the time line important events that happened in the Apollo program during their year. When each group has completed its part, have the groups assemble the five-year time line on a bulletin board or on a wall in your room.

(VISUAL/TACTILE)

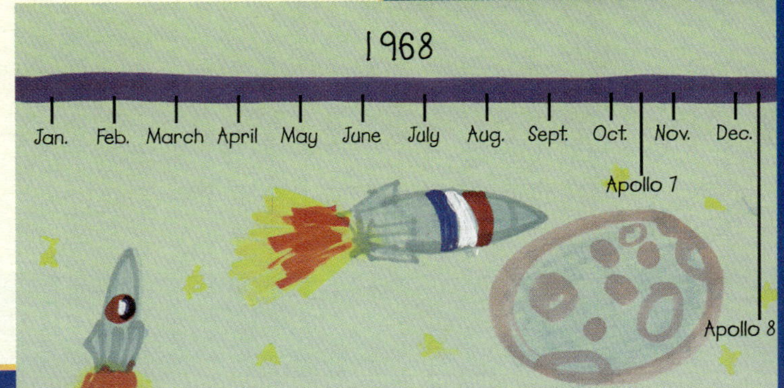

My Special Day Time Line

Materials: **string, drawing paper, construction paper strips, tacks, clothespins, scissors, crayons or markers**

Have children ask adult family members to help them choose a special date, such as their birthday or a special family holiday. Then suggest children draw a picture of themselves on their special day and write the date of their special event under their picture. Then have them cut out the picture. At school, hang a piece of string with 12 knots tied in it at equal intervals, low enough for children to reach. Write the name of each month on a separate paper strip and place the strips in order above each of the twelve segments of string. Have children use a clothespin to clip the cutout picture to the string under the appropriate month and in chronological order by date. When you complete the activity, challenge children to pose questions that can be answered by using information on the time line.

(VISUAL/TACTILE/AUDITORY)

Examine Primary Sources

Learning About the Past

OBJECTIVES

- Name sources of information, such as people, places, and artifacts.
- Obtain information about a topic using a variety of sources.
- Compare sources of information about the past.

RESOURCES

Pupil Book/Unit Big Book, pp. 222–225

Word Cards V59–V60

Internet Resources

Vocabulary

history p. 222 **source** p. 222 **artifact** p. 224

1 Motivate

Remind children that Earnest says to look for the *story* in *history*. Explain that history is the story of what happened in the past. Historians—or people who study history—look at things from long ago to learn about the way people lived. Historians also find out about the past by talking with people, reading what people have written, and visiting places such as museums or monuments.

Q Why do you think historians study different sources about the past?

A Historians need to compare sources to find the truest story about the past.

Help children understand that there are often several interpretations of any event depending on the reporter's point of view.

Access Prior Knowledge

Ask children if they have ever asked an older family member or friend, "What were things like when you were a child?" Ask volunteers to tell what they have learned about the past when they asked questions such as this one or listened to older adults tell stories about the old days. As children share, encourage them to compare how the childhood experiences of older family members were alike and different.

2 Teach

Read and Respond

History Read aloud the text on pages 222 and 223. Be sure children understand that a source is where something comes from. Stress that a story about the past is called history. Point out to children that learning about family history can teach them about world history because they can learn what family members experienced as they lived through world events.

Link History and Geography. Explain to children that today's current events will be tomorrow's history. As a class, list some important events that are happening in the community, state, or world today. On a map, help children find where the events are taking place. Then discuss why some of the events on the list might become important events in history.

Visual Learning

Pictures Ask volunteers to suggest who the people shown in the pictures might be. Have children point out visual clues that might help them identify who each person is.

Invite children to list items pictured around the trunk.

Q What can people use to tell about their family's history?

A photographs, letters, souvenirs

Learning About the Past

History is made up of the stories people tell about the past. The past can be as long ago as ancient times or as near in time as yesterday. One way to learn about the past is through sources. A **source** is someone or something that can give information.

1 How are people sources?

grandparent

reenacter

librarian

222

INTEGRATE READING

Share a Book Read aloud two books that relate the history of people in North America, such as *Pearl* by Debby Atwell (Houghton Mifflin, 2001) and *Meema's Memory Quilt: Treasured Stories of Watauga County History* by Jane Wilson (Parkway Publishers, 1999). Then have a discussion comparing the ways the people in the stories share their histories.

REACH ALL LEARNERS

English as a Second Language Help children create a web showing people who might be sources.

People who are sources: grandmother, father, grandfather, teachers, sister, brother, aunt, uncle, librarians, mother

BACKGROUND

Jamestown King James I of England sent members of the Virginia Company to North America with the hopes of settling Virginia and finding gold and a water route to East Asia. In 1607 the settlers landed on Jamestown Island. They were successful in building a settlement, but they did not find gold or a route to East Asia. Instead, they grew tobacco and sometimes traded copper and iron tools with the Powhatan Indians for food. Jamestown was the capital of Virginia until 1698, when the capital was moved to Williamsburg.

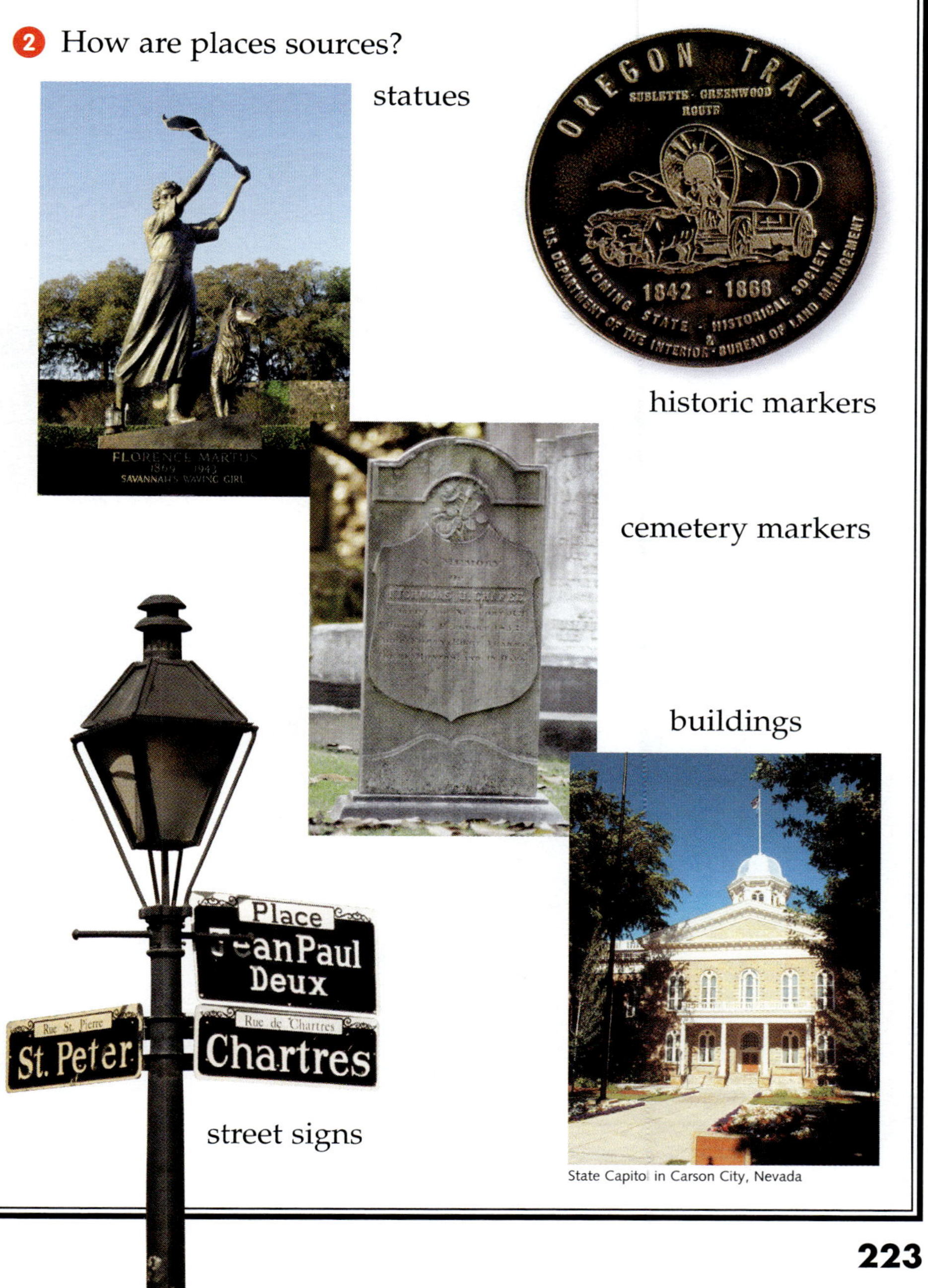

State Capitol in Carson City, Nevada

223

Read and Respond

History Discuss ways children can use places to help them learn about the past. Point out that some places, such as libraries and history museums, are built specially to house materials that show or tell how people before us have lived. Other places, such as monuments or historical markers, remind us of special people or events from history. In cemeteries, names, dates, and other information carved into tombstones can provide historical information. Buildings can help us learn how people lived and worked in the past, while the names of streets can tell us the names of important people and places of the past.

Q What streets in our town are named after people? Why do you think the streets got these names?

A Children may say that Washington Street, for example, was named after our first President. This tells them that people in their town long ago thought Washington was important and wanted to honor him.

Point out that the language on street signs can also tell about cultures of the area.

Visual Learning

Pictures Discuss the images shown in each picture. Ask children to identify similar places in your area. Have them note similarities and differences between local places and the ones shown in the photographs.

Point out the picture of the county courthouse. Explain that in addition to being historic landmarks, old courthouses like this one have stored countless records of births, deaths, marriages, and land transactions.

Q Why do you think county courthouses are important sources?

A They keep records that can tell people about their history.

MAKE IT RELEVANT

In Your Community Provide a street map of your area. Have partners choose a place named after someone—Franklin Square, Madison Park, Clara Barton School, for example—and then do research to find out who that person was and why he or she was important. Let children present their information to the class.

INTEGRATE LANGUAGE ARTS

Write About a Place Ask children to think about a historic place in your area. Have them write a paragraph explaining what they have learned about the past from visiting the place. Invite volunteers to read their paragraphs to the class.

Read and Respond

History Explain that an artifact is an object from another time or place. Point out that letters and notes can help us learn about people's everyday lives, and that newspapers and ticket stubs can give information about important events at a certain place and time. Review the artifacts in the trunk on page 222.

Q **What artifact would you place in a time capsule to help people in the future know about your life today? Why?**

A Children should be able to justify the importance of their selected artifact in letting people know something about their life today.

Visual Learning

Artifact Ask children to tell about family heirlooms, or keepsakes, they have seen. Have them describe the pocketwatch on this page and explain how it can be a source. (Children should note the inscription and the age of the watch.)

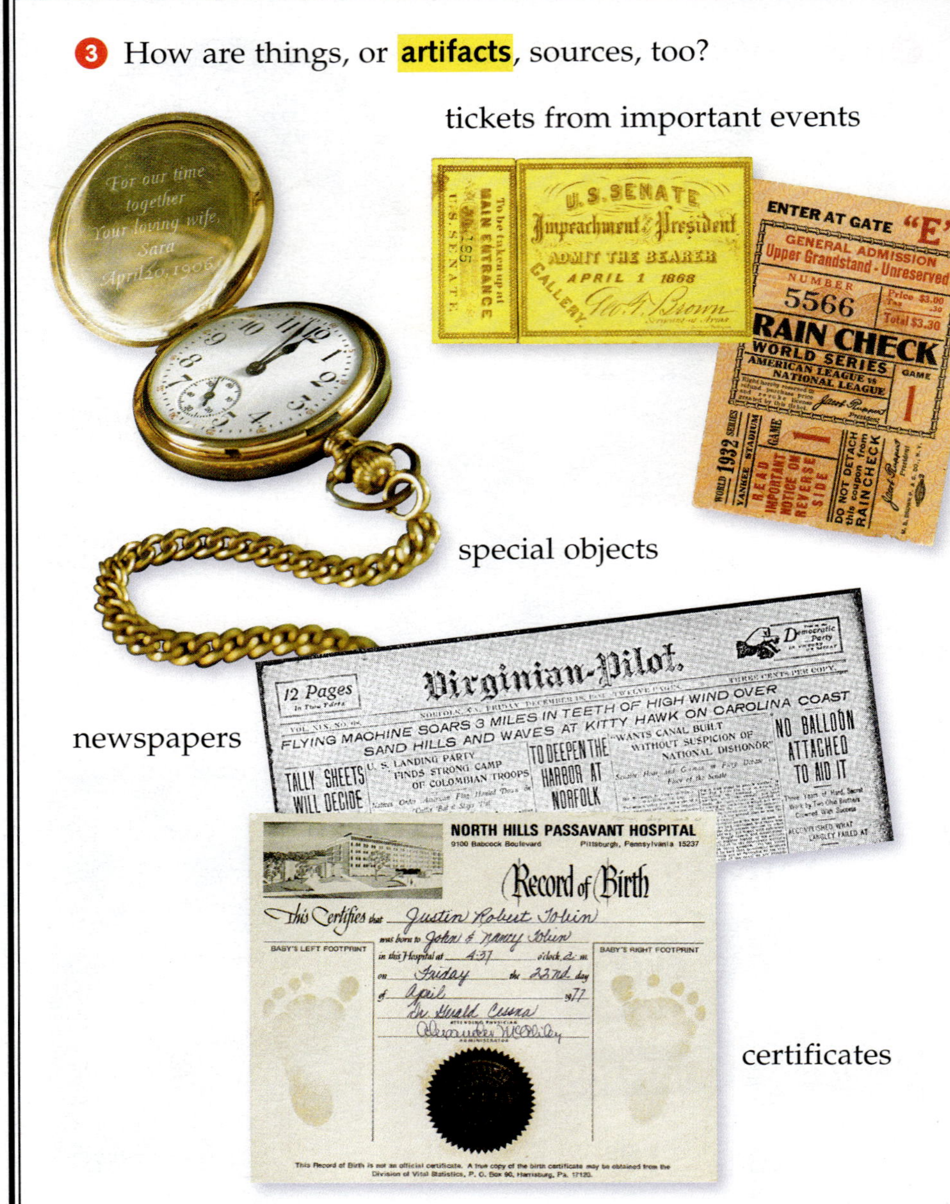

MAKE IT RELEVANT

At Home Have children interview people in their family. Explain that the interview should include their family's origin, legends, or adventures. Have children bring in any artifacts that will help them share with the class the information they obtained in the family interviews.

INTEGRATE LANGUAGE ARTS

Diary Tell children that diaries or journals are important sources of information about daily life at a certain place and time. Encourage them to begin keeping their own diaries. For each entry, have them include the date and then write a few sentences describing anything that stands out about that day's experience. Emphasize that diaries are personal and private and that they will not have to share their diaries with you or with the class.

QUESTIONS KIDS ASK

Q **Why should I care about what happened long ago?**

A It is interesting to compare how people lived a long time ago with how we live today. Also, many things we use and enjoy today come from the past. Another reason is that people at all times have made mistakes. We can learn not to do the same things.

Activity

Find out three interesting facts about your community's history. Get one from a person, one from a place, and one from a thing.

Research

Visit The Learning Site at
www.harcourtschool.com
to research other primary sources.

225

Read and Respond

History Ask children to look at the artifacts shown on this page. Have them identify each artifact and discuss what kinds of information might be collected by studying it.

Q What might someone in the future learn about your school by looking at a photograph of your class?

A They could learn how people dress, what kinds of furniture we use, how many children are in a class, and what kinds of materials we use.

Q How can videos, film, and television help people learn about the past?

A They can show how things looked; they can be used to record things happening now for future study.

3 Close

Activity

Refer children to the examples of sources in this lesson for ideas about the kinds of people, places, and things they can investigate.

Research

Children will find a variety of other history sources at The Learning Site at **www.harcourtschool.com.** Encourage children to select one source and find out what story of past events that source has to tell.

EXTEND AND ENRICH

Research and Report Have small groups of children use a variety of reference sources to find photographs of automobiles from the 1920s up to the present time. Have each group make a time line showing how automobiles looked in each decade. If necessary, have them review the time line on pages 220 and 221. Encourage children to add illustrations to show the automobiles described for each decade on the time line.

RETEACH

Write Questions Invite children to choose one of each kind of source—person, place, and artifact—shown or discussed in this lesson. Have them write a question for each that they might ask to learn about the past. Use the following model as an example: Librarian— Do you have a book about how the Pilgrims lived?

Name ______________________ Date __________

Examine Primary Sources

How can each of the following help you learn?

storyteller ______________________

____

statue ______________________

____

old photograph ______________________

____

Answer the questions.

1. How are people sources?

____

2. How are places sources?

____

3. How are things, or artifacts, sources, too?

____

SKILLS

Predict a Likely Outcome

OBJECTIVES

- Recognize the importance of knowing the past to predict the future.
- Follow steps for making a prediction.

RESOURCES

Pupil Book/Unit Big Book, pp. 226–227

Word Cards V59–V60

Activity Book, p. 54

Skill Transparency 5-2

Vocabulary

predict p. 226

1 Motivate

Ask children to imagine they are on the playground. They hear a rumbling noise and look up to see dark clouds in the sky. Lightning flashes, thunder claps, and a teacher carrying an umbrella comes outside and begins rushing them indoors. Ask children what they think will happen next. Explain that they have just predicted an outcome.

Why It Matters

Tell children that they used details from the story and their own past experience to help them figure out what would happen next.

INTEGRATE READING

Share a Poem Write the poem on the board (leaving off the last line) and read it aloud. Ask children to predict how the poem will end. Then write the last line and compare it to children's predictions.

Surprise Party

Janny Jo is turning seven.
It's time to throw a party!
Her parents asked May and Kevin,
Melissa, Kat, and Marty.
Everyone is told to hide
'Til Janny Jo is brought inside.
We wonder what she'll have to say
When we all yell
Happy Birthday!

Extension Activities For Home and School

Predictions Game

Materials: strips of writing paper, container, pencils

Give each child a strip of paper. Ask children to write on the strip an event or activity that can be described either as predictable or unpredictable. For example, predictable events might include birthdays, lunch period, and various holidays. Unpredictable events could include a fire drill, finding a nickel, or running into a friend at the park. Have children fold their completed strips and place them in a container. Next, write in large letters on two sides of the board the words *Predictable* and *Unpredictable*. Have children take turns drawing strips from the container. Ask them to read the information on the strip aloud and then decide whether the event is predictable or unpredictable. Have them explain their decision and then show it by going to stand under one of the words you have written on the board. Encourage discussion of any decisions the class disagrees with.
(VISUAL/AUDITORY)

How Does It End?

Materials: a variety of predictable comic strips, drawing paper, crayons or markers, glue

Provide a variety of predictable comic strips from which you have cut off the final panel. You may want to duplicate strips to make sure you have enough to go around. Give each child a strip. Ask children to glue their strips onto a sheet of drawing paper, leaving room to draw in the last panel. Ask children to read the cartoon strip and to predict how the strip will end. Then have them draw a picture showing their ending. Invite volunteers to share their completed cartoon strips with the class. Encourage children who completed the same strip to compare their endings.
(VISUAL/TACTILE)

How Does the Story End?

Materials: story below in a sealed envelope, one per child

Give each child an envelope containing the story below. Tell them to take the envelope home (no peeking!) and give it to an adult family member. The adult should read the story to the child and then ask the child to think of an ending for the story. Together they can write the ending. Ask children to bring their endings to class to share and compare.

Once upon a time, four friends were having a picnic in the yard. One friend spread a cloth on the grass. Another friend put out the paper plates. The third friend poured lemonade into paper cups. The fourth opened the picnic basket and took out four yummy sandwiches. Just then, the first friend jumped up and yelled, "Ants!"
(AUDITORY)

SKILLS

Identify Cause and Effect

OBJECTIVES

- Explain how one event can cause another.
- Analyze the effects of change.
- Recognize that history is a series of causes and effects.

RESOURCES

Pupil Book/Unit Big Book, pp. 234–235

Word Cards V61–V62

Activity Pattern P10

Activity Book, p. 56

Skill Transparency 5-3

Vocabulary

cause p. 234 **effect** p. 234

1 Motivate

Remind children that when the railroad came to Fort Myers in 1905, it brought more people to the area. The railroad also helped citrus growers ship their fruit to new parts of the country. Ask: *What caused more people to come to the area?* Lead children to see that advancements in transportation technology caused a population increase in Fort Myers.

Why It Matters

Explain to children that knowing what causes something to happen can help people decide what to do today and help them make plans for the future. Discuss the following examples: If children know that eating a whole box of crackers gives them a stomachache, they may decide not to eat all the crackers next time. If city officials know that a large number of cars causes traffic jams, they can plan to build more roads to meet the needs of a larger population.

REACH ALL LEARNERS

Auditory Learners Create a tape recording of various sound effects, such as the sounds of thunder, glass breaking, someone laughing, a baby crying, or the roar of the crowd at a ball game. Play each sound and ask children to suggest what might have caused it. Extend the activity by asking children to suggest how the listener might act when hearing each of the sounds.

2 Teach

What You Need to Know

Ask a volunteer to read aloud page 234. Then illustrate cause and effect by drawing on the board three boxes connected by right-pointing arrows. In the first box, write *Railroad is built.* Ask children what happened after the railroad was built. *What was the effect of the railroad?* Lead them to see that the building of the railroad caused more people to move to Fort Myers. Write *People move to Fort Myers* in the second box. Ask: *What happened when more people moved to Fort Myers?* Elicit that this caused the city to grow. Write *City grows* in the last box. Discuss how children might add to this cause-and-effect chain. For example, they might add a fourth box saying *More schools are built.*

Q What were some effects of more people's moving to Fort Myers?

A Children might suggest that more houses, stores, and schools were built.

Visual Learning

Pictures Ask volunteers to identify what they see in each of the pictures on page 235. Discuss what the pictures help the children know about Fort Myers and its surrounding area.

Skills

Identify Cause and Effect

Vocabulary
cause
effect

Why It Matters

Changes happen for many reasons. It can be helpful to know why something happened.

What You Need to Know

What makes something happen is a **cause**. What happens is an **effect**. You read that the building of the railroad caused more people to move to Fort Myers. The effect was a growing city.

234

Fort Myers

INTEGRATE ART

Draw Pictures Review the concept of cause and effect with children. Then have them choose a historical event discussed in Lesson 2 that clearly demonstrates cause and effect, such as the coming of the railroad that caused more people to visit Fort Myers. Ask children to draw pictures to illustrate the cause and effect of this event.

INTEGRATE SCIENCE

Changing Water Ask children what happens to water when they put it into the freezer. Ask what happens to water when they heat it in a pot on the stove. In each case, have children identify the cause-and-effect relationship.

EXTEND AND ENRICH

Add to the Cause-and-Effect Chain Review the cause-and-effect chain you wrote on the board for What You Need to Know. Challenge children to add at least three more boxes to the chain, showing a progression of causes and effects. For example, *New teachers are hired. The teachers need houses. New houses are built.* Invite volunteers to share their cause-and-effect chains with the class.

Practice the Skill

There are other reasons that more people go to Fort Myers. Look at the following pictures. Explain how the building of an airport could affect the growth of Fort Myers.

1. Why do you think an airport was built in Fort Myers?
2. How can more visitors help Fort Myers grow?

Apply What You Learned

Look for changes taking place in your community. Find out what has caused the changes.

READING SKILLS

Practice the Skill—Answers

1. People wanted a faster way to get to Fort Myers.
2. Some visitors might like Fort Myers so much that they decide to move there.

3 Close

Apply What You Learned

Suggest that children look for something brand-new, such as a building or road, and ask older family members and friends what caused it to be built.

RETEACH THE SKILL

What's the Cause? Prepare a list of specific events or situations, such as a clap of thunder, a child's being late for school, a baby's laughing, and a dog's barking. Read the items on the list one by one, and ask children to suggest causes for each. Then discuss other effects that might result from the suggested causes.

ACTIVITY BOOK

Name ____________ Date ________

READING SKILLS

Cause and Effect Pictures

Draw the beginning or ending for each story.

1

2

3

56 • Activity Book

Use after reading Unit 5, Skill Lesson 3.

PAGE 56

TRANSPARENCY

Use SKILL TRANSPARENCY 5-3.

Extension Activities For Home and School

What Happened and Why?

Materials: **copies of a cause-and-effect chain, current events articles from newspapers and magazines, paper, pencils**

Draw a cause-and-effect chain on paper and make a copy for each child. Also, give each child a simple newspaper or magazine article dealing with current events. (If possible, use articles from magazines written for children.) Ask children to take their articles home and to read and discuss them with a family member. Then have each child use the cause-and-effect chain to show the progression of events discussed in the article. Finally, have children retell for the class what they read in the article, explaining what happened and why.
(VISUAL/AUDITORY)

People voted for a new park.
↓
A new park was built.
↓
There was a big opening party at the park.

History Films

Materials: **Activity Pattern P10 (filmstrip), crayons or markers, box, construction paper, tape**

Provide children with the Activity Pattern P10. Then remind them of what they read about the history of Fort Myers. Have them illustrate the events on the filmstrip, showing the cause-and-effect progression. For example, they might show Spanish explorers arriving in Florida, followed by planting crops, and so on. After children complete their drawings, have them tape the filmstrips end to end. Provide a viewer by cutting a frame-sized hole in a small box that you have covered with dark-colored construction paper. Above the viewer, insert a pencil through the sides of the box lid to use as a roller. Help children tape the top of their filmstrip to the roller. Show children how to turn the pencil to cause the filmstrip to move, frame by frame, behind the viewer. Invite volunteers to show their filmstrips to the class, providing narration about what is happening in the film and why.
(VISUAL/KINESTHETIC/TACTILE)

Role-Playing Effects

Write on strips of paper actions that children can role-play—for example, shooting a basketball toward the basket, dropping a dish on the kitchen floor, hitting a baseball with a bat, dancing, playing the tuba in a parade, and stirring batter in a mixing bowl. Fold the strips and place them in a container. Have children take turns choosing a strip and role-playing the action. Then have the class suggest what will happen next. Extend the activity by having children guess what happened to cause the action.
(KINESTHETIC/AUDITORY/VISUAL)

Celebrating Our Country's History

OBJECTIVES

- Explain the significance of various national celebrations.
- Compare early Native American groups.
- Sequence early American history.
- Identify places that remind us of our history.

Sequence pp. 209, 240, 260

RESOURCES

Pupil Book/Unit Big Book, pp. 236–241

Word Cards V63–V64

Activity Book, p. 57

Reading and Vocabulary Transparency 5-4

Internet Resources

READING SOCIAL STUDIES

Make a Prediction Ask children to name the holidays they can recall. Have them read the lesson title and predict what holidays they will read about in this lesson. Save the predictions for use at the end of the lesson.

Guess	Check
Fourth of July and Flag Day	

USE READING AND VOCABULARY TRANSPARENCY 5-4.

Vocabulary

colony p. 238 **independence** p. 238 **freedom** p. 238 **landmark** p. 239

When Minutes Count

Have pairs of children read the lesson together. Then ask them to write a summary sentence for the lesson.

Quick Summary

This lesson focuses on ways we celebrate our country's history, including the reasons we celebrate Thanksgiving, Independence Day, and Memorial Day.

1 Motivate

Set the Purpose

Big Idea Read aloud the Big Idea statement. As children read the lesson, have them look for details about how our country's history is celebrated on certain holidays.

Access Prior Knowledge

Before reading the lesson, show children pictures that suggest certain holidays. For example, you might show the Norman Rockwell illustration of a Thanksgiving dinner. Ask children to identify the holiday being celebrated in each image. Have volunteers discuss what they like best about each holiday.

Read and Respond

History Read aloud and discuss pages 238 and 239. On a map, point out England and then the eastern coast of the United States. Stress that the colonists were ruled by a king who lived far away and who did not understand their problems and needs. Explain to children that England had just fought the French and Indian War to protect the 13 colonies. The English government felt that the colonists should help pay for the war through higher taxes. The colonists felt the taxes were unfair, especially since no one represented them in the English government.

Q Why were the colonists upset with England's government?

A The colonists felt that they should not be taxed without having a say in the government.

Explain that leaders among the colonists got together and decided that people in America could do a better job of governing themselves than a king in England could. Point out the date on which these leaders signed the Declaration of Independence—July 4. Note the time line.

Q What is another name we call the Fourth of July celebration?

A Independence Day

Q How can you tell that freedom was important to the colonists?

A They were willing to fight a war to gain freedom from England.

Visual Learning

Map Ask a volunteer to read aloud the title of the map. Explain that the map shows only the Atlantic, or eastern, side of the country.

Ask students to locate each colony as you name it.

Q Which colony was the farthest north? south?

A Massachusetts; Georgia

CAPTION ANSWER: Massachusetts

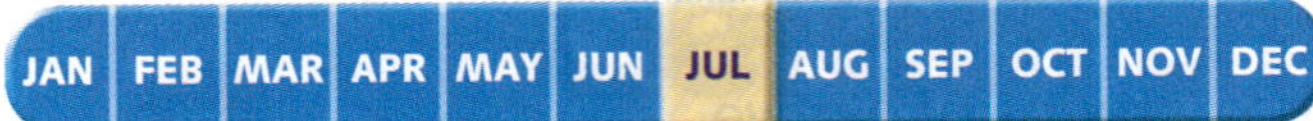

Independence Day

The first English settlers in North America built their colonies along the Atlantic Ocean. A **colony** is a place ruled by another country. England was very far away. The colonists were not always happy about following English laws.

On July 4, 1776, leaders in the colonies signed the Declaration of Independence. **Independence** is being free from rule by another country. The colonists said they were Americans and should have **freedom**, or the right to make their own choices. The English king did not agree.

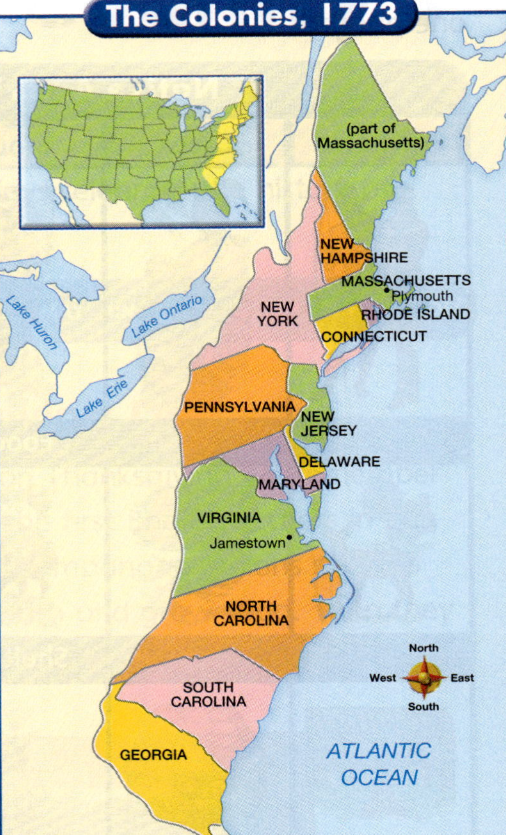

GEOGRAPHY THEME In which colony is Plymouth?

238

INTEGRATE MUSIC

Sing a Song Explain that "Yankee Doodle" was a popular song of the American Revolution. Teach children the lyrics, and if you have a recording of the music, play the song and invite children to sing along.

INTEGRATE LANGUAGE ARTS

American Revolution Have students use the library or Internet to learn more about the causes of the American Revolution. Then have children use the information they have learned to write a paragraph explaining why the Revolution happened.

For six years the Americans fought English soldiers. This war was called the American Revolution. The Americans finally won the war. This was the beginning of the United States of America.

Today you can visit landmarks of that war. A **landmark** is a building, statue, or other large thing that reminds people of an important event.

The Minuteman Statue stands in Concord, Massachusetts. The first shots of the American Revolution were fired there.

The Declaration of Independence was signed at Independence Hall in Philadelphia, Pennsylvania.

INTEGRATE READING

Read a Poem Read aloud "Fourth of July." Ask children to compare their own Independence Day experiences with those in the poem.

Fourth of July, Fourth of July.
That's when the flag goes waving by.
And the crackers crack, and the popguns pop,
And the big guns boom and never stop.
And we watch parades, and listen to speeches,
And picnic around on all the beaches.
And it usually rains, and it's always hot;
But we all like Fourth of July a lot.

by Marchette Chute

Visual Learning

Pictures Help children identify the images included in the pictures on page 239. Ask volunteers to read the captions and to describe what they see in each image. Then discuss the importance of the landmarks with regard to the American Revolution.

Q **What are some important landmarks in our area? What do they mark?**

A Children's answers should indicate an understanding of what a landmark is.

Explain that Independence Hall is a historical building located in Philadelphia, Pennsylvania. It was built between 1732 and 1741. Today, it is a museum. Point out that the Hall was the meeting place for the Continental Congress, a group of colonists who directed the war for independence against England.

Q **Where was the Declaration of Independence signed?**

A Independence Hall

Read and Respond

History Help children create a cause-and-effect chart using information they have learned in this lesson. (You can use copying master T8.) The following are possible causes and effects:

Cause—The Wampanoag Indians showed the Pilgrims how to grow food.

Effect—The Pilgrims celebrated by giving thanks with a feast.

Cause—The colonists were unhappy with English laws.

Effect—The colonists declared their freedom.

Cause—Southern states wanted to form their own country.

Effect—The Civil War was fought.

Extension Activities For Home and School

Make a Group Presentation

Materials: posterboard, crayons or markers, magazines, scissors, glue, holiday props

Arrange children in groups of four or five. Assign each group one of the holidays addressed in the lesson. Have the group plan a presentation that will explain why the holiday is important and describe ways it might be celebrated. Ask them to make a poster to illustrate their points and to gather any other props that might be useful in the presentation. Then have groups take turns making their presentation to the class. **(VISUAL/AUDITORY/KINESTHETIC)**

Comparison Diagram

Powhatan	Both	Creek
Eat corn and game	Eat corn	Eat corn, beans, and squash

Materials: paper, pencil

Have children turn to the table on page 237. Ask them to choose two of the Indian groups to compare. Then have children draw a three-column table. At the top of the first column, have them write the name of one of the groups they selected. At the top of the second column, have them write the word *Both.* Have them write the name of the second group at the top of the third column. Then have children complete the table by making entries that note differences between the two groups in columns one and three. Have them write ways that the two groups are similar in column two. Ask volunteers to display their completed tables for the class and explain the similarities and differences they have listed. **(VISUAL/KINESTHETIC)**

What Happened Here?

Materials: paper, pencil, crayons or markers

Have children talk with family members about important historical landmarks in your area or state and make a list of as many as possible. Encourage them to look for information in the library and on the Internet. Then ask children to choose one historical landmark, draw a picture of it, and write a label telling its name, location, and historical importance. Assemble all the drawings in a class booklet titled "Historical Landmarks of Our Area." **(VISUAL/AUDITORY/KINESTHETIC)**

History Sequence Game

Materials: index cards, pencils, markers

Arrange children in groups. Have each group do research to identify and date five events that happened between the time the Pilgrims arrived in America (1620) and the time the United States won its independence from England (1783). Have them write each event and date on an index card. Encourage group members to draw illustrations on each card to show something about the time or event. Have each group shuffle their cards and exchange with another group. Then have groups arrange the new set of cards in chronological order, beginning with the earliest. **(VISUAL/TACTILE)**

Read a History Map

OBJECTIVES

- Learn about the past from a history map.
- Draw maps to show places and routes.

RESOURCES

Pupil Book/Unit Big Book, pp. 242–243
Word Cards V65–V66
Activity Book, p. 58
Skill Transparency 5–4
GeoSkills CD-ROM

Vocabulary

history map p. 242 **region** p. 242 **settlement** p. 242

Review the kinds of things a map can show. As necessary, remind children that maps show the names and borders of countries and states, capitals and important cities, lakes, rivers, mountains, grasslands, and deserts. Tell children that in this lesson, they will learn about a different kind of map.

Why It Matters

Explain that a history map shows what a place looked like long ago. Point out that children can compare a history map with a present-day map of the same place to determine changes that have occurred over time. For example, they can see how boundaries and areas of settlement have changed.

MENTAL MAPPING

Am I in the Wrong Room? Before children come to class, rearrange the classroom so that the desks are in a circle rather than rows, your desk is facing in another direction, the globe is on the other side of the room, and so on. You do not have to move everything; just be sure the room is noticeably different. Tell children to try to remember how their room looked yesterday and to draw maps showing it. Have children compare their maps with the way the room looks today. Then have children help put the classroom back the way it was.

2 Teach

What You Need to Know

Help children recall that the people who moved westward to settle new lands were called pioneers. Explain that pioneers would pack their belongings in a covered wagon. Then they would set out on a journey to a new place—usually somewhere that was unexplored and completely unfamiliar to the pioneers. Discuss that, after this difficult and often risky trip, the pioneers could claim lands for farming or ranching.

Review the cardinal directions with children and remind them how to use a compass rose on a map. Then have children look at the map on page 243 and trace the westward path of the trails with their fingers. Ask them to look back at a map of the original thirteen colonies on page 238. Have them compare the size of the settled area on the two maps.

Q What changes can you see by comparing the two maps?

A Children might say that there are more settlements and the area where people live is larger in the second map.

Skills

Read a History Map

Vocabulary

history map region settlement

Why It Matters

A **history map** shows what places were like long ago. You can compare maps from different times to see how a place changes.

What You Need to Know

Long ago, people moved to new **regions**, or parts, of our country. They built new homes to start **settlements**, or communities, across the West.

242

REACH ALL LEARNERS

Kinesthetic Learners Place an assortment of objects in a box or on a large square of cardboard or butcher paper. Have children study the arrangement and then draw a map showing what they see. Next, remove or rearrange some of the objects in the box. Have children compare their maps with the new arrangement to determine what has been changed.

BACKGROUND

Louisiana Purchase In 1803 the United States purchased from France part of the Western area of the Mississippi River basin. The United States paid just three cents an acre for the 828,000 square miles of land, which doubled the size of the country. The Louisiana Purchase gave strength to the movement toward westward expansion in the United States.

EXTEND AND ENRICH

State History Maps Display a history map of your state along with a current map. Then arrange children in small groups. Have each group complete a two-column table with the headings *Then* and *Now*. Ask them to note in the table differences they see in the two maps. Finally, have groups share and discuss their tables.

Practice the Skill

Study the history map to find the trails the settlers followed to move west.

1. Where does the California Trail begin?
2. Where does the Old Spanish Trail end?
3. Which two trails follow the Platte River?

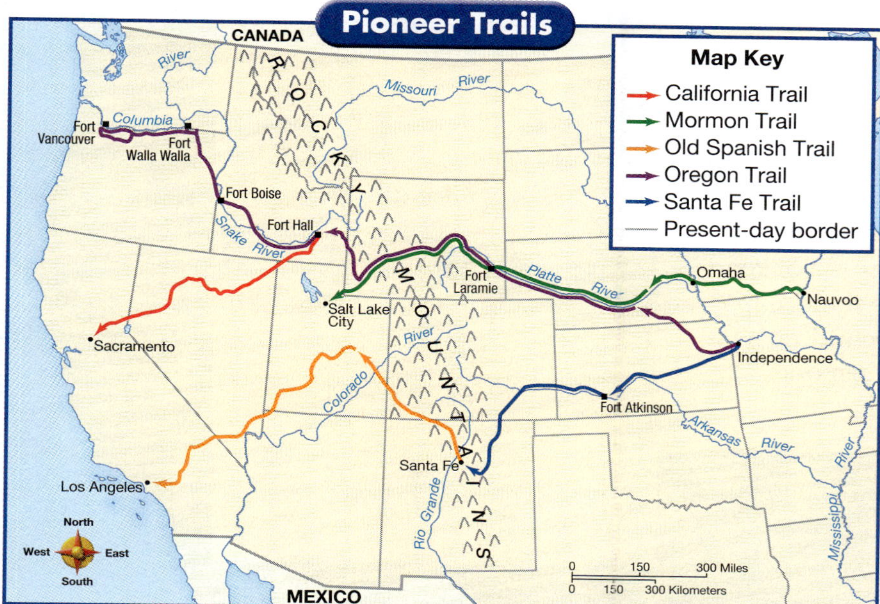

Apply What You Learned

Compare the trail map to a highway map today to see how the country has grown.

Practice your map and globe skills with the **GeoSkills CD-ROM**.

243

MAP AND GLOBE SKILLS

Practice the Skill—Answers

1. Fort Hall
2. Los Angeles
3. Oregon Trail; Mormon Trail

Close

Apply What You Learned

Children should correctly note changes between the two maps in settlement patterns, boundaries, and so on.

RETEACH THE SKILL

Use a History Map Challenge children to use the history map on this page, along with a copy of a current United States map, to determine which present-day states are crossed by each of the pioneer trails.

ACTIVITY BOOK

Name ______ Date ______

MAP AND GLOBE SKILLS

Journeys

The people who settled the West faced a long journey. Early pioneers traveled by wagon train on the Oregon Trail. Later the Transcontinental Railroad helped people transport goods faster and more safely.

Use the map to answer the questions below.

The Oregon Trail and Transcontinental Railroad

Map Key
Oregon Trail, 1843 to 1869
Transcontinental Railroad, complete 1869

What landform did pioneers cross at Independence Rock?

mountains

How many states did the Transcontinental Railroad cross?

five

58 ▪ Activity Book   Use after reading Unit 5, Skill Lesson 4.

PAGE 58

TRANSPARENCY

Use SKILL TRANSPARENCY 5-4.

CD-ROM

Explore GEOSKILLS CD-ROM to learn more about map and globe skills.

Extension Activities For Home and School

City History Maps

Materials: **paper, crayons or markers, pencils**

Display and discuss a current map of your city. Ask children to think about what your city might have looked like 100 years ago. Encourage children to talk to older family members about the way their community may have looked in the past. Then have children use their ideas to draw city history maps. Be sure they realize that 100 years ago very few people owned cars and there were no skyscrapers, movie theaters, supermarkets, or malls. Ask them to include details such as major roadways, landmarks, parks, and so on. Have volunteers share their maps with the class. Discuss similarities and differences among children's maps, as well as how children's maps differ from the modern one.
(VISUAL/TACTILE)

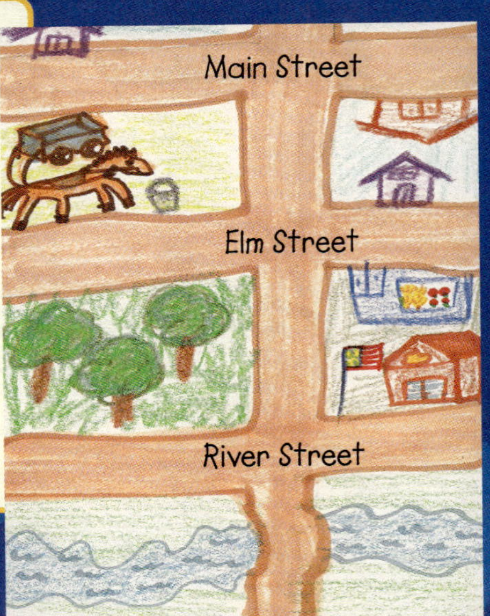

Trail Maps

Materials: **large paper, crayons or markers**

Explain to children that explorers drew maps as they discovered new places. Have children imagine they are explorers or early pioneers traveling across unknown lands. Ask children to think about places, such as rivers, mountains, or forests, that they might see. Invite them to draw maps of their journey, naming landmarks and trails along the way. Make sure they include a compass rose. Children might enjoy displaying their maps and writing or telling stories about adventures on their journey.
(VISUAL/TACTILE/AUDITORY)

Celebrating Heroes of the Past

OBJECTIVES

- Identify contributions of historical figures who have influenced the community, state, and nation.
- Describe ways people honor their heroes.
- Give examples of places in the community where individuals are remembered.

 **Sequence** pp. 209, 249, 260

RESOURCES

Pupil Book/Unit Big Book, pp. 244–249

Word Cards V65–V68

Activity Book, p. 59

Reading and Vocabulary Transparency 5-5

Internet Resources

READING SOCIAL STUDIES

Anticipation Guide Have children copy the following statements and write whether they think each one is true or false. Have children save their guesses for use during Close.

1. A monument is built to honor ordinary people. False
2. The Washington Monument was built to honor Franklin Roosevelt. False
3. Thurgood Marshall was the first African American appointed to the Supreme Court. True
4. Nobel Prizes are awarded for reading, writing, and arithmetic. False

USE READING AND VOCABULARY TRANSPARENCY 5-5.

Vocabulary

monument p. 244 **memorial** p. 244 **hero** p. 244

When Minutes Count

Have children examine the pictures on pages 244–249. Use the pictures to discuss the Big Idea of the lesson.

Quick Summary

This lesson focuses on ways we remember and honor people who have helped make the world a better place. Thurgood Marshall, Louis Pasteur, Golda Meir, Marie Curie, Albert Einstein, and Dr. Martin Luther King, Jr., are among the individuals discussed.

1 Motivate

Set the Purpose

Big Idea Read aloud the Big Idea statement. Ask volunteers to name someone they think of as a hero. It could be a person who did something "big" or the school crossing guard who keeps them safe every day. Tell children that they will learn about ways Americans remember their heroes.

Access Prior Knowledge

Ask children if they have ever seen any monuments or memorials in the United States. Have children who have visited a monument or memorial share their experience.

2 Teach

Read and Respond

Culture and Society Have children identify the monuments and memorials shown on pages 244 and 245. Explain that the people honored by these memorials are national heroes and that this means that people all over our country are grateful for what they have done for us. Point out that all of the monuments shown honor United States Presidents and a First Lady, and have children tell why these people are important to us.

You may also wish to find and display pictures or have children search the Internet for Arlington National Cemetery, the African American Civil War Memorial, the Korean War Memorial, and the Vietnam Veterans Memorial. The Arlington National Cemetery honors soldiers who served our country, while the African American Civil War Memorial, the Korean War Memorial, and the Vietnam Veterans Memorial honor men and women who died helping our country during those wars.

Q Why do you think so many monuments and memorials honoring heroes are located in Washington, D.C.?

A It is our country's capital, so it belongs to all the people.

Lesson

Celebrating Heroes of the Past

Big Idea
Americans remember their heroes in many ways.

Vocabulary
monument
memorial
hero

Americans have built **monuments** and **memorials** to honor the country's **heroes**. Many of these statues and buildings are located in Washington, D.C.

President Abraham Lincoln sits tall in the Lincoln Memorial. Lincoln guided the country through the Civil War and freed the slaves.

The Thomas Jefferson Memorial honors our third President, who helped write the Declaration of Independence.

244

BACKGROUND

Thomas Jefferson Thomas Jefferson is best known as the main writer of the Declaration of Independence. He later became the third President of the United States. In addition to politics, Jefferson was also interested in science, agriculture, and architecture. He designed his home, Monticello. It is near Charlottesville, Virginia. In 1819 he founded the University of Virginia.

INTEGRATE ART

Design a Monument Tell children the story of Maya Lin, the architecture student who won a contest to design the Vietnam Veterans Memorial. Then ask children to think about a hero or a group of people who work heroically in the community every day. Invite children to design a monument or memorial to honor their heroes. Encourage interested children to construct a scale model of their design.

REACH ALL LEARNERS

Advanced Learners Ask children to choose one of the monuments shown on these pages and do research to learn more about it and the person or people who inspired it. Have them find information about the monument's size, when it was built, what it is made of, and other interesting facts. Invite volunteers to report their findings to the class.

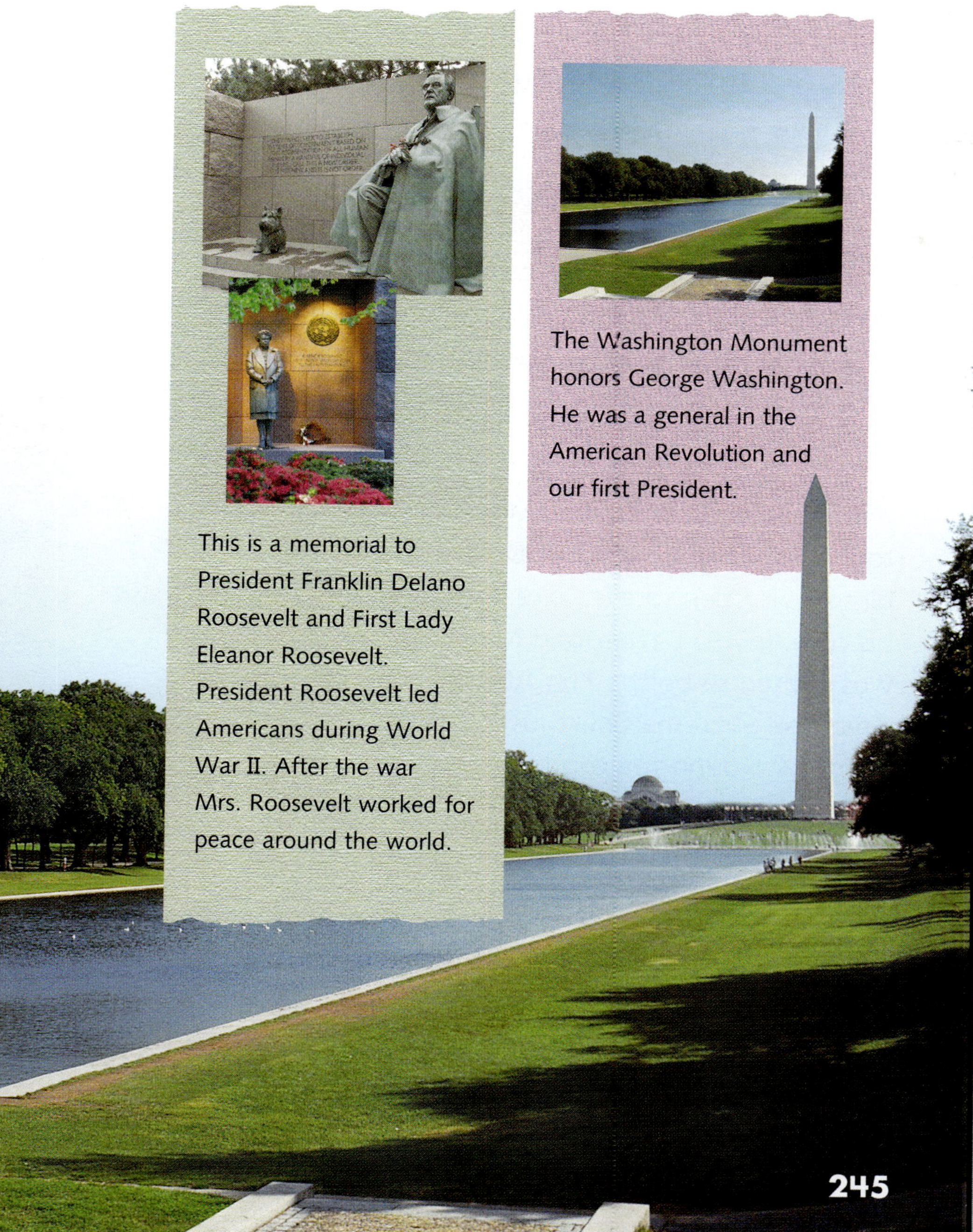

This is a memorial to President Franklin Delano Roosevelt and First Lady Eleanor Roosevelt. President Roosevelt led Americans during World War II. After the war Mrs. Roosevelt worked for peace around the world.

The Washington Monument honors George Washington. He was a general in the American Revolution and our first President.

245

Visual Learning

Pictures Invite children to study the photographs on pages 244 and 245. Have them note and compare details of each memorial, including size, material, style, setting, and so forth.

Q Why do you think the memorials are made from stone or metal?

A These materials are strong, so the memorials will last a long time.

Children might enjoy researching Washington, D.C., the National Mall, and monuments and memorials. Have them visit The Learning Site at **www.harcourtschool.com**

BACKGROUND

The National Mall The monuments and memorials on these pages are located on the National Mall in Washington, D.C. The National Mall is a national park. It was commissioned by George Washington and designed by Pierre L'Enfant to be a place citizens could visit to learn about and remember those who have served our country well. The mall contains gardens, pools, fountains, and monuments. The Reflecting Pool stretches from the Washington Monument to the Lincoln Memorial. The Smithsonian Institution, the Capitol Building, and the White House are also found at the Mall. This combination makes the National Mall so appealing that it is one of the most visited sites in the world.

MAKE IT RELEVANT

In Your Community or State Ask children to name local or state heroes they know of. Discuss why these people are heroes and, if possible, show photographs of monuments or memorials honoring them.

Read and Respond

Civics and Government Read aloud page 246 with children. Review that the Supreme Court heads the judicial branch of our national government. Explain that the job of a Supreme Court justice is very important, with responsibilities as great as those of the President, senators, and representatives.

Q **What was special about Thurgood Marshall's appointment as a Supreme Court justice?**

A He was the first African American appointed to that job, and it opened doors for other minorities and for women to serve in such positions.

Culture and Society Ask children to think of parks, streets, or buildings in your area that are named for people. Discuss why these people have been honored by having a place named for them. If your school is named for a person, discuss that person's contribution to your community or to our country.

Q **Why do we name buildings, parks, and streets for people?**

A to show respect for the people and to honor and remember them

Monuments and memorials are found in many communities. People also honor heroes by naming schools, parks, and other places for them.

Thurgood Marshall

Thurgood Marshall wanted to be a lawyer. His mother, who was a teacher, encouraged him. However, the first law school Marshall tried to enter would not take African Americans.

Years later, as a lawyer, Marshall spoke to the Supreme Court about making all schools open to everyone. He won his case. In 1971 Thurgood Marshall was chosen to be the first African American Supreme Court justice. Now buildings around the country are named for him.

246

INTEGRATE LANGUAGE ARTS

Write a Letter Have children write a class letter to the school board suggesting a local hero for whom a school might be named. Ask them to tell something about the person and to give reasons why the person should be honored in such a way. You may want to provide a letter format template for children to use in writing their letter.

BACKGROUND

Thurgood Marshall Thurgood Marshall was born in 1908 in Baltimore, Maryland. He was educated at Lincoln University in Pennsylvania and at Howard University Law School in Washington, D.C., where he graduated first in his class. As an attorney, in 1954 he argued before the Supreme Court in the landmark case of *Brown* v. *Board of Education* that declared racial segregation in U.S. public schools unconstitutional. Marshall won 29 of the 32 cases that he argued before the Supreme Court.

STUDY/RESEARCH SKILLS

Note Taking You may wish to help children prepare to write biographies of the heroes in this lesson or others that interest them. The following template may be used as a model.

Name ______
Date and place of birth ______
Family history ______
Achievements and contributions ______
______
Special skills, talents, or awards ______
______
Quotes ______

Louis Pasteur

A middle school in Orangevale, California, is named for Louis Pasteur. You can think about Pasteur every time you drink milk. He learned that some kinds of illness are caused by germs. He found a way to kill germs that get into milk and other foods.

Golda Meir

At the University of Wisconsin, students study in the Golda Meir Library. Golda Meir was a Russian immigrant who grew up and taught school in Wisconsin. Later she moved to Israel. At the age of 71 she became the first woman to be the leader of Israel.

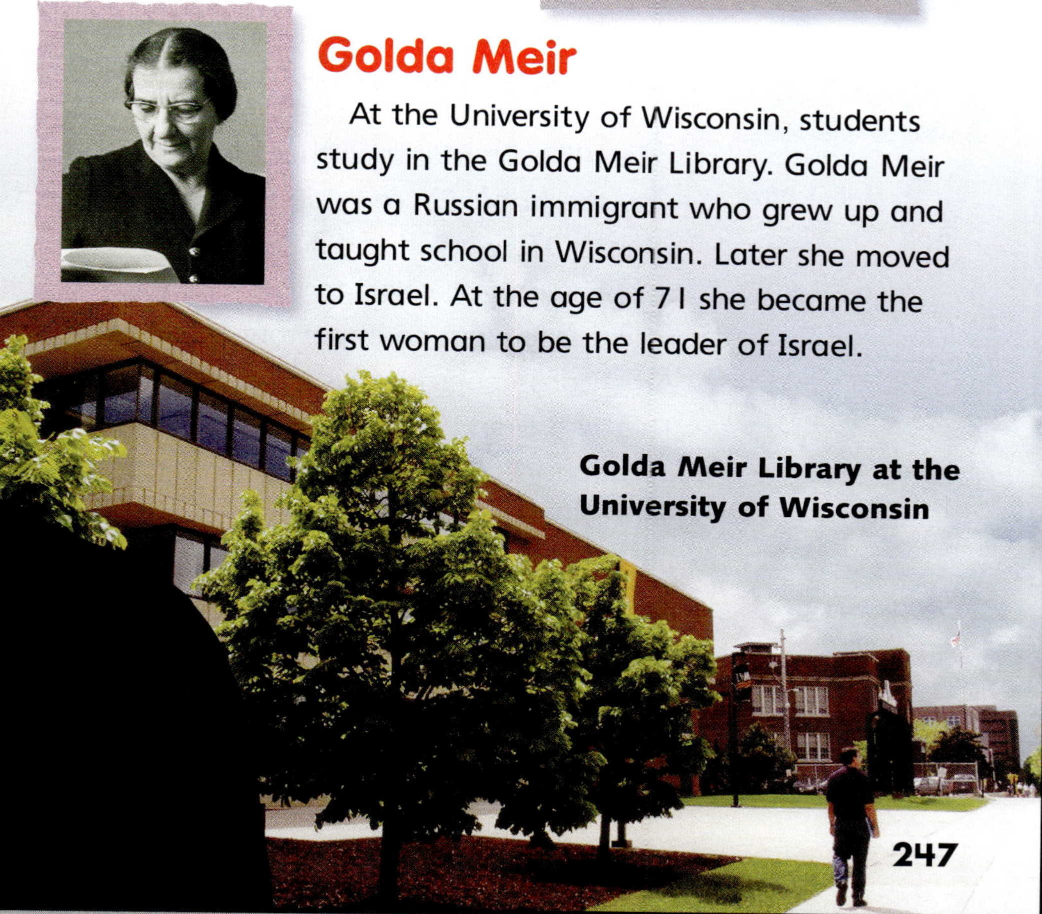

Golda Meir Library at the University of Wisconsin

247

BACKGROUND

Golda Meir Born in Kiev, Russia, in 1898, Golda Meir moved with her family to Milwaukee, Wisconsin, in 1906. There she grew up and attended college. Later she and her husband immigrated to Palestine, where they joined the Merhavya kibbutz. In Palestine, Golda Meir worked hard for political and social causes. She was a founder of the State of Israel and, in 1969, became its fourth prime minister.

WORD WORK

Words Named for People Tell children that we use the word *pasteurize* to name the process of heating milk to make it safe to drink. There are other words that come from people's names, such as *sandwich* and *graham cracker.* Have children use a dictionary to find out about the origins of *sandwich* and *graham cracker.*

Read and Respond

Culture and Society After reading the page aloud, stress to children that not all the people we honor as heroes were born in the United States. Point out that Golda Meir was born in Russia but moved to the United States, while Frenchman Louis Pasteur never lived in our country.

Q **Why do we in the United States consider people from other countries to be heroes?**

A People become heroes because their actions and contributions help everyone all over the world, not just where they live.

Discuss with children the process Louis Pasteur discovered for making milk and other products free from germs that cause illness. Point out that long ago, people often became sick from drinking milk. Explain that Pasteur learned that if he heated the milk to 161°F (72°C), the germs that caused illness were killed. To help children understand how hot that is, tell them that water boils at 212°F (100°C).

Q **What did Pasteur learn about germs in milk?**

A He learned that heat killed the illness-causing germs in the milk.

NOTE: Caution children against trying this at home.

Help children recognize that people like Marshall, Meir, and Pasteur make contributions in different ways. They are honored for helping other people, being leaders, and inventing new ways of doing things.

Q **How does naming buildings after scientists like Pasteur show an American love of inventiveness?**

A Americans honor those who find new ways to help improve people's lives.

Q **What symbols show an American love of inventiveness?**

A Responses might include prizes, awards, stamps, coins, and statues.

Read and Respond

Culture and Society Discuss that giving prizes is one way to recognize and show respect for the work people do. Point out awards presented by your school or community, such as Student of the Week or Citizen of the Year. Discuss what individuals must do to win such awards. Explain that the Nobel Prize is a very special award and that only those people who have made very important contributions to the whole world receive it.

Next, discuss that another way to honor heroes is to place their pictures on coins or stamps. Ask children to identify people whose pictures they recognize on the coins and stamps shown in their textbooks. Then discuss each person, and read aloud the caption to identify that person's contribution.

Q **Whose picture would you like to see on a coin or stamp? Why?**

A Children's answers should indicate an awareness of positive attributes that deserve recognition.

Civics and Government As you discuss the people on pages 248 and 249, ask children to describe characteristics of good citizenship in each of them.

Link Civics and Government with Culture and Society Explain to children that civil rights are the rights guaranteed to all citizens by the Constitution. People such as Thurgood Marshall and Dr. Martin Luther King, Jr., worked hard to change laws that denied certain people their civil rights. Remind children that Marshall went before the Supreme Court to make sure that all children were provided an equal education. Tell children that Dr. King worked for civil rights using peaceful ways, such as making speeches. In 1964 Congress passed the Civil Rights Act of 1964. This law said that people of all races could go to the same places and that they should have equal job opportunities.

Nobel Prize Winners

Each year people around the world who have done important work receive Nobel prizes. These prizes are given for work done in different kinds of science, in literature, and in keeping peace.

Marie Curie and Albert Einstein were scientists who won Nobel prizes. Marie Curie discovered a metal that could be used to cure illness. Albert Einstein used math to explain difficult ideas about time and space.

Nobel Prize

In 1964, Dr. Martin Luther King, Jr., won the Nobel Peace Prize. Dr. King was a minister. He worked to find peaceful ways for people of all colors to live together. His message was so important that Americans honor him with a holiday. The third Monday in January each year is Dr. Martin Luther King, Jr., Day.

248

INTEGRATE READING

Share a Poem Read aloud the poem "Martin Luther King." Ask children to suggest "real good ways" to overcome hatred.

Got me a special place
For Martin Luther King.
His picture on the wall
Makes me sing.
I look at it for a long time
And think of some
Real good ways
We will overcome.

by Myra Cohn Livingston

EXTEND AND ENRICH

Monument Bulletin Board Have children find pictures of monuments, memorials, stamps, coins, and other things that honor a local, state, or national hero. Have them cut these out and create a bulletin board collage. Then have children agree on a title for their bulletin board display.

LESSON 4 Review

1. **Sequence** What events led to Thurgood Marshall speaking to the Supreme Court?
2. **Vocabulary** Where in the United States can you find many **monuments** and **memorials**?
3. Make a poster showing what buildings in your community are named for people who have done important things.

3 Close

Summarize Key Content

- Americans have built monuments and memorials to honor their heroes.
- People honor heroes by naming buildings after them.
- The Nobel Prize is awarded each year to people who have done important work.
- Some people have been honored by having their pictures placed on coins or stamps.

READING SOCIAL STUDIES

Anticipation Guide Have children check their responses. Ask them to correct statements that proved to be false.

1. A monument is built to honor ~~ordinary people~~. heroes
2. The Washington Monument was built to honor ~~Franklin Roosevelt~~. George Washington
3. Thurgood Marshall was the first African American appointed to the Supreme Court. true
4. Nobel Prizes are awarded for ~~reading, writing, and arithmetic~~. science, literature, and keeping peace

USE READING AND VOCABULARY TRANSPARENCY 5-5.

5-5 TRANSPARENCY

RETEACH THE LESSON

Write Riddles Ask children to write riddles about the heroes described in this lesson, giving clues about when and where they lived and what their contributions were. Then have children take turns reading and answering each other's riddles.

ACTIVITY BOOK

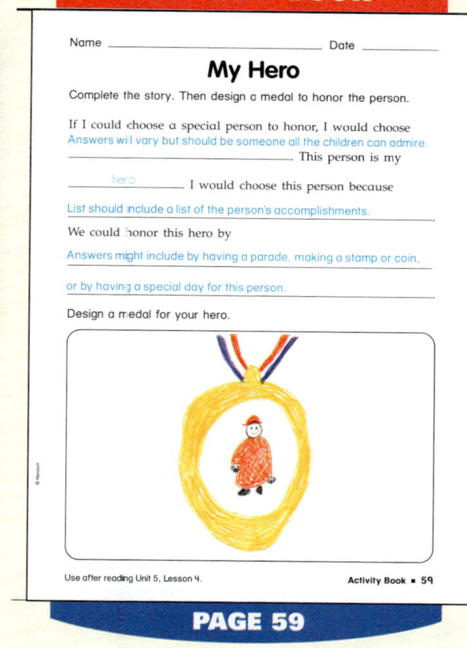

Name ______ Date ______

My Hero

Complete the story. Then design a medal to honor the person.

If I could choose a special person to honor, I would choose
Answers will vary but should be someone all the children can admire. This person is my
hero. I would choose this person because
List should include a list of the person's accomplishments.
We could honor this hero by
Answers might include by having a parade, making a stamp or coin,
or by having a special day for this person.

Design a medal for your hero.

Use after reading Unit 5, Lesson 4. Activity Book ▪ 59

PAGE 59

Assess

Lesson 4 Review—Answers

1. **Sequence** He wanted to be a lawyer, but the first law school he tried to go to wouldn't let him because he was African American; schools weren't open to all people and he wanted to change that.
2. Washington, D.C.
3. 

   Performance Assessment Guidelines Ask children to display their posters and tell about the person for which the building was named.

Extension Activities For Home and School

Make a Memorial Map

Materials: **paper, pencils, crayons or markers**

Have children seek help from family members and friends in identifying places in your community where individuals are remembered. Then have children draw a community map that shows these places. Have them label the buildings or memorials along with major streets and landmarks that might help someone find the places. Encourage children to color their maps, adding illustrations for parks, landmarks, and so on. **(VISUAL/TACTILE)**

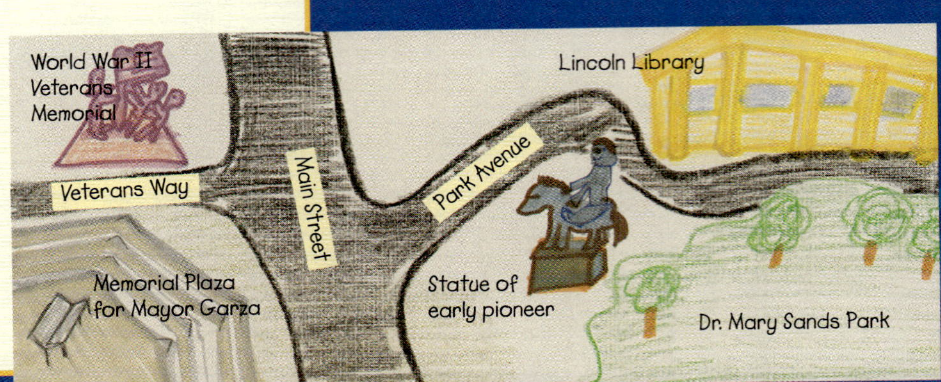

Memorial Play

Materials: **paper, pencils, props as necessary**

Arrange children in groups of five or six. Have the groups plan a play in which one child is a visitor to a memorial park and the others are statues in the park. As the visitor approaches each statue, it comes to life and tells about the contributions the person made that resulted in his or her being honored. Tell children that the statues can represent local, state, or national heroes. Encourage children to collect props, such as a cowboy hat, a briefcase, or a nurse's cap, that show something about the people whose statues they are portraying. After children have planned their play, have them perform it for the class. **(VISUAL/AUDITORY/KINESTHETIC)**

It's an Honor!

Materials: **paper, pencil, crayons or markers, small boxes, cardboard tubes, glue, tape, various found objects**

Have children name people they consider to be heroes. Write their suggestions on the board. Then have each child select one person from the list and design an appropriate way to honor him or her. Children might draw a portrait to place on a stamp or a coin, or they might create a three-dimensional monument or memorial using available materials. When children complete the activity, have volunteers show their work to the class and explain why it is a good way to honor their hero. Finally, arrange all the work in a class memorial corner. Place the three-dimensional memorials on a table and place the drawings on the wall behind the table. Have children invite other classes to visit their memorial corner.

Read a Map Grid

OBJECTIVES

- Read a grid.
- Use a map grid to locate places on the map.
- Draw a map grid of a familiar place.

RESOURCES

Pupil Book/Unit Big Book, pp. 250–251

Word Cards V67–V68

Activity Book, p. 60

Skill Transparency 5-5

GeoSkills CD-ROM

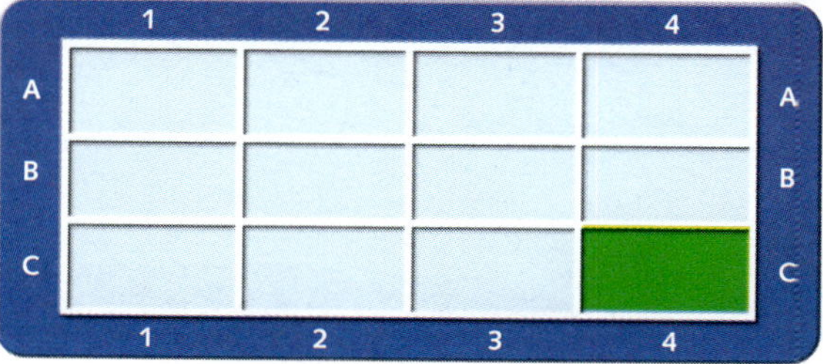

Vocabulary

map grid p. 250

1 Motivate

Display a street map of any city other than yours, the bigger and more complicated the better. Choose a place on the map that is not obvious (not a big park) and ask children to find it. If they give up, tell them that in this lesson they will learn an easy way to find things on a map.

Why It Matters

Tell children that having a map is of no use if they cannot find the place they are looking for. Stress that map grids help users easily locate places on a map.

REACH ALL LEARNERS

Tactile Learners Prepare for each child a 10-by-10 grid with large boxes. Have children locate and color in squares as you call out directions. For example, tell them to begin in the top left-hand square, move right three squares and down four squares, and color that square blue. After several squares have been colored, have partners compare their grids to see if they have followed the same paths.

2 Teach

What You Need to Know

Review left and right with children by asking them to raise their left hand and then their right one. Explain that map grids are arranged from left to right and from top to bottom. Point out that the rows are identified by letters located to the left and right of the map and that the columns are identified by numbers located at the top and bottom of the map. Have children practice finding squares as volunteers suggest combinations of letters and numbers.

Q Why do you think that letters and numbers appear on all four sides of the map?

A It helps you double-check that you have found the right square.

Skills

Read a Map Grid

Vocabulary
map grid

Why It Matters

One way to find places on a map is to use a map grid. A **map grid** is a set of lines that form columns and rows on a map. Knowing how to use a map grid makes it easy to find places on a map.

What You Need to Know

Look at the grid on this page. Put your finger on the green square. Slide your finger to the left or right. You are on row C. Put your finger on the green square again. Slide your finger to the top or bottom. You are in column 4. To say where the green box is on the grid, you would say it is at C-4.

REACH ALL LEARNERS

Below-Level Learners Use visual aids to reinforce row and column. Show a picture of someone rowing a boat and a picture of a tall building. Explain that the person is rowing the boat from one side of a lake to the other, just as rows go from one side of the map (or table) to the other. Similarly, the building goes up and down, just as columns on a map (or table) go from top to bottom.

INTEGRATE MATHEMATICS

Math Problem Grid Create a large grid on the classroom floor. Prepare a set of cards with the number and letter of a square on each. On each grid square, place a card on which you have written a simple mental math problem. Invite children to take turns drawing cards, locating the square, and then answering the mental math problem they find there.

EXTEND AND ENRICH

Neighborhood Maps Have children use blocks, boxes, or construction-paper cutouts to make a tabletop model of your school neighborhood. Then have them make a grid map of their model. Ask children to use the map to practice identifying places and to plan routes from one place to another.

Practice the Skill

1. Find the Petrified Forest. It is in square A-1. In which square is the Medora Visitor Center?
2. In which square are the Saddle Horse Rides?
3. Where is Prairie Dog Town?

Apply What You Learned

Make a map of your neighborhood. Put a map grid on it. Tell a classmate the row and column of the square in which your home is located. See if he or she can find it.

Practice your map and globe skills with the **GeoSkills CD-ROM**.

MAP AND GLOBE SKILLS

Link Geography and History Tell children that the map grid shows a small part of the Theodore Roosevelt National Park in the North Dakota Badlands. Help them locate it on a map of North Dakota. Explain that the park was changed from a memorial to a national park in 1978 by President Jimmy Carter. Children might be interested to know that President Roosevelt first visited Little Missouri in the Dakota Territory in 1883. He returned often to live like a cowboy at Elkhorn, the ranch he built there.

Practice the Skill—Answers

1. C-2
2. B-2
3. C-4

3 Close

Apply What You Learned

Children should arrange the map grid correctly, with letters on each side and numbers across the top and bottom. They should be able to correctly identify the letter and number for the square in which their home is located.

RETEACH THE SKILL

Use a City Map Provide children copies of a simple city map. Ask them to locate places, based on grid coordinates that you give them. For example, *What park is located in square C-6?* Extend the activity by having partners ask each other questions about the map.

ACTIVITY BOOK

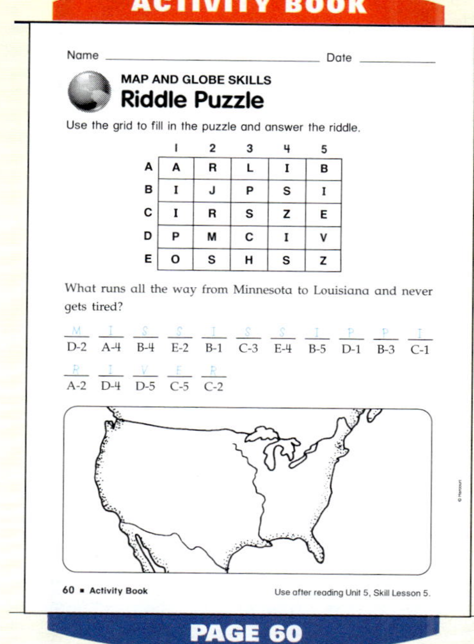

Name ______________ Date ______

MAP AND GLOBE SKILLS
Riddle Puzzle

Use the grid to fill in the puzzle and answer the riddle.

	1	2	3	4	5
A	A	R	L	I	B
B	I	J	P	S	I
C	I	R	S	Z	E
D	P	M	C	I	V
E	O	S	H	S	Z

What runs all the way from Minnesota to Louisiana and never gets tired?

D-2 A-4 B-4 E-2 B-1 C-3 E-4 B-5 D-1 B-3 C-1

A-2 D-4 D-5 C-5 C-2

60 • Activity Book   Use after reading Unit 5, Skill Lesson 5.

PAGE 60

TRANSPARENCY

Use SKILL TRANSPARENCY 5-5.

CD-ROM

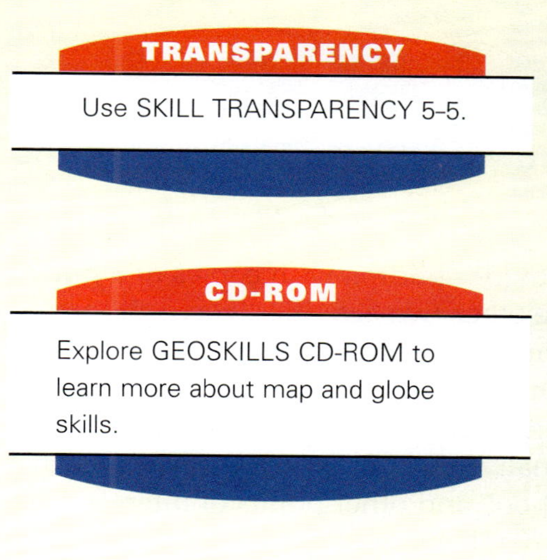

Explore GEOSKILLS CD-ROM to learn more about map and globe skills.

Extension Activities For Home and School

Make a Grid Picture

Materials: copies of a 7-by-7 grid, crayons or markers, pencils

Provide each child with a simple 7-by-7 grid. Leave room on all four sides for children to label the rows A–G and the columns 1–7. After children label the rows and columns, have them follow your instructions to create a picture. Write the following instructions on the board and read them aloud:

- Color these squares red: A-5, A-6, A-7, C-5, C-6, C-7, E-1, E-2, E-3, E-4, E-5, E-6, E-7, G-1, G-2, G-3, G-4, G-5, G-6, and G-7.
- Color these squares blue: A-2, A-4, B-1, B-3, C-2, and C-4.

Ask children to display their completed grid drawings and tell what they show.
(VISUAL/TACTILE)

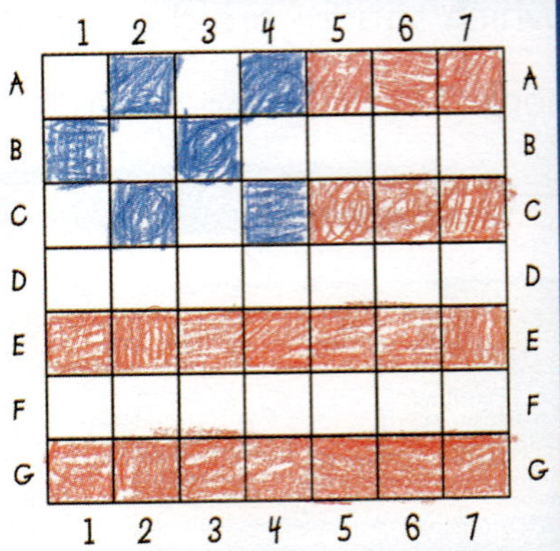

Treasure Hunt

Materials: copies of a 7-by-7 grid, small "treasure" items, crayons or markers, pencils

Provide small groups with copies of a grid and have them label it as they did in the activity Make a Grid Picture. Next, have children create a map of the room within the grid. Then, provide each group with a small treasure to hide in the room and allow time for groups to hide their treasure when the other groups are out of the room. Have them mark an X on their map to show where the treasure is located. Have groups exchange maps and go on a treasure hunt. After groups locate the treasures, have them tell how they found the treasure and ask them to name the coordinates on the grid where the treasure was located.
(VISUAL/KINESTHETIC/TACTILE)

Draw a Map from Home to School

Materials: copies of a 7-by-7 grid, pencils

Provide children with copies of a grid and have them label it as they did in the other two activities. Have children work with a family member to create a map showing the area between their home and school. Squares on the grid can represent one or more city blocks. After their home and the school have been placed on the map, have children add other details or points of interest. Finally, have them create a map key that gives the coordinates for home, school, and other points of interest. Have children bring their completed maps to display in class.
(VISUAL/TACTILE)

Home A-2
Green grocery store E-3
Apartment building A-6
School F-5
Park D-7

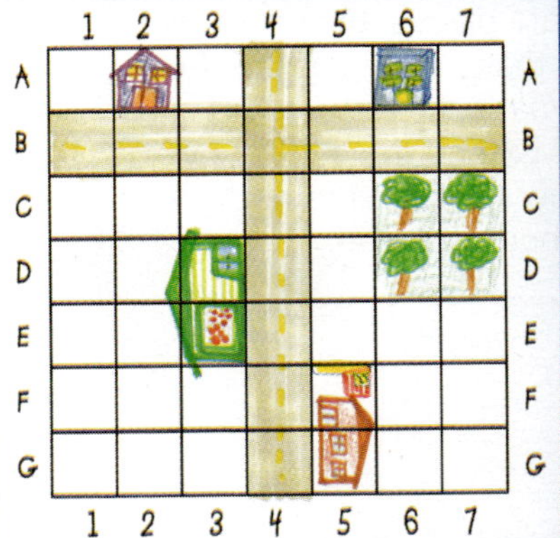

Contributions in World History

OBJECTIVES

- Understand that cultures and civilizations existed in ancient times.
- Identify contributions made by ancient Egyptians, Chinese, and Native Americans.
- Trace the history of writing.

Sequence pp. 209, 260

RESOURCES

Pupil Book/Unit Big Book, pp. 252–255

Word Cards V67–V70

Activity Book, p. 61

Reading and Vocabulary Transparency 5-6

Internet Resources

READING SOCIAL STUDIES

Make Word Webs As children read, have them make a word web for each of the ancient cultures in the lesson. Have them write the name of the culture in the middle of the web and then write details about that culture in the surrounding circles.

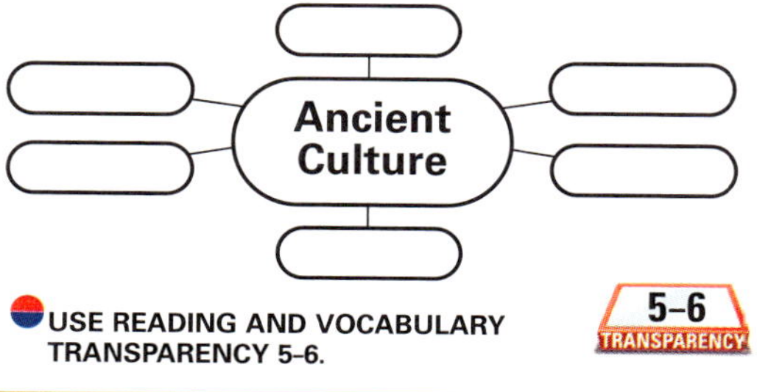

USE READING AND VOCABULARY TRANSPARENCY 5-6.

5-6 TRANSPARENCY

Vocabulary

scribe p. 252 **papyrus** p. 252 **maize** p. 255

When Minutes Count

Have children skim the lesson to find the meanings of the lesson vocabulary words. Encourage children to tell how each word relates to the Big Idea of the lesson.

Quick Summary

This lesson focuses on cultural contributions made by ancient cultures in Egypt, China, and Central and South America.

1 Motivate

Set the Purpose

Big Idea Have a volunteer read aloud the Big Idea statement before children begin the lesson. Then, as children read and discuss the lesson, help them identify the specific contributions of each ancient culture.

Access Prior Knowledge

Ask volunteers to describe something they have learned from a grandparent or another older adult. Then ask them how that person might have learned it. Discuss that much of what we know has been passed down for hundreds—sometimes even thousands—of years from generation to generation.

Read and Respond

Culture and Society Read pages 254 and 255 with children. Ask them to repeat aloud some of the unfamiliar words, such as *Tenochtitlán* (tay•nohch•teet•LAHN), *Texcoco* (tes•KOH•koh), and *maize,* after you read them. On a map, point out central Mexico and Peru, where the Aztecs and Incas lived.

Q **What is one way that people today can learn about the ancient Americans?**

A People can learn about them by studying the remains of their buildings and cities.

Link Government with Culture and Society Help children relate what they know about the need for government to ancient cultures. Emphasize that the Aztecs and Incas were advanced cultures.

Q **Why do you think the Aztecs and Incas needed organized governments?**

A Children might mention the need for control over the building of cities and roads, trade, and food supplies.

• GEOGRAPHY •

Inca Highways

Human Systems The Inca highway system was made up of paved and unpaved roads, many of which connected to a main highway that spanned 3,450 miles from the present-day Colombia-Ecuador border to what is now central Chile. The highway system included paved roads as wide as 24 feet, tunnels, bridges, and stepped pathways cut into rock. Along the network of roads, the Inca government maintained post houses so that people could drop off and receive messages or packages. The highway and postal systems helped the government build and control a vast empire. Ask children to explain how a postal system helps connect people.

Ancient Americans

Thousands of years ago Native Americans lived in Central and South America. These ancient Americans built great cities.

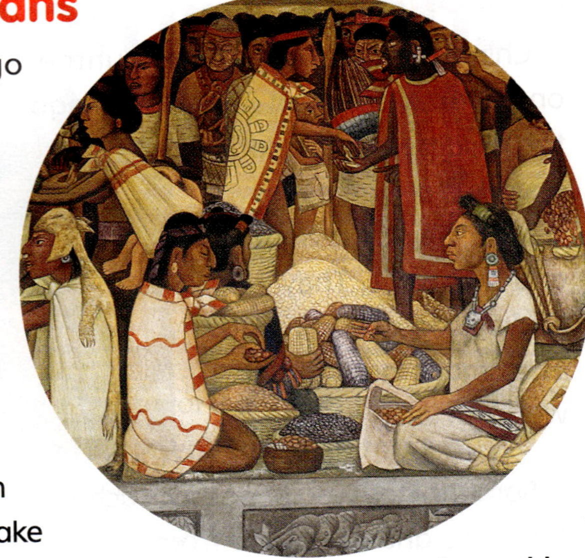

A mural by Diego Rivera

The Aztecs lived in what is now Mexico. They built a huge city called Tenochtitlán on an island in the middle of Lake Texcoco. It had straight, wide streets. In the center was a giant pyramid used as a temple. In its marketplace sixty thousand people could gather to buy and sell goods. The Aztecs built this amazing city without all the machines we have for building today.

FAST FACT A legend tells how the Aztecs saw an eagle perched on a cactus at Lake Texcoco. This was a sign showing them where to build their great city.

254

BACKGROUND

Machu Picchu Machu Picchu is an ancient Inca ruin. It is located in the Andes Mountains between two peaks, at an elevation of 7,710 feet. Machu Picchu was found nearly intact by a Yale professor who was searching for the "lost city of the Incas." It turned out that this was not the city he was searching for. Still, this 1911 discovery eventually led to the ruins being designated as a United Nations Education, Scientific and Cultural Organization (UNESCO) World Heritage site in 1983.

EXTEND AND ENRICH

Write a Paragraph Have children write a paragraph about how the contributions of one of the ancient cultures affect modern life. For example, they might write about the fact that we read books printed on paper in part because of the contributions of the ancient Egyptians and Chinese or the fact that we enjoy certain foods made from corn, tomatoes, chili, and squash because of the early American civilizations.

Another large group of Native Americans, the Incas, lived in what is now Peru. They, too, built cities. They had a strong government that ruled large areas of land. The government made laws and provided services, such as food storage, to keep the Incas safe and healthy. Many of the foods that we eat today have come from the early Americans. Chilies, tomatoes, squash, and a kind of corn called **maize** are some of the foods they grew.

• GEOGRAPHY •

Inca Highways

Human Systems

The Incas lived in the high Andes Mountains of Peru. They built wide, paved roads to connect their cities. They had no horses, so mail was carried by runners. By passing it from one person to another, the runners could carry it 150 miles in a day.

LESSON 5 Review

1. **Vocabulary** Why do you think **scribes** were important in ancient times?
2. What groups of Native Americans built cities?
3. Read a book about one of the ancient peoples in this lesson. Write a book report telling something you learned.

255

RETEACH THE LESSON

Make a Table Ask children to make a four-column table titled "Four Ancient Cultures." Have them write *Egyptians, Chinese, Aztecs,* and *Incas* as column heads. Then have them list two or three things they have learned about each culture in the lesson. Suggest that children reread each section as they make their list on the table.

ACTIVITY BOOK

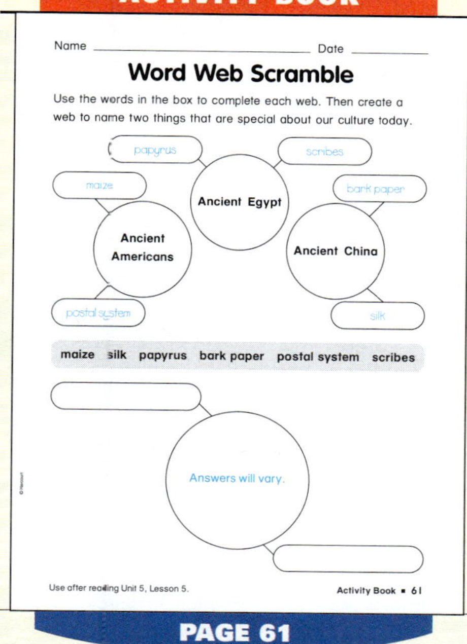

Name ______ Date ______

Word Web Scramble

Use the words in the box to complete each web. Then create a web to name two things that are special about our culture today.

Ancient Egypt: papyrus, scribes, bark paper

Ancient Americans: maize, postal system

Ancient China: bark paper, silk

maize silk papyrus bark paper postal system scribes

Answers will vary.

Use after reading Unit 5, Lesson 5. Activity Book • 61

PAGE 61

3 Close

Summarize Key Content

- People in ancient Egypt developed a system of writing and a kind of paper.
- More than 3,000 years ago in China, people made silk and paper and beautiful artworks.
- The Aztecs and Incas built great cities in Central and South America.

READING SOCIAL STUDIES

Make Word Webs Discuss the details children added to their word webs while reading. Invite volunteers to draw their word webs on the board.

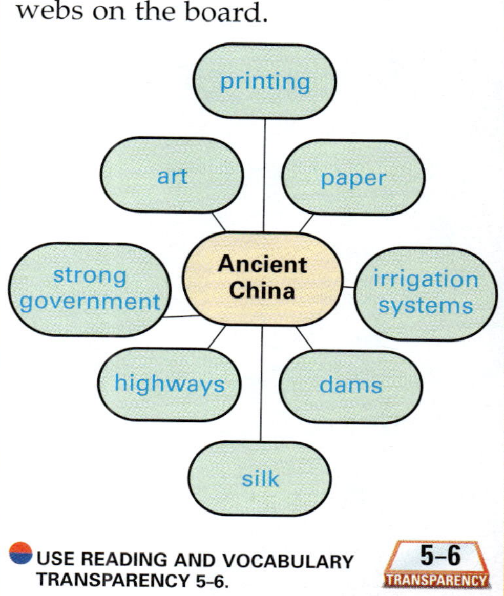

USE READING AND VOCABULARY TRANSPARENCY 5-6.

5-6 TRANSPARENCY

Assess

Lesson 5 Review—Answers

1. Scribes wrote down what people needed to know and remember.
2. the Aztecs and Incas
3. 

Performance Assessment Guidelines Ask the school librarian to help children find books. Below-level readers and ESL children might want to read with partners.

Extension Activities For Home and School

Writing with Pictures

Materials: construction paper, markers

Review the word *hieroglyphic* and its meaning on page 252. Then ask children to imagine what it would be like if they were scribes living long ago in ancient Egypt. Have them share the experience of making up a new way of writing. Ask children to think of a word or phrase and then to design a hieroglyphic to illustrate it. Encourage them to draw the hieroglyphic with a black marker and then color it to make details stand out. When children complete the activity, assemble all the hieroglyphics, along with their meanings, on a bulletin board to resemble an Egyptian painted wall.
(VISUAL/TACTILE)

Ancient World Mural

Materials: craft paper, paints, paintbrushes, reference materials

Ask children to look again at part of a mural by Diego Rivera on page 254. Explain that the mural offers a "slice-of-life" view of the Aztec culture. Have children draw their own mural to show one of the ancient civilizations mentioned in the lesson. Organize children into small groups and have each group select a different people. Help children locate more information and pictures of their groups in reference materials. Provide paper, paints, and paintbrushes. Encourage children to plan their pictures and then have each child choose a part of the mural to paint. Suggest that children use bold colors, as Diego Rivera did.
(VISUAL/TACTILE)

SKILLS

Read a Diagram

OBJECTIVES

- Explain how diagrams are used.
- Read a cross-section diagram of a pyramid.

RESOURCES

Pupil Book/Unit Big Book, pp. 256–257

Word Cards V69–V70

Activity Book, p. 62

Skill Transparency 5-6

Vocabulary

diagram p. 256

1 Motivate

Ask volunteers to tell about times when they or their family members have had to assemble a bicycle, a toy, or a piece of furniture. Explain that there is usually a picture or a diagram to go along with the written instructions. Tell children that in this lesson, they will learn how to use diagrams to gain information.

Why It Matters

Ask children if they have ever heard the saying, "A picture is worth a thousand words." Tell them that diagrams show pictures of things. Explain that it is sometimes easier to understand something by looking at a diagram than by reading a detailed explanation.

REACH ALL LEARNERS

English as a Second Language Help children understand that they can interpret information from simple drawings. Draw several circles on the board to represent faces. On each face, vary the features to express different emotions, such as happiness, sadness, and anger. Have children identify the feeling expressed by each drawing.

2 Teach

What You Need to Know

Have children turn back to page 216 to look at the photograph of the Egyptian wall painting. Explain that paintings like these were found inside pyramids, like the one shown on page 257. Point out that another way to show what is inside the pyramid is to draw a diagram, like the one on these pages. Discuss the differences in the kinds of information presented in photographs and diagrams.

Q Why would someone look at a diagram instead of a photograph to get information about the inside of a pyramid?

A The diagram gives an overall view of the inside and shows how the parts are related.

Read a Diagram

Vocabulary
diagram

Why It Matters

You can find out how things work or how things are made by looking at a kind of picture called a **diagram**.

What You Need to Know

The picture on the next page is a diagram of a pyramid. Pyramids were tombs built by the ancient people of Egypt.

Practice the Skill

Study the diagram.

1. Where were bodies mummified?
2. What connected the Valley Temple to the pyramid?
3. Where was the queen buried?
4. What happened in the Mortuary Temple?

1 The Valley Temple
Here the king's body was mummified.

BACKGROUND

Pyramids Ancient pyramids were built as monuments to house the tombs of Egyptian pharaohs. Thousands of slaves worked many years to construct the pyramids. Scientists are unsure how the builders were able to move and stack blocks of stone weighing tons. After the death of a pharaoh, the body was mummified and hidden with its worldly treasures inside the pyramid. The largest pyramid, the Great Pyramid, is taller than the Statue of Liberty, and its base would cover seven city blocks.

INTEGRATE ART

Make a Drawing Have children select a diagram from some you have provided, or ask them to find a diagram in a book or magazine. Have them use ideas in the diagram to create a drawing of the thing shown in the diagram. Stress that the drawing will contain more form and detail than the image presented in the diagram. Then each child can display his or her drawing next to a copy of the diagram that inspired it.

EXTEND AND ENRICH

Explain a Diagram Ask each child to find a book or magazine that includes a diagram. For example, they might find a diagram of a plant or a rocket in a science book, a diagram of a bedroom in a decorating magazine, or a diagram of a car's engine in an instruction manual. Have each child study her or his diagram and then take turns sharing the diagrams with the class and explaining what they show.

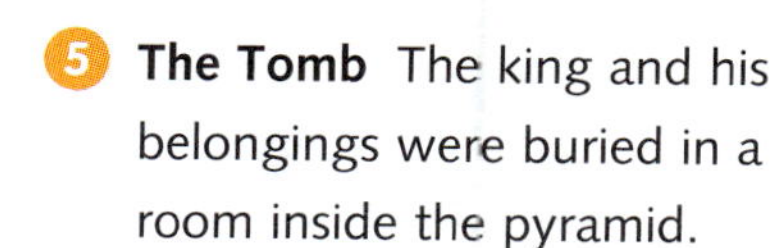

5 The Tomb The king and his belongings were buried in a room inside the pyramid.

3 The Mortuary Temple Priests prayed to the king's spirit every day.

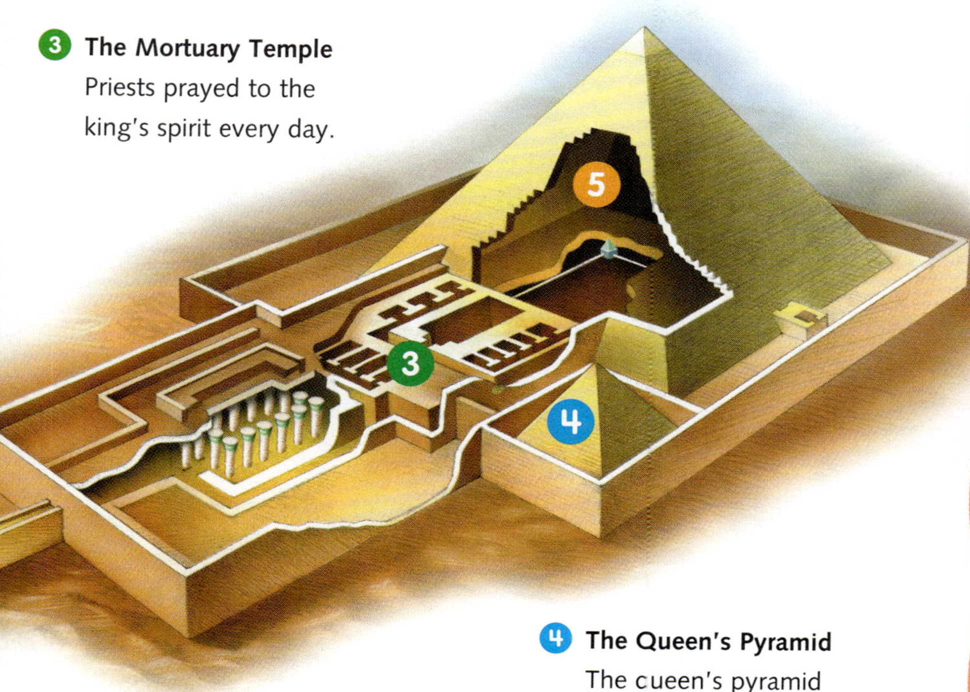

4 The Queen's Pyramid The queen's pyramid was much smaller.

2 The Causeway A walkway led to the pyramid.

Apply What You Learned

Look for diagrams at home. Show or describe them to the class and explain how they are used.

Practice the Skill—Answers

1. The Valley Temple (1)
2. The Causeway (2)
3. The Queen's Pyramid (4)
4. Priests prayed every day. (3)

3 Close

Apply What You Learned

Children might find diagrams that explain how to open packages, put together a toy, use a tool, play a game, and so forth. Their descriptions should reflect the process shown in the diagram.

RETEACH THE SKILL

Make a Chart Have children make a two-column chart to compare what they know about a pyramid by looking at a photograph and the diagram. Show children a photograph of an Egyptian pyramid. Encourage children to realize that the photograph is limited in what it can show and the diagram can give more information.

Pyramid Photograph	Pyramid Diagram
Made of stone blocks	Hidden rooms and hallways inside

ACTIVITY BOOK

Name ______________ Date ________

CHART AND GRAPH SKILLS

Chinampas

The Aztecs had an interesting way of growing crops. They made floating gardens called chinampas. These gardens were held in place by stones and trees. The Aztecs could grow several crops a year on the chinampas.

Use the diagram to answer the questions.

crops, water, trees, stones, stakes, plant fiber matting

1. Which parts of the chinampas are above the water? trees, crops
2. What goes on top of the plant fiber matting? stones
3. What natural resource is in between the rows of crops? water

62 • Activity Book — Use after reading Unit 5, Skill Lesson 6.

PAGE 62

TRANSPARENCY

Use SKILL TRANSPARENCY 5-6.

Extension Activities For Home and School

Write a Description

Materials: **paper, pencils**

Have children use information from the diagram on pages 256 and 257 to write a description of a pyramid. Have them include in their description details describing all parts of the pyramid included in the diagram. Encourage them to use words that can help the reader "see" what they are describing. Invite volunteers to read aloud their descriptions for the class. **(VISUAL/AUDITORY)**

How Does That Work?

Materials: **pencil, paper**

Brainstorm with children electrical items they use at school or at home, such as radio, toaster, telephone, VCR, television, microwave oven, electric pencil sharpener, and computer. Write the suggestions on the board. Then have each child select one of the items to diagram. Tell them to include labels identifying various parts. When children complete the assignment, have volunteers display their diagrams for the class. Have them explain how each diagram might help a person learn how to use the item. Encourage a discussion of similarities and differences between two or more diagrams of the same item. **(VISUAL/AUDITORY)**

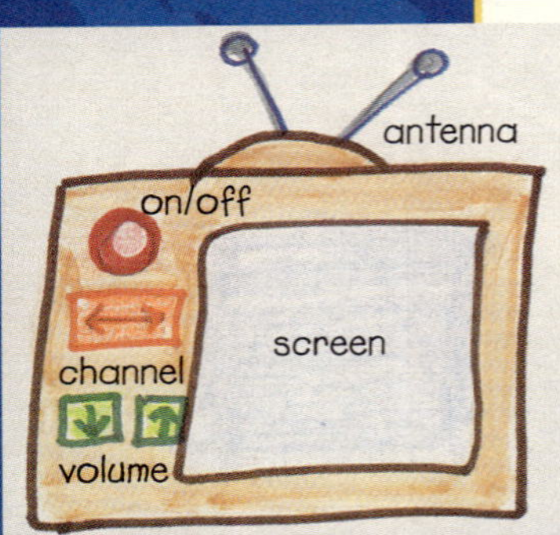

Food Diagrams

Materials: **copies of illustrated recipes from children's cookbooks**

Show children the recipes. Explain that cookbooks often include pictures to show the steps and what the finished dish should look like. Let each child choose one or two recipes to take home and cook with a family member. Tell children as they make the dish to talk about how the diagram helps them.

(AUDITORY/VISUAL)

Peanut Butter Cookies

Makes about 60 cookies—enough to share with lots of friends

What you need:
1/2 cup brown sugar
1/2 cup granulated sugar
1/2 cup butter
1 egg
1 cup smooth peanut butter
1/2 teaspoon salt
1/2 teaspoon baking soda
1 1/2 cups flour, sifted
1/2 teaspoon vanilla extract

What to do:
1. Mix together the sugars and the butter until the mixture is creamy.
2. Add the egg, peanut butter, salt, and baking soda,and beat some more.
3. Add the flour and vanilla. Beat until the mixture is smooth.
4. Roll the mixture into balls. The size of table-tennis balls is good.
5. Place the balls on a greased cookie sheet and press them flat with a fork to make a criss-cross design.
6. Bake for about 15 minutes at 375°F.

VISIT

Mount Rushmore

OBJECTIVES

- Identify and explain the significance of various community, state, and national memorials such as Mount Rushmore.
- Obtain information about a topic using a variety of visual sources.

RESOURCES

Pupil Book/Unit Big Book, pp. 258–259

Take a Field Trip Video

Internet Resources

Summary

In this lesson children will visit Mount Rushmore, the national memorial designed by Gutzon Borglum and sculpted in the Black Hills of South Dakota. The 60-foot busts of George Washington, Thomas Jefferson, Theodore Roosevelt, and Abraham Lincoln represent the first 150 years of American history.

1 Motivate

Get Ready

Tell children they will be visiting the Mount Rushmore National Memorial in South Dakota, honoring four American Presidents and our nation's history. Ask if any children have visited Mount Rushmore. If so, invite them to tell about their experiences. To help children read for main ideas, have them record the answers to the questions *who, what, where, when, why,* and *how* as they read.

BACKGROUND

Gutzon Borglum American painter and sculptor Gutzon Borglum, the son of a Danish immigrant, was born near Bear Lake, Idaho, in 1867. After studying art in San Francisco, Borglum traveled to Paris, where he continued his studies from 1890 to 1893. His work received recognition in France and in England, where he later traveled. Establishing himself in New York City in 1901, he began sculpting the busts of American leaders and heroic figures, including an enormous head of President Lincoln from a six-ton marble block. Referring to Mount Rushmore, Borglum said, "A monument's dimensions should be determined by the importance to civilization of the events commemorated.... Let us place there, carved high, as close to heaven as we can, the words of our leaders, their faces, to show posterity what manner of men they were."

2 Teach

What to See

As children study the pictures on pages 258 and 259 of Mount Rushmore and the four Presidents honored by the memorial, help them recall how each President contributed to the history of the United States.

Q If you were going to carve a memorial in a mountain to honor four great Americans, whom would you choose? Why?

A Choices will likely vary but children should be able to tell how each person contributed to United States history.

Direct children's attention to the first photograph on page 259, noting that Gutzon Borglum is the man wearing the hat.

Q Do you think Gutzon Borglum created the Mount Rushmore sculpture by himself? Why or why not?

A No, because it is too big.

As children study the photograph of the plaster models, explain that Borglum also made plaster copies of these studio models for the workers to use as guides on the mountain. Explain that the studio models were sized so that one inch on the model equaled one foot on the mountain.

Point out that at first Borglum did not want to use dynamite.

Q Why do you suppose he did not want to use dynamite?

A He would not be able to add rock if he accidentally blasted too much away.

Explain that Borglum quickly discovered that dynamite was the only way to remove the large pieces of extremely hard granite. Emphasize that Borglum used very skilled workers who were able to dynamite to within inches of his measurements.

Encourage children to compare the pictures of the Presidents with the stone sculptures.

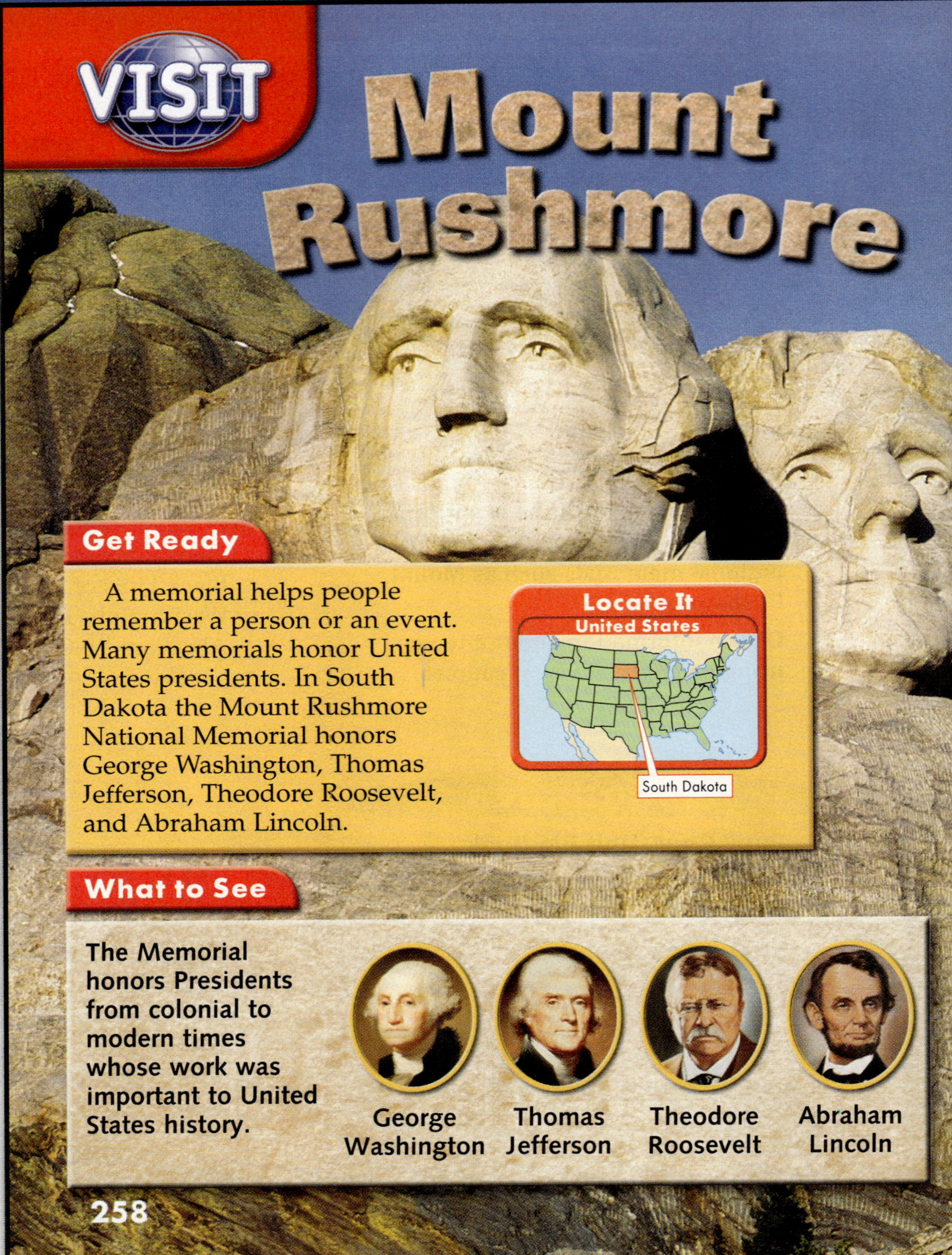

INTEGRATE MATHEMATICS

Scale Recall with children that one inch on Borglum's models equaled one foot, or 12 inches, on the mountain. Have children answer questions such as the following: *If George Washington's mouth is 12 feet wide on the mountain, how wide is it on the model? If Abraham Lincoln's nose is 15 1/2 inches long on the model, how long is it on the mountain?*

MAKE IT RELEVANT

In Your Community Help children identify memorials and monuments in the community, noting where they are located on a map and the people or events they honor. Then arrange to take children on a tour to observe the memorials and monuments so they can gather details about each one. If possible, take photographs or make a video. Use the video in the classroom to review and discuss what children observed and learned.

In 1927 artist Gutzon Borglum planned the memorial at Mount Rushmore. The sculpture took more than 14 years to complete.

Borglum made plaster models of the Presidents' faces. He used information from paintings, photographs, and written descriptions.

Workers used drills and dynamite to carve the solid rock of the cliff. The faces on Mount Rushmore are 60 feet high!

Take a Field Trip

A VIRTUAL TOUR
Visit The Learning Site at **www.harcourtschool.com** to take virtual tours of other monuments and memorials.

A VIDEO TOUR
Check your media center or classroom library for a video featuring a segment from Reading Rainbow.

259

3 Close

Tape a large picture of Mount Rushmore to the board. Invite children to pretend they are tour guides. Ask them to prepare what they would say to a group of children who have come to see Mount Rushmore. Have children write or record their presentations.

Take a Field Trip

A Virtual Tour Depending on the availability of computers, have children work individually, in pairs, or in small groups to view the virtual tour. Suggest they research other monuments and memorials and learn more about the people and events they honor.

INTERNET RESOURCES

THE LEARNING SITE

Go to **www.harcourtschool.com** for a listing of Web sites focusing on other important monuments and memorials.

A Video Tour Have children watch the Reading Rainbow video in small groups. As they watch the video ask them to jot down five to ten facts about how the Mount Rushmore National Memorial was constructed. Then have them rewrite the facts, replacing an important word in each fact with a blank space. For example, *Each face is ____ feet high.* Then have groups exchange facts and fill in the blanks. You may want to show the video a second time before groups complete the activity.

VIDEO

Use the Reading Rainbow TAKE A FIELD TRIP videotape of the history of the construction of the Mount Rushmore National Memorial.

BACKGROUND

More About the Memorial at Mount Rushmore The memorial was begun in 1927 and completed in 1941, but work was intermittent. Actual work time totaled six and a half years. Gutzon Borglum supervised most of the project and its 400 workers but died without seeing the completed memorial. Borglum's son Lincoln took over after his death. Carved on the northeast face of the 5,725-foot Mount Rushmore, the memorial is taller than the Great Pyramid of Egypt.

EXTEND AND ENRICH

Research and Report Challenge children to name other national memorials and monuments, such as the Statue of Liberty, the Vietnam Veterans Memorial, Devil's Tower National Monument, the Lincoln Memorial, the Washington Monument, and the Alamo. Then have children form groups. Ask each group to choose and research a different monument or memorial and to create a poster showing what they learned. As the groups share their posters, have them locate each place on a map.

Unit 5 Review and Test Preparation

PAGES 260–264

Sequence

Children may use the graphic organizer that appears on page 63 of the Activity Book. Children should write the following events in the First, Next, Last boxes in this order:

The English started colonies.

The Americans wrote the Declaration of Independence.

Americans won their freedom in the American Revolution.

ACTIVITY BOOK

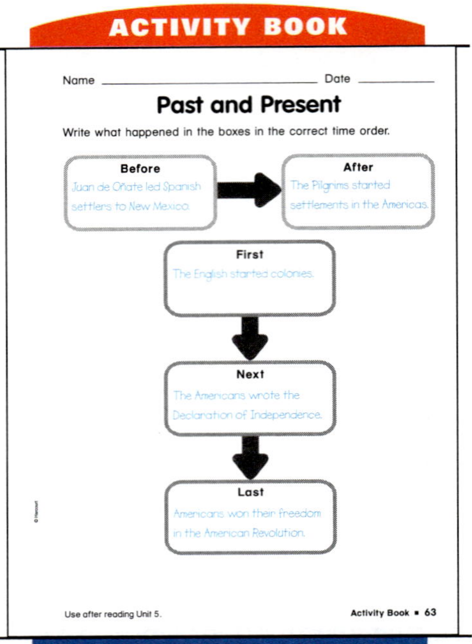

Name ______ Date ______

Past and Present

Write what happened in the boxes in the correct time order.

Before: Juan de Oñate led Spanish settlers to New Mexico.
After: The Pilgrims started settlements in the Americas.

First: The English started colonies.

Next: The Americans wrote the Declaration of Independence.

Last: Americans won their freedom in the American Revolution.

Use after reading Unit 5. Activity Book • 63

PAGE 63

Think & Write

Children's news reports should be about a real historical event and should include facts from research sources. Children should be able to point out the words in their reports that answer the questions *who, what, when,* and *where.*

Unit 5 Review and Test Preparation

Sequence

Put these events in the correct order.

Americans won their freedom in the American Revolution.
The Americans wrote the Declaration of Independence.
The English started colonies.

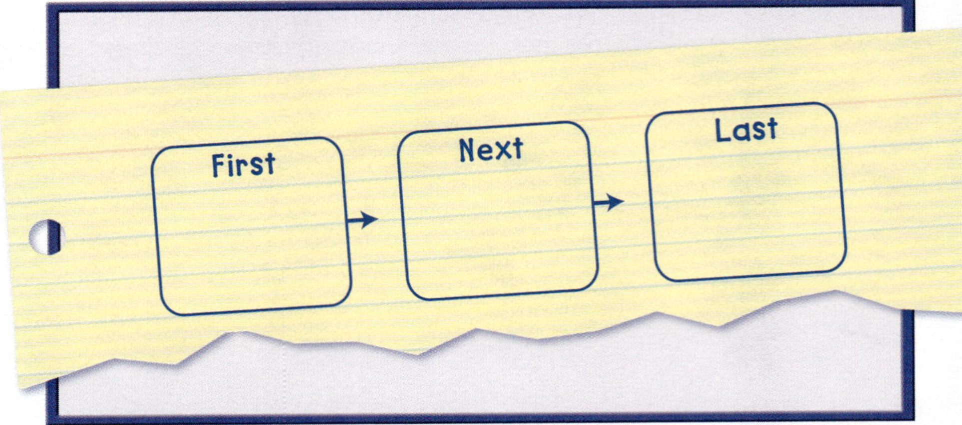

THINK & WRITE

Go Back in History Think of an event that happened in history. Use books and the Internet to find out about the event.

Report the News Write a news article telling about your event. Answer the questions who, what, when, and where.

260

TEST PREPARATION

Review these tips with children.

- Read the directions before reading the questions.
- Read each question twice, focusing the second time on all the possible answers.
- Take the time to think about all the possible answers before deciding on an answer.
- Move past questions that are giving you trouble, and answer the ones you know. Then return to concentrate on the difficult items.

TRANSPARENCY

This graphic organizer appears on READING AND VOCABULARY TRANSPARENCY 5-7.

Use Vocabulary

Change the underlined words to the correct vocabulary word.

history (p. 222)
artifact (p. 224)
settler (p. 229)
colony (p. 238)
landmark (p. 239)

1. A person who built a home on the frontier was a pioneer who helped our country grow.
2. The Gateway Arch, a familiar sight in St. Louis, reminds us of early pioneers.
3. Virginia was a land ruled by another country.
4. We studied an object from the past to learn more about ancient Egyptians.
5. The study of the past tells us who we are.

Recall Facts

6. What tools do we use to measure time?
7. Who were the first people to live in Fort Myers?
8. Tell something you learned about a hero in this unit.
9. On which holiday do we remember the American Revolution?
   - **A** Thanksgiving
   - **B** Labor Day
   - **C** Memorial Day
   - **D** Independence Day
10. Who was President during the Civil War?
    - **F** George Washington
    - **G** Abraham Lincoln
    - **H** Thomas Jefferson
    - **J** Franklin Roosevelt

Use Vocabulary

1. settler
2. landmark
3. colony
4. artifact
5. History

Recall Facts

6. We use clocks and calendars to measure time.
7. The Calusa Indians
8. Children should be able to identify one of the heroes from the unit and write one fact about that person.
9. D—Independence Day
10. G—Abraham Lincoln

Think Critically

11. We can learn about the past by reading about it or by studying artifacts that were used in the past.
12. Ancient people are a part of our history because all the people who lived before us are a part of our history. Some of the words and place names we use come from the languages of ancient people. Inventions from ancient people are still being used.

Apply Chart and Graph Skills

13. solar panels
14. truss
15. the laboratories
16. Destiny

Think Critically

11. What are some ways to learn about the past?
12. How are ancient people a part of our history?

Apply Chart and Graph Skills

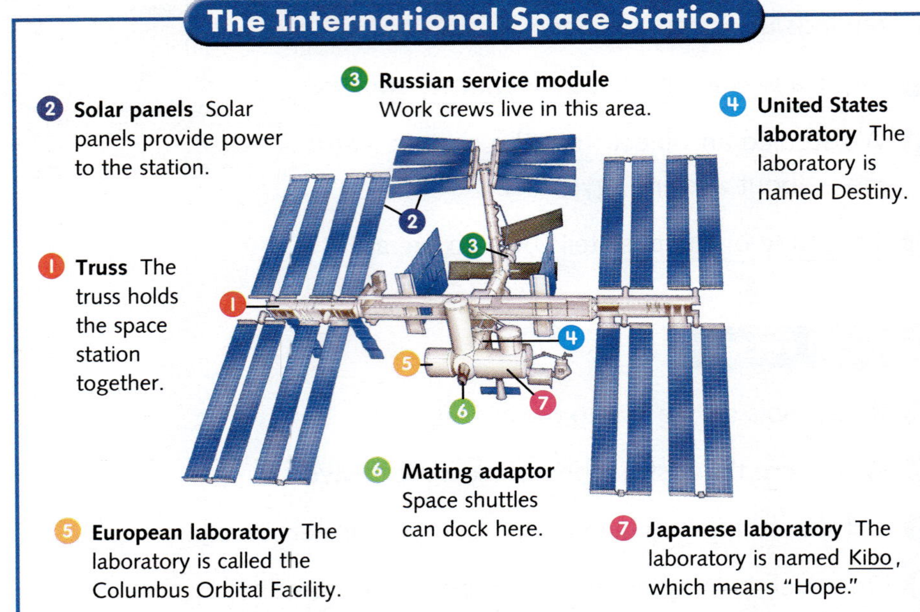

13. What is the source of power for the space station?
14. What holds the space station together?
15. Where will experiments be done?
16. What is the name of the U.S. laboratory?

262

Apply Map and Globe Skills

Early Roads

17. Name two cities on the Coastal Post Road.
18. Which road crossed the Appalachian Mountains into Kentucky?
19. What road went from Cumberland to Vandalia?
20. Which road connected Pittsburgh to the Coastal Post Road?

ASSESSMENT

Use the UNIT 5 TEST on pages 17-20 of the Assessment Program.

Apply Map and Globe Skills

17. Children may name any two of the following cities: Portland, Maine; Boston, Massachusetts; New York, New York; Philadelphia, Pennsylvania; Baltimore, Maryland; Washington, D.C.; Richmond, Virginia; Raleigh, North Carolina; or Charleston, South Carolina.
18. Wilderness Road
19. National Road
20. Forbes Road

ACTIVITY BOOK

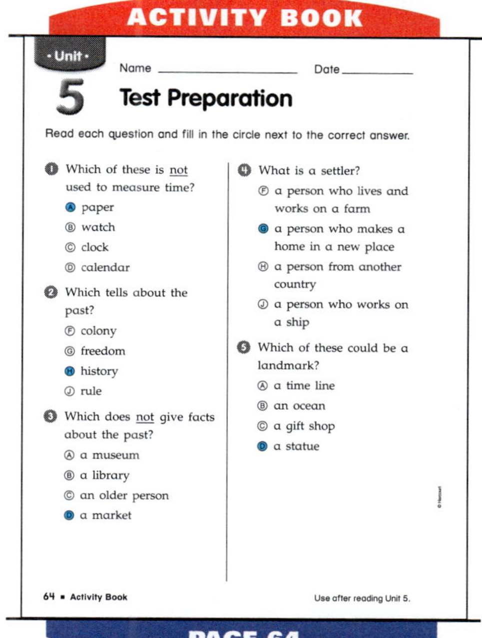

Unit 5 Name ______ Date ______

Test Preparation

Read each question and fill in the circle next to the correct answer.

1. Which of these is not used to measure time?
   - Ⓐ paper
   - Ⓑ watch
   - Ⓒ clock
   - Ⓓ calendar
2. Which tells about the past?
   - Ⓕ colony
   - Ⓖ freedom
   - Ⓗ history
   - Ⓙ rule
3. Which does not give facts about the past?
   - Ⓐ a museum
   - Ⓑ a library
   - Ⓒ an older person
   - Ⓓ a market
4. What is a settler?
   - Ⓕ a person who lives and works on a farm
   - Ⓖ a person who makes a home in a new place
   - Ⓗ a person from another country
   - Ⓙ a person who works on a ship
5. Which of these could be a landmark?
   - Ⓐ a time line
   - Ⓑ an ocean
   - Ⓒ a gift shop
   - Ⓓ a statue

64 • Activity Book Use after reading Unit 5.

PAGE 64

Unit Activities

In advance, obtain an aluminum canister and label it in indelible ink. Display the canister, and explain that children will be making a time capsule to show children of the future what life was like in the early part of the twenty-first century. Brainstorm a list of things children use every day that represent today's culture. Take a class vote to decide which items on the list they would like to include in their time capsule. Then assign small groups of children to be responsible for locating one of the objects on the list.

Where to Get Information

Encourage children to use a wide variety of reference sources, including encyclopedias, library books, travel brochures, social studies books, picture atlases, magazines, and the Internet.

Ways to Share

When children bring in their artifacts, display them on a table. Ask a volunteer from each group to describe the object the group brought and explain what the object will tell future children who open the time capsule. After writing the class letter, suggest children make personal copies and save them to read when they are older. Then seal the time capsule and place it in an appropriate spot in the school or on the school grounds.

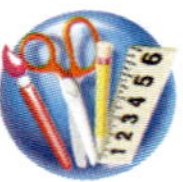

Performance Assessment Guidelines Call on volunteers to explain the purpose of a time capsule. As children explain the importance of their artifacts, listen to note whether children understand that to children of the future, the objects in the canister will be artifacts from the past.

Visit Your Library

Encourage independent reading with these books or others of your choice after children have completed their study of the past. Additional books are listed in the Multimedia Resources on pages 209J–209K of this Teacher's Edition.

Unit Activities

Complete the Unit Project Work with your class to finish the unit project. Decide what you will put in your time capsule and where you will store it.

Visit The Learning Site at **www.harcourtschool.com** for additional activities.

Choose Artifacts

List and collect items such as these that tell about you, your school, and your community.

- newspapers or magazines
- photographs
- symbols and models

Write a Letter

Work together to write a class letter to a class of the future. Tell about things you like to do. Describe the important events and people of your time. Place the letter in the capsule with your artifacts.

Visit Your Library

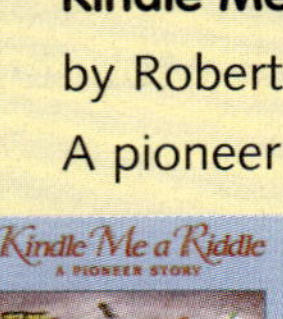

Right Here on This Spot by Sharon Hart Addy. Objects dug from the ground give clues to the past.

Kindle Me a Riddle by Roberta Karim. A pioneer father shares riddles with his daughter to explain the past.

The Tomb of the Boy King: A True Story in Verse by John Frank. Explore the mysteries of Egypt's King Tutankhamen.

264

Easy *Right Here on This Spot* by Sharon Hart Addy. Houghton Mifflin, 1999. As Grandpa works on his Wisconsin farm, he finds objects from the past that tell about the people who lived in the same place years ago.

Average *Kindle Me a Riddle* by Roberta Karim. Greenwillow, 1999. The everyday objects the pioneer family uses in their riddles have changed, but present-day children can still enjoy playing the same riddle game to guess the names and origins of modern products.

Challenging *The Tomb of the Boy King: A True Story in Verse* by John Frank. Farrar, Straus & Giroux, 2001. The author uses the style of an epic poem to tell the true story of archaeologist Howard Carter's discovery of King Tut's tomb.

People at Work

A manual typewriter, early 1900s

1
2
3
4
5
6

Unit 6 Planning Guide People at Work

Unit 6 deals with economics. Children will identify goods and services and the people who provide them. They will distinguish between producers and consumers and ways in which people are both. They will learn about resources needed to produce goods in a factory, work and income, volunteer work, the history of money, and trade around the world. In addition, children will learn how to follow a flow chart, make choices when buying, and read a product map.

LESSON	PACING	OBJECTIVES	VOCABULARY
Introduce the Unit pp. 265R–265 **Preview the Vocabulary** pp. 266–267A **Start with a Poem** pp. 268A–271A	**3 Days**	■ Use a visual to predict content. ■ Interpret a quotation. ■ Use a summary chart to prepare for the unit. ■ Use visuals to determine word meanings. ■ Use words and visuals to predict the content of the unit. ■ Obtain information about a topic using a variety of visual sources, such as literature. ■ Recognize the variety of jobs that people do. ■ Explain how people depend on one another in their daily lives.	**Word Work,** pp. 267A, 268
1 Goods and Services pp. 272A–275A	**2 Days**	■ Distinguish between goods and services. ■ Identify people who provide goods and services to the community.	**goods** **services**
2 Producers and Consumers pp. 276A–279A	**2 Days**	■ Distinguish between producing and consuming. ■ Identify ways in which people are both producers and consumers. ■ Recognize what is needed to run a business.	**business** **producer** **consumer** **Word Work,** p. 276
3 A Visit to a Factory pp. 280A–283A	**2 Days**	■ Identify three kinds of resources needed to produce goods. ■ Describe the jobs of factory workers. ■ Recognize that technology affects the way people work.	**raw material** **factory** **manufacture**

Time Management

6 WEEKS	WEEK 1	WEEK 2	WEEK 3	WEEK 4	WEEK 5	WEEK 6
	Introduce the Unit	Lessons 1–3		Lessons 4–6		Wrap Up the Unit

READING	INTEGRATE LEARNING	REACH ALL LEARNERS	RESOURCES
Focus Skill **Summarize,** p. 265 Reading Social Studies: **Preview the Unit,** p. 266 Reading Social Studies: **Graphic Organizer,** pp. 268A, 270 Reading Social Studies: **Use Picture Clues,** p. 270	**Theme Time,** p. 265I Language Arts **Write Captions,** p. 265 Art **Make a Poster,** p. 267 Reading **Books About Jobs,** p. 269 Health **Time to Rest,** p. 270	**English as a Second Language,** pp. 265N, 266 **Below-Level Learners,** p. 265N **Advanced Learners,** p. 265N **Tactile Learners,** p. 269 **Extension Activities for Home and School,** p. 271A	**Pupil Book/Unit Big Book,** pp. 265–271 **Audiotext, Unit 6** **Reading and Vocabulary** Transparency 6–1 Internet Resources
Reading Social Studies: **Graphic Organizer,** pp. 272A, 275	Mathematics **What Do Stores Earn?** p. 273 Language Arts **Advertisement,** p. 274	**English as a Second Language,** p. 273 **Extend and Enrich,** p. 274 **Reteach the Lesson,** p. 275 **Extension Activities for Home and School,** p. 275A	**Pupil Book/Unit Big Book,** pp. 272–275 **Word Cards V71-V72** **Activity Book,** p. 65 **Reading and Vocabulary** Transparency 6–2 Internet Resources
Reading Social Studies: **Anticipation Guide,** pp. 276A, 279 Focus Skill **Summarize,** p. 276 Reading Social Studies: **Use Context Clues,** p. 276	Reading **Lemonade for Sale,** p. 277	**Auditory Learners,** p. 277 **Extend and Enrich,** p. 278 **Reteach the Lesson,** p. 279 **Extension Activities for Home and School,** p. 279A	**Pupil Book/Unit Big Book,** pp. 276–279 **Word Cards V71-V74** **Activity Book,** p. 66 **Reading and Vocabulary** Transparency 6–3 Internet Resources
Reading Social Studies: **Make a Prediction,** pp. 280A, 283	Art **Create Can Labels,** p. 280 Science **Technology,** p. 280	**English as a Second Language,** p. 281 **Tactile Learners,** p. 282 **Extend and Enrich,** p. 282 **Reteach the Lesson,** p. 283 **Extension Activities for Home and School,** p. 283A	**Pupil Book/Unit Big Book,** pp. 280–283 **Word Cards V73-V74** **Activity Book,** p. 67 **Reading and Vocabulary** Transparency 6–4 Internet Resources

Unit 6 Planning Guide

LESSON	PACING	OBJECTIVES	VOCABULARY
CHART AND GRAPH SKILLS **Follow a Flow Chart** pp. 284A–285A	1 Day	■ Describe the purpose of a flow chart. ■ Trace the development of a product from a natural resource to a finished product.	**flow chart** **product** **Word Work,** p. 284
4 **Work and Income** pp. 286A–289A	2 Days	■ Explain how work provides income to purchase goods and services. ■ Explain the choices people in the United States free enterprise system make about spending and saving money.	**income** **free enterprise** **bank** **interest**
CITIZENSHIP SKILLS **Make Choices When Buying** pp. 290A–291A	1 Day	■ Use a decision-making process to identify a situation that requires a decision. ■ Recognize that scarcity and demand affect cost. ■ Explain the opportunity costs and trade-offs of spending money.	**scarce**
EXAMINE PRIMARY SOURCES **A History of Money** pp. 292A–295A	2 Days	■ Describe various means of exchange. ■ Compare the use of money and barter. ■ Discuss modern methods of payment.	**barter**
5 **People Make a Difference** pp. 296A–297A	1 Day	■ Distinguish volunteers from other kinds of workers. ■ Identify community volunteers.	**volunteer**

READING	INTEGRATE LEARNING	REACH ALL LEARNERS	RESOURCES
	Music **Sequencing Songs,** p. 285	**Kinesthetic Learners,** p. 284A **Extend and Enrich,** p. 284 **Reteach the Skill,** p. 285 **Extension Activities for Home and School,** p. 285A	**Pupil Book/Unit Big Book,** pp. 284–285 **Word Cards V75–V76** **Activity Book,** p. 68 **Activity Pattern P11** **Skill Transparency 6-1** Internet Resources
Reading Social Studies: **Study Questions,** pp. 286A, 289	**Reading** **Books About Money,** p. 287 **Mathematics** **How Much Is Left?** p. 287	**English as a Second Language,** p. 286 **Advanced Learners,** p. 288 **Extend and Enrich,** p. 288 **Reteach the Lesson,** p. 289 **Extension Activities for Home and School,** p. 289A	**Pupil Book/Unit Big Book,** pp. 286–289 **Word Cards V75–V78** **Activity Book,** p. 69 **Reading and Vocabulary** Transparency 6–5 Internet Resources
		English as a Second Language, p. 290 **Extend and Enrich,** p. 290 **Reteach the Skill,** p. 291 **Extension Activities for Home and School,** p. 291A	**Pupil Book/Unit Big Book,** pp. 290–291 **Word Cards V77–V78** **Activity Book,** p. 70 **Skill Transparency 6-2**
	Art **Design New Money,** p. 294 **Reading** **More Money,** p. 294	**Advanced Learners,** p. 292 **Extend and Enrich,** p. 295 **Reteach,** p. 295	**Pupil Book/Unit Big Book,** pp. 292–295 **Word Cards V77–V78** Internet Resources
Reading Social Studies: **Graphic Organizer,** pp. 296A, 297		**Extend and Enrich,** p. 296 **Reteach the Lesson,** p. 297 **Extension Activities for Home and School,** p. 297A	**Pupil Book/Unit Big Book,** pp. 296–297 **Word Cards V79–V80** **Activity Book,** p. 71 **Reading and Vocabulary** Transparency 6–6 Internet Resources

Unit 6 Planning Guide

LESSON	PACING	OBJECTIVES	VOCABULARY
6 Goods from Near and Far pp. 298A–303A	3 Days	■ Explain that people around the world depend on one another through trade. ■ Describe how science and technology have changed transportation. ■ Identify historic figures who have exhibited a love of individualism and inventiveness.	trade transportation
MAP AND GLOBE SKILLS **Read a Product Map** pp. 304A–305A	1 Day	■ Compare information from different sources about places and regions. ■ Use symbols to find products on a map. ■ Recognize jobs associated with resources in a place.	product map
Visit a Crayon Factory pp. 306A–307	1 Day	■ Explain the basic steps in a manufacturing process. ■ Identify natural resources used in making a product. ■ Sequence and categorize information.	
Unit 6 Review and Test Preparation pp. 308–312	3 Days		

READING	INTEGRATE LEARNING	REACH ALL LEARNERS	RESOURCES
Reading Social Studies: **Graphic Organizer,** pp. 298A, 303 **Summarize,** p. 302	**Languages** **Product Information,** p. 298 **Language Arts** **Write a Poem,** p. 299	**Below-Level Learners,** p. 298 **Auditory Learners,** p. 300 **English as a Second Language,** p. 301 **Extend and Enrich,** p. 302 **Reteach the Lesson,** p. 303 **Extension Activities for Home and School,** p. 303A	**Pupil Book/Unit Big Book,** pp. 298–303 **Word Cards V79–V80** **Activity Book,** p. 72 **Activity Pattern P12** **Reading and Vocabulary** Transparency 6–7 **Internet Resources**
		Visual Learners, p. 304A **English as a Second Language,** p. 304 **Extend and Enrich,** p. 304 **Reteach the Skill,** p. 305 **Extension Activities for Home and School,** p. 305A	**Pupil Book/Unit Big Book,** pp. 304–305 **Word Cards V79–V80** **Activity Book,** p. 73 **Skill Transparency 6-3** **GeoSkills CD-ROM**
	Science **Make Cupcake Crayons,** p. 306	**Extend and Enrich,** p. 307	**Pupil Book/Unit Big Book,** pp. 306–307 **Internet Resources** **Take a Field Trip Video**
Summarize, p. 308			**Pupil Book/Unit Big Book,** pp. 308–312 **Activity Book,** pp. 74–75 **Reading and Vocabulary** Transparency 6–8 **Assessment Program, Unit 6 Test,** pp. 21–24

Unit 6 Skills Path

Unit 6 features the reading skill of summarizing. It also highlights the social studies skills of reading a product map, making choices when buying, and following a flow chart.

FOCUS SKILLS

UNIT 6 READING SKILL

SUMMARIZE

- INTRODUCE p. 265
- APPLY pp. 276, 302, 308

READING SOCIAL STUDIES

- Preview the Unit, p. 266
- Graphic Organizer, pp. 268A, 270, 272A, 275, 296A, 297, 298A, 303
- Use Picture Clues, p. 270
- Anticipation Guide, pp. 276A, 279
- Use Context Clues, p. 276
- Make a Prediction, pp. 280A, 283
- Study Questions, pp. 286A, 289

CITIZENSHIP SKILLS

MAKE CHOICES WHEN BUYING

- INTRODUCE pp. 290A–291A

CHART AND GRAPH SKILLS

FOLLOW A FLOW CHART

- INTRODUCE pp. 284A–285A
- APPLY p. 310

MAP AND GLOBE SKILLS

READ A PRODUCT MAP

- INTRODUCE pp. 304A–305A
- APPLY p. 311

STUDY AND RESEARCH SKILLS

- Look Ahead at Review Questions, p. 286
- Television, p. 298

Theme Time: Working World

MATH CENTER

Bartering Bargains

Display real items or pictures of groceries, toys, school supplies, and clothing. Mark each with a price. Remind children that bartering is a way of making a fair trade without using money. Have partners make two groups of items they could barter to make a fair trade. Ask children to record their bartering transactions by drawing pictures of the two groups of items they could trade. Have them list the prices of the items and show the method they used to prove the trade is fair.

SCIENCE CENTER

A Better Cargo Plane

Invite children to design paper airplanes that will carry several drinking straws ten feet. Mark off a ten-foot-long "airfield," and provide paper, tape, and drinking straws. Explain to children that shippers want to put as much freight as they can on a cargo plane but that too much freight will cause problems in flying the plane. If children create a successful design, have them display their plane in the science center and write a summary giving the number of straws it carried over the length of the airfield and why they think the design works well. Challenge children to improve their designs to carry more straws.

READING/LANGUAGE ARTS CENTER

Chain Stories

Cut large sheets of drawing paper into strips. Have each child fold a strip accordion-style to use in writing and illustrating a story about shopping and selling. Explain to children that they should write the title of the story and their name on the first square. Then children should start the story by telling about someone buying something from a store. Next have them tell how that store owner used the money to buy something. Have children continue the chain until they have described three or four transactions. Ask them to illustrate their stories and display their chain stories in the center.

BULLETIN BOARD: WAYS WE USE MONEY

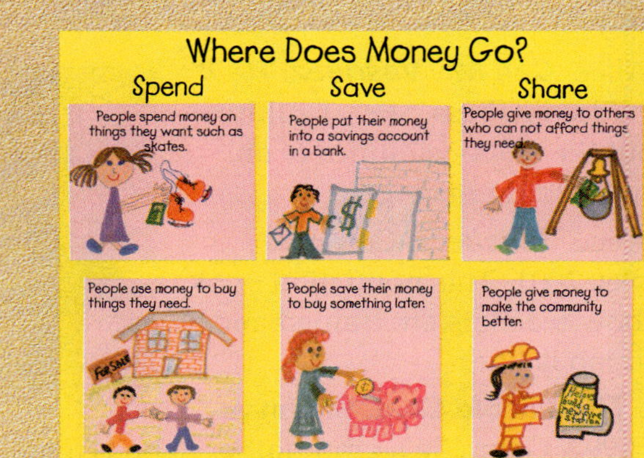

Prepare a bulletin board with the title "Where Does Money Go?" and create columns labeled *Spend*, *Save*, and *Share*. Discuss specific examples of ways people spend their money, save their money, and share their money with others who need help. Have each child draw a picture of a person using money in one of those ways. Ask children to write captions explaining their drawings. Then have them tell in which category on the bulletin board each of their pictures should be displayed.

Multimedia Resources

The Multimedia Resources can be used in a variety of ways. They can supplement core instruction in the classroom or extend and enrich children's learning at home.

Independent Reading

Easy

Aliki. ***Milk: From Cow to Carton.*** HarperTrophy, 1992. This is an illustrated tour showing how foods made from milk are produced.

Banks, Kate. ***The Night Worker.*** Farrar, Straus & Giroux, 2000. A boy goes along to find out what his father's job as a night construction engineer is like.

Best, Cari. ***Taxi! Taxi!*** Orchard, 1997. Tina's father works as a taxi driver. He does not live with Tina, but every Sunday he takes her on fun outings.

Gardella, Tricia. ***Just Like My Dad.*** Boyds Mills Press, 2000. A child enjoys working alongside his father as a cowhand.

Gershator, David and Phillis. ***Bread Is for Eating.*** Henry Holt, 1995. A song in English and Spanish tells how bread is made.

Hall, Donald. ***Ox-Cart Man.*** Viking, 1983. This classic story traces an early nineteenth century New England family through the seasons.

Hayward, Linda. ***A Day in the Life of a Dancer.*** Dorling Kindersley, 2001. This nonfiction book shows what a typical day is like for a ballet student.

Hayward, Linda. ***A Day in the Life of a Firefighter.*** Dorling Kindersley, 2001. Through photographs and simple text, children learn what a firefighter's day is like.

Lobel, Arnold. ***On Market Street.*** Greenwillow, 1981. A young boy visits Market Street and buys gifts beginning with each letter of the alphabet.

Pilkey, Dav. ***The Paperboy.*** Orchard, 1996. A boy enjoys the early morning as he delivers newspapers.

Rockwell, Anne. ***Career Day.*** HarperCollins, 2000. Relatives of the children in Mrs. Madoff's class visit the school to tell the class about their occupations.

Average

Bloom, Becky. ***Crackers.*** Orchard, 2001. A cat finds it is hard to keep a job until he finds the perfect work for him.

Davis, Wendy. ***From Metal to Music.*** Children's Press, 1997. Follow the steps for making brass instruments.

Dubois, Muriel. ***I Like Sports: What Can I Be?*** Bridgestone Books, 2001. This nonfiction book spotlights sports-related jobs.

Kajikawa, Kimiko. ***Yoshi's Feast.*** Dorling Kindersley, 2000. A Japanese folktale takes a humorous look at a fishmonger's business relationship with a miserly neighbor.

Murphy, Stuart J. ***Lemonade for Sale.*** ScottForesman, 1998. Children start their own business.

Ready, Dee. ***Mail Carriers.*** Bridgestone Books, 1998. This nonfiction book explains what a mail carrier's job is like.

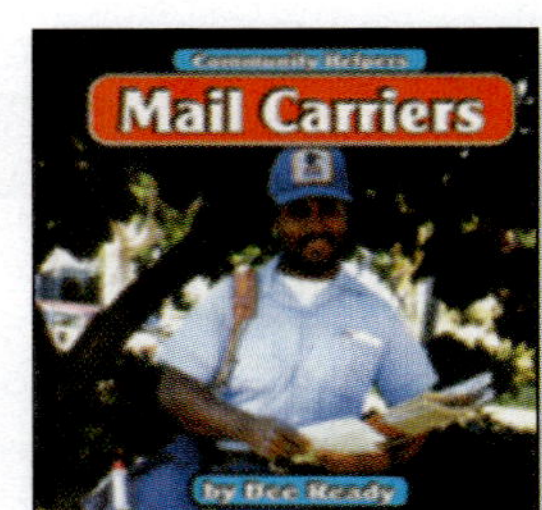

Sommer, Carl. ***Your Job Is Easy.*** Advance, 2000. A mother and father gain new respect for each other after exchanging jobs for a day.

Challenging

Burleigh, Robert. ***Messenger, Messenger.*** Atheneum, 2000. Interesting illustrations and rhyming couplets show what it is like to be a bike messenger in a busy city.

Carle, Eric. ***Walter the Baker.*** Simon & Schuster, 1998. This engaging story is based on a German tale about how the pretzel was invented.

Flanagan, Alice. ***A Busy Day at Mr. Kang's Grocery.*** Children's Press, 1997. Children learn how hard a grocery store owner works to provide what his customers come to buy.

Flanagan, Alice. ***Call Mr. Vasquez, He'll Fix It!*** Children's Press, 1997. Children learn about the responsibilities of an apartment building manager.

Flanagan, Alice. ***Teachers.*** Compass Point Books, 2001. This nonfiction book explains how teachers are trained and what their job is like.

Hest, Amy. ***The Purple Coat.*** Simon & Schuster, 1992. Gabrielle's grandfather, who is a tailor, finds a way to make her exactly what she wants—even though the girl's mother has a different idea.

Lewin, Ted. ***Market!*** Lothrop, Lee & Shepard, 1996. Read about marketplaces around the world and the goods they sell.

Madrigal, Antonio Hernandez. ***Erandi's Braids.*** G. P. Putnam's Sons, 1999. A young girl makes a difficult and unselfish decision to help buy the fishing net her family needs.

Maestro, Betsy and Giulio. ***The Story of Money.*** Mulberry, 1995. From trading feathers, shells, and animal teeth, find out how people through the ages have bartered and spent money to meet their needs.

Schaefer, Lola. ***We Need Dentists.*** Capstone Press, 1999. In this clear, informative book, children learn why dentists are important to the community.

Schaefer, Lola. ***We Need Farmers.*** Capstone Press, 1999. Through photographs and informative text, children learn about the work that grain and dairy farmers do.

Audiocassettes

All About Money. Educational Activities. The songs on this cassette introduce children to the days before money, to money in other countries, and to the concepts of earning and spending.

The Gardener. Live Oak Media, 1998. This read-along set tells the story of a young girl who helps her uncle in his bakery during the Depression. Her love for gardening transforms more than just a barren plot of ground.

People in Our Neighborhood. Kimbo Educational. Ronno sings about nurses, doctors, computer programmers, astronauts, and more.

Computer Software

The Airport. Junior Field Trips. Maxis. Windows. Children try their hand at different jobs at the airport, including ticket counter sales, flying the Concorde, and working on the ground crew.

Classroom Storeworks. Tom Snyder Productions. Mac/Windows. This program provides a cash register and allows for customizing product information and job descriptions so children can set up an in-classroom store.

Farmer Greenfield's Virtual Harvest. Ohio Distinctive Software. Mac/Windows. Children learn how to grow and harvest as many kinds of flowers and vegetables as possible by managing resources and responding to weather problems and garden pests.

Monopoly Junior. Hasbro Interactive. Windows. Children conduct transactions at the bank, buy cotton candy, and play amusement park games.

Videos and DVDs

Bob's Job Series. Library Video. Bob introduces children to careers by leading them on an on-the-job tour. Series includes two titles: *An Airline Pilot* and *Home Builder*.

Neighborhood and Community. My America: Building a Democracy Series. Library Video, 1997. Children see a variety of urban and rural communities and a group of school children working on a project to help their community.

Supply and Demand. Economics in Our Age Series. Library Video, 1999. A child host helps children understand economic terms and principles through the story of two children running a lemonade stand.

Worksong. Reading Rainbow/Lancit Media. This video version of Gary Paulsen's verse includes an introduction discussing a variety of jobs people do.

Additional books also are recommended at point of use throughout the unit.
Note that information, while correct at time of publication, is subject to change.

ISBNs and other publisher information can be found at www.harcourtschool.com

The Learning Site: Social Studies Center

The Learning Site at www.harcourtschool.com offers a special Social Studies Center. The center provides a wide variety of activities, Internet links, and online references.

Find all this at The Learning Site at www.harcourtschool.com

- Activities and Games
- Content Updates
- Current Events
- Free and Inexpensive Materials
- Multimedia Biographies
- Online Atlas
- Primary Sources
- Video Updates
- Virtual Tours
- Your State

and more!

Here are just some of the HARCOURT Internet resources you'll find!

Multimedia Biographies

www.harcourtschool.com

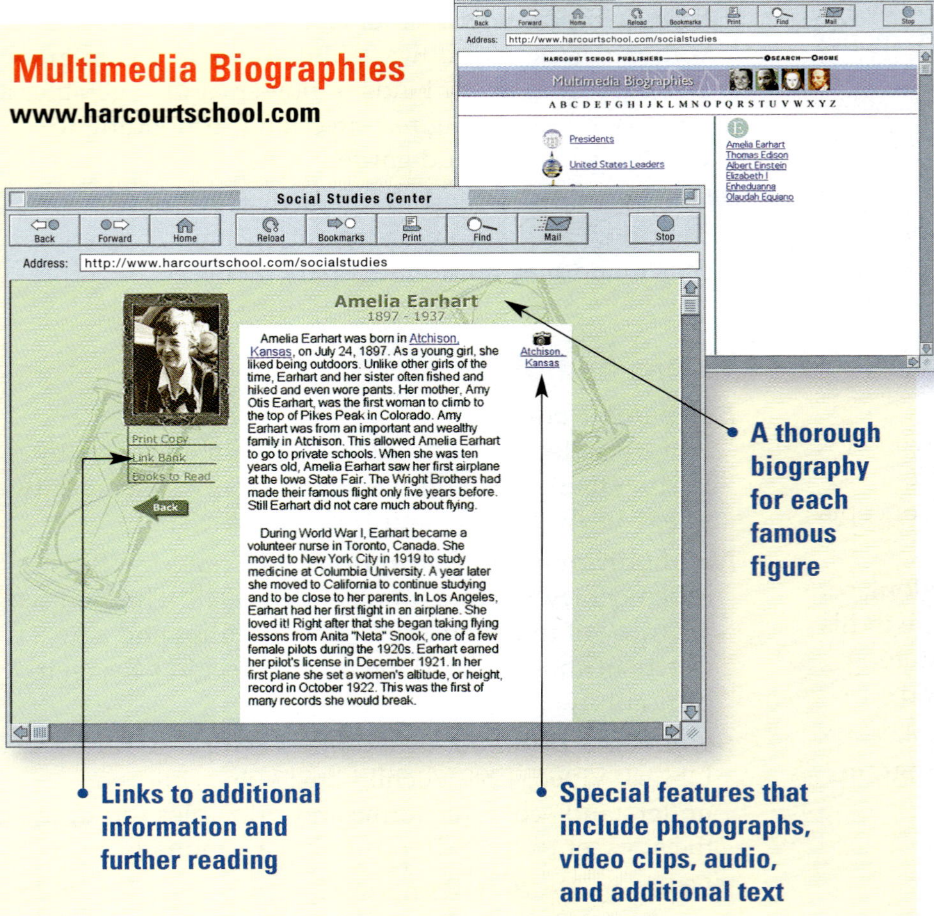

- A thorough biography for each famous figure
- Links to additional information and further reading
- Special features that include photographs, video clips, audio, and additional text

Free and Inexpensive Materials

- Addresses to write for free and inexpensive products
- Links to unit-related materials
- Internet maps
- Internet references

www.harcourtschool.com

Primary Sources

- Artwork
- Clothing
- Diaries
- Government Documents
- Historical Documents
- Maps
- Tools

and more!

www.harcourtschool.com

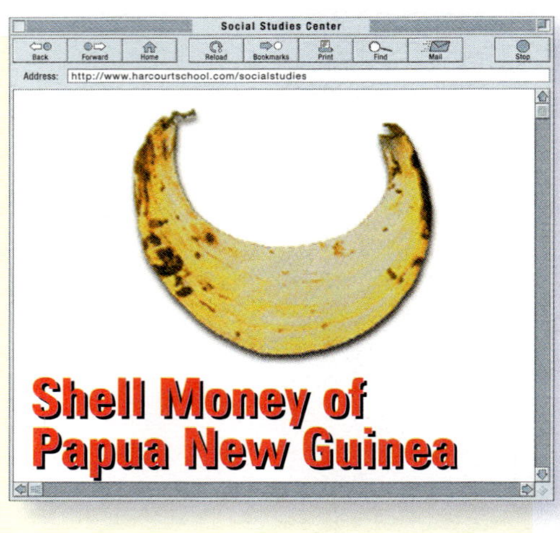

Virtual Tours

- Capitols and Government Buildings
- Cities
- Countries
- Historical Sites
- Museums
- Parks and Scenic Areas

and more!

www.harcourtschool.com

Integrate Learning Across the Curriculum

Use these topics to help you integrate social studies into your daily planning. See the page numbers indicated for more information about each topic.

Social Studies

Art

Make a Poster, p. 267
Create Can Labels, p. 280
Design New Money, p. 294

Science

A Better Cargo Plane, p. 265I
Make Cupcake Crayons, p. 306

Health

Time to Rest, p. 270

Language Arts

Chain Stories, p. 265I
Write Captions, p. 265
Advertisement, p. 274
Write a Poem, p. 299

Languages

Product Information, p. 298

Computer/Technology

Go Online, pp. 271, 284, 295, 307
GeoSkills CD-ROM, p. 305
Take a Field Trip Video, p. 307

Reading/Literature

Mole and Shrew Have Jobs to Do, p. 269
Fox on the Job, p. 269
Goods Around the World, p. 271
The Mint, p. 271
Robert Fulton, p. 271
Lemonade for Sale, p. 277
The Coin Counting Book, p. 287
The Big Buck Adventure, p. 287
Coin County: A Bank in a Book, p. 287
The Story of Money, p. 294
The Paperboy, p. 312
From Metal to Music, p. 312
Market! p. 312

Mathematics

Bartering Bargains, p. 265I
What Do Stores Earn? p. 273
How Much Is Left? p. 287

Music

Sequencing Songs, p. 285

Reach All Learners

Use these activities to help individualize your instruction. Each activity has been developed to address a different level or type of learner.

English as a Second Language

Materials

- chart with rhymed conversation
- table with items for buying and selling

MARKETPLACE CONVERSATION **Have children role-play shoppers and vendors while using a rhyme.**

- Set up a classroom market by placing things on a table that people might want to buy and sell.
- Help children learn the *Shop Talk* rhyme. Make sure they understand what each line means.
- Review the names of the items on the table and model using the words in the rhyme.
- Invite pairs of children to take turns role-playing a shopper and a vendor.
- The shopper should choose an item and say the lines of the rhyme as the shopper and vendor act out the shopping scene.

Shop Talk	
Shopper	I want to buy a ________.
Vendor	I'll sell you one, my friend.
Shopper	Thank you! Here's my money.
Vendor	You're welcome. Come again!

Below-Level Learners

Materials

- clay, small boxes
- construction paper
- action figures

MARKETPLACE MODEL **Have small groups of children work together to create a model of a marketplace.**

- Organize children into small groups.
- Provide groups with materials to create a model of a marketplace.
- After children make their models, have them add labels to describe the people there and what is happening in the marketplace.
- You may wish to display a list of terms such as *producers, consumers, money, credit card, business, products, goods,* and *services* for children to use in making and labeling their models.
- Invite children to explain their models to the class.

Advanced Learners

Materials

- posterboard
- art materials

PRODUCT PROMOTION **Invite children to make an advertisement poster.**

- Invite children to think of a favorite product or a new invention they would like to sell.
- Have them make a poster showing an advertisement for the product.
- Ask them to make up an interesting name for their product and include a description of how it is used, what it is made of, and why consumers should buy it.
- Encourage children to think of a catchy jingle or slogan to make consumers remember their product.

Assessment Options

The assessment program gives all learners many opportunities to show what they know and can do. It also provides ongoing information about each child's understanding of social studies.

Formal Assessment

- **LESSON REVIEWS:** pp. 275, 279, 283, 289, 297, 303
- **UNIT REVIEWS AND TEST PREPARATION,** pp. 308–311
- **UNIT ASSESSMENT**
  Standard Test
  Assessment Program, pp. 21–23
  Individual Performance Task
  Assessment Program, p. 24

Student Self-Evaluation

- **GEOGRAPHY THEME QUESTIONS** within lessons of Pupil Book
- **INDIVIDUAL END-OF-PROJECT CHECKLIST** Assessment Program, p. viii
- **GROUP END-OF-PROJECT CHECKLIST** Assessment Program, p. ix
- **INDIVIDUAL END-OF-UNIT CHECKLIST** Assessment Program, p. x

Informal Assessment

- **THINK ABOUT IT,** p. 271
- **EXAMINE PRIMARY SOURCES,** p. 292–295
- **SOCIAL STUDIES SKILLS CHECKLIST** Assessment Program, pp. vi–vii
- **SKILLS**
  Practice the Skill, pp. 284, 291, 304
  Apply What You Learned, pp. 285, 291, 305

Performance Assessment

- **PERFORMANCE ACTIVITY** in Lesson Reviews
- **UNIT ACTIVITIES,** p. 312
- **COMPLETE THE UNIT PROJECT,** p. 312
- **INDIVIDUAL PERFORMANCE TASK** Assessment Program, p. 24

Portfolio Assessment

STUDENT SELECTED ITEMS MAY INCLUDE:

- **THINK AND WRITE,** p. 308
- **UNIT ACTIVITIES,** p. 312
- **COMPLETE THE UNIT PROJECT,** p. 312

TEACHER SELECTED ITEMS MAY INCLUDE:

- **UNIT ASSESSMENT**
  Assessment Program, pp. 21–24
- **PORTFOLIO SUMMARY**
  Assessment Program, p. xv
- **GROUP END-OF-PROJECT CHECKLIST**
  Assessment Program, p. ix
- **INDIVIDUAL END-OF-UNIT CHECKLIST**
  Assessment Program, p. x

Unit 6 Test

STANDARD TEST

Unit 6

Name ______________ Date ______________

Test

Vocabulary (5 points each)

Write the correct word or words on each line.

producer	consumer	income
factory	free enterprise	transportation

1. This is where oranges are made into juice.
   factory
2. My parents decided to start their own business.
   free enterprise
3. We buy fresh bread at a bakery every week.
   consumer
4. We use cars, airplanes, and buses to go places.
   transportation
5. Farmers grow corn and sell it to grocery stores.
   producer
6. I earn money by raking leaves for neighbors.
   income

STANDARD TEST

Name ______________ Date ______________

Main Ideas (5 points each)

7. Which of these is a raw material needed to make a bicycle?
   - A factory
   - B metal (filled in)
   - C worker
   - D machine
8. When is a producer who makes bread also a consumer?
   - F when she is paid money for the bread
   - G when she is slicing the bread
   - H when she bakes the bread
   - J when she buys flour to make the bread (filled in)
9. Write three things a person can do with income.
   Possible answers: spend it, donate it, save it
10. Put a check mark (✔) next to each service worker.
    - ✔ teacher
    - ✔ gardener
    - ___ farmer
    - ✔ news reporter

Complete a sentence to explain how each person made transportation better. (10 points each)

11. Amelia Earhart
    tested air travel.
12. Robert Fulton
    improved the steamboat.

NOTES

6

1 2 3 4 5

STANDARD TEST

Name ________________ Date ________

Skills (4 points each)

Follow the flow chart and answer the questions below.

1. Farmers harvest cotton.
2. Trucks take cotton to factory.
3. Cotton is used to make thread and cloth.
4. Machines cut and sew cloth.
5. Clothing is sold in stores.

13. What does this flow chart show about cotton?
Cotton can be used to make cloth.

14. Where does the cotton come from? It grows on a plant.

15. How does the cotton get to the factory?
A truck takes it there.

16. What happens after the cotton is made into cloth?
The cloth is cut and sewn into clothes.

17. What is the last step? The cotton clothes are sold in stores.

STANDARD TEST

Name ________________ Date ________

Performance Task

You have decided to open a lemonade stand. Think about the supplies you will need. Fill in the chart below.

What supplies do I need?	lemons, sugar, water, ice, cups
How will I use them?	I will use the lemons, sugar, and water to make the lemonade. I will use the ice and cups to serve the lemonade.
What might happen if I charge too much for the lemonade?	People might not buy it.
What might happen if I charge too little for the lemonade?	I might not be able to earn enough money to pay for my supplies and make a profit.
How much should a cup of your lemonade cost?	Answers will vary.

RUBRICS FOR SCORING

SCORING RUBRIC The rubric below lists the criteria for evaluating the tasks above. It also describes different levels of success in meeting those criteria.

INDIVIDUAL PERFORMANCE TASK

SCORE 4	SCORE 3	SCORE 2	SCORE 1
▪ Many details are provided.	▪ Some details are provided.	▪ Few details are provided.	▪ No details are provided.
▪ Demonstrates strong understanding of the development of a product.	▪ Demonstrates understanding of the development of a product.	▪ Demonstrates some understanding of the development of a product.	▪ Does not demonstrate understanding of the development of a product.
▪ Economic details are accurate.	▪ Economic details are mostly accurate.	▪ Economic details are sometimes accurate.	▪ Economic details are not accurate.

1 2 3 4 5 6

Introduce the Unit

OBJECTIVES

- Use a visual to predict content.
- Interpret a quotation.
- Use a summary chart to prepare for the unit.

Access Prior Knowledge

Help children make connections between work that people do and products they make and buy. Ask children to name a product that people buy, such as shoes, a bicycle, or bread. Create an *H* chart for the product. In the horizontal area, write the name of the product. On the left side of the chart, write jobs associated with making the product. On the right side, write ways that people are able to get the product.

people make car parts; people put parts together; people sell cars	***car***	people work to earn money; people save money; people borrow money from a bank; people buy the car

Visual Learning

Picture Have children examine the images of the typewriter and workers in an office. Explain that before people used computers in offices, office workers typed letters, bills, and other information on typewriters. Invite volunteers to name other changes in workplaces. Ask children if they would want to work in an office such as the one shown. Encourage them to explain their responses. Have children predict the kinds of jobs they will learn about in this unit.

BACKGROUND

Typewriter First placed on the market in 1874, the typewriter is a machine that produces characters when a steel type strikes paper through an inked ribbon. United States inventor Christopher Sholes developed the first practical typewriter. Electric typewriters came into use in the 1920s. The arrangement of keys on a typewriter keyboard is called "QWERTY," which stands for the first six letters in the top alphabet row of a keyboard.

MAKE IT RELEVANT

At Home Suggest children interview family members about the work they do. Before the interview, have children make a list of questions about the work, such as *How did you choose this type of work? What do you like best about the work? What are some things you do with the money earned from your work?* Invite volunteers to share with the class information they gained from the interviews.

Unit 6

People at Work

"Whatever your life's work is, do it well."

—Dr. Martin Luther King, Jr., in a speech at Montgomery, Alabama, 1956

Summarize

As you read this unit, do the following.

- List main ideas about the work people do and the way they spend their money.
- Summarize what you learned.

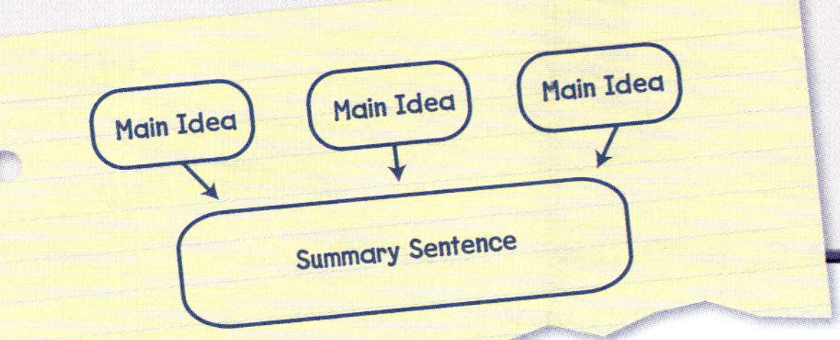

265

Analyze Primary Sources

Typewriter Help children identify the artifact at the beginning of the unit as a typewriter. Explain that the typewriter shown is an antique, meaning that it was made many years ago. Have children compare and contrast the typewriter keyboard with a present-day computer keyboard.

Quotation Invite a volunteer to read the quotation aloud. Tell children that Dr. Martin Luther King, Jr., was an African American minister. His life's work was to try to bring about equal and fair treatment of Americans regardless of their race. He wanted all people to live and work together peacefully.

Q What rewards might come from doing a job well?

A Children may say that they would feel a sense of pride and satisfaction in knowing that they are doing their best work.

Summarize

Point out that using a summary chart can help children keep track of important ideas when they read. Explain that as children read each lesson, they can write the key ideas from the lesson in the *Idea* boxes. After they finish the lesson, children can use the key ideas to write a summary of the lesson.

- A blank graphic organizer appears on page 74 of the Activity Book.
- A completed graphic organizer can be found on page 308 of this Teacher's Edition.

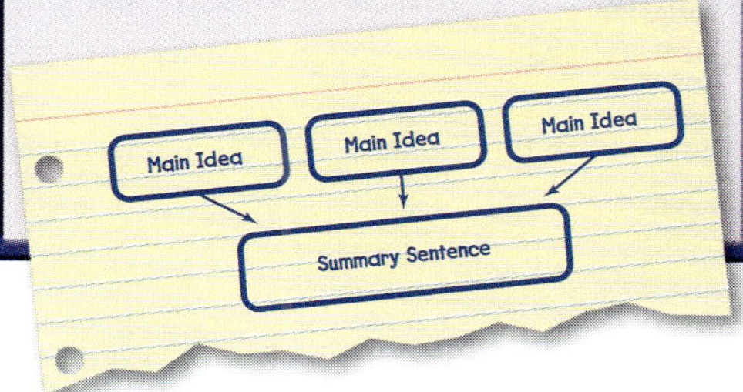

INTEGRATE LANGUAGE ARTS

Write Captions Have children bring to class pictures of people at work in various jobs. Ask them to compare the pictures and organize them according to fields such as *the food industry, health care,* or *child care.* Then have children work in groups to glue related photographs onto one poster and write captions that describe each job.

BACKGROUND

About the Quotation Dr. Martin Luther King, Jr. (1929–1968), became famous in the 1950s and 1960s for his use of nonviolent action to oppose segregation. He helped organize a march on Washington, D.C., in 1963 that drew more than two hundred thousand supporters of civil rights. His famous "I have a dream" speech was delivered at this march. Americans honor King with a national holiday celebrated each January.

AUDIOTEXT

Use the Unit 6 AUDIOTEXT for a reading of the Unit narrative.

Preview the Vocabulary

PAGES 266–267

OBJECTIVES

- Use visuals to determine word meanings.
- Use words and visuals to predict the content of the unit.

Access Prior Knowledge

Ask children to suggest some of the jobs people do in your community. As necessary, stimulate suggestions by asking questions such as, *Who sells food? Who grows food? Who sells clothing? Who repairs automobiles? Who works at the library?* Then elicit from children that people receive money in return for their work. Discuss the kinds of things people buy with the money they earn from working.

Make Connections

Link Pictures and Words Tell children that all the words on these pages have to do with earning and spending money. Ask volunteers to read each word and definition aloud. Then discuss with children how the illustration for that word shows something about earning or spending money.

Visual Learning

Pictures Tell children that the pictures on page 266 tell a story about one woman's small business. Ask children to name the characters and to tell the story aloud.

Preview the Vocabulary

producer A person who makes, grows, or sells goods. (page 277)

income The money people earn for the work they do. (page 286)

free enterprise The freedom to start and run any kind of business. (page 286)

consumer A person who buys and uses goods and services. (page 279)

266

READING SOCIAL STUDIES

Preview the Unit Display the following flow chart. Encourage children to refer to it as they read the unit.

A producer makes or grows goods.
↓
A producer earns income for the work.
↓
A producer uses income to buy goods.
↓
A producer then becomes a consumer.

REACH ALL LEARNERS

English as a Second Language Pair fluent English speakers with children who speak another language. Have children say each word aloud, pronouncing it carefully. Then have the pair discuss the meaning of each word and how the illustration helps make the meaning clear.

Work hard and spend wisely.

factory A building in which people use machines to make goods. (page 282)

transportation Ways of carrying people and goods from one place to another. (page 300)

Visual Learning

Pictures Have children recall the woman making strawberry jam on page 266. Invite them to look at the picture of a factory on page 267. Ask them to compare hand-made goods with factory-made goods.

Point out the picture of the truck.

Q What other ways can goods be moved?

A trains, planes, ships

DEMOCRATIC VALUES

Individual Rights

Have a volunteer read aloud what Earnest says, and discuss it with children. Point out that when people work hard at a job, they feel good about themselves and about the work they have done. They also think carefully about how to spend the money—they try not to waste it. Help children recognize that in the United States there are many opportunities for people to choose the work they do and to spend their earnings freely.

Q What are some wise ways to spend money? What are some unwise ways?

A Rent, food, and clothing are wise ways. Buying a book to read and a toy to play with can be wise purchases, too, but only if you have enough money for the things you need. Unwise spending might include buying things you cannot afford or things you do not really need.

INTEGRATE ART

Make a Poster Have children create a poster showing things people in your community make and things they buy. Draw a line down the center of the poster and label the sides *Things We Make or Grow* and *Things We Buy.* Have children draw or cut from magazines pictures that fit each category. Then have them paste the pictures on the poster in a pleasing arrangement. Display the finished collage in your classroom.

SCHOOL TO HOME

Use the Unit 6 SCHOOL TO HOME NEWSLETTER on pages S11–S12 to introduce the unit to family members and suggest activities they can do at home.

Word Work

The following activities may be used to preteach vocabulary. You may also wish to duplicate and distribute the word cards found in the back of this book on pages V71–V80. Children can use them as flash cards to practice saying and defining each word. Remind children to use the glossary at the back of their books to help them define these words.

CATEGORY QUIZ GAME

Make sets of word cards with vocabulary words that name categories, such as *goods, services, producer, consumer, business, raw materials,* and *products*. Have partners challenge another pair of children to a category game. Model how one partner should read the first word card and the other partner should name examples that fit in that category. Players may give just one example or as many as three. Teams win a point for each correct example.

CLASS TIC-TAC-TOE

Choose nine vocabulary terms to write in the spaces of a tic-tac-toe board on an overhead transparency. Divide the class into two teams, and give each player a word card showing one of the remaining vocabulary words or another key word related to the content of the unit. Have teams alternate turns. To claim a space, one of the players on the team volunteers to show a connection between the word on his or her card and the word in the desired space on the tic-tac-toe board. If the player correctly makes a sentence that includes both words, mark an *O* or *X* for that team over the word used.

goods	services	~~factory~~
business	scarce	trade
income	savings	credit card

raw material

WHAT'S MY WORD?

Have children take turns selecting a vocabulary word card from a basket and giving two clues about the word. The other children guess the word. Suggest that children give one clue about the word's meaning and one clue about the word's spelling or pronunciation. Model clues such as *This word means "to make things." It has four syllables.*

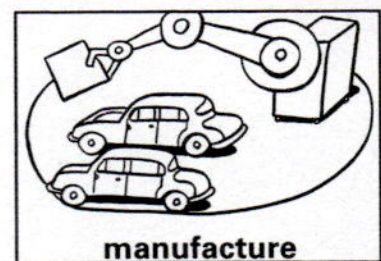

MY PLACE IN THE COMMUNITY

JOURNAL Ask children to record the following words in their journal. Have children draw a picture to illustrate each word or use the words to describe the process that helps people get things that they need and want. Children may choose to describe how one specific product reaches the market.

Start with a Poem

Worksong

Summary

This poem describes many of the jobs that people do and gives examples of ways those jobs affect our lives.

1 Motivate

Set the Purpose

Have children read the title of the poem. Ask them how some poems are like songs. If children do not know, point out that many poems rhyme and have a rhythm or a beat. Explain that people write poems and songs for different reasons—to tell a story, to share a feeling, to honor or thank someone, or just for fun. Have children read to discover why this poem is called "Worksong."

Access Prior Knowledge

Before reading the poem with children, ask them to name a job they would like to have when they grow up. Then ask them to share reasons why they would like that particular job.

OBJECTIVES

- Obtain information about a topic using a variety of visual sources, such as literature.
- Recognize the variety of jobs that people do.
- Explain how people depend on one another in their daily lives.

RESOURCES

- Pupil Book/Unit Big Book, pp. 268–271
- Reading and Vocabulary Transparency 6–1
- Internet Resources
- Audiotext, Unit 6

READING SOCIAL STUDIES

Graphic Organizer Ask children to suggest occupations that fit into each category on the table below. Write children's suggestions in the appropriate column. As children read, have them identify jobs noted in the poem that are not included in either list. Add those jobs as children point them out.

Outdoor Jobs	Indoor Jobs
Construction worker	Teacher
Crossing guard	Store clerk
Park ranger	Factory worker
Horse trainer	Secretary

USE READING AND VOCABULARY TRANSPARENCY 6–1.

2 Teach

Read and Respond

Understand the Poem Read aloud the first stanza of the poem with children. Discuss the meaning of *It* in the first line. Lead children to see that *It* refers to the many kinds of work people do. Challenge children to identify as many jobs as they can that fit the descriptions in the first stanza. Help them understand that carpenters, mechanics, plumbers, and others use hammers in their work; carpenters, plumbers, electricians, roofers, masons, and others build houses; gardeners, farmers, foresters, and nursery workers plant and care for trees; and truck drivers and delivery people work behind the wheel of a truck.

Then read aloud the next two stanzas. Ask children to identify the workers involved in providing food, building and cleaning sidewalks, building skyscrapers, working in offices, and making steel beams.

Q What kinds of choices can people in our country make about work?

A Children's responses should explain that Americans are free to choose the work they do and how they do it.

Visual Learning

Illustrations Focus children's attention on the illustrations on pages 269 and 270.

Q Which workers need safety equipment?

A steel workers, carpenter

Q Which worker is wearing a uniform?

A nurse

Children who are familiar with this book may note that not all the illustrations are shown here. Encourage them to match illustrations with text. Invite children to visualize unillustrated text. You may wish to assign volunteers to illustrate some additional scenes.

START with a POEM

GARY PAULSEN WORK SONG ILLUSTRATED BY RUTH WRIGHT PAULSEN

WORK

by Gary Paulsen
illustrated by Ruth Wright Paulsen

It is keening noise and jolting sights,
and hammers flashing in the light,
and houses up and trees in sun,
and trucks on one more nighttime run.

268

BACKGROUND

About the Author Gary Paulsen was born in 1939 in Minneapolis, Minnesota. His interest in books began one very cold day when he went to the library to keep warm. Paulsen held many kinds of jobs before he became a writer, including carnival hand, migrant farm worker, truck driver, soldier, field engineer, ranch hand, and magazine editor. He lives in New Mexico with his wife, Ruth, who sometimes illustrates his books.

WORD WORK

Unfamiliar Words Point out the words *keening* and *jolting* in the first line of the poem. Explain that *keening* means "wailing" and that *jolting* means "in a sudden, jerky way." Discuss how the poet uses these words to help the reader see, feel, and hear the patterns of work he is describing.

SONG

It is fresh new food
to fill the plates,
and flat, clean sidewalks
to try to skate,
and towering buildings
that were not there,
hanging suddenly
in the air.

It is offices filled with glowing screens
and workers making steel beams,
and ice-cream cones to lick and wear,
and all the pins that hold your hair.

269

Read and Respond

Economics Discuss reasons besides earning money that people might have for doing a job. Point out that people often enjoy their work, they like contributing to society, and they enjoy staying busy. Explain that people who enjoy their work are usually successful at what they do.

Q What are some ways workers contribute to society?

A Children should be able to name jobs and tell why those jobs are important to people in society. For example, firefighters help keep people safe, farmers provide food that people eat, and doctors help keep people healthy.

INTEGRATE READING

Books About Jobs Ask the school librarian to help children find books about jobs, such as *Mole and Shrew Have Jobs to Do* by Jackie French Koller (Random House, 2001) or *Fox on the Job* by James Marshall (Puffin, 1995). Invite children to report to the class about the book they read.

INTERNET RESOURCES

Go to **www.harcourtschool.com** for economic problem-solving activities.

REACH ALL LEARNERS

Tactile Learners Place a selection of simple tools in a large bag. You might include: pen, paintbrush (large and small), tape measure, cell phone, stethoscope, wrench, hammer, badge, computer mouse, spade, wooden spoon. Invite children to reach into the bag without looking and bring out a tool. Ask them to describe someone who might use the tool in his or her job.

Read and Respond

Understand the Poem Continue reading the poem and discussing what the lines mean. Then tell children that people do not get paid for all the work that they do. Point out examples, such as parents cooking meals for their families, children sharing in household chores or doing tasks in the classroom, and family members and friends helping one another with projects.

Q How do you think the mother and father in the poem feel about their work?

A They look forward to their work because it helps them provide for the needs of people they love.

Q Why do you think Gary Paulsen wrote the poem "Worksong"?

A He wanted to tell a story about people working; he wanted to thank workers for making life better for everyone.

3 Close

Summarize the Reading

- People do many kinds of work.
- Workers make many things we have and share and see.
- After the workday, people rest with loved ones and prepare to work another day.

READING SOCIAL STUDIES

Graphic Organizer Review with children the table you created at the beginning of the lesson. Invite children to suggest jobs they can add after reading the poem.

Outdoor Jobs	Indoor Jobs
Construction worker Crossing guard Park ranger Horse trainer Gardener Farmer Firefighter	Teacher Store clerk Factory worker Secretary Doctor Nurse

USE READING AND VOCABULARY TRANSPARENCY 6-1.

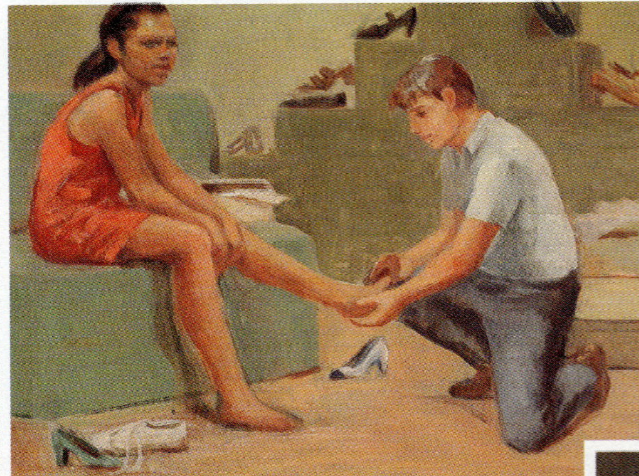

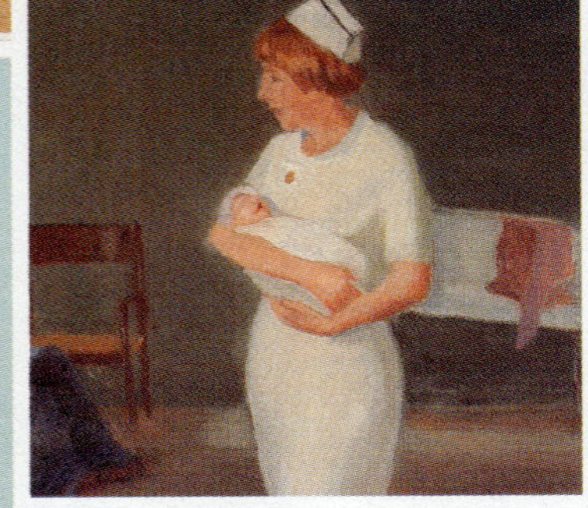

It's gentle arms that lift and hold,
and all the soldiers brave and bold,
and help to fit the brand-new shoes,
and hands to show you books to use.

It is people here and people there,
making things for all to share;
all the things there are to be,
and nearly all there is to see.

270

READING SOCIAL STUDIES

Use Picture Clues Encourage children to use clues in the pictures to help them understand the meaning of the poem.

INTEGRATE HEALTH

Time to Rest Remind children that the mother and father in the poem rest after a long day's work. Explain that all animals, including people, need rest, and that sleep is necessary for the brain as well as the body. Point out that most children between the ages of 5 and 12 need 8 to 10 hours of sleep each night, or more. If people don't get enough sleep, they may be cranky and have trouble paying attention. People can also get sick if they don't get enough rest.

And when the day is paid and done,
and all the errands have been run,
it's mother, father in a chair,
with tired eyes and loosened hair.
Resting short but loving long,
resting for the next day's song.

Think About It

1. How do farmers and truck drivers depend on one another?
2. Write a job description for a job that interests you.

Read a Book

Start the Unit Project

Career Day Your class will plan a Career Day to find out about different jobs. As you read this unit, think about the kind of work people do and what interests you.

Use Technology

Visit The Learning Site at **www.harcourtschool.com** for additional activities, primary sources, and other resources to use in this unit.

271

Think About It

Answers

1. Farmers need truck drivers to deliver the food they grow to market. Truck drivers need customers, such as farmers, so that they can earn money.
2. Children's answers should indicate an awareness of what is involved in performing the job and why the job interests them.

AUDIOTEXT

Use the Unit 6 AUDIOTEXT for a reading of the Unit poem.

Read a Book

Children may enjoy reading these leveled independent Readers. Additional books are listed on pages 265J–265K of this Teacher's Edition.

Easy *Goods Around the World* by Susan Ring. This book tells about the many things we buy that have come from other countries.

Average *The Mint* by Susan Ring. Learn about the jobs of workers at the United States Mint as well as the process of making coins.

Challenging *Robert Fulton* by Susan Ring. Learn about the man who invented the first commercially successful steamboat.

Start the Unit Project

Hint Before children begin the Unit Project, suggest they look over Preview the Content on page 265. As children read each lesson, encourage them to make a list of jobs that interest them and to find out about the tools and skills needed to do each job.

Use Technology

THE LEARNING SITE

Go to **www.harcourtschool.com** to view Internet resources for this unit.

Go to **www.harcourtschool.com** for the latest news in a student-friendly format.

Extension Activities For Home and School

Career Day

Materials: paper, pencils, markers

Arrange a date for a Job Fair. Have children invite family members and friends to come and talk to the class about the work they do. Help children prepare for the event by making a list of questions they might like to ask the visitors about their work. Tell children that they may ask only questions they have prepared ahead of time. This should prevent problems that might arise from embarrassing or personal questions being asked of the visitors. Following the Job Fair activities, discuss the different jobs with children and ask them to tell which jobs sounded most interesting to them and why. Then have children write thank-you notes to send to each visitor. Encourage them to make drawings on each note that show something about the job the person described.

(VISUAL/AUDITORY)

Thank you for telling our class what you do and how we can stay healthy.

Book Reports

Materials: selection of books, paper, pencils

Assemble a selection of fiction and nonfiction books that relate in some way to jobs or working. For example, you might choose *The Piñata Maker/El Piñatero* by George Ancona (Harcourt, 1994), *Mr. Griggs' Work* by Cynthia Rylant (Orchard, 1993), *Bruno the Baker* by Lars Klinting (Henry Holt, 1997), *Riding the Ferry with Captain Cruz* by Alice K. Flanagan (Children's Press, 1997), and *What Do Authors Do?* by Eileen Christelow (Houghton Mifflin, 1997). Help children select a book that interests them and that is at an appropriate reading level. Then invite children to take their books home and read them with a family member. Encourage children to get help and support from that family member as they write a short book report that describes the characters in the book, tells what happens, and explains what the child thought about the book. Ask volunteers to bring their reports to school and share them with the class.

(VISUAL/AUDITORY)

Related Jobs Mural

Materials: long strip of butcher paper, markers, magazines, scissors, glue

Discuss the way people in communities depend on one another to do jobs and provide services. Then discuss how some jobs are related to others. As an example, begin with the work a farmer does. Then explain that a truck driver takes the farmer's produce to market. The market owner sells the produce to many consumers, including a restaurant owner. The restaurant owner uses the produce to make food for customers to eat. Have children use this example or another of their own choosing and create a mural showing the way the jobs are connected. Have them divide the mural paper into panels. Small groups can draw scenes showing each job. Then the panels can be reassembled and displayed on a wall in your room.

(VISUAL/TACTILE)

LESSON 1

Goods and Services

OBJECTIVES

- Distinguish between goods and services.
- Identify people who provide goods and services to the community.

Summarize pp. 265, 275, 308

RESOURCES

Pupil Book/Unit Big Book, pp. 272–275

Word Cards V71–V72

Activity Book, p. 65

Reading and Vocabulary Transparency 6-2

Internet Resources

READING SOCIAL STUDIES

Graphic Organizer Have children make two word webs—one labeled *goods* and the other *services*. Then ask *Does a teacher provide goods or services?* Have children record the word *teacher* on one of their webs. Repeat by naming other goods and people who provide services. Have children save their webs for use at the end of the lesson.

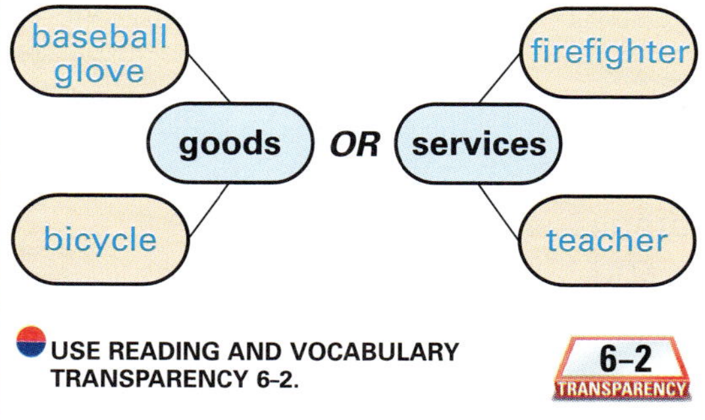

USE READING AND VOCABULARY TRANSPARENCY 6-2.

6-2 TRANSPARENCY

Vocabulary

goods p. 272 **services** p. 274

When Minutes Count

Direct children to examine the pictures in the lesson. Have them predict what they think is the Big Idea of the lesson. Encourage them to read the lesson to find out if they were correct.

Quick Summary

This lesson focuses on goods and services and on the people in communities who provide them.

1 Motivate

Set the Purpose

Big Idea Have a volunteer read aloud the Big Idea statement before children begin the lesson. Then, as children read and discuss the lesson, encourage them to think about goods and services they use or depend on every week.

Access Prior Knowledge

Have children name things that they can buy in a store. Then ask children to give examples of stores that would sell each item that they named.

2 Teach

Read and Respond

Economics Read aloud pages 272 and 273. Focus on one or two examples and expand the discussion by asking questions such as these: *Who makes the fabric that the sewer uses to make the clothing? Who are some other people who help in getting clothing to your closet?* Lead children to see that all sorts of workers are involved in making clothing, including people who make the sewing machines that sewers use, and so on.

Share with children some of the job requirements you have as a teacher. Then point out the workers in the pictures on pages 272 and 273. Ask children to think of some job requirements these workers may have.

Q What do you think the cashier needs to know to do his job?

A He needs to know how much the books cost and how to count money.

Point out that people have different ways of learning the skills they need to do a good job. Some people go to colleges or universities; some learn what they need while working; some take special classes to become better skilled.

Explain to children how you know you've done a good job as a teacher. Remind children that they too have a job at school. Their job is to learn.

Q How do you know when you've done a good job at school?

A I finish my class work; I get good grades.

Invite children to discuss how other workers know they've performed their work well.

Visual Learning

Pictures Ask children what the pictures on this page show and which goods they own or use.

Q How would your lives be different without these goods?

A We wouldn't have books to read, food to eat, or clothes to wear.

Lesson 1

Goods and Services

Big Idea
Everyone depends on people who provide goods and services.

Vocabulary
goods
services

In "Worksong" you met many people with different kinds of jobs. You depend on people like these every day. Some workers, such as the grocer, the shoe seller, and the steelmaker, provide goods. **Goods** are things that can be bought and sold.

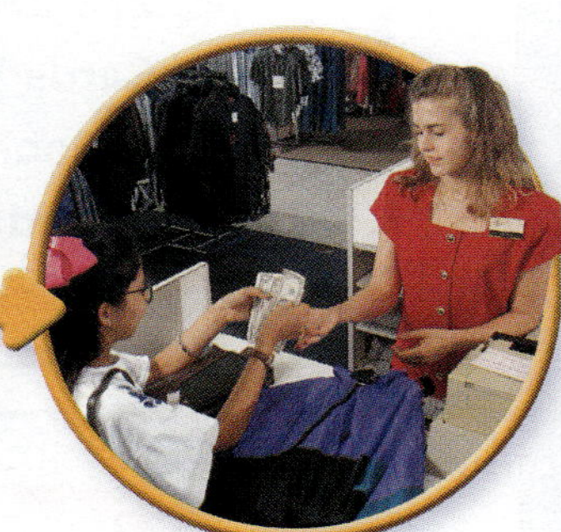

QUESTIONS KIDS ASK

Q Why don't the people who make a product sell it too?

A Sometimes they do, such as people at a farmers' market. Usually, though, it is too much work to make something and run a store to sell it. Also, some people who are good at making things aren't so good at selling them, and some people who are good at selling things don't know how to make them.

MENTAL MAPPING

Stores in the Neighborhood Ask children to think about an area near their home or school and about the stores on those blocks. Then have children draw simple maps showing all the stores they remember. Encourage children to compare their finished maps with the real streets and add any stores they forgot.

Think about the things you use every day. Some workers grow or make these goods and others sell them.

Stores are places where people can buy all kinds of goods. What goods can you buy in your community?

273

Visual Learning

Pictures Identify and discuss the stores shown on page 273. Ask which of these kinds of stores children included on their mental maps. Invite children to name things that might be sold in each of the stores. Extend the discussion by asking where the goods children mentioned come from.

Q **How do stores help people?**

A They gather goods from many places and sell them under one roof, so people do not have to travel around to buy what they want or need.

Read and Respond

Economics Lead children in a discussion about workers in the community that supply people's daily needs. Help children differentiate between the workers who produce and process the things they need and the workers who distribute the products.

Link Economics with Civics and Government Explain to children that our government provides citizens with services such as police protection, fire protection, an educational system, and garbage collection. To pay for these important services, the government collects taxes from citizens.

REACH ALL LEARNERS

English as a Second Language Brainstorm with children kinds of stores in your community, such as grocery store, department store, bookstore, and bakery. Write these words on the board, and have children read them aloud with you. Ask children to write the name of each store at the top of a page. Then have them cut out magazine pictures that show goods that might be sold in the store. Have them glue the pictures onto the correct pages.

INTEGRATE MATHEMATICS

What Do Stores Earn? Remind children that stores have to buy the goods they sell. Point out that in order for stores to earn money, they have to charge more for a product than they paid for it. Read the following word problems to children and ask them to figure out how much the store earns. *The Apple Store pays the farmer 20¢ each for apples. Then it sells the apples for 30¢ each. How much does the Apple Store earn for each apple it sells?* (10¢) *How much does the Apple Store earn if it sells 5 apples?* (50¢) *If it sells 10 apples?* (100¢ or $1.00) *If you had 75¢, how many apples could you buy?* (2 apples)

Read and Respond

Economics Discuss with children the difference between goods and services. Tell them that goods are things you can hold in your hands, such as an orange or a yo-yo, while services are those things we pay other people to do for us, such as clean the streets and deliver our mail. Encourage children to name workers in your community who provide services. You may want to ask questions such as the following: *Who cuts your hair? Who puts out fires? Who repairs cars? Who treats you when you are sick?*

Q **Why do we pay people to provide services?**

A We pay people because they do something we don't know how to do or don't have time to do.

Economics Explain to children that markets are places where people can buy and sell goods and services. Point out that a store is one kind of market. Have children tell about markets they have been in, such as a farmer's market, a supermarket, or a mall. Encourage volunteers to give examples of markets for various goods and services.

Culture and Society Explain to children that advances in technology help doctors and nurses perform their jobs better. With these advances, the health care profession is able to treat more illnesses and make people's lives healthier and longer.

Visual Learning

Pictures Have children describe what the people in the pictures are doing. Invite volunteers to tell about experiences they have had with the service providers shown in the pictures.

In "Worksong" you also met many people who provide services. A **service** is work done by others for pay. The construction worker, the truck driver, and the nurse provide services. What services can you buy in your community?

274

INTEGRATE LANGUAGE ARTS

Advertisement Have children think of a make-believe service company. Then have them write a newspaper advertisement telling why people should do business with the company. Encourage children to design the advertisement as it might look in a newspaper, adding a logo or other visual features.

EXTEND AND ENRICH

Goods and Services Have children work with a partner. Ask each pair of children to make a chart with two columns. Have them label one column *Goods* and the other *Services*. Each pair of children should fill in the chart with the goods and services produced/provided in their community and state.

LESSON 1
Review

Focus Skill ❶ **Summarize** How do you depend on people in your community?

❷ **Vocabulary** What is the difference between **goods** and **services**?

❸ Interview your neighbors about their work. Make a table showing which ones provide goods and which ones provide services.

275

3 Close

Summarize Key Content

- Some workers provide goods, which are things that can be bought or sold.
- Stores are places where people can buy goods.
- Some workers provide services, or work that is done for payment.

READING SOCIAL STUDIES

Graphic Organizer Have children add to the webs they began earlier.

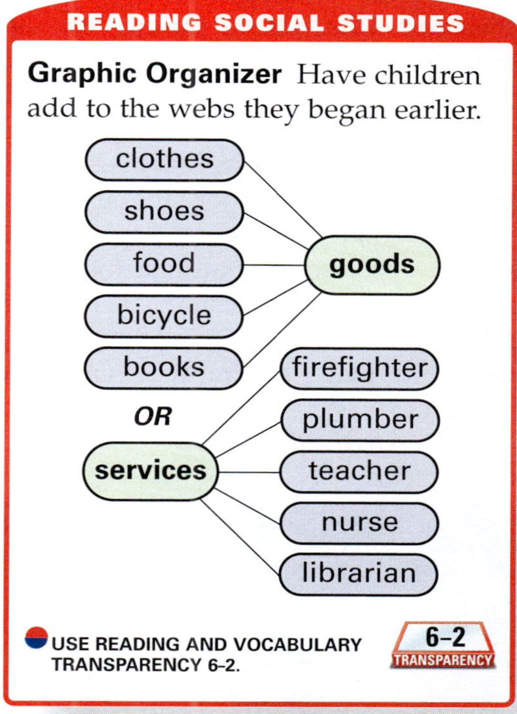

USE READING AND VOCABULARY TRANSPARENCY 6-2.

6-2 TRANSPARENCY

RETEACH THE LESSON

Sort Pictures Provide many pictures of goods and services. Have children sort the pictures into the two categories and explain how they decided where to put each picture.

ACTIVITY BOOK

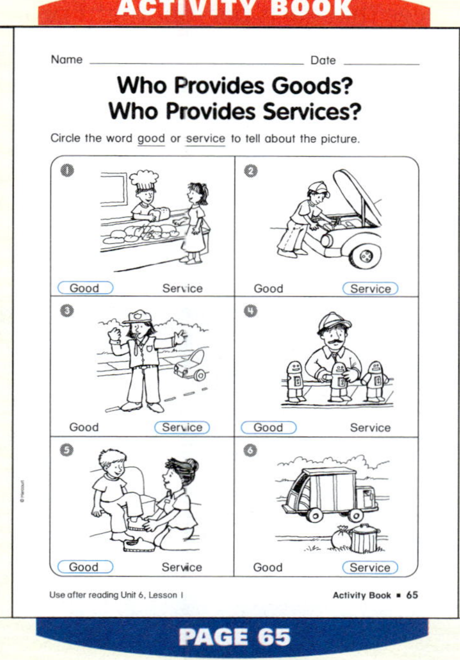

Name ____________ Date ______

Who Provides Goods?
Who Provides Services?

Circle the word good or service to tell about the picture.

❶ Good Service	❷ Good Service
❸ Good Service	❹ Good Service
❺ Good Service	❻ Good Service

Use after reading Unit 6, Lesson 1 — Activity Book ▪ 65

PAGE 65

Assess

Lesson 1 Review—Answers

❶ Focus Skill **Summarize** Children's responses should indicate an awareness of how people in the community depend on one another to provide goods and services.

❷ Goods are things that are made or grown. Services are jobs people do for others for money.

❸

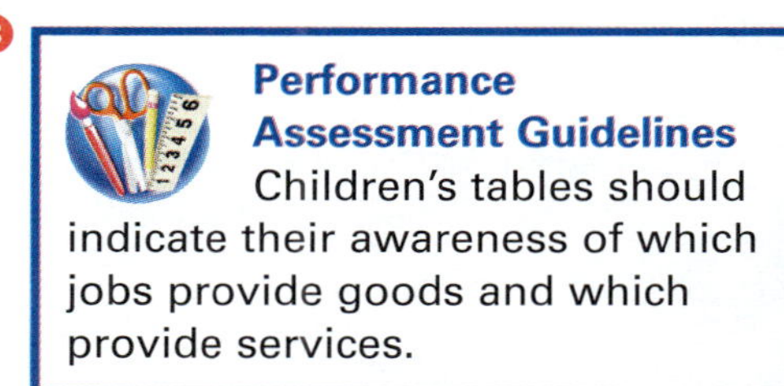

Performance Assessment Guidelines Children's tables should indicate their awareness of which jobs provide goods and which provide services.

Extension Activities For Home and School

Class Community

Materials: shoe boxes with lids, construction paper, scissors, crayons or markers, magazines, found objects, glue

Have children build a class community. First, as a class, have children brainstorm the kinds of stores and services they would like to include in their community. Write the suggestions on the board and then choose four or five stores and three or four services for children to work with. Arrange children in groups and assign one of the selected stores or services to each. Have groups use the shoe box and materials to create a model of their business. Ask them to cover the box with construction paper and then cut a "door" in the lid of the box. Around the door, they might draw signs, windows, displays, and so forth. Inside the box, have them draw or place cutouts and found objects to show what is happening inside the store or business. When the interior is completed, have children replace the lid on the box. Finally, have all groups arrange their boxes to simulate a downtown area. Invite children to walk around, looking inside each of the buildings.
(VISUAL/KINESTHETIC/TACTILE)

Goods and Services Game

Materials: index cards

Prepare a set of game cards. On individual index cards, write the names of people who provide goods or services. For example, you might have cards reading *grocer, bookseller, department store clerk, plumber,* and *baseball coach.* On a separate set of cards, write at least two goods or services that each person might provide. For example, for *department store clerk,* you might have cards reading *shoes* and *sweater.* Have volunteers each choose one card from the first set and then stand at the front of the room. Distribute the goods and services cards among the remaining children. Have them locate the children in the first group who have the cards naming the providers of their goods or services. Repeat the activity, with different children holding job cards, as time permits.
(VISUAL)

grocer

orange juice

cheese

Producers and Consumers

OBJECTIVES

- Distinguish between producing and consuming.
- Identify ways in which people are both producers and consumers.
- Recognize what is needed to run a business.

Summarize pp. 265, 276, 308

RESOURCES

Pupil Book/Unit Big Book, pp. 276–279

Word Cards V71–V74

Activity Book, p. 66

Reading and Vocabulary Transparency 6-3

Internet Resources

READING SOCIAL STUDIES

Anticipation Guide Ask children to predict which of the following statements are true and which are false. Children may correct their predictions as they read.

1. A business can make goods or sell services. true
2. Producers make goods. true
3. Consumers provide services. false
4. A person can be both a producer and a consumer. true

USE READING AND VOCABULARY TRANSPARENCY 6-3.

Vocabulary

business p. 276 **producer** p. 277 **consumer** p. 279

When Minutes Count

Have children examine the pictures on pages 276–279. Use the pictures to discuss the Big Idea in the lesson.

Quick Summary

This lesson uses imaginary student entrepreneurs to focus on people who produce goods and services and on the consumers who buy them. It illustrates how people can be both producers and consumers.

1 Motivate

Set the Purpose

Big Idea Read aloud the Big Idea statement. Then paraphrase it: Businesses need both people who make things and people who buy things. As children read, encourage them to think about people who are producers and consumers in your community.

Access Prior Knowledge

Have children who have made a lemonade stand or engaged in some similar enterprise tell about the experience.

2 Teach

Read and Respond

Economics Read aloud pages 276 and 277. Invite children to give examples of businesses in your community as well as large, national businesses that they know about. Discuss the fact that businesses must provide quality goods and services if they want to make money. Explain that if a business does not keep its customers happy, the customers will stop using that business. If that happens, the business will probably have to close.

Then discuss the business that the children in the story are planning. Invite volunteers to tell in their own words why the children in the story are producers. Help children realize that they are producers because they are making things to sell.

 **Are the producers in the story providing goods or services to sell? Explain your answer.**

A The children in the story are providing goods to sell. They are making office supplies.

Explain to children that what people want to buy influences what businesses will produce and sell. Point out that the supply of products is affected by the demand from consumers or buyers. Businesses watch what consumers buy, and they produce those goods.

Lesson 2

Producers and Consumers

Big Idea
Businesses need both producers and consumers.

Vocabulary
business
producer
consumer

My class needed money for a field trip. We decided to start a business. A **business** is an activity in which people make or sell goods or provide services.

We decided we would make and sell goods. We liked the idea of office supplies. Everyone offered ideas. Warren suggested we paint interesting rocks to make paperweights.

276

Focus Skill — READING SKILL

Summarize Create a concept web to answer the question *Why do businesses need producers and consumers?* After each page of the lesson is read, stop to add new concepts to the web. At the end of the lesson, have children use the web to write a sentence summarizing the lesson.

WORD WORK

Suffixes The vocabulary words in this lesson all end with a suffix: *-er* or *-ness.* Tell children that the suffix *-er* means "someone who" and the suffix *-ness* means "a state or way of being." Explain that children can use the knowledge of these suffixes to figure out the meanings of the words: *producer* means "someone who produces," *consumer* means "someone who consumes," and *business* means "a state of being busy."

READING SOCIAL STUDIES

Use Context Clues Review with children that they can use clues surrounding an unfamiliar word to help them figure out the meaning of that word. Point out the word *supplies* in the text. Ask children to identify context clues that might help them figure out the meaning of this word. Children might point out each of the resources children in the lesson will use.

Judy knew how to decorate wooden clothespins to hold papers. Linsey showed us how to glue pretty scraps of paper to cardboard to make bookmarks.

Everyone in the class became a producer. **Producers** make the goods or provide the services people buy in a community.

Visual Learning

Pictures Discuss the pictures on pages 276 and 277. Ask volunteers to identify what individual children in the pictures are producing. Discuss how visual clues in the pictures can help readers figure out the meanings of unfamiliar words in the surrounding text, as well as the meaning of the text in general. Ask children to point out examples of clues in the pictures that help them better understand what is being described in the text.

Q Which of the products shown on this page might you be interested in buying? Why?

A Children might suggest that if they had a pretty paperweight, their desk at home might be neater. A colorful bookmark would be useful too, because they know they should never bend down the corner of a page in a book, especially not a library book.

REACH ALL LEARNERS

Auditory Learners Arrange children in small groups to play a guessing game. Each child will think of a product and then give the others clues to help them guess the product. For example, a child might give the following clues: *I am red on the outside and white on the inside. I am crunchy and sweet. I am a fruit. People like to eat me. What am I?* Once the other children have guessed that the product is an apple, the next child can take a turn describing a product.

MAKE IT RELEVANT

In Your School and Community Discuss fund-raising events your school or community has been involved with. Elicit from children whether the fund-raiser provided goods or services in order to raise money. For example, if children sold wrapping-paper kits, they were providing goods, whereas if they sold car washes, they were providing a service.

INTEGRATE READING

Lemonade for Sale Read with children *Lemonade for Sale* by Stuart J. Murphy (Scott Foresman, 1998). This, too, is a fictional story about children who start a business. Like the children who make school supplies, the children who open a lemonade stand need the money for a reason. As you read, stop periodically to ask children how the two stories are similar and different.

Read and Respond

Economics Read aloud pages 278 and 279; then have children tell in their own words what is happening in the story. Discuss what makes a person a consumer. Then have volunteers tell about times when they have been consumers.

Q When is the child telling the story a producer? When is he or she a consumer?

A The child is a producer when he or she makes office supplies. The child is a consumer when he or she buys the picture frame.

Point out that the children in the story had to price the office supplies they produced before they could sell them. Ask children to think about things they like to buy. Then have them share examples of how much they have paid for a new toy or an ice cream cone. Explain that the price of goods and services is determined by the interaction between buyers and sellers. When an item is in demand—meaning more people want to buy it—the price is increased. When an item is not in demand the price is typically lowered.

Q What do you think would happen if the children in the story lowered the prices on the items toward the end of the day?

A They would probably sell all of their office supplies.

Explain to children that prices also influence how much of an item people will buy.

Q Why do you think people buy more when prices are low?

A Because people can afford to buy more when prices are low; people might buy more than one of the same item and use one now, saving the other one for a later time.

After we produced the goods, we were ready to sell them. We set out the office supplies and decided on prices. Then we invited our families and friends to come and shop.

278

MAKE IT RELEVANT

In Your Community Put children into groups based on the neighborhoods they live in. Ask children to think about the people who live in their neighborhoods. Have them predict what the needs and wants of these consumers are. Have each group of children write down the needs and wants and share them with the class.

EXTEND AND ENRICH

Research and Report Ask children to take a survey of 10 people to learn what most of them buy on a weekly basis. Have children record their findings in a list and then write a paragraph explaining what they learned about consumers' buying habits.

Warren's mother was the first to buy. She bought a paperweight. She was a consumer. A **consumer** buys goods or services. We are all consumers.

My classmate Lisa had made a picture frame. I thought it might look good with a picture of my cat Goldie in it. So I bought the picture frame. Now you can call me a producer *and* a consumer!

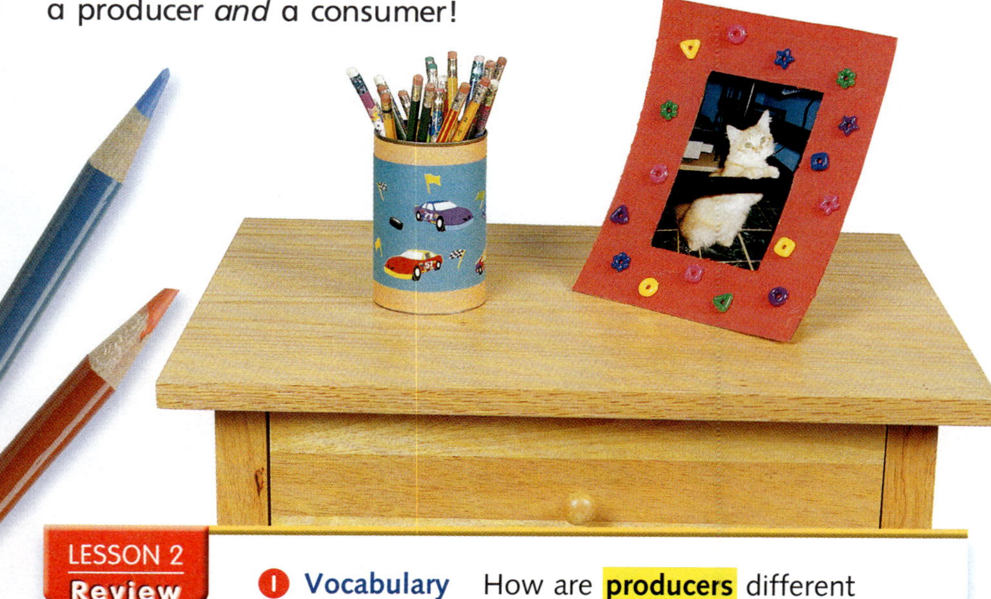

LESSON 2 Review

1. **Vocabulary** How are **producers** different from **consumers**?
2. Explain how you can be both a producer and a consumer.
3. Write a paragraph telling what you think makes a business successful.

3 Close

Summarize Key Content

- Children decided to start a business by making office supplies.
- The children in the class became producers.
- Consumers bought the office supplies the children made.

READING SOCIAL STUDIES

Anticipation Guide Have children check their answers to the anticipation guide at the beginning of the lesson.

1. A business can make goods or sell services. true
2. Producers make goods. true
3. Consumers provide services. false Consumers buy goods and services.
4. A person can be both a producer and a consumer. true

USE READING AND VOCABULARY TRANSPARENCY 6-3.

Assess

Lesson 2 Review—Answers

1. Producers make or sell things. Consumers buy the things that producers make or sell.
2. Anyone who works is a producer, because he or she is providing either goods or a service. Producers are consumers when they use the money they earn to buy the things they need or want, such as food and clothing.
3. 
   Performance Assessment Guidelines Children's paragraphs should indicate an awareness that successful businesses provide a good product or service at a reasonable price. They should also note that to be successful, a business needs to make a profit.

RETEACH THE LESSON

Make a Consumer List Have children make a list of four things they would like to buy. Then, have them write the name of a business where they could purchase each item. Finally, have them list at least two producers (such as the salesperson, the grower, or the manufacturer) for each item on their list.

ACTIVITY BOOK

Name ______ Date ______

Producers and Consumers

In each row, draw a picture to show what happens next. Then write P under the pictures of producers and C under the pictures of consumers.

66 • Activity Book — Use after reading Unit 6, Lesson 2.

PAGE 66

Extension Activities For Home and School

What a Production!

Materials: paper, pencils, markers or crayons, drawing paper

Tell children that it is now their turn to create a business. First, brainstorm reasons your class might need to earn money. Then have children discuss goods or services they would like to sell. For example, they might sell potted plants, baked goods, or used books, or they might wash cars, walk dogs, or weed gardens.

When children have decided on a purpose for their project and a way to earn the money to pay for it, have them plan how to operate their class business. For example, all children might participate in creating the products or providing the services. Then children might form groups to advertise the product or service, coordinate sales, and solicit parent and community involvement.

After children carry out the project, help them use the proceeds from sales in the way they planned. Discuss the various relationships between producers and consumers that children experienced during the project.
(VISUAL/AUDITORY/TACTILE/KINESTHETIC)

Chain Game

Materials: index cards

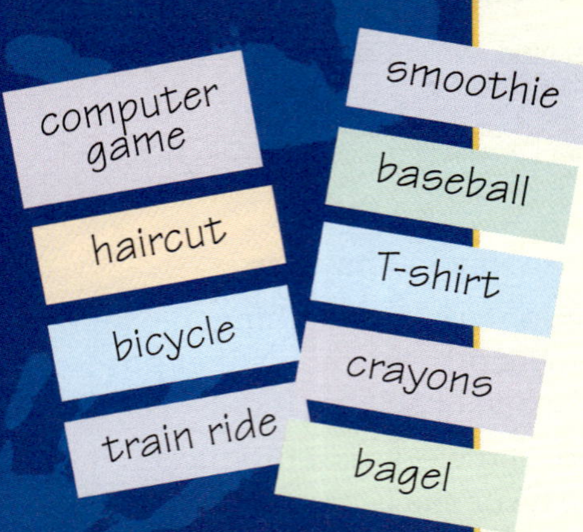

Before class, prepare a set of game cards. On a number of index cards equal to the number of children in your class, write goods or services children might be interested in. For example, you might have cards reading *computer game, haircut, bicycle, train ride,* and *smoothie.* Have each child choose a card, and then arrange the class in large groups. Start the game in each group by saying, "I am a consumer when I buy ______." Then point to one member of the group and have that child read what is on his or her card—*smoothie,* for example. Use *smoothie* to complete your sentence. Then have that child repeat the process, saying, "I produce smoothies, but I am a consumer when I buy ______." The child will then point to another who will fill in the blank and begin the process again. Have children continue the game until all group members have had a turn. As time allows, rearrange groups and repeat the activity.
(AUDITORY)

Produce/Consumer

Materials: mail order catalogs and newspaper advertisements, markers, drawing paper, glue, scissors

Have children and a family member look through catalogs or newspaper advertisements for an interesting product and cut out a picture of the item. Next, have children glue their cut-out pictures onto the top of a page of drawing paper that has a line drawn down the middle. Beneath the picture, on the left-hand side of the page, ask children to draw a scene showing how the product might have been produced. Encourage children and the family member to brainstorm ideas for the drawing. Then, on the right-hand side, have them draw a picture showing the product being used by a consumer. Invite volunteers to bring their drawings to school to share with the class and describe what is shown on the page.
(VISUAL/TACTILE)

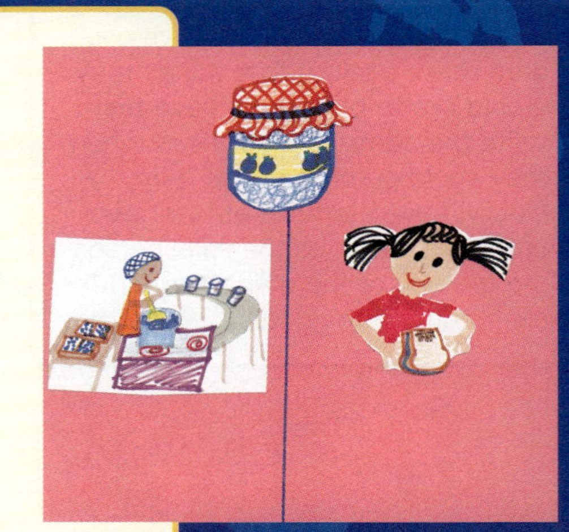

LESSON 3

A Visit to a Factory

OBJECTIVES

- Identify three kinds of resources needed to produce goods.
- Describe the jobs of factory workers.
- Recognize that technology affects the way people work.

Focus Skill **Summarize** pp. 265, 283, 308

RESOURCES

Pupil Book/Unit Big Book, pp. 280–283

Word Cards V73–V74

Activity Book, p. 67

Reading and Vocabulary Transparency 6-4

Internet Resources

READING SOCIAL STUDIES

Make a Prediction To help prepare children for the lesson, ask them to scan the lesson to predict the kinds of resources that are used to produce canned tomato products. Have children write their predictions before they begin to read.

Guess	Check
tomatoes cans	

USE READING AND VOCABULARY TRANSPARENCY 6-4.

Vocabulary

raw material p. 281 **factory** p. 282 **manufacture** p. 283

When Minutes Count

Have children read the Big Idea of the lesson. Then have them read the lesson and find at least one sentence that supports the Big Idea.

Quick Summary

This lesson focuses on a tomato canning factory. It describes the many people and machines involved in providing manufactured goods for sale.

1 Motivate

Set the Purpose

Big Idea Have a volunteer read aloud the Big Idea statement. Review that resources are things needed to make other things. Three important resources are raw materials, workers, and machines. Tell children to look for examples of these resources as they read about a tomato canning factory.

Access Prior Knowledge

Ask children to look around the classroom and at one another and tell what things they see that were made in a factory. Children should soon realize that almost everything they use, including the clothes they wear and the food they eat, is made in a factory.

Extension Activities For Home and School

Plan a Factory

Materials: **paper, pencils, markers or crayons, drawing paper**

Arrange children in small groups. Have them brainstorm a new and unusual product they think people would like to buy. For example, they might think of canned peanut butter and jelly sandwiches or super-soft soccer balls. Then have the groups plan a factory to manufacture their product. Ask them to identify the types of raw materials, workers, and machines the factory would need. Then have them draw pictures to show the manufacturing process and the final product. Have each group appoint a spokesperson to present its ideas to the class.
(VISUAL/AUDITORY/TACTILE/KINESTHETIC)

Division of Labor

Materials: **poster board, labels, colored markers, clipboards, pencils, pens**

Arrange children in groups. Tell them that they will be organizing a neighborhood garage sale. Have children assign the following jobs:

- sign makers
- people to price items
- people to set up the items for sale
- people to collect the money from the garage sale

Have group members discuss what their duties will be. Then reassemble the class and have volunteers discuss the importance of dividing the jobs to make the garage sale easier and faster to set up.
(VISUAL/AUDITORY/KINESTHETIC)

Interview Workers

Materials: **paper, pencil**

Ask children to interview at least three family members or adult friends about how technology affects the way they work. Encourage children to prepare a list of questions prior to the interviews. For example, they might ask *What kinds of machines do you use at work? How do the machines help you do your job? How would your job be different if you did not have these machines?* Have children make notes about each interview. Then have them report to the class about what they learned.
(AUDITORY)

Follow a Flow Chart

OBJECTIVES

- Describe the purpose of a flow chart.
- Trace the development of a product from a natural resource to a finished product.

RESOURCES

Pupil Book/Unit Big Book, pp. 284–285
Word Cards V75–V76
Activity Book, p. 68
Activity Pattern P11
Skill Transparency 6-1
Internet Resources

Vocabulary

flow chart p. 284 **product** p. 284

1 Motivate

Hold up a picture of a wheat field and a picture of a loaf of bread. Ask children to tell how they think wheat from the field ends up in a loaf of bread they buy at the store.

Why It Matters

Tell children that a flow chart shows in pictures and writing the steps involved in doing something. Showing steps in order this way makes the process easier to understand.

REACH ALL LEARNERS

Kinesthetic Learners Provide simpler three- or four-step flow charts showing familiar processes—put on socks, put on shoes, tie shoelaces; get leash, attach leash to dog's collar, walk dog; put two slices of bread on plate, spread peanut butter on one slice, spread honey on other slice, put halves together. Ask children to act out what is happening in each step and to tell why the steps have to be done in the proper order.

put slices of bread on a plate → spread peanut butter and honey on slices → put slices together

2 Teach

What You Need to Know

Read aloud the title of the flow chart. Explain that the title tells what is included in the flow chart. Then discuss that the arrows show how one step leads to the next. Read aloud each step involved in canning tomatoes. Stress that the steps are arranged in the order they occur in the process. Discuss the way the pictures help the reader understand what is being described in each step.

Q What are some other products that are canned?

A Children may suggest other fruits and vegetables.

Q Do you think they follow the same steps? Why or why not?

A The steps would be the same, except that for peaches and other fruits you would need to remove the pits, for corn you would need to take the kernels off the cob, and for peas you would need to remove the pods.

Follow a Flow Chart

Vocabulary
flow chart
product

Why It Matters

A **flow chart** shows the steps needed to make or do something. You can use a flow chart to show the steps workers follow to produce a product. A **product** is something that is made by nature or by people.

What You Need to Know

The title of the flow chart tells what it is about. Each picture has a sentence that describes the step. Arrows show you the order of the steps.

Practice the Skill

1. What does the flow chart show you?
2. What is the first step?
3. What happens after the tomatoes are put into cans?

284

INTERNET RESOURCES

GO ONLINE

THE LEARNING SITE

Go to **www.harcourtschool.com** for a virtual flow chart tracing a product from its source to its use in the home.

WORD WORK

Use Picture Clues Point to the words *harvested* and *conveyor* in the flow chart. Tell children that they can use clues from the pictures to help them figure out the meaning of the words. Invite volunteers to tell what they think the words mean, based on clues they find in the pictures.

EXTEND AND ENRICH

Garden-to-Table Flow Chart Have children think of a fruit or vegetable that might grow in a backyard garden or orchard. Have them create a flow chart showing the steps involved in bringing that fruit or vegetable from the garden or orchard to the table. Ask children to include steps showing preparation and presentation of the product.

Canning Tomatoes

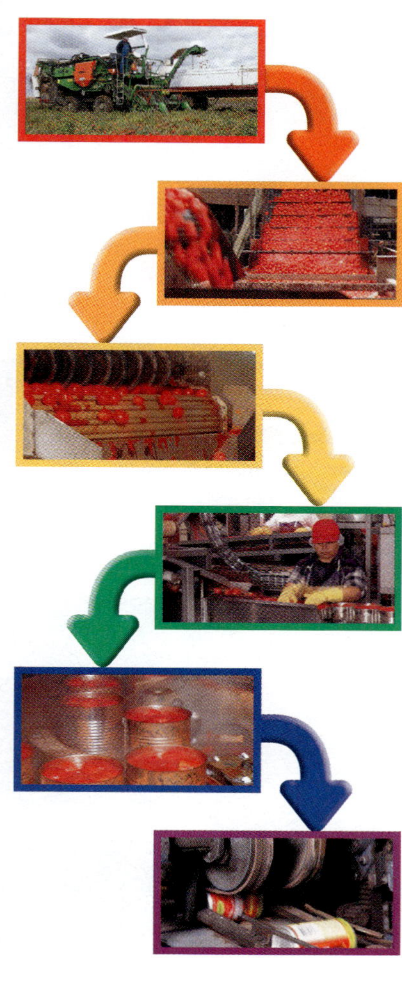

1. The tomatoes are harvested.
2. A conveyor takes the tomatoes to be washed.
3. A machine peels the tomatoes.
4. The tomatoes are put into cans.
5. The tomatoes are cooked in cans.
6. The cans are sealed and put into boxes.

Apply What You Learned

Think about a job you know how to do. For example, list the steps for setting the table or making your bed. Use your list to make a flow chart. Share it with a family member.

CHART AND GRAPH SKILLS

Practice the Skill—Answers

1. The flow chart shows the steps in canning tomatoes.
2. harvesting tomatoes
3. cooking tomatoes

3 Close

Apply What You Learned

Children's flow charts should correctly show the ordered steps in a process. Flow charts should include a title, arrows, and pictures, as well as words describing each step.

RETEACH THE SKILL

Build a Flow Chart Assemble the following items (or pictures) and display them in random order: four arrows drawn on pieces of cardboard (bent to stand up), a picture of a corn field, an ear of corn, a package of popcorn kernels, a covered pot, and a bowl of popped corn. Ask children to help you arrange the items in order to build a flow chart showing the process of making popcorn.

ACTIVITY BOOK

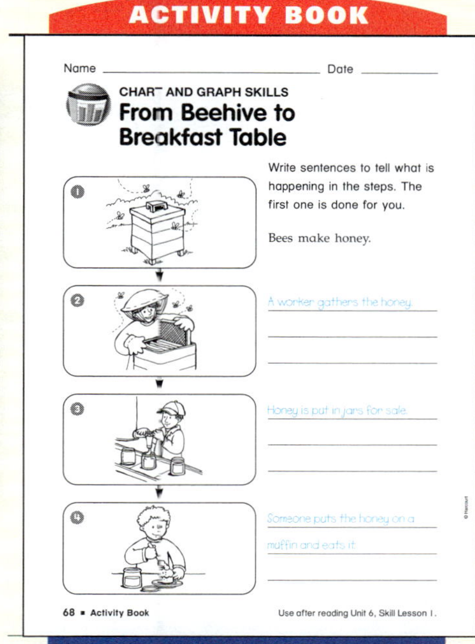

Name ______________ Date ________

CHART AND GRAPH SKILLS

From Beehive to Breakfast Table

Write sentences to tell what is happening in the steps. The first one is done for you.

1. Bees make honey.
2. A worker gathers the honey.
3. Honey is put in jars for sale.
4. Someone puts the honey on a muffin and eats it.

© Harcourt

68 ■ Activity Book

Use after reading Unit 6, Skill Lesson 1.

PAGE 68

INTEGRATE MUSIC

Sequencing Songs
Provide children with copies of a popular song, such as "Polly Put the Kettle On," "There's a Hole in My Bucket," or "Peanut Butter and Jelly." Discuss the step-by-step pattern in the song you choose. Then assign children parts to sing, making sure they sequence the steps correctly.

TRANSPARENCY

Use SKILL TRANSPARENCY 6-1.

Extension Activities For Home and School

Chant a Flow Chart

Materials: **drawing paper, markers**

Write the following camp chant on the board:

Peanut Butter
Peanut, peanut butter (and jelly).
Peanut, peanut butter (and jelly).

First you dig the peanuts, and you dig them, you dig them.
Then you smash the peanuts, and you smash them, you smash them.
Then you pick some grapes, and you pick them, you pick them.
Then you squish the grapes, and you squish them, you squish them.
Then you take some bread, and you spread it, you spread it.
Then you take the sandwich, and you eat it, you eat it.

Peanut, peanut butter (and jelly).
Peanut, peanut butter (and jelly).

Read the words to the chant, emphasizing the rhythm by clapping your hands. Then lead children in chanting the song. Finally, have children use the words of the song to help them as they create a flow chart showing the steps in making a peanut butter and jelly sandwich. **(VISUAL/AUDITORY/TACTILE)**

From Field to Store

Materials: **Activity Pattern P11, crayons or markers, scissors, tape**

Have children work with a family member to make a flow chart book illustrating six steps involved in getting frozen peas to their grocery store. Ask them to use Activity Pattern P11 and draw the steps, from planting or picking the peas to putting the package in the grocery's freezer. After children have drawn the pictures in their book, they should tape the two parts together at the tab and then carefully fold along the dotted lines. Then, when the book is folded shut, have them create a cover. Invite children to bring their completed books to class to share. **(VISUAL/TACTILE)**

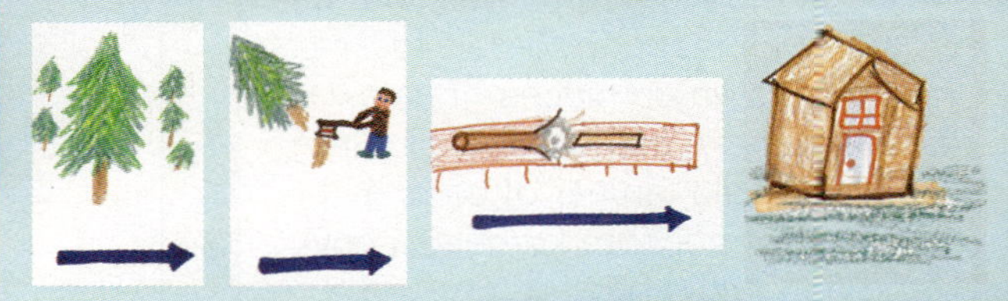

Group Flow Charts

Materials: **index cards, markers**

Arrange children in small groups. Have each group think of a process they can show with a flow chart. Then, have the group members draw each step on individual index cards. Ask them to draw right-pointing arrows on each card except that showing the last step in the process. Next, have groups shuffle the cards and exchange with another group. Ask each group to reassemble the flow charts in the correct order. **(VISUAL/TACTILE)**

Work and Income

OBJECTIVES

- Explain how work provides income to purchase goods and services.
- Explain the choices people in the United States free enterprise system make about spending and saving money.

Summarize pp. 265, 308

RESOURCES

- **Pupil Book/Unit Big Book,** pp. 286–289
- **Word Cards V75–V78**
- **Activity Book,** p. 69
- **Reading and Vocabulary Transparency 6-5**
- **Internet Resources**

READING SOCIAL STUDIES

Study Questions In order to help prepare children for the lesson, write the following questions on the board. Ask children to write their answers on a sheet of paper, leaving room to add information as they read the lesson.

1. What are some ways people earn money?
2. What do people do with the money they earn?

USE READING AND VOCABULARY TRANSPARENCY 6-5.

Vocabulary

income p. 286 **free enterprise** p. 286
bank p. 287 **interest** p. 287

When Minutes Count

Have children skim the lesson to find the meaning of the lesson vocabulary words. Encourage children to tell how each word relates to the Big Idea of the lesson.

Quick Summary

This lesson focuses on ways that people earn and use income. It emphasizes the value of saving money and of sharing it with others.

1 Motivate

Set the Purpose

Big Idea Have children read the Big Idea statement before starting the lesson. Point out that *earn* means "to get something, such as money, for what you do" and that *spend* means "to give money to buy things." Remind children to look for details that support the main idea as they read.

Access Prior Knowledge

Have children imagine that a neighbor has offered to pay them $10.00 to feed and play with her cat while she is away on a trip. Discuss with children what they might do with the money they would earn from this job.

2 Teach

Read and Respond

Economics Have children give examples of goods and services that people provide to earn money. Ask them whether Hector earns money by making goods or by providing services. If necessary, point out that he provides services: watering plants and shoveling snow. Then lead children to understand that Hector does three things with the money he earns: he saves some of it, he shares some of it, and he spends some of it. Expand on the definition of *free enterprise* by explaining that in this type of system, people are free to start any business they want. Add that people can charge what they want for goods or services with little or no interference from the government.

Q What choices do you have for earning money?

A Children can earn money by doing chores around the house or for neighbors.

Q What choices do you have for using money that you earn?

A Children can use money they earn to buy things such as books and CDs, or they can save some of the money for a large purchase such as a bicycle.

Explain to children that money flows back and forth between businesses and families' households. People work for businesses, and businesses make products or provide services that people buy. Businesses use the money from the sale of these goods and services to pay employees.

Visual Learning

Picture Direct children's attention to the picture on page 286. Ask children if they have done work like Hector's to earn money. Have volunteers tell ways they have worked to earn money and how they used the money.

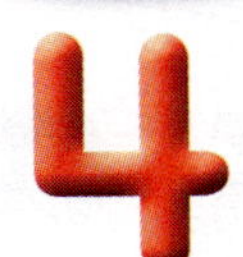

Lesson 4

Work and Income

Big Idea
People plan how to earn and spend their money.

Vocabulary
- income
- free enterprise
- bank
- interest

People make or sell goods or provide services to earn money. Hector earns money by watering plants for his neighbors. He also shovels snow in the winter. The money he earns for his services is his **income**.

Hector saves some of the money he earns. He shares some, too, and spends the rest. The freedom to decide how to make money and what to do with it is called **free enterprise**.

286

STUDY/RESEARCH SKILLS

Look Ahead at Review Questions Have children look at the Review questions on page 289. Tell them that keeping these questions in mind as they read the lesson will help them pay attention to what they read and remember the most important ideas.

REACH ALL LEARNERS

English as a Second Language Pair children proficient in English with English-language learners and have them take turns pantomiming ways to earn money. Ask the proficient English speaker to begin by pantomiming one of Hector's actions while narrating the action, as in, "Hector waters plants to earn money." Partners can take turns demonstrating other ways to make money.

Saving

Hector saves some of his money in a bank until he wants to spend it. A **bank** is a business that keeps money safe. Money in a bank earns more money. This extra money is called **interest**.

Hector's grandmother gave him money on his birthday. Since he wants to save money for college, he puts that money in the bank.

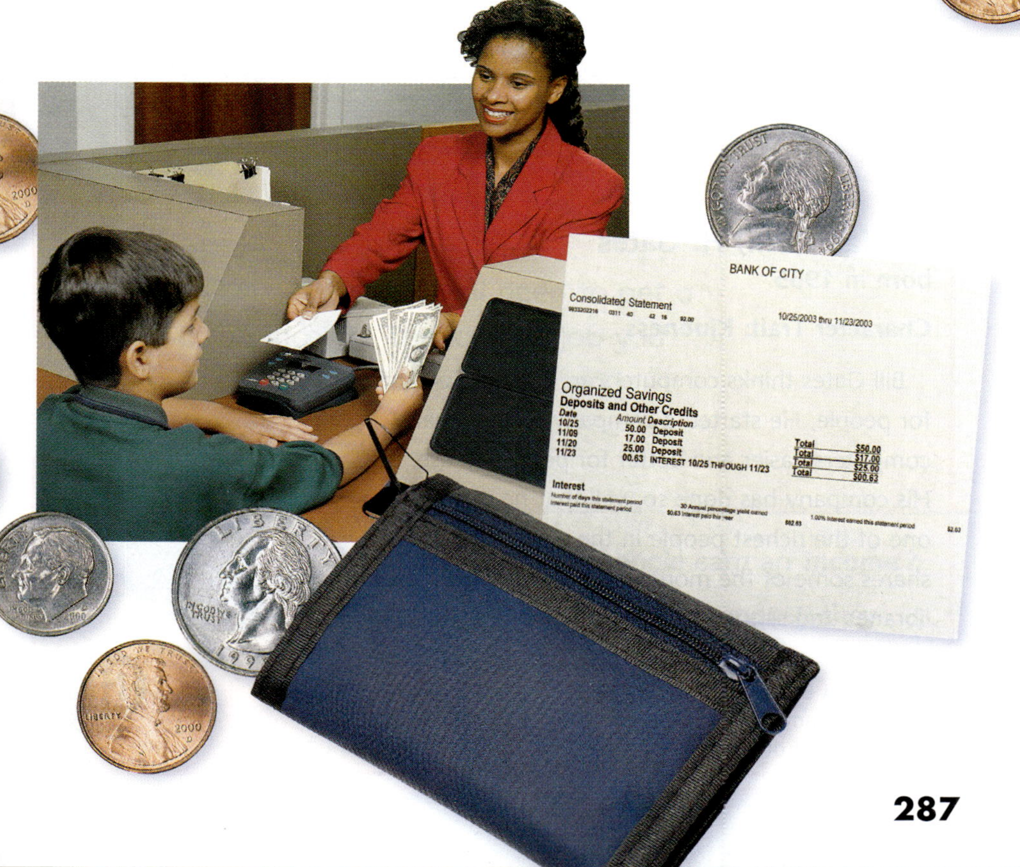

287

Visual Learning

Pictures Have children look at the pictures on this page and describe what they show. Invite children who have visited a bank to describe their experiences. Point out that bank statements tell customers how much money is in their accounts and that statements are mailed to customers or can be viewed electronically on a computer.

Read and Respond

Economics Ask children to explain why people save money. Point out that people put money aside for specific needs and wants, such as to buy a car or pay for a vacation, as well as for unplanned needs, such as home repairs or an illness. Help them understand the concept of interest by explaining that the bank adds some of its own money to a customer's money. That is one reason it is a good idea to put your money in a bank. Tell children that other people can borrow money from the bank, and they are charged interest on the money borrowed. Point out that banks can loan money to businesses in the form of investments.

Q Why is your money safer in a bank than in a box at home or in your pocket?

A Banks have strong safes that protect customers' money. People are less likely to lose money or spend it unwisely if they keep it in a bank.

BACKGROUND

Origin of *Bank* Long ago, religious temples were places where one country's money could be exchanged for another country's money. The word *bank* comes from the word *bench* and refers to the benches in temples that money-changers used during the Middle Ages.

INTEGRATE READING

Books About Money Have volunteers read from one or more of the books listed below. Invite children to discuss the information as it relates to this lesson.

The Coin Counting Book by Rozanne Lanczak Williams. (Charlesbridge, 2001)

The Big Buck Adventure by Shelly Gill, Deborah Tobola, and Grace Lin. (Charlesbridge, 2000)

Coin County: A Bank in a Book by Jim Talbot. (Innovative Kids, 1999)

INTEGRATE MATHEMATICS

How Much Is Left? Write this problem on the board for children to solve: Hector has earned $40. He wants to buy a CD that costs $15 and a book that costs $5. After Hector buys these items, how much money will he have left? Next, have children work with partners to make up math problems based on Hector's income, which can vary. Ask pairs to exchange problems and solve them.

Extension Activities For Home and School

Ways to Make Money

Materials: **drawing paper, construction paper, pencils, crayons or markers, stapler**

Have children work in small groups to make booklets suggesting ways for children to earn money at home and in their communities. Ask children to brainstorm a list of ways to make money. Then tell them to divide the list into jobs that provide goods, such as baking and selling cookies or selling original artworks, and jobs that provide services, such as helping to wash cars and walking neighbors' dogs. Have them draw a picture of each job and write a sentence or two describing the job. Invite children to use construction paper for the front and back covers of their booklets. Then have them staple together the pages and design cover art for the booklets. Display children's booklets in the class reading center.
(VISUAL/TACTILE)

How We Use Money

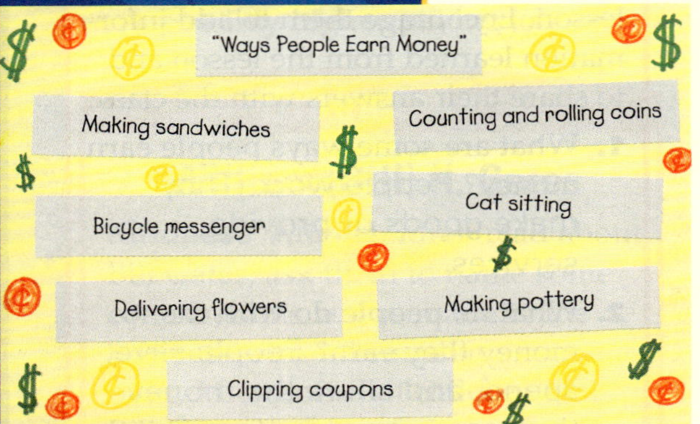

Materials: **paper, pencils, scissors, posterboard, glue**

Ask children to interview friends and family members to learn interesting ways they have earned money. Have children write a brief description of each way people earned their money, leaving a line or two of space between the descriptions. When children have finished their interviews, have them bring the descriptions to class. Ask them to cut out each description. Then have them take turns gluing each strip of paper onto posterboard. Invite a volunteer to write a title at the top of the posterboard. Display children's completed collage in the classroom. Ask children to explain what they learned about the choices people make about work.
(VISUAL/KINESTHETIC/TACTILE)

Idea Bank

Materials: **shoe boxes with tops, index cards, crayons or markers, magazines, scissors, glue**

Have children work in small groups to create an idea bank that shows reasons saving money is important. Provide each group with a shoe box that has a slot in the top cut slightly larger than the width of an index card. Ask members of each group to think of at least four important reasons for saving money. Then have them illustrate index cards with one reason per card. Encourage them to make original drawings, in addition to cutting out magazine pictures that suggest reasons for saving money and gluing the pictures onto index cards. Then have children put their cards through the slots into their boxes. Invite groups to exchange boxes, open the boxes, and discuss what is shown on each card.
(VISUAL/TACTILE)

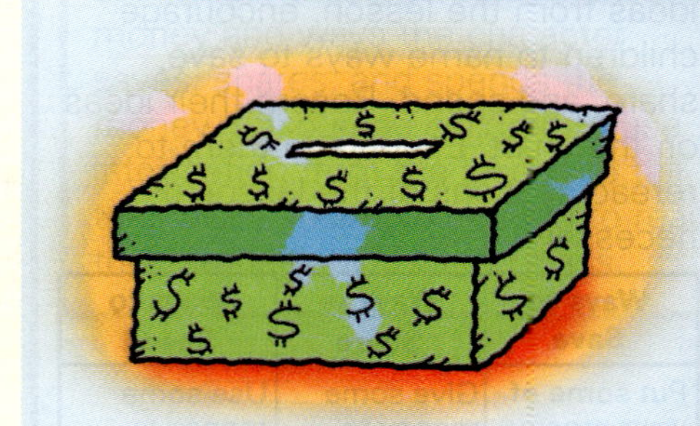

Make Choices When Buying

OBJECTIVES

- Use a decision-making process to identify a situation that requires a decision.
- Recognize that scarcity and demand affect cost.
- Explain the opportunity costs and trade-offs of spending money.

RESOURCES

Pupil Book/Unit Big Book, pp. 290–291

Word Cards V77–V78

Activity Book, p. 70

Skill Transparency 6-2

Vocabulary

scarce p. 290

Motivate

Invite children to tell about their favorite stores. Ask them to describe the items that are available in the stores. Discuss with them how they make choices about what things to buy (or ask family members to buy for them) in the stores.

Why It Matters

Ask children for examples of when they've had to make all-or-nothing choices. For example, they can choose to turn on the radio, or they can choose to leave it off. Point out that some choices require more thought. Explain to children that no one—not even a very rich person—can buy everything he or she wants. We all have to make choices about how we spend our money. If we learn to make wise choices, then we won't waste our money.

MAKE IT RELEVANT

At Home Have children talk to adults at home to learn how they make choices when buying goods and services. Ask them to write down responses to their questions about spending. Then have them share their answers with the class. Lead a discussion of how children can use some of the information to make wise spending choices.

2 Teach

What You Need to Know

Discuss reasons money can be scarce—for example, there is less income, or there is more spending, or both. Then discuss reasons a resource can be scarce—for example, bad weather destroys most of an orange crop one year, causing the fewer oranges to be more expensive. Discuss how a drought would require people to make choices about goods and services in the food industry.

Have children think about how they might be affected if a resource became scarce.

Q How might things in your community change if there were a drought?

A People wouldn't be able to water their lawns; people wouldn't be able to wash their cars; fountains would be turned off.

Introduce to children the idea of a budget as a written plan that shows how much income a person has and the amount he or she spends. Point out that budgets help people manage money and make wise spending choices. Explain that individuals, families, businesses, organizations, and even governments use budgets. Emphasize that making wise choices helps people avoid spending more money than they have.

Q What is an example of giving up something to get what you want?

A Children might suggest not buying a snack each day after school to save money to buy a T-shirt.

Ask children about recent choices: *What did you give up to get what you want? Was the choice worth it?* Help them see that to make wise choices when buying, they need to think about what they will want tomorrow as well as what they want today.

Skills

Make Choices When Buying

Vocabulary
scarce

Why It Matters

When you go shopping, you see many things you want to buy. You need to make a choice about how to spend your money wisely.

What You Need to Know

When there is not enough of something, we say that it is **scarce**. Money can be scarce. Resources can also be scarce, causing goods to be more expensive. You have only a certain amount of money to spend, so you cannot buy everything. You must decide what you are willing to give up to get what you want.

290

REACH ALL LEARNERS

English as a Second Language Write the word *expensive* on the board. Explain or pantomime that things that are expensive cost a lot of money. Pair English-language learners with fluent English speakers and provide each pair with an old magazine that features advertisements for expensive items. Have pairs work together to identify and cut out pictures of expensive goods.

EXTEND AND ENRICH

Produce a Product Tell children that they will be choosing which of two products they would like to produce. Explain that both products require the same amount of resources. Then give children the two choices, and have each child write down which product he or she would like to produce. Lead a discussion in which children share the reasons for their choice of product.

Practice the Skill

Imagine that you have five dollars to spend. You want to buy a book. You also want to rent a movie. You do not have enough money to do both.

1. If you decide to buy the book, what do you give up?
2. If you decide to rent the movie, what do you give up?

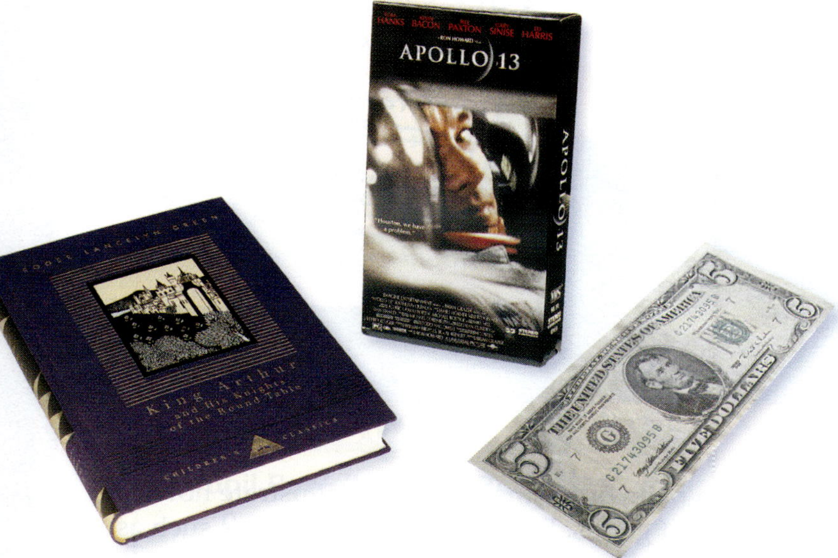

Apply What You Learned

Think about your choices the next time you go shopping. Write down how you spend your money. Then explain your choices to a family member.

CITIZENSHIP SKILLS

Point out to children that people in communities also make decisions. For example, they think about what they give up when they build new hospitals, businesses, parks, homes, and more. Have children imagine that an undeveloped area of land in your community is going to be developed. Ask children to think about what purpose the land should have. For example, should the land be used to build new homes, a hospital, or a park? Have children discuss what would be the best use of the land and what they would be giving up by making that choice.

Practice the Skill—Answers

1. I give up renting the movie.
2. I give up buying the book.

Children might also argue that buying the book is a better choice. They would own the book, whereas they would have to return a movie rental.

3 Close

Apply What You Learned

Children should include meals, snacks, drinks, and other incidentals in the list of things they buy, along with reasons for each purchase.

RETEACH THE SKILL

Buying Choices Set out some items or pictures of items for children, such as one large candy bar, five pieces of gum, three mini candy bars, and a bag of balloons. Explain to children that each costs one dollar, even though their amounts vary. Have children share with the class what they would buy and their reasons for making that choice.

ACTIVITY BOOK

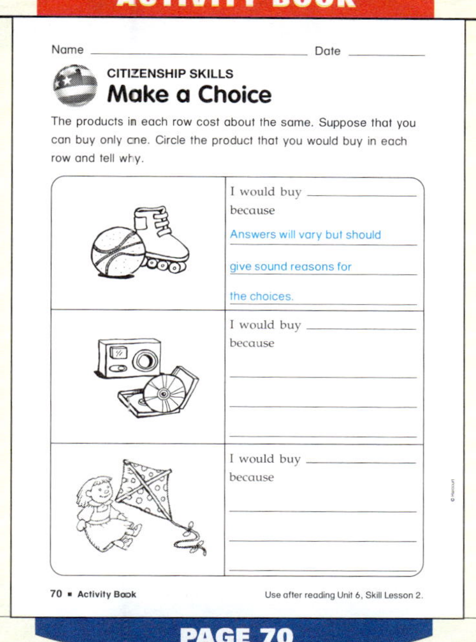
Name ________ Date ________

CITIZENSHIP SKILLS
Make a Choice

The products in each row cost about the same. Suppose that you can buy only one. Circle the product that you would buy in each row and tell why.

I would buy ________
because
Answers will vary but should give sound reasons for the choices.

I would buy ________
because

I would buy ________
because

70 ■ Activity Book

Use after reading Unit 6, Skill Lesson 2.

PAGE 70

TRANSPARENCY

Use SKILL TRANSPARENCY 6-2.

UNIT 6 ■ 293

Read and Respond

Geography As you read the name of each country and its money, point out the country on a world map or globe. Have children repeat the country and money names after you.

Visual Learning

Artifacts Ask children to examine the examples of foreign money and to compare them to United States coins and bills.

Q **Who do you think these people are on the foreign money?**

A They are probably presidents or kings or other people who are important in these countries.

Be sure children understand that these forms of money are not equivalent. For example, one Indian rupee does not equal one American dollar.

As you discuss what money is called, tell children that the Euro is a new currency. Ask children if they have ever seen francs, lire, or marks (the names of money in France, Italy, and Germany). Help them understand that the countries of Europe are so close together that they are trying to make things easier for people by having just one kind of money.

3 What do other countries call their money?

294

INTEGRATE ART

Design New Money Remind children that money typically has on it something or someone a country values or believes in. Have children imagine that they have been asked to design a new type of coin or paper money. Ask them to think about what the coin or paper money would be worth and what it would look like. Whose picture would be on their money? Why? Then have them draw a picture of the new money. Invite children to share their creations with classmates.

INTEGRATE READING

More Money Children might enjoy finding out more about the history of money and seeing pictures of other forms of exchange. Suggest that they go to the library and find *The Story of Money* by Giulio and Betsy Maestro (Mulberry, 1995).

4 How can checks and credit cards be used to pay for things today?

Checks

Credit cards

Bank statement

Activity

Draw a diagram of a dollar bill. Write what the symbols on it mean.

Research

Visit The Learning Site at **www.harcourtschool.com** to research other primary sources.

295

Read and Respond

Economics Explain the differences in paying for things with a bank check, a credit card, and a bank card. When you write a check, your bank takes money out of your account and puts it in someone else's bank account. With a credit card, you do not pay any money when you buy something, but you promise to pay it later when you receive a bill. A bank card is like a check. When you use a bank card, your bank again takes money from your account and puts it in someone else's account.

Q What is the most common way people pay for things in the United States?

A with money

Q Why might people prefer using credit cards?

A With credit cards you can buy something that you want now and pay for it later.

3 Close

Activity

Give children real dollar bills to use as they draw their diagrams. Remind them to write their labels around the outside of the diagram and to draw a line from each label to the item it describes.

Research

Children will find links to sites that can help them find this information at The Learning Site at **www.harcourtschool.com** Encourage children to select one feature on the dollar bill and tell why that feature is important to them.

Use Technology

INTERNET RESOURCES

THE LEARNING SITE

Go to **www.harcourtschool.com** for a DIRECTORY OF PRIMARY SOURCES.

EXTEND AND ENRICH

Invent a System of Money Have children work in small groups to invent a new system of money. Ask them to choose objects that will be used as money to buy items. Have them create a chart that shows what various units of the money are worth. Allow children time to create the new money from clay, construction paper, or other art materials or from everyday objects such as beads. Ask a volunteer from each group to explain the new money system.

RETEACH

Draw Cartoon Panels Have children choose three events in the history of money to show in pictures. Ask them to divide a piece of drawing paper into three sections. Show examples of cartoon drawings. Then have them draw pictures of the three events, one event per panel. Ask children to write one or two sentences in each panel to explain the event. Invite volunteers to share their draw ngs with the class.

Name ______________________ Date ____________

Examine Primary Sources

Write a sentence about each of these kinds of money.

____

____

____

____

Answer the questions.

1. Why do you think people started to use kinds of money?

____

2. Why do you think money changes over time?

____

3. What do other countries call their money?

____

4. How can checks and credit cards be used to pay for things today?

____

295A ■ UNIT 6

People Make a Difference

OBJECTIVES

- Distinguish volunteers from other kinds of workers.
- Identify community volunteers.

Summarize pp. 265, 308

RESOURCES

Pupil Book/Unit Big Book, pp. 296–297

Word Cards V79–V80

Activity Book, p. 71

Reading and Vocabulary Transparency 6-6

Internet Resources

READING SOCIAL STUDIES

Graphic Organizer Create a concept web to answer the question *What is a volunteer?* Record children's responses on the web and save it for use at the end of the lesson.

What is a volunteer?

someone who helps without being asked

someone who does good deeds

USE READING AND VOCABULARY TRANSPARENCY 6-6.

6-6 TRANSPARENCY

Vocabulary

volunteer p. 296

When Minutes Count

Have children read the Big Idea of the lesson. Then have them read the lesson and find at least one sentence that supports the Big Idea.

Quick Summary

This lesson focuses on ways volunteers serve their community.

1 Motivate

Set the Purpose

Big Idea Have children read the Big Idea statement before starting the lesson. As they read and discuss the lesson, encourage them to look for ways volunteers help their community.

Access Prior Knowledge

Ask children to describe ways they have helped others in their family, neighborhood, or community. List responses on the board. Encourage children to describe feelings associated with helping others.

2 Teach

Read and Respond

Culture and Society As children read the text, help them understand that volunteers give their services without pay, yet the rewards can be great. Explain that one reward is the good feeling that comes from helping others. Another reward is gaining valuable experience. Lead a discussion of ways communities benefit from the work of volunteers, especially when a disaster happens.

Visual Learning

Pictures Direct attention to the pictures on pages 296 and 297. Ask children to tell how the people in each picture are making a difference in their community.

• Biography •

Jimmy and Rosalynn Carter

Civic Virtue Emphasize that persons with civic virtue work to make their community a better place in which to live. Tell children that besides working for Habitat for Humanity, the Carters have written several books on ways people can help others. Jimmy Carter also works for world peace.

Q **Why do you think the Carters are good role models?**

A They not only talk about doing good deeds, they also volunteer.

Democratic Values

Common Good

Ask a volunteer to read aloud what Earnest says. Lead a discussion of actions that constitute good deeds. Remind children that good deeds can benefit both the giver and the receiver of the deeds.

Lesson 5

Big Idea
Volunteers help their community.

Vocabulary
volunteer

People Make a Difference

Some people work without being paid. These people are volunteers. A **volunteer** spends his or her free time making the community a better place to live.

Volunteers provide services in a neighborhood or community. Some volunteers run food banks, where food is collected and given to people who need it. Some volunteers help people after an earthquake or flood. They collect food, clothing, and blankets for people who need them.

296

Make It Relevant

In Your Community Ask children to find out about volunteer opportunities in their community, such as with a library or nature center. Provide them with the yellow pages of a local telephone book, or direct them to Internet sites that tell about ways to volunteer in their area. Have children list three opportunities and tell how this work would help the community. Encourage children to share their findings with the class.

Extend and Enrich

Helping Volunteers Have children discuss the volunteer groups they researched during the lesson. Ask them to choose one organization to help. Direct them to think of ways to help this organization as a class or as individual volunteers. Children may want to write a class letter to the organization with their suggestions.

• BIOGRAPHY •

Jimmy Carter born in 1924
Rosalynn Carter born in 1927
Character Trait: Respect

Jimmy Carter was once President of the United States. His wife, Rosalynn, was First Lady. After they left the White House, the Carters served as volunteers on a project called Habitat for Humanity. A habitat is a place to live, and humanity is people. These volunteers build or repair homes for people who need this help.

MULTIMEDIA BIOGRAPHIES
Visit The Learning Site at
www.harcourtschool.com
to learn about other famous people.

GO ONLINE

Do a good deed.

LESSON 5 Review

1. **Vocabulary** How can **volunteers** help a community?
2. What can you do to help volunteers?
3. Make a list of volunteer groups in your community.

3 Close

Summarize Key Content

- A volunteer is someone who works without being paid.
- Volunteers help make their community a better place in which to live.
- Examples of volunteer jobs are providing food to people in need and helping people who have suffered from disasters.

READING SOCIAL STUDIES

Graphic Organizer Have children look at the web they started at the beginning of the lesson. Invite them to add information they learned from reading the lesson.

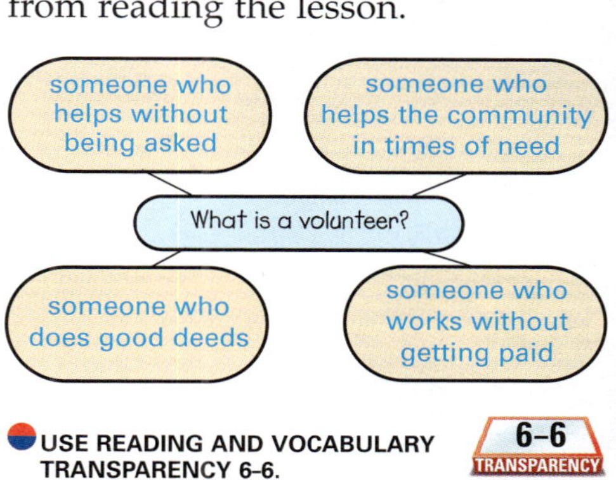

USE READING AND VOCABULARY TRANSPARENCY 6-6.

6-6 TRANSPARENCY

Assess

Lesson 5 Review—Answers

1. They can help people in need by providing food, clothing, and medicine. They can raise money to buy the things people need. They can be volunteer firefighters.
2. Children should mention making and serving food, asking friends and neighbors for donations, and telling others about volunteer opportunities.
3. 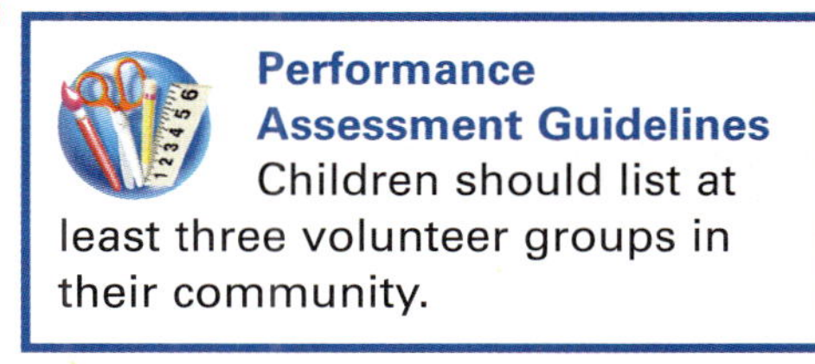

Performance Assessment Guidelines Children should list at least three volunteer groups in their community.

RETEACH THE LESSON

Write a Speech Have children write a brief speech about the importance of being a volunteer in the community. Encourage them to tell how helping others also helps the volunteer. Invite children to read their speeches to the class.

ACTIVITY BOOK

Name ______ Date ______

Help Wanted!

Match each volunteer with a volunteer job. Draw a line from the person on the left to the job on the right.

1. Ana likes animals.
2. Ben enjoys cooking.
3. Nhan makes balloon toys.

Use after reading Unit 6, Lesson 5. Activity Book • 71

PAGE 71

Extension Activities For Home and School

Volunteer Interviews

Materials: **paper, pencils**

Have children interview friends and family members about volunteer work they have done. Suggest that children prepare questions in advance of the interviews, such as *Why did you want to volunteer? What kinds of volunteer work have you done? How did it help others? How did volunteering make you feel?* Have children write a summary of the information they learned from their interviews. Collect children's summaries in a binder. Place the binder in the classroom reading center and invite children to read the information.
(VISUAL/TACTILE/AUDITORY)

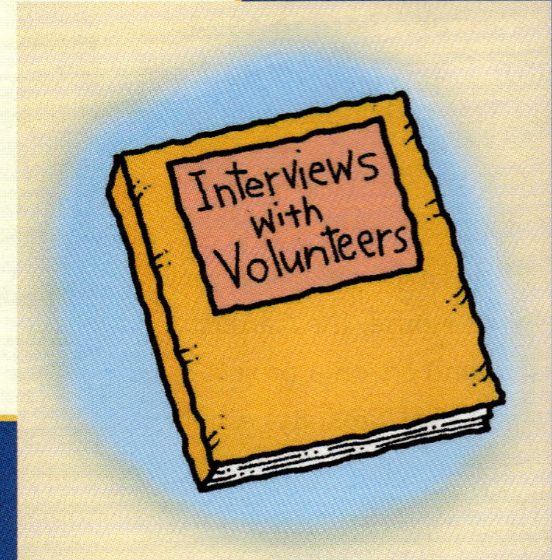

People Make a Difference

Materials: **local newspapers, magazines, scissors, posterboard, glue, crayons or markers**

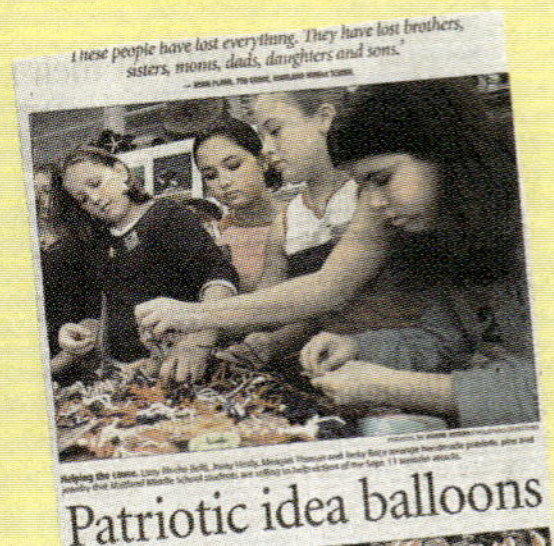
'These people have lost everything. They have lost brothers, sisters, moms, dads, daughters and sons.'

Patriotic idea balloons

A student project at Maitland Middle School grew into a nonprofit enterprise to aid terrorists' victims.

Children make pins to raise money.

Have children work in small groups to make posters that show people in the community (or in other areas) who have made a difference by helping others. Ask them to first look through local newspapers to find and cut out information about volunteers in their community. Children can also find articles in newspapers and magazines about other volunteers. Direct them to glue this information onto posterboard and to label each article or picture with information about how the person is making a difference. Display the posters in the classroom.
(VISUAL/TACTILE)

Idea Box

Materials: **index cards, pencils or crayons, a shoebox or other container**

Have children work in small groups to think of volunteer jobs they could do alone or with family members in their neighborhoods and at school. Provide them with index cards and have them describe one volunteer job per card. Collect the cards and place them in a shoebox or other container. Invite volunteers to draw cards from the box and read what is written on them. Keep the box in the classroom. Children may want to perform the volunteer tasks at school or in their neighborhood.
(VISUAL/TACTILE/KINESTHETIC)

School:
Clean off lunch tables.

School:
Put library books back on shelves.

Neighborhood:
Bring toys to children's home.

Goods from Near and Far

OBJECTIVES

- Explain that people around the world depend on one another through trade.
- Describe how science and technology have changed transportation.
- Identify historic figures who have exhibited a love of individualism and inventiveness.

Summarize pp. 265, 302, 308

RESOURCES

Pupil Book/Unit Big Book, pp. 298–303

Word Cards V79–V80

Activity Book, p. 72

Activity Pattern P12

Reading and Vocabulary Transparency 6-7

Internet Resources

READING SOCIAL STUDIES

Graphic Organizer Create a K-W-L chart. Ask children what they know and would like to know about ways goods are traded around the world. Together with children, fill in the first and second columns of the chart.

What We Know	What We Want to Know	What We Learned
Many of the things we buy come from other countries.	How do the things we buy from other countries get to our city?	

USE READING AND VOCABULARY TRANSPARENCY 6-7.

6-7 TRANSPARENCY

Vocabulary

trade p. 298 **transportation** p. 300

When Minutes Count

Have pairs of children read the lesson together. Then ask them to write a sentence summarizing the lesson.

Quick Summary

This lesson focuses on ways that countries depend on one another for goods. It explores forms of transportation used to move these goods from one place to another.

Motivate

Set the Purpose

Big Idea Write in a vertical list each word of the Big Idea statement. Help children define each word, writing the definition to the right of the word. Rewrite the main idea, using these definitions.

Access Prior Knowledge

Ask children to look at the objects around them. Explain that many of the objects came from other countries. Have children speculate about how the objects were moved from the places they were made to the classroom.

2 Teach

Read and Respond

Economics Discuss the kinds of goods that people and countries exchange with one another. Point out that people and countries can also exchange money for goods and services that they need. Ask children to name some benefits from trading with other countries, such as discovering new ideas and sharing cultures. Explain that some products, such as computers, televisions, and cars, are partially assembled in other countries and then shipped to the United States to be finished. In some cases, parts for products are manufactured in other countries and are sent here to be put together.

Q **What are some products you use at home that come from other countries?**

A Children may mention foods such as fruits and vegetables, clothing, and electronic devices such as TVs, VCRs, CD players, and telephones.

Visual Learning

Pictures Direct attention to the picture on page 298. Have children name the items shown in the picture and identify where the items came from.

Lesson

Big Idea
Transportation helps countries trade around the world.

Vocabulary
trade
transportation

Goods from Near and Far

No country can grow or make all the goods its people need and want. Countries get goods from one another by making a trade. **Trade** is the exchange of one thing for another.

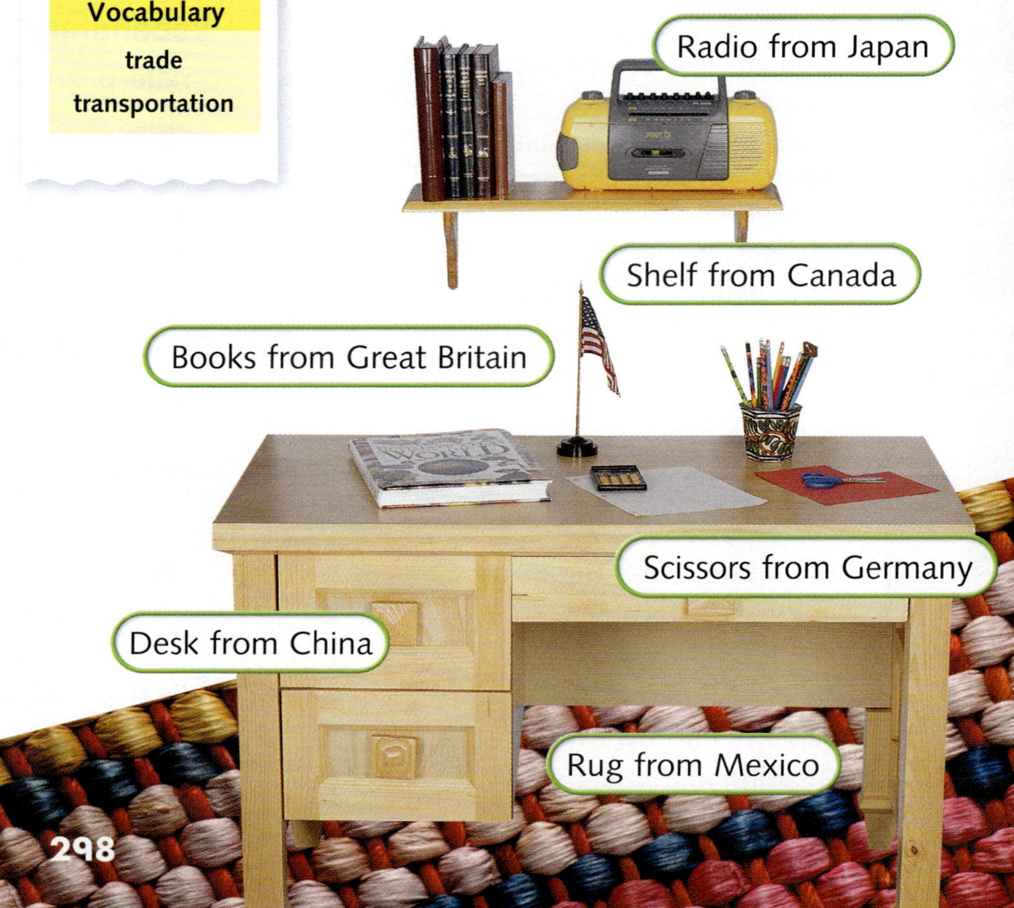

298

STUDY/RESEARCH SKILLS

Television Discuss with children how television can be a source of information. Children should recognize that in addition to providing entertainment, television carries ideas around the world. Invite children to make notes as they watch television. Have them look for information about how people around the world meet their needs. Challenge children to identify products from other countries. Ask them to share their notes with classmates.

INTEGRATE LANGUAGES

Product Information
Bring to class examples of product information printed in several languages, such as that accompanying some watches, VCRs, or computer components. Distribute the information for children to review. Ask them to identify the languages in which the information is printed. Have children speculate as to why manufacturers print their product information in different languages.

REACH ALL LEARNERS

Below-Level Learners
Have children work in pairs to read the lesson. Ask them to make notes to answer the questions: *What goods do we get from other countries? How do these goods get to us?* Children should take turns reading and making notes. Suggest that children pause while reading to discuss whether the information in the text answers one or both questions.

Trading Partners			
Country	**Products**		
Canada	lumber	maple syrup	newsprint
Mexico	fruit/vegetables	pottery	rugs
Japan	cameras	computers/games	CD players
Germany	clocks	tools	toys
Great Britain	books	clothing	silverware
China	furniture	silk cloth	tea

What product made in Germany might you buy?

Visual Learning

Table Ask children what the table on page 299 shows. Explain that countries that trade with one another are called trading partners. The countries shown on the table are trading partners with the United States. Display a world map or a globe. Ask volunteers to take turns locating the countries listed on the table. As one child points to a country, have another child read the names of products that come from that country.

Q **Which countries shown on the table trade items that help meet people's needs?**

A food: Canada, Mexico, China; clothing: Great Britain, China; shelter: Canada

CAPTION ANSWER: Children may choose a clock, tool, or toy.

Read and Respond

Link History and Economics Remind children that people in different parts of the world have traded with one another for many years. Point out that hundreds of years ago, Christopher Columbus, Marco Polo, and other explorers traveled to new lands so that countries could exchange goods. Marco Polo traveled the Silk Road, a trade route that linked China with the West, for 24 years. He found the farthest route east all the way to China, where he served in Kublai Khan's court for many years. He also wrote a travelogue of his journeys to the East.

INTEGRATE LANGUAGE ARTS

Write a Poem Invite children to write a poem about trading with other countries. Suggest they use the information in the table of products to help them come up with ideas. Encourage children to illustrate their poems. Invite volunteers to read their completed poems aloud for classmates.

MAKE IT RELEVANT

At Home Have children identify products in their home that come from one or more of the countries listed in the table on page 299. Direct children to make a list of the names of the countries shown on the table. Ask them to check labels on items or ask family members to help them identify the item's country of origin. Ask children to list these items next to their country of origin. Invite children to bring their lists to school and share the information with classmates.

Visual Learning

Diagram Ask a volunteer to tell what the diagram on pages 300 and 301 shows. Remind children that trading partners are countries that exchange goods with one another. Have children identify the United States's trading partners that are on some of these continents: North America, South America, Asia, Europe, Africa, and Australia.

Q How are goods sent from one country to another?

A Goods are sent by boat, plane, truck, or train.

Help children locate Louisiana.

Q How many ports in Louisiana are shown on this diagram?

A four

Q Why do you think this is a good location for shipping goods into and out of the country?

A Critical thinkers may recall that the Mississippi River flows through Louisiana into the Gulf of Mexico.

CAPTION ANSWER: by truck and by train

Read and Respond

Link Economics and Geography Have children locate on a map or globe island countries such as Japan and Australia. Discuss how trade is different within these countries as compared to trade within the United States. Point out that being an island country may make trade more necessary or difficult. Then help children learn what goods are produced and which services are performed in those countries. Compare these goods and services to those found in the United States.

Economics Explain to children that importing is bringing goods into a country, while exporting is sending goods out of the country to other countries. Point out some examples of goods that the United States imports, such as Japanese and European cars. Some examples of goods that the United States exports are textiles such as blue jeans and farm products such as wheat.

Countries use many kinds of **transportation** to move goods from one place to another. Goods travel between countries by train, truck, ship, and plane.

How are goods moved from the United States to Canada and Mexico?

REACH ALL LEARNERS

Auditory Learners Have children use the table on page 299 and the diagram of trading partners to write "trade" slips. For example: *China trades silk to Mexico; Mexico trades pottery to the United States;* and so on. Have children use their trade slips in a relay game. One child reads his or her slip. The turn passes to the first child who has a slip that begins as the other ends and who can identify how the product is transported.

BACKGROUND

Canada Canada is the second-largest country in the world after Russia. Canada is the United States's largest trading partner. The two countries share similar ways of life and a common language, although French is the primary language of many people in the Canadian province of Quebec. Forestry and fisheries are major industries there, and Canada is a leading producer of minerals.

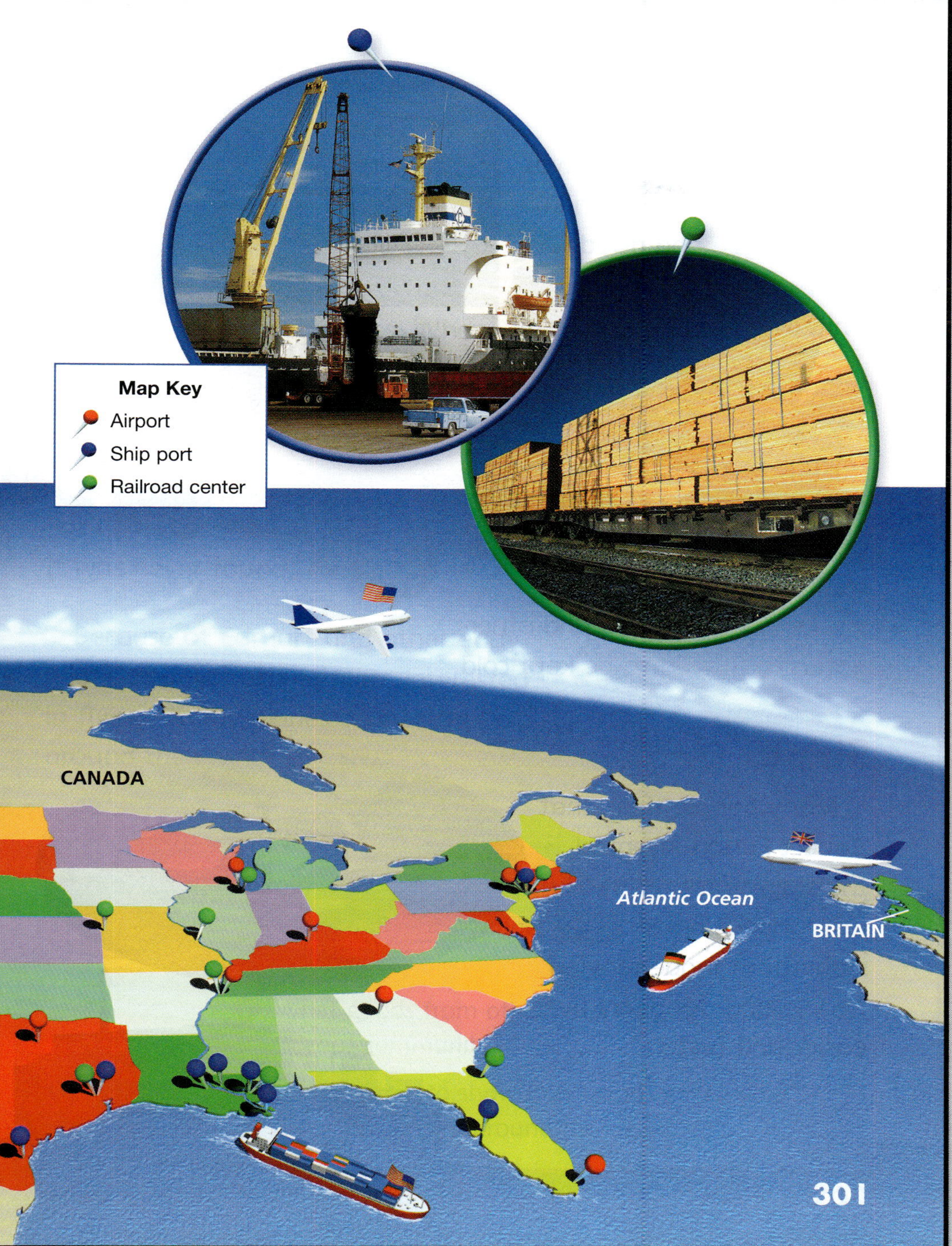

Read and Respond

Geography As children continue to view the diagram, have them describe how trading with other countries is becoming easier and faster because of technology. Orders for products can be sent by telephones, computers, or fax machines. Traders from all over the world can be linked. Orders for goods from faraway places can arrive in a matter of days or weeks instead of months or years.

Link Economics and Geography Have children look again at the table on page 299 and note the products that come from each place.

Q **Why do we need to trade with other countries?**

A Because many of those countries have special things that we do not have in this country but would like to have.

You may also want to explain that some countries do not have everything they need for their people and so they must trade with other countries to provide for their people.

Link Economics with Civics and Government Explain to children that we have a free market economy in the United States based on supply and demand. Point out that the government has little control over what is produced and sold in the United States. Tell children the United States economy interacts with other countries through trade agreements and importing and exporting of goods and services.

REACH ALL LEARNERS

English as a Second Language Invite volunteers to point out on a world map their country of origin. Ask them to draw a picture of the country. Encourage them to include drawings of goods that are produced in that country. Display children's drawings in the classroom.

MAKE IT RELEVANT

In Your State Discuss with children goods that are produced in their state. Ask them if any of these goods are traded with other states or countries. If necessary, provide resources such as encyclopedias and almanacs so children can investigate products or resources that are shipped from their state to faraway places.

Unit 6 Review and Test Preparation

PAGES 308–312

Summarize

Children's summary sentences should tie together the main ideas from the unit. Their responses should be written in their own words and should demonstrate an understanding of how the main ideas are related. Children may use the graphic organizer that appears on page 74 of the Activity Book.

ACTIVITY BOOK

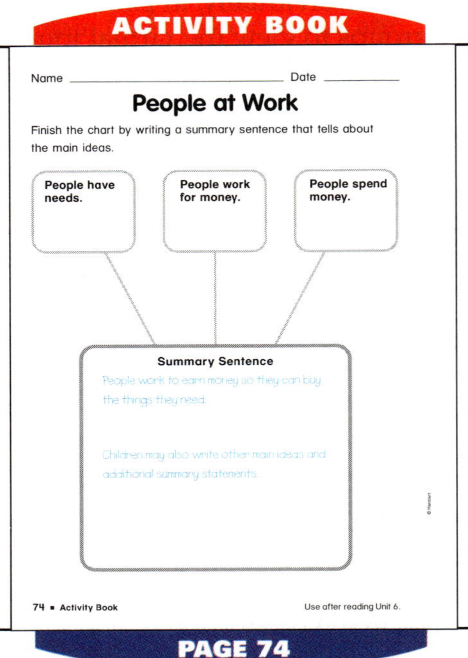

Name ______________ Date ________

People at Work

Finish the chart by writing a summary sentence that tells about the main ideas.

People have needs.

People work for money.

People spend money.

Summary Sentence

People work to earn money so they can buy the things they need.

Children may also write other main ideas and additional summary statements.

74 • Activity Book | Use after reading Unit 6.

PAGE 74

Think & Write

Children should clearly describe their products and what the products do. In their ads children should use vivid adjectives to persuade people to buy the existing or invented products.

TRANSPARENCY

This graphic organizer appears on READING AND VOCABULARY TRANSPARENCY 6-8.

Unit

Review and Test Preparation

Summarize

Write what you have learned in this unit about summarizing.

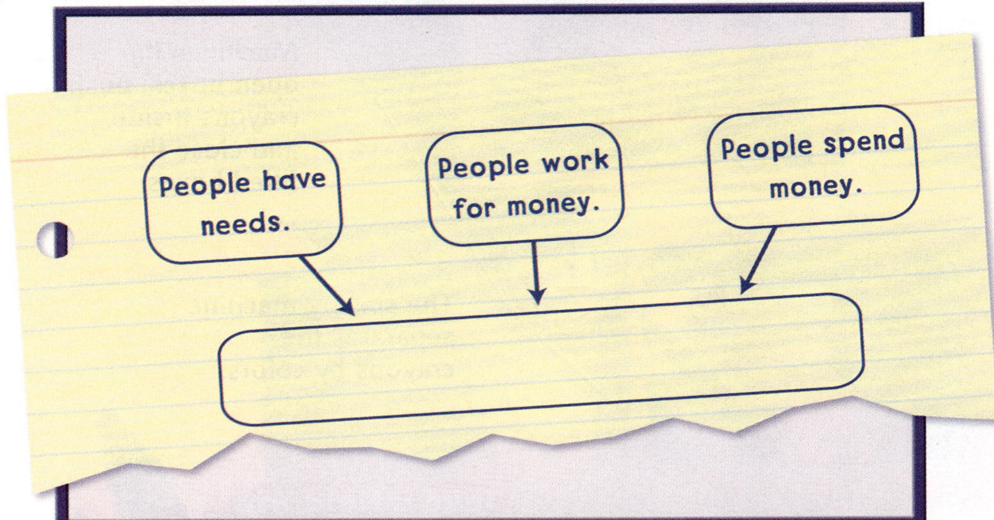

THINK & WRITE

Invent a Product Think of a new product. Ask yourself why people might need or want to have your product.

Write an Advertisement Write an advertisement about your product. Use words that will make people want to buy it.

308

TEST PREPARATION

Review these tips with children.

- Read the directions before reading the questions.
- Read each question twice, focusing the second time on all the possible answers.
- Take the time to think about all the possible answers before deciding on an answer.
- Move past questions that are giving you trouble, and answer the ones you know. Then return to concentrate on the difficult items.

Use Vocabulary

Match each word with its definition.

1. The freedom to start and run any kind of business
2. A person who makes, grows, or sells goods
3. Ways of carrying people and goods from place to place
4. A person who buys and uses goods and services
5. The money people earn for the work they do
6. A building in which people use machines to make goods

producer (p. 277)
consumer (p. 279)
factory (p. 282)
income (p. 286)
free enterprise (p. 286)
transportation (p. 300)

Recall Facts

7. How can a person be both a producer and a consumer?
8. What three things do factories need to make goods?
9. Why do people work?
10. Which of these workers sells a service?
   A farmer
   B baker
   C potter
   D plumber
11. Which kind of transportation is <u>not</u> used to move goods?
   F bus
   G plane
   H train
   J boat

309

Use Vocabulary

1. free enterprise
2. producer
3. transportation
4. consumer
5. income
6. factory

Recall Facts

7. A producer can earn money by making a product and then use the money as a consumer to buy the goods or services that he or she needs.
8. Factories need raw materials, workers, and machines.
9. People work to earn money.
10. D—plumber
11. F—bus

Think Critically

⓬ Children may say that if a product is scarce, it will be hard to find in stores. Also, a scarce product is likely to be expensive.

⓭ Children's responses might include that trade with other countries allows people to buy products that are not grown or made in their own country. Responses may also include benefits such as exposure to new products and ideas and increased understanding among people of different countries.

Apply Chart and Graph Skills

⓮ Trucks take corn to factories.

⓯ It is cooked in giant kettles.

⓰ Dried corn is pressed into flakes.

Think Critically

⓬ How can scarcity affect what you buy?

⓭ Why is trade with other countries important?

Apply Chart and Graph Skills

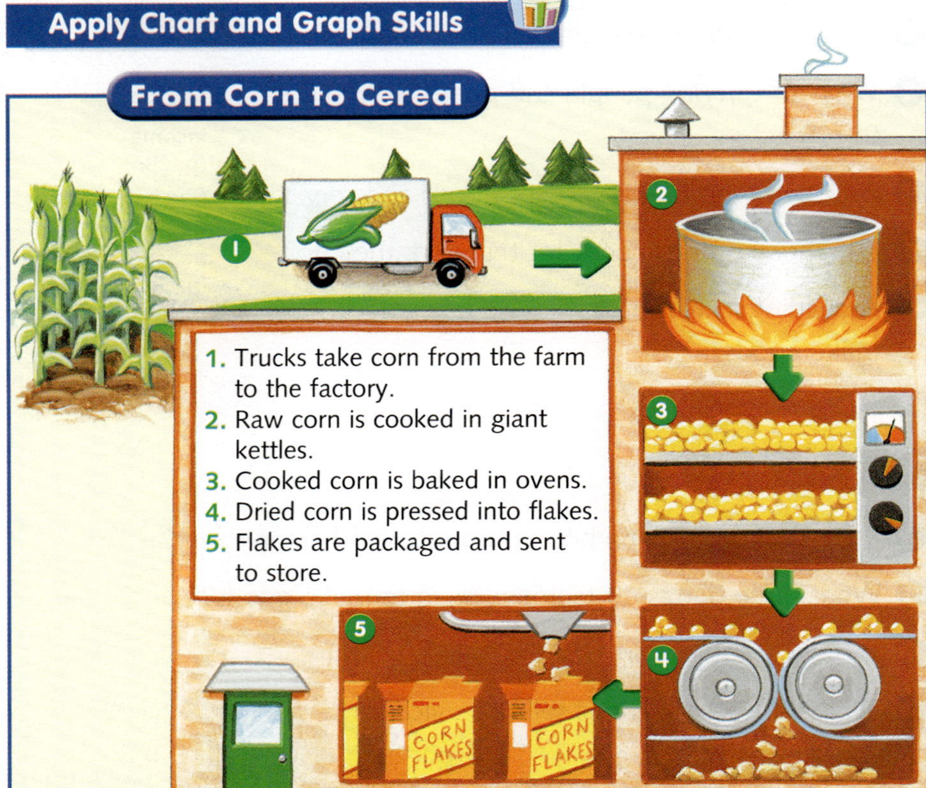

⓮ How does corn get to the factory?

⓯ How is raw corn cooked?

⓰ What happens after the corn is baked?

310

Apply Map and Globe Skills 

17. What is the largest crop in Alabama?
18. In what part of Alabama is wheat grown?
19. Near what cities is coal found?
20. What crop is grown near Mobile?

Apply Map and Globe Skills

17. cotton
18. in the north, south, and central
19. Huntsville, Gadsden, Birmingham, Tuscaloosa
20. accept soybeans, peanuts, vegetables, cotton, or wheat

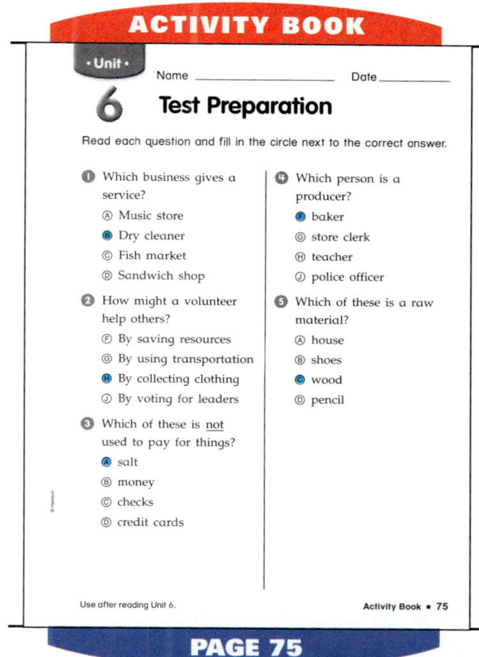
ACTIVITY BOOK

• Unit • 6 Name ______ Date ______

Test Preparation

Read each question and fill in the circle next to the correct answer.

1. Which business gives a service?
   - Ⓐ Music store
   - ● Dry cleaner
   - Ⓒ Fish market
   - Ⓓ Sandwich shop
2. How might a volunteer help others?
   - Ⓕ By saving resources
   - Ⓖ By using transportation
   - ● By collecting clothing
   - Ⓙ By voting for leaders
3. Which of these is not used to pay for things?
   - ● salt
   - Ⓑ money
   - Ⓒ checks
   - Ⓓ credit cards
4. Which person is a producer?
   - ● baker
   - Ⓖ store clerk
   - Ⓗ teacher
   - Ⓙ police officer
5. Which of these is a raw material?
   - Ⓐ house
   - Ⓑ shoes
   - ● wood
   - Ⓓ pencil

Use after reading Unit 6. Activity Book • 75

PAGE 75

ASSESSMENT

Use the UNIT 6 TEST on pages 21–24 of the Assessment Program.

Unit Activities

Organize children into small groups for the unit project. Explain that some schools offer a Career Day, in which people who work in various jobs speak to students about the work they do. Tell children that these people often set up booths that provide information about what the work involves and about how to prepare for careers in these fields. Help children brainstorm questions about the skills and tools required for various jobs. List their responses on the board. Discuss how best to set up booths that offer answers to the questions.

Have children think of specific jobs within each category of careers. Encourage children with family members who work in these areas to discuss what they know about the work. Suggest that they use a combination of written materials and pictures in their booths.

Where to Get Information

Encourage children to use a wide variety of reference sources, including encyclopedias, library books, travel brochures, social studies books, picture atlases, magazines, and the Internet.

Ways to Share

After guests have spoken to the class, invite children to take turns exploring one another's booths. Encourage them to ask questions about the information displayed in the booths. Children may also want to invite another class to attend Career Day.

Performance Assessment Guidelines The written information and pictures displayed in the booths should show that children researched the careers highlighted in their displays.

Visit Your Library

Encourage independent reading with these books or others of your choice after children have completed their study of the work people do. Additional books are listed in the Multimedia Resources on pages 265J-265K of this Teacher's Edition.

Easy *The Paperboy* by Dav Pilkey. Orchard, 1996. A boy celebrates the quiet joys of performing a routine job while others sleep.

Average *From Metal to Music* by Wendy Davis. Children's Press, 1997. Detailed photographs help show the transformation of raw metal ore into musical instruments.

Challenging *Market!* by Ted Lewin. Lothrop, Lee & Shepard, 1996. The diverse marketplaces show a colorful array of settings, goods, and people.

Unit Activities

Complete the Unit Project Work in a group to plan a Career Day. Find out about the skills and tools people need to do their jobs.

Visit The Learning Site at **www.harcourtschool.com** for additional activities.

Choose Jobs

Gather information about different kinds of jobs.

- office jobs
- factory jobs
- service jobs
- sales jobs
- travel jobs
- outdoor jobs

Display Job Information

Set up booths to display information.

- Make pamphlets.
- Write job descriptions.
- Show pictures of workers.
- Invite guest speakers.

Visit Your Library

The Paperboy by Dav Pilkey. A boy enjoys the early morning as he delivers newspapers.

From Metal to Music by Wendy Davis. Follow the steps for making brass instruments.

Market! by Ted Lewin. Read about marketplaces around the world and the goods they sell.

312

For Your Reference

313

Biographical Dictionary

The Biographical Dictionary lists many of the important people introduced in this book. The page number tells where the main discussion of each person starts. See the Index for other page references.

Anthony, Susan B. (1820–1906) Women's rights leader. She helped get women the same rights that men have. p. 83

Armstrong, Neil (1930–) American astronaut. He was the first person to walk on the moon. p. 220

Austen, Alice (1866–1952) Photographer. She took real-life photographs of immigrants. p. 27

Barton, Clara (1821–1912) Founder of the American Red Cross. She was its first president. p. 84

Bush, George W. (1946–) 43rd President of the United States. His father was the 41st President. p. 225

Carson, Rachel (1907–1964) American biologist and science writer. She told people about the dangers of pesticides. p. 249

Carter, Jimmy (1924–) and **Rosalynn** (1927–) Jimmy was the 39th President of the United States. He and his wife Rosalynn work for peace and justice. p. 297

Carver, George W. (1864–1943) African American scientist. He worked on ways to improve farming in the South. p. 133

Chavez, Cesar (1927–1993) American farm worker. He worked to get fair treatment for all farm workers. p. 85

Chavez, Dennis (1888–1962) Second Hispanic American to serve in the United States Senate. p. 249

Curie, Marie (1867–1934) French scientist. She was the first woman to win a Nobel Prize. p. 248

Earhart, Amelia (1897–1937?) American pilot. She was the first woman to fly across the Atlantic Ocean alone. p. 303

Edison, Thomas (1847–1931) American inventor. He is most famous for inventing the light bulb. p. 230

Einstein, Albert (1879–1955) One of the greatest scientists of all time. He wrote about time, space, and energy. p. 248

Fulton, Robert (1765–1815) American inventor and engineer. He is known for building a steamboat. p. 302

Gates, William (Bill) H. (1955–) Businessperson. He gives money to build and improve libraries and schools. p. 288

Glenn, John (1921–) First American astronaut to orbit Earth. p. 220

Grasso, Ella (1919–1981) First woman elected governor in the United States. p. 64

Greer, Pedro José (1956–) Florida doctor who started a walk-in clinic for people who are homeless. p. 86

Jefferson, Thomas (1743–1826) Third U.S. President. He wrote most of the Declaration of Independence. p. 244

314

Keller, Helen (1880–1968) American who overcame physical disabilities at an early age. She became a writer. p. 84

Key, Francis Scott (1779–1843) Lawyer and poet who wrote the words of "The Star-Spangled Banner." p. 77

Khan, Kublai (1216–1294) Ruler of China from 1279 to 1294. p. 59

King, Martin Luther, Jr. (1929–1968) African American civil rights leader. He received a Nobel Prize for working to change unfair laws. p. 248

Lincoln, Abraham (1809–1865) 16th President of the United States during the Civil War. He made it against the law to own slaves. p. 241

Ma, Yo-Yo (1955–) One of the world's most popular cello players. p. 86

Marshall, Thurgood (1908–1993) First African American justice of the United States Supreme Court. p. 246

Meir, Golda (1898–1978) Prime Minister of Israel from 1969 to 1974. p. 247

Mother Teresa (1910–1997) Roman Catholic nun who spent most of her life helping poor people. She received a Nobel Peace Prize. p. 85

Muñoz Marín, Luis (1898–1980) First elected governor of Puerto Rico. p. 249

Pasteur, Louis (1822–1895) French scientist who discovered that germs spread diseases. His work saved many lives. p. 247

Polo, Marco (1254–1324) Explorer from Venice, Italy. He traveled to Asia. p. 59

Ramses II Egyptian pharaoh, or king. He built many temples. p. 58

Revere, Paul (1735–1818) Messenger who warned American leaders they were in danger from the British. p. 83

Rice, Condoleezza (1954–) Advisor to President George W. Bush. p. 86

Ride, Sally (1951–) Astronaut and first American woman in space. p. 175

Robinson, Jackie (1919–1972) First African American to play modern major league baseball. p. 82

Roosevelt, Eleanor (1884–1962) Wife of President Franklin Roosevelt. She worked for people in need around the world. p. 245

Roosevelt, Franklin (1882–1945) 32nd President of the United States. He was President longer than any other person. p. 64

Roosevelt, Theodore (1858–1919) 26th President of the United States. He protected natural resources and wilderness. p. 251

Sacagawea (1786?–1812?) Shoshone woman. She helped explorers Lewis and Clark communicate with Native Americans. p. 249

Shakespeare, William (1564–1616) English writer whose plays are still performed today. p. 12

Sitting Bull (1834?–1890) Sioux Indian leader. p. 249

Truth, Sojourner (1797?–1883) African American woman who spoke out against slavery. She was once a slave. p. 83

Washington, George (1732–1799) First President of the United States. He chose the place for the nation's capital city, Washington, D.C. p. 72

315

PICTURE GLOSSARY

Picture Glossary

ancestor
A family member who lived a long time ago. My **ancestors** arrived here before my grandfather was born. (page 182)

anthem
The official song for a country. Our national **anthem** is played at special events. (page 76)

ancient
Very old. The pyramids are **ancient** buildings in Egypt. (page 216)

appoint
To name or choose for a public office or job. The President **appoints** helpers. (page 61)

316

artifact
An object from another time or place. This **artifact** was found in Greece. (page 224)

bar graph
A graph that uses bars to show how many or how much. This **bar graph** shows the money I saved each month. (page 184)

ballot
A piece of paper that shows the choices for voting. The voter marked her choices on the **ballot**. (page 62)

barter
To trade goods and services. People can **barter** instead of using money. (page 292)

bank
A business that looks after people's money. People put money in the **bank** to keep it safe. (page 287)

blizzard
A heavy snowstorm. The **blizzard** covered the roads with snow. (page 144)

317

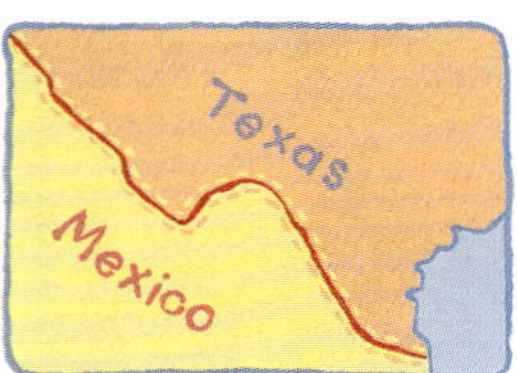

border

A line on a map that shows where a state or country ends. The red line shows the **border** between Texas and Mexico. (page 68)

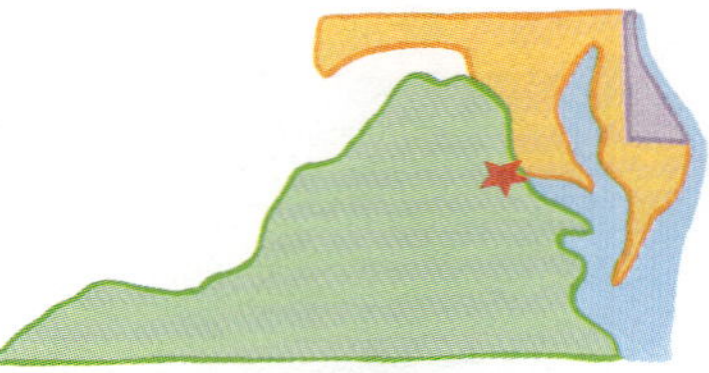

capital

A city in which a state's or country's government meets and works. Washington, D.C., is the **capital** of the United States. (page 68)

business

The making or selling of goods or services. My parents have their own **business** selling flowers. (page 276)

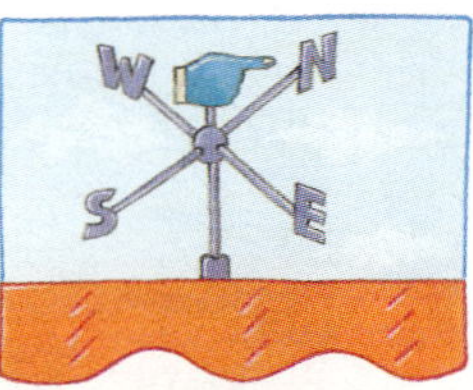

cardinal directions

The main directions of north, south, east, and west. The **cardinal directions** help you find places on a map. (page 124)

S	M	T	W	T	F	S
		1	2	3	4	5
6	7	8	9	10	11	12
13	14	15	16	17	18	19
20	21	22	23	24	25	26
27	28	29	30	31		

MAY

calendar

A chart that shows the days, weeks, and months in a year. The **calendar** shows there are seven days in a week. (page 30)

cause

What makes something happen. My cat's action was the **cause** of a spill. (page 234)

318

change

To become different. The leaves **change** color when the weather gets cooler. (page 26)

climate

The kind of weather a place has over a long time. The rain forest has a very wet **climate**. (page 143)

citizen

A person who lives in and belongs to a community. Nick is a **citizen** of the United States. (page 8)

colony

A place that is ruled by another country. Virginia was the first English **colony** in America. (page 238)

city

A very large town. There are many tall buildings in my **city**. (page 20)

communication

The sharing of ideas and information. The firefighter uses a radio for **communication** with other firefighters. (page 196)

319

community
A group of people who live or work together in the same place. My family has lived in our **community** for many years. (page 6)

consequence
Something that happens because of what a person does. The **consequence** of wearing muddy shoes is a dirty floor. (page 49)

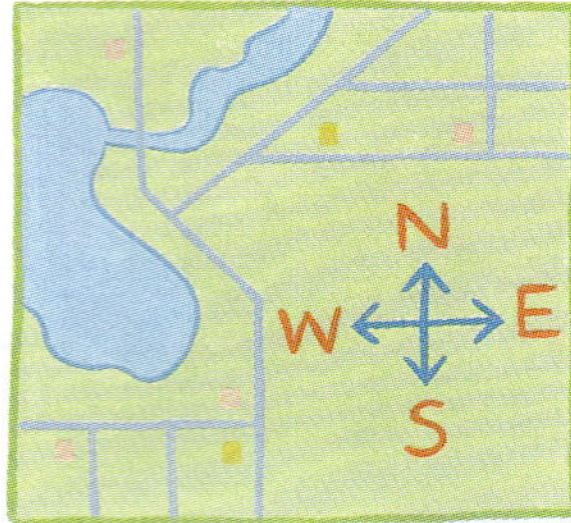

compass rose
Arrows on a map that show direction. The **compass rose** shows directions. (page 126)

conservation
Working to save resources or make them last longer. **Conservation** of electricity is a good idea. (page 148)

Congress
The group of citizens chosen to make decisions for the country. **Congress** votes on new laws. (page 71)

Constitution
The plan of government for the United States. The **Constitution** says every adult citizen has the right to vote. (page 73)

consumer
A person who buys and uses goods and services. This **consumer** is buying food for a picnic. (page 279)

council
A group of citizens chosen to make decisions for all the people. The **council** is discussing where to build the playground. (page 53)

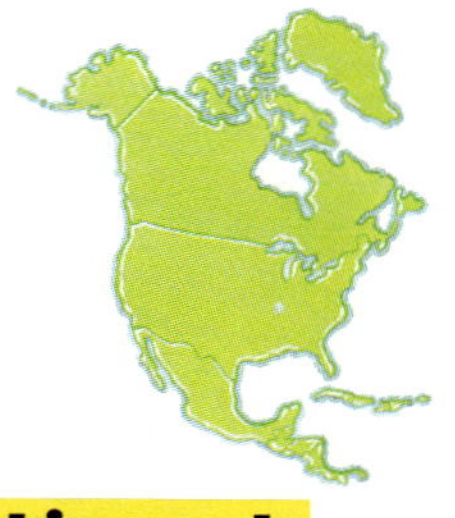

continent
One of the seven main land areas on the Earth. We live on the **continent** of North America. (page 122)

country
An area of land with its own people and laws. We are proud of our **country**. (page 22)

cooperate
To work together. My family likes to **cooperate** on projects. (page 16)

court
A place where a judge decides whether a person has broken the law, and if so, what the consequence should be. Mr. Jackson broke the law and had to go to **court**. (page 54)

321

crop
A plant people grow for food or other needs. Corn is an important **crop** in the United States. (page 132)

culture
A group's way of life. Music and dance are part of my **culture**. (page 169)

custom
A group's way of doing something. One Hawaiian **custom** is to give flowers to visitors. (page 186)

decision
A choice. Tom made a **decision** about what shirt to buy. (page 152)

desert
A large, dry area of land. Very little rain falls in the **desert**. (page 108)

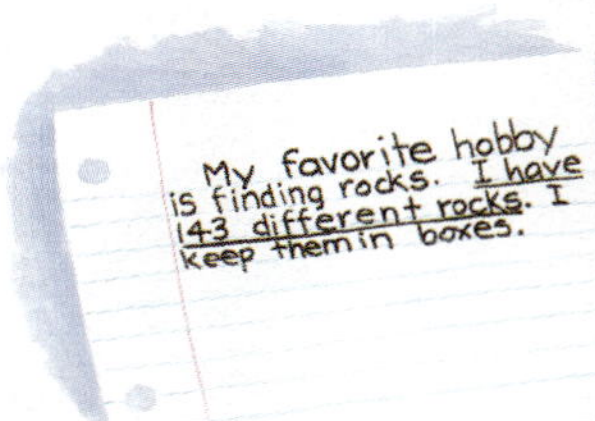

detail
An extra piece of information about something. The number of rocks Sara has is a **detail**. (page 10)

322

diagram
A drawing that shows the parts of something or explains how it works. The **diagram** helped me put my toy together. (page 256)

equator
An imaginary line that divides Earth in half between north and south. Most of South America is south of the **equator**. (page 125)

effect
What happens because of a cause. My cat was surprised by the **effect** of its action. (page 234)

explorer
A person who goes first to find out about a place. Lewis and Clark were famous **explorers**. (page 172)

election
A time when people vote for their leaders. The **election** to choose the President is held in November. (page 60)

fact
A piece of information that is true. It is a **fact** that humans have walked on the moon. (page 88)

323

factory

A building in which people use machines to make goods. The car was made in a **factory** in Detroit. (page 282)

forest

A very large area of trees. This is a **forest** of pine trees. (page 140)

fair

Done in a way that is right and honest. To be **fair**, my brother pours and I choose the glass I want. (page 8)

freedom

The right of people to make their own choices. Americans have the **freedom** to vote. (page 238)

flow chart

A chart that shows the steps needed to make or do something. The **flow chart** shows how to make a picture frame. (page 284)

free enterprise

The freedom to start and run any kind of business. **Free enterprise** helps these children earn money. (page 286)

324

fuel
A resource, such as oil, that can be burned for heat or energy. Gasoline is a **fuel** used in cars. (page 141)

goods
Things that can be bought and sold. This store sells many kinds of **goods**. (page 272)

geography
The study of Earth and its people. **Geography** teaches us about Earth and the people on it. (page 100)

government
The group of citizens that runs a community, state, or country. Our **government** needs strong leaders. (page 47)

globe
A model of Earth. We can find countries on our classroom **globe**. (page 124)

government service
A service that a government provides for citizens. Police officers provide a **government service**. (page 55)

325

governor

The leader of a state's government. Every state has a **governor**. (page 64)

hero

A person who has done something brave or important. This **hero** saved someone's life. (page 244)

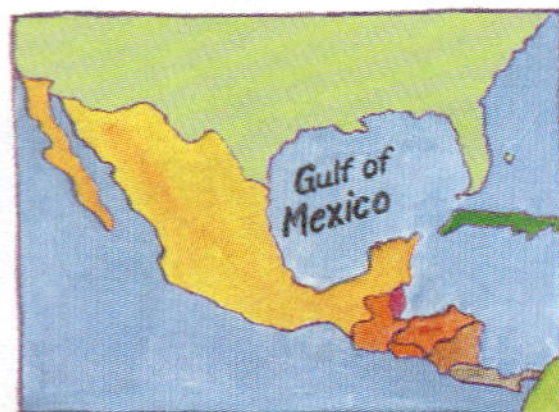

gulf

A large body of ocean water that is partly surrounded by land. The **Gulf** of Mexico is between Mexico and the United States. (page 118)

hill

Land that rises above the land around it. It is fun to slide down a snowy **hill** in winter. (page 112)

H

heritage

The culture and traditions handed down to people by their ancestors. My grandmother teaches me about my **heritage**. (page 178)

history

The study of what happened to people in the past. The **history** of our country is interesting. (page 222)

326

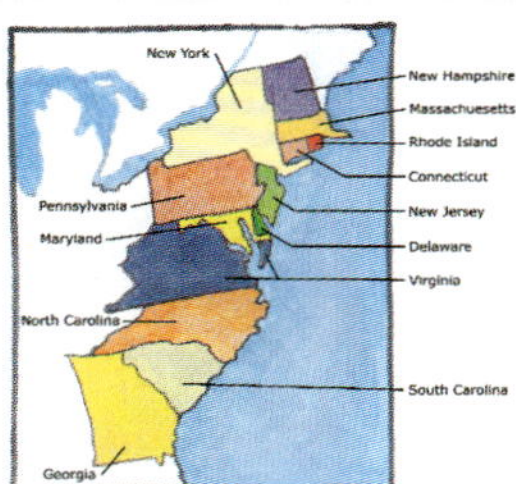

history map
A map that shows how a place looked in an earlier time. This **history map** shows the original thirteen colonies. (page 242)

income
The money people earn for the work they do. Miguel will use his **income** to buy lemonade. (page 286)

holiday
A day to celebrate or remember something. Many African Americans celebrate a **holiday** called Kwanzaa. (page 186)

independence
The freedom of people to choose their own government. George Washington fought for **independence**. (page 238)

immigrant
A person who comes from somewhere else to live in a country. My great-grandfather was an Irish **immigrant**. (page 174)

interest
Money that money earns in a bank. My savings have earned **interest**. (page 287)

327

island
A landform with water all around it. Deep blue water surrounds the **island**. (page 115)

judge
The leader of a court. The **judge** punished the lawbreaker. (page 54)

justice
Fairness. Americans believe in **justice**. (page 85)

lake
A body of water that has land all around it. We enjoy fishing in the **lake**. (page 117)

landform
A kind of land with a special shape, such as a mountain, hill, or plain. A mountain is a large **landform**. (page 112)

landmark
A familiar object at a place. The Alamo is a Texas **landmark**. (page 239)

328

language
The words or signs people use to communicate. Some people use sign **language** to communicate. (page 190)

law
A rule that people in a community must follow. A speed limit **law** keeps people safe. (page 48)

legislature
A group of citizens chosen to make decisions for a state. The **legislature** will decide where to build a new road. (page 65)

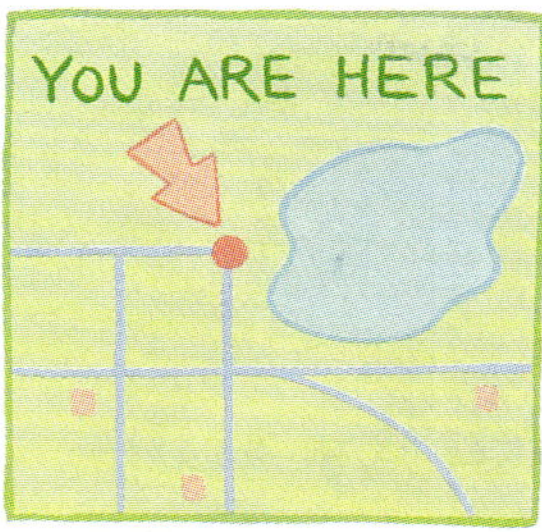

location
The place where something is. The map will help you find your **location**. (page 19)

main idea
What the information you are reading is mostly about. Every paragraph should have a **main idea**. (page 10)

maize
A kind of corn. **Maize** is one crop grown in Mexico. (page 255)

329

majority rule
Rule by more than half of the people in a community. Building a new school was decided by **majority rule**. (page 62)

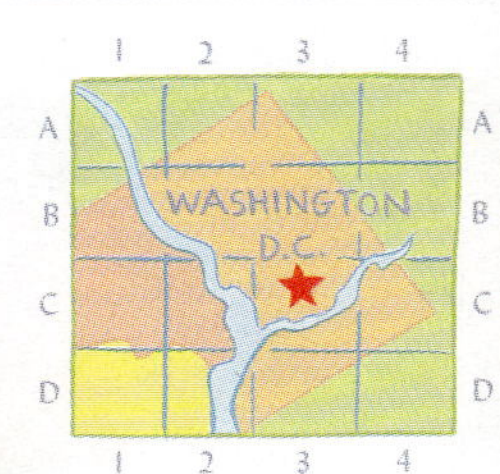

map grid
A set of columns and rows placed on a map to help people find a location. The star is at square C-3 on the **map grid**. (page 250)

manufacture
To make with machines. Robots are used to **manufacture** car parts. (page 283)

map key
The part of a map that shows what the symbols mean. Look for the symbol of the bridge in the **map key**. (page 24)

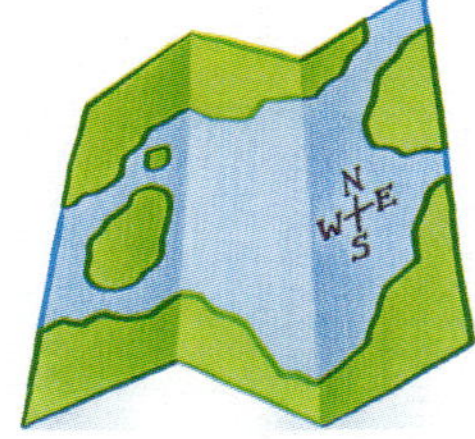

map
A drawing that shows where places are. Can you find an island on this **map**? (page 19)

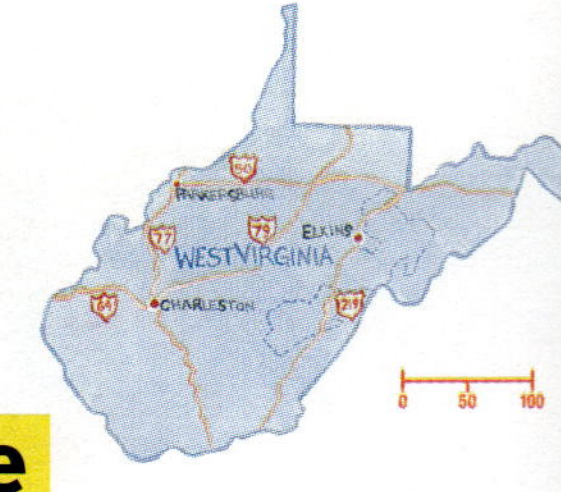

map scale
The part of a map that helps you find distance. The **map scale** can help you find out how far it is from Charleston to Weston. (page 146)

330

map symbol
A small picture that stands for a real thing on Earth. This **map symbol** stands for a mountain. (page 24)

modern
Of the present time. **Modern** technology helps us do our jobs. (page 216)

mayor
The leader of a city or town government. The **mayor** makes important decisions for our community. (page 52)

monument
A statue or marker created to honor a person or an event. This **monument** honors George Washington. (page 244)

memorial
A monument created to honor and remember a hero. This **memorial** reminds us of a brave American. (page 244)

mountain
The highest kind of land. The eagle soared over the top of the **mountain**. (page 114)

museum
A building in which objects from other times and places are displayed. Famous paintings hang in this **museum**. (page 228)

natural resource
Something found in nature that people can use to meet their needs. Oil is a **natural resource**. (page 128)

needs
Things people must have to live. Food, clothing, and a place to live are **needs**. (page 32)

neighborhood
The part of a community in which a group of people lives. The people in my **neighborhood** are friendly. (page 18)

ocean
A very large body of salty water. Ships sail across the **ocean**. (page 109)

opinion
A statement of what a person believes to be true but cannot prove. My friend and I have different **opinions** about the movie. (page 88)

papyrus

A kind of paper made from a certain kind of plant. Ancient Egyptians wrote on **papyrus**. (page 252)

peace

A time of quietness and calm when people are getting along. We wish everyone could live in **peace**. (page 78)

patriotic symbol

A picture or object that stands for something the people of a country believe in. The bald eagle is a **patriotic symbol** for our country. (page 74)

peninsula

A landform that has water on only three sides. Part of Florida is a **peninsula**. (page 115)

patriotism

A feeling of pride people have for their country. People show **patriotism** when they wave the flag. (page 74)

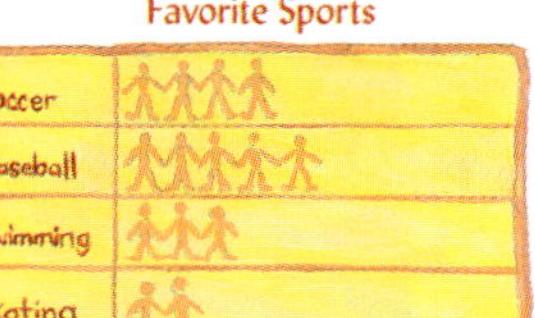

picture graph

A graph that uses pictures to stand for numbers of things. The **picture graph** shows that baseball got the most votes as favorite sport. (page 80)

333

raw material
A resource used to make a product. Wood is a **raw material** used to make furniture. (page 281)

region
An area. We live in a mountain **region**. (page 242)

recreation
The things people do in their spare time, such as playing sports or having hobbies. Sailing is my favorite kind of **recreation**. (page 164)

religion
A belief in a god or gods. Americans enjoy freedom of **religion**. (page 180)

recycle
To use things again. We can **recycle** newspapers to make new paper. (page 149)

responsibility
Something that a citizen should take care of or do. It is my **responsibility** to take these glasses I found to the store owner. (page 9)

336

rights
Freedoms. Freedom of speech is one of our many **rights**. (page 73)

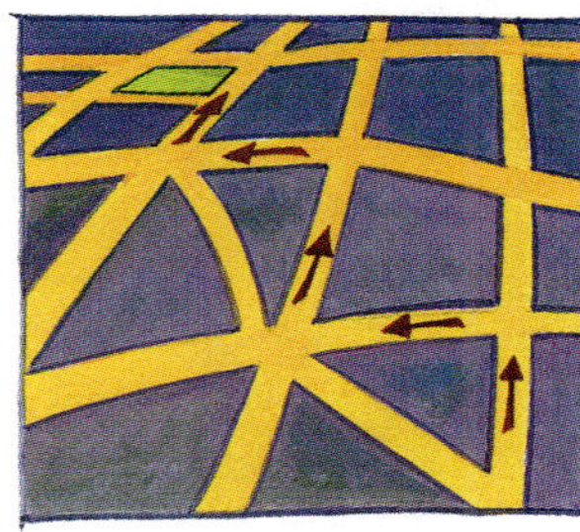

route
A way to go from one place to another. The **route** on this map is easy to follow. (page 176)

river
A stream of water that flows across the land. The Mississippi **River** is the longest river in the United States. (page 116)

rule
An instruction telling what must or must not be done. There is a **rule** against talking loudly in the library. (page 8)

role
The part a person plays in a group or community. The **role** of a goalie is to keep the other team from scoring. (page 12)

S

scarce
Not in good supply, or hard to find. When money is **scarce**, George cannot buy candy. (page 290)

337

PICTURE GLOSSARY

scribe
A person who records things in writing. Long ago, a **scribe** wrote in clay. (page 252)

settlement
A small community started in a new place. The pioneers built a **settlement**. (page 242)

season
One of the four parts of the year that have different kinds of weather. My favorite **season** is fall. (page 212)

settler
One of the first people to make a home in a new place. The **settler** worked hard on his land. (page 229)

services
Work done for others for money. We paid the waiter for his **services**. (page 274)

solution
The way people agree to solve a problem. The **solution** to the leaky pipe is to replace it. (page 50)

338

source
The place where something comes from. An encyclopedia is a good **source** of information. (page 222)

Supreme Court
The highest court in the United States. The **Supreme Court** decides the most important cases. (page 73)

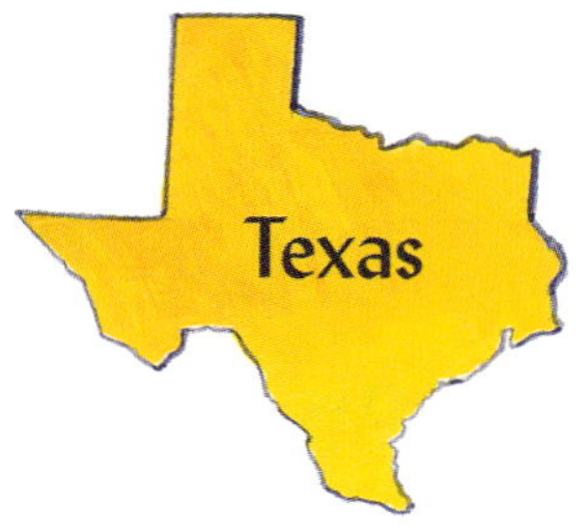

state
A part of a country. Texas is one of our fifty **states**. (page 22)

Class Rides

	BIKE	SCOOTER
Mike		✓
Jane	✓	
Maya		✓
Eric		✓

table
A chart that shows information in rows and columns. A **table** can be used to compare things. (page 134)

suburb
A community near a large city. This **suburb** is about thirty miles from the city. (page 21)

tax
Money paid to the government that is used to pay for services. The **tax** we pay at the store helps pay for building roads. (page 56)

339

technology
The use of new inventions in everyday life. Computers are a useful **technology**. (page 136)

trade
The exchange of one thing for another. Is this a fair **trade**? (page 298)

time line
A line that shows when events happen. This **time line** shows holidays. (page 220)

tradition
A way of doing something that is passed on from parents to children. Wearing kilts is a Scottish **tradition**. (page 181)

tornado
A strong, whirling wind that causes great damage to land and buildings. A **tornado** is a dangerous storm. (page 144)

transportation
Ways of carrying people and goods from one place to another. Buses and airplanes are two types of **transportation**. (page 300)

340

unique
One-of-a-kind. Would you say this painting is **unique**? (page 168)

vote
A choice that gets counted. The person who gets the most **votes** is the winner. (page 60)

valley
Low land between hills or mountains, often with a river or stream flowing through it. A small river runs through the **valley**. (page 114)

volunteer
A person who works without being paid. I am a **volunteer** for my favorite charity. (page 296)

wants
Things people would like to have but do not need. I have more **wants** than I can afford. (page 33)

341

O

P

R

S

T

U

INDEX

347

INDEX

348

For permission to reprint copyrighted material, grateful acknowledgment is made to the following sources:

Charlesbridge Publishing, Inc.: Cover illustration from *Different Just Like Me* by Lori Mitchell. Copyright © 1999 by Lori Mitchell.

Cobblehill Books, an affiliate of Dutton Children's Books, a division of Penguin Putnam Inc.: Cover photograph from *Chidi Only Likes Blue: An African Book of Colors* by Ifeoma Onyefulu. Photograph copyright © 1997 by Ifeoma Onyefulu.

Farrar, Straus and Giroux, LLC: Cover illustration by Tom Pohrt from *The Tomb of the Boy King* by John Frank. Illustration copyright © 2001 by Tom Pohrt.

Harcourt, Inc.: Cover illustration by Thomas Locker from *Between Earth and Sky: Legends of Native American Sacred Places* by Joseph Bruchac. Illustration copyright © 1996 by Thomas Locker. Cover illustration from *Moon Rope* by Lois Ehlert. Copyright © 1992 by Lois Ehlert. From *Worksong* by Gary Paulsen, illustrated by Ruth Wright Paulsen. Text copyright © 1997 by Gary Paulsen; illustrations copyright © 1997 by Ruth Wright Paulsen.

HarperCollins Publishers: From *The Egyptian Cinderella* by Shirley Climo, illustrated by Ruth Heller. Text copyright © 1989 by Shirley Climo; illustrations copyright © 1989 by Ruth Heller. From *The Korean Cinderella* by Shirley Climo, illustrated by Ruth Heller. Text copyright © 1993 by Shirley Climo; illustrations copyright © 1993 by Ruth Heller. Cover illustration by Bethanne Andersen from *Kindle Me a Riddle: A Pioneer Story* by Roberta Karim. Illustration copyright © 1999 by Bethanne Andersen. Cover illustration from *Market!* by Ted Lewin. Copyright © 1996 by Ted Lewin. Cover photograph by Comstock Inc./David Lokey from *Teamwork* by Ann Morris. Photograph © by Comstock Inc./David Lokey. Cover illustration by Lynn Sweat from *Amelia Bedelia 4 Mayor* by Herman Parish. Illustration copyright © 1999 by Lynn Sweat. From *Some Things Go Together* by Charlotte Zolotow, cover illustration by Karen Gundersheimer. Text copyright © 1969 by Charlotte Zolotow; illustration copyright © 1983 by Karen Gundersheimer.

Holiday House, Inc.: Cover illustration from *Celebrate the 50 States!* by Loreen Leedy. Copyright © 1999 by Loreen Leedy.

Henry Holt and Company, Inc.: Cover illustration from *Chinatown* by William Low. Copyright © 1997 by William Low.

Houghton Mifflin Company: Cover illustration by John Clapp from *Right Here on This Spot* by Sharon Hart Addy. Illustration copyright © 1999 by John Clapp.

Alfred A. Knopf Children's Books, a division of Random House, Inc.: Cover illustration by Reynold Ruffins from *Misoso: Once Upon a Time Tales from Africa* by Verna Aardema. Illustration copyright © 1994 by Reynold Ruffins. Cover illustration by Michael McCurdy from *American Tall Tales* by Mary Pope Osborne. Illustration copyright © 1991 by Michael McCurdy.

Little, Brown and Company (Inc.): Cover illustration from *Bravo, Maurice!* by Rebecca Bond. Copyright © 2000 by Rebecca Bond. Cover illustration by Kathy Jakobsen from *This Land Is Your Land* by Woody Guthrie. Illustration copyright © 1998 by Kathy Jakobsen. Cover illustration by Isabelle Brent from *The Golden Bird*, retold from the Brothers Grimm by Neil Philip. Illustration copyright © 1995 by Isabelle Brent.

The Millbrook Press, Inc., Brookfield, CT 06804: Cover illustration by Elisa Kleven from *Our Big Home: An Earth Poem* by Linda Glaser. Illustration copyright © 2000 by Elisa Kleven.

Joan Miller: From "Valentine For Earth" in *The Little Naturalist* by Frances Frost. Text copyright © 1959 by the Estate of Frances Frost; © renewed 1987.

G. P. Putnam's Sons, an imprint of Penguin Putnam Books for Young Readers, a division of Penguin Putnam Inc.: Cover illustration from *Officer Buckle and Gloria* by Peggy Rathmann. Copyright © 1995 by Peggy Rathmann. From *Growing Seasons* by Elsie Lee Splear, cover illustration by Ken Stark. Text and cover copyright © 2000 by Carolyn Splear Pratt.

Scholastic Inc.: Cover illustration from *The Paperboy* by Dav Pilkey. Copyright © 1996 by Dav Pilkey. Published by Orchard Books, an imprint of Scholastic Inc. *Tulip Sees America* by Cynthia Rylant, illustrated by Lisa Desimini. Text copyright © 1998 by Cynthia Rylant; illustrations copyright © 1998 by Lisa Desimini. Published by The Blue Sky Press, an imprint of Scholastic Inc.

Sports Illustrated For Kids: From "Eskimo Games" by Andrew Gutelle, illustrated by Brad Hamann in *Sports Illustrated For Kids*, April 1993. Copyright © 1993 by Time Inc.

Viking Penguin, an imprint of Penguin Putnam Books for Young Readers, a division of Penguin Putnam Inc.: Cover illustration by S. D. Schindler from *Are We There Yet, Daddy?* by Virginia Walters. Illustration copyright © 1999 by S. D. Schindler.

Albert Whitman & Company: Cover illustration by Cornelius Van Wright and Ying-Hwa Hu from *Mei-Mei Loves the Morning* by Margaret Holloway Tsubakiyama. Illustration copyright © 1999 by Cornelius Van Wright and Ying-Hwa Hu.

ILLUSTRATION CREDITS:

ATLAS

Page A1-A13, MAPQUEST.COM.; A12, Studio Liddell.

UNIT 1

Page 4-5, Brenda Joysmith; 8-9, Laura Ovresat; 11, Renee Preston; 14, Jennifer Dingess; 19, Ken Batelman/Brian Ashe; 22-23, Ken Batelman; 24-25, 39 Stephanie Darden.

UNIT 2

Pages 44-45, Andy Cook; 50-51, Darin Johnston; 63, Renee Preston; 81 Stephanie Darden.

UNIT 3

Page 100-112, Lisa Desimini; 130, Jon Edwards; 135, Ken Batelman/Brian Ashe; 160, Wendy Walenberg.

UNIT 4

Page 206, Stephanie Darden; 208, Renee Preston.

UNIT 5

Pages 212-215, Doug Bowles; 218, 256-257, 262, Jon Edwards; 237, Wayne Still; 251, Stephanie Darden.

UNIT 6

Page 268-271, Ruth Wright Paulsen; 299, Ken Batelman/Stephanie Darden; 300-301, Studio Liddell; 310, Scott Schiedly.

PICTURE GLOSSARY

Page 316, 317, 318, 319, 320, 321, Denise Fraifeld; 316, 322, 325, 331, 332, 333, 334, 335, 336, 337, 338, Franklin Ayers; 317, 326, 327, 336, 337, 338, Everett Magie; 318, 322, 323, 324, 325, 327, 328, 329, Robert Dellinger; 318, 319, 320, 329, 330, 333, Steven Royal; 321, 326, 327, Jeff Wilson; 325, 326, 327, 336, 337, 338, 339, 340, 341, Navin Patel; 330, 333, 340, Darrin Johnston.

PHOTO CREDITS

Cover: Doug DuKane (fireman, fire engine); Rafael Macia/Photo Researchers, Inc. (flag); Ed Castle/Folio (building).

PAGE PLACEMENT KEY: (t)-top (c) center, (b)-bottom, (l)-left, (r)-right, (bg) background, (fg)-foreground;

TITLE PAGE AND TABLE OF CONTENTS: iv Shelburne Museum; v Terry Heffernan Films; vi The Chester County Historical Society, vii Superstock; viii Smithsonian Institution;

UNIT 1

Opener (fg) Shelburne Museum, 1 Shelburne Museum; 2 (tr) Joseph Sohm, Chromosohm/Corbis; 2 (br) Ted Rose/Unicorn Stock Photos; 3 (cr) Bob Daemmrich/The Image Works; 6,7 (b) Panoramic Images; 6 J. Sohm/The Image Works; 7 (tl)(tr) PhotoVault.com; 7 (cr) Jay Taffet/Affordable Aerials.com; 8 (tr) Cathy Fox Raphaelson/Houserstock; 8 (bl) M.Anyman/The Image Works, Inc.; 8 (br) Bob Daemmrich Photos; 8 (cl) John P. Kelley/The Image Bank; 8 Steve Jessmore/Dembinsky Photo Associates; 8 (cr) Peter Essick /Aurora /PictureQuest; 9 (tr) A. Ramey/Stock, Boston; 9 (cr) M. Ferguson/PhotoEdit; 9 (cr) Frozen Images/The Image Works, Inc.; 18 (b), (c) Richard Hamilton Smith Photography; 20 (cr) C. E. Mitchell/Black Star; 21 (b) Jeff Greenberg/Unicorn Stock Photos; 26 (br) Eric & Nathalie Cumbie; 26 (cr) Eric & Nathalie Cumbie; 27 © Eric & Nathalie Cumbie; 27 (tr) Staten Island Historical Society; 27 Siede Preis/PhotoDisc; 28 (l) The Mariners Museum/Corbis; (r) E.O Hoppe/Corbis; 29 Stephen Morton/Getty Images; 30 (tl), (cl) Culver Pictures/Picture Quest; 32 (c) Ecoscene/Corbis; 32 and 33 (b) Kelvin Murray/Stone; 32 (cl), (bl) David & Peter Turnley/Corbis; 32 (cl), (bl) Jason Laure/Laure Communications; 33 (c) Aaron Haupt/Photo Researchers; 33 (tl) Spencer Grant/PhotoEdit; 33 (tr) Loren Santow/Stone; 33 (cr) Yann Guichaoua/Allsport Photography; 34-35 (c) PhotoEdit; 34 (br) Judith F. Baca/Great Wall Images; 35 (tl) Sparc Murals; 35 (tr) PhotoEdit.

UNIT 2

Opener (fg) Terry Heffernan Films, (bg) Wilton S. Tifft Photography, (spread) Wilton S. Tifft Photography; 41 Terry Heffernan Films; 42 (tl) Mark Morgan/Black Star/Harcourt; 42 (tl) Bob Daemmrich/The Image Works; 43 (tl) Mark Burnett/Stock, Boston; 43 (cr) Bob Daemmrich/The Image Works; 48-49 Spencer Grant/PhotoEdit; 52 (c) Kelly Culpepper/Harcourt; 52 Ron Wurzer/Getty Images; 53 (t) Ron Wurzer/Getty Images; 53 (br) Mark Richards/PhotoEdit; 53 (cr) Candace C. Mundy/Tampa Tribune/Silver Image; 54 Bob Daemmrich/Stock, Boston/Picture Quest; 55 (t) Michael Leschisin/Silver Image; 55 (b) David R. Frazier; 56 (t) Image Farm/PictureQuest; 56 Eric Berndt/Unicorn Stock Photos; 57 (t) Steven

Rubin/The Image Works; 57 (cr) Philip Kaake/Corbis; 58 Harvey Lloyd/FPG International; 59 (b) Dean Conger/Corbis; 59 (tr) National Palace Museum; Taiwan/E.T. Archive, London/Superstock; 60-61 (b) PhotoEdit; 61 (cr) Bob Daemmrich Photos; 64 (l) Time Pix; 64 (r) Hulton/Archive; 65 (t) Bob Daemmrich/Stock, Boston; 66 (t) Mike Booher/Transparencies, Inc.; 66 (t) & (c) David Ulmer/Stock, Boston; 67 Agence France Presse/Corbis; 70 Harcourt; 71 Doug Armand/Stone; 72 (t) Richard Nowitz/Photo Researchers; 72 (b) Jon Feingersh/Stock, Boston; 73 (t) Alan Schein/Corbis Stock Market; 73 (b) Joseph Sohm; Visions of America/Corbis; 74 (l) Richard Hobbs/Silver Image; 74 (tr), (br), (cr) One Mile Up; 76 (inset) The Granger Collection, New York; 77 (t) Corbis; 77 (b) Richard Hutchings/PhotoEdit; 78 (l) Tommy Dodson/Unicorn Stock Photos; 78 (t) Planet Earth Pictures/FPG International; 78-79 (b) Jon Feingersh/Uniphoto; 78 (bl) James Strawser/Grant Heilman Photography; 78 (bc) Ken Reid/Taxi/Getty Images; 78 (br) Patrick Johns/Corbis; 79 (t) Lee Snider/The Image Works; 79 (cr) Jimmy Rudnick/Corbis Stock Market; 80 Jim Zipp/Photo Researchers; 80 Superstock; 81 (t) Tom Tietz/Stone; 81 (c) Rod Planck/Photo Researchers; 81 (b) Superstock; 81 (tc) Ted Rose/Unicorn Stock Photos; 81 (bc) John Cancalosi/Stock, Boston; 82 Hulton Archive; 83 (l) Superstock; 83 (r) Corbis; 83 (c) Hulton Archive; 84 TIME LIFE PICTURES/Time Life Pictures/Getty Images; 85 (l) Archive Photos/PictureQuest; 85 (r) Bob Parent/Archive Photos; 86 (l) Reuters NewMedia Inc./Corbis; 86 (c) MHPC; 87 (r) Robert Pepper/Getty/Liason; 87 (c) Reuters NewMedia Inc./Corbis; 90 (tl) Joe McDonald/Corbis; 90 (bl) Gwyn McKee/George Miksch Sutton Avian Research Center; 90 (cr) Craig Koppie/George Miksch Sutton Avian Research Center; 91 (tl) Gwyn McGee/George Miksch Sutton Avian Research Center; 91 (tr) George Miksch Sutton Avian Research Center; 91 (cr) Gwyn McKee/Steve Sherrod/George Miksch Sutton Avian Research Center; 91 (bl) Superstock..

UNIT 3

Opener (fg) The Chester County Historical Society; (bg) L. Burton/H. Armstrong Roberts, Inc., (spread) L. Burton/H. Armstrong Roberts, Inc.; 97 The Chester County Historical Society; 98 (c) Library Intern/Corbis; 98 (bl) Jon Feingersh/Corbis Stock Market; 99 (tl) Thomas Wiewandt/Masterfile; 99 (tr) Peter Christopher/Masterfile; 99 (bl) Dave Reed/AgStock; 112 Phil Schermeister/Corbis; 113 (t) Grant Hellman; 113 (b) Karen Holsinger Muller/Unicorn Stock Photos; 114 Doug Berry/Telluride Stock; 115 (b) NASA/Harcourt; 115 (tr) Robert Fried; 116 H. Abernathy/H. Armstrong Roberts, Inc.; 117 (t) Susie Leavines; 117 (b) Grant Heilman; 118 (tr) PhotoDisc; 118 (b) Jeff Greenberg/PhotoEdit; 120 (bl) Tom Bean; 120 (tr) Phil Schermeister/Corbis; 120 (bl) Doug Berry/Telluride Stock; 120 (br) Grant Heilman; 122-123 (b) David Ball/Corbis Stock Market; 126-127 Jon Feingeresh/Corbis Stock Market; 129 (t) Index Stock Photography; 129 (cr) Orion Press/Black Sheep Stock Photography; 129 (br) Orion Press/Black Sheep Stock Photography; 129 (inset) David Madison/Stone; 130 (bg) H.R. Bramaz/Peter Arnold, Inc.; 131 (c) George Lepp/AgStock USA; 131 (b) Mark E. Gibson; 131 Jim Cummins/Corbis Stock Market; 132-133 (b) Larry Lefever/Grant Hellma Photography; 132 (tl) Barry L. Runk/Grant Hellman Photography; 132 (cl) Michael A. Keller/Corbis; 132 (cr) Steven Needham/Envision; 132 (bl) Siede Preis/PhotoDisc; 132 (br) Steven Needham/Envision; 133 (tr) National Portrait Gallery, Smithsonian Institution/Art Resource, NY; 133 (cl) Scott Sinklier/AgStock USA; 134-135 Bryan Peterson/Corbis Stock Market; 135 (t) Momatiuk Eastcott/The Image Works; 135 (ct) Bryan Peterson/Corbis Stock Market; 135 (cb) John Cancalosi/Stock, Boston; 135 Superstock; 136 (cr) Hulton-Deutsch Collection/Corbis; 137 (c) Brown Brothers; 137 (b) Larry LeFever/Grant Heilman Photography; 137 (tc) Brown Brothers; 137 (all) Siede Preis/PhotoDisc; 138 (t) Alan Pitcairn/Grant Heilman Photography; 138 (b) Bill Barksdale/AGStock USA; 139 (t) John Colwell/Grant Heilman Photography; 139 (c) Arthur C. Smith III/Grant Heilman Photography; 140, 141 Ed Jackson; 142 Ed Jackson; 143 (tr) Bob Daemmrich Photos Photography; 143 (cr) Kelly-Mooney Photography/Corbis; 143 (c) Kindra Clineff/International Stock; 143 (br) David Brownell Photography; 144 (t) Harold M.Lambert/Superstock; 144 (b) Bob Daemmrich/Stock, Boston, 145 (t) Jim Richardson/Corbis; 145 (inset) U.S. Army Corps of Engineers; 148 (b) Keith Wood/Stone; 148 (inset) Bob Daemmrich/The Image Works; 150 (tr) Simon Fraser/Northumbrian Environmental Management/Science Photo Library/Photo Researchers; 150-151 Geri Engberg Photography; 151 D. Young-Wolff/PhotoEdit; 152 (both) Myrleen Cate/PhotoEdit; 153 (c) David Oliver/Stone; 153 (inset) PhotoEdit; 154-155 (all) Jerry Jacka Photography.

UNIT 4

Opener (fg) Superstock, (bg) Nik Wheeler/Corbis, (spread) Nik Wheeler/Corbis; 161 Superstock; 162 (tr) Lester Sloan/Woodfin Camp & Associates; 162 (b) D. Lada/H. Armstrong Roberts; 163 (tl) Con Mason/Corbis; 163 (tr) Ohio Historical Society; 163 (bl) Robert Brenner/PhotoEdit; 168 (tr) Chronis Jons/Stone; 168 (cl) PhotoEdit; 168 (c) Charles Gupton/Stock, Boston; 168 (cr) Tom Pantages; 168 (bl) Walter Hodges/Corbis; 168 (bc) Kelley-Mooney Photography/Corbis; 168 (br) Don Smetzer/Stone; 169 (tr) Agence France Presse/Corbis; 169 (cl) Ariel Skelley/Corbis Stock Market; 169 (cl) Steve Bourgeois/Unicorn Stock Photos; 169 (cr) Michael Dwyer/Stock, Boston; 169 (bl) Michael Newman/PhotoEdit; 169 (bc) (br) Bob Daemmrich Photos; 171 (tl) Mike Yamashita/Woodfin Camp & Associates; 171 (tr) Dennis Cox/ChinaStock Photo Library; 171 (bl) Ariel Skelley/Corbis Stock Market; 172 (b) Corbis; 173 (tr) Danny Lehman/Corbis; 173 (br) Gene Aherns/Corbis; 174 (tr) George Rinhart/Corbis; 174 (c) Bob Krist/Corbis; 174-175 Brown Brothers; 175 (tr) NASA/Harcourt; 175 Everett C. Johnson/Leo De Wys, Inc.; 178 (r) (inset) Don Couch Photography/TX General Land Office; 178 Felicia Martinez/PhotoEdit; 179 (b) (inset) Timothy Fuller/Harcourt; 179 (b) Timothy Fuller/Harcourt; 180 (t) Brown Brothers; 180 (b) Roger Ressmeyer/Corbis; 182 (tr) Library of Congress/Corbis; 182 (cl) PhotoEdit; 183 (cr) Owen Franken/Stock, Boston; 186 (bl) H. Rogers/Art Directors & TRIP Photo Library; 186-187 A. Ramey/Stock, Boston; 187 (tr) Siede Preis/PhotoDisc; 187 (tr) (inset) Jerry Koser/H. Armstrong Roberts; 187 (tl) Jules Frazier/PhotoDisc; 187 (b) Christopher Morrow/Stock, Boston; 188 (tl) Superstock; 188 (cr) Peter Johansky/Envision; 188 (bl) Lawrence Migdale; 188 (br) D. Young-Wolff/PhotoEdit; 189 (tr) Lawrence Migdale/Stock, Boston; 189 (br) PhotoEdit; 192 (t) M & E Bernheim/Woodfin Camp & Associates; 192 (c) Penny Tweedie/Corbis; 193 (tr) Catherine Karnow/Woodfin Camp & Associates; 193 (cl) R. Krubner/H. Armstrong Roberts; 193 (cr) Kunio Owaki/Corbis Stock Market; 193 (b) Craig Tuttle/Corbis Stock Market; 194 (tl) David Ball/Corbis Stock Market; 194 (c) Jose Carrillo/Stock, Boston; 194 (bl) Jean Higgins/Envision; 195 (c) Superstock, 196 (bl) Giraudon/Bridgeman Art Library; 197 (tr) The Granger Collection; 197 (inset) PhotoEdit; 197 (b) Mark E. Gibson Photography; 198 (tr) Bettman Archive/Corbis; 198 (cl) Brown Brothers; 198 (bl) Corbis/PictureQuest; 198 (br) Don Mason/Corbis; 199 (c) Kury Wittman/Omni-Photo Communications, Inc.; 199 (cr) David Mcglynn/FPG International; 202 (both) Ann Hawthorne; 203 (tl), (tr), (cr) Ann Hawthorne; 203 (bl) Penland School of Crafts; 203 (br) Ann Hawthorne/Penland School of Crafts.

UNIT 5

Opener (fg) Smithsonian Institution, (bg) McConnell & McNamara, (spread) McConnell & McNamara; 209 Smithsonian Institution; 210 (t) Pictor, 210 (b) John McGrail; 211 (tl) Todd Gipstein/Corbis; 211 (b) Superstock; 216 Robert Caputo/Stock, Boston, 217 (r) Jean Higgins/Unicorn Stock Photos; 217 (cl) Tony Freeman/PhotoEdit; 217 (c) Superstock; 217 (cr) Ancient Art and Architecture Collection; 217 (bl) Chuck Scheiser/Unicorn Stock Photos; 217 (bc) Richard Pasley/Stock, Boston; 218 (t) ChinaStock Photo Library; 218 (c) Richard S. Calhoun; 219 Giraudon/Art Resource, NY; 220 (bl) NASA; 220 (bc) Bettann/Corbis; 220 (t), (br) NASA; 221 (all) NASA; 222 (bl) Tim Wright/Corbis; 223 (tl) Jan Butchofsky-Houser/Corbis; 223 (tr) James L. Amos/Corbis; 223 (c) Stephen Morton/Getty Images; 223 (bl) Robert Burch Communications; 223 (br) AP Photo/Nevada Appeal, Cathleen Allison; 224 (tl) Jon Feingersh/Corbis Stock Market; 224 (tc) Library of Congress; 224 (tr) National Baseball Hall of Fame & Museum/National Baseball Hall of Fame Library; 224 (b) Bettmann/Corbis; 225 (tl) Karen Roush; 225 (cr) Reuters NewMedia, Inc./Corbis; 226 Frank Siteman/Stock, Boston Inc./PictureQuest; 227 (l) Superstock; 227 (r) Robert W. Ginn/Envision; 228 Paul Wayne Wilson; 229 Fort Myers Downtown Redevelopment Agency; 230 Paul Wayne Wilson; 231 Halgrim; 232 (t) Fort Myers Historical Society; 232 (b) Henry Bartley; 233 South Florida Water Management District; 234 2002-2003 PicturesFrom.com; 235 (tl) Mark Peterson/Corbis; 235 (cr) 2002-2003 PicturesFrom.com; 235 (bl) Alamy Images; 236 (b) Bettman/Corbis; 239 (inset) National Park Service/ Minuteman National Historic Park, MA; 239 (b) Dennis Degnan/Corbis; 240 (b) Stone; 240 (inset) Gregory Smith/Associated Press; 241 Superstock; 242 Bettmann/Corbis; 244 (l) Henryk T. Kaiser/Transparencies; 244 (r) Superstock; 244-245 Mark Burnett/Stock, Boston; 245 (tl) Alison Wright/Stock, Boston; 245 (cl) Jeff Lawrence/Stock, Boston; 246 (br) Bettman/Corbis; 247 (tl) Steve Yeater/Black Star; 247 (tr) Hulton/Archive/Getty Images; 247 (cl) FPG International; 247 (b) University of Wisconsin, Milwaukee; 248 (tl), (cl) Superstock; 248 (bl) Ted Spiegel/Corbis; 248 (br) Mike Smith/FPG International; 249 (tl) Tony Freeman; 249 (tr) David R. Frazier; 252 (bl) Scala/Art

Resource; 252 (br) Newberry Library, Chicago/Superstock; 253 (t) David Forbert/Superstock; 253 (c) Peter Harholdt/Superstock; 253 (b) Superstock; 254 (t) Macduff Everton/The Image Works, Inc.; 254 (b) Newberry Library, Chicago; 255 Michael J. Pettypool/Houserstock, Inc.; 256 Karen Roush; 257 (br) Hulton/Archive Photos; 258 (bl) Museum of the City of New York/Corbis; 258 (bcl) The Granger Collection, New York; 258 (bcr) The Granger Collection, New York; 258 (br) The Granger Collection, New York; 258-259 Paul A. Souders/Corbis; 259 (tr) Lionel Green/Archive Photos.

UNIT 6

Opener (bg) Aneal N. Vohra/Unicorn Stock Photos, (spread) Aneal N. Vohra/Unicorn Stock Photos; 266 (tl) David Butow/Corbis SABA; 267 (tl) Superstock; 267 (cr) Randy Vaughn-Dotta/AGStock USA; 272 (tc) Michael Newman/PhotoEdit; 272 (tr) PhotoEdit; 272 (cl) Joel W. Rogers/Corbis; 272 (c) Bob Daemmrich Photos; 272 (bc) Pictor; 272 (br) Bob Daemmrich Photos; 273 (tl) Matthew Borkoski/Stock, Boston; 273 (bl) Bob Daemmrich Photos; 273 (r) Daniel Grogan/Pictor; 274 (tl) Bob Daemmrich Photos; 274 (c) Superstock; 274 (bl) Karen Roush; 274 (br) PhotoEdit; 275 (tr) Bill Gallery/Stock, Boston; 275 (c) VCG/FPG International; 275 (bl) Bob Daemmrich/The Image Works; 275 (bg) David Wagner/Phototake/PictureQuest; 280 (both) McGuire Studio Midwest; 280-281 John Colwell/Grant Heilman Photography; 281 (t) John Colwell/Grant Heilman Photography; 281 (c) McGuire Studio Midwest; 282, 283, 284, 285, McGuire Studio Midwest; 288 (b) Reuters NewMedia Inc./Corbis; 289 (tr) Karen Roush; 292 (cr) Museum of the City of New York Toy Collection; 292 (bl), (br) British Museum; 293 (tl) W.S. Nawrocki/Nawrocki Stock Photo; 293 (tr) British Museum; 293 (c) Larry Stevens/Nawrocki Stock Photo; 293 (bl), (br) British Museum; 294 (tl), (tr) Feldman & Associates; 294 (c), (cl) Smithsonian Institution National Numismatic Collection; 294 (cr) Feldman & Associates; 294 (bl) AFP/Corbis; 294 (bl) Corbis; 294 (br) Smithsonian Institution National Numismatic Collection; 296 (cr) Richard T. Nowitz/Corbis; 296 (bl) Bob Daemmrich Photos; 297 Mark Peterson/Corbis SABA; 300 Pictor; 301 (tl) Bob Daemmrich Photos; 301 (tr) Joseph Sohm;ChromoSohm Inc./Corbis; 302 (tr) Ian Clark/International Stock; 302 (c) Bob Daemmrich Photos; 302 (b) (inset) The Granger Collection, New York; 302 (br) Paul A. Souders/Corbis; 303 (tr) Corbis; 306 (l) Gale Zucker; 303 (r) Joe Towers/Corbis Stock Market; 306 (cr) Gale Zucker 2001; 307 (tr) Gale Zucker 2001; 307 (c) Binney & Smith Inc.; 307 (b) Gale Zucker 2001.

All other photos by Harcourt Photographers, Ken Kinzie, Weronica Ankarorn, Victoria Bowen, and US Color.

Activity Patterns

The reproducible patterns in this section are for use with the extension activities described in your lesson plans. You may also want to use the patterns to create other activities appropriate for children in your class.

Contents

Rules Puzzle

Geography Cube

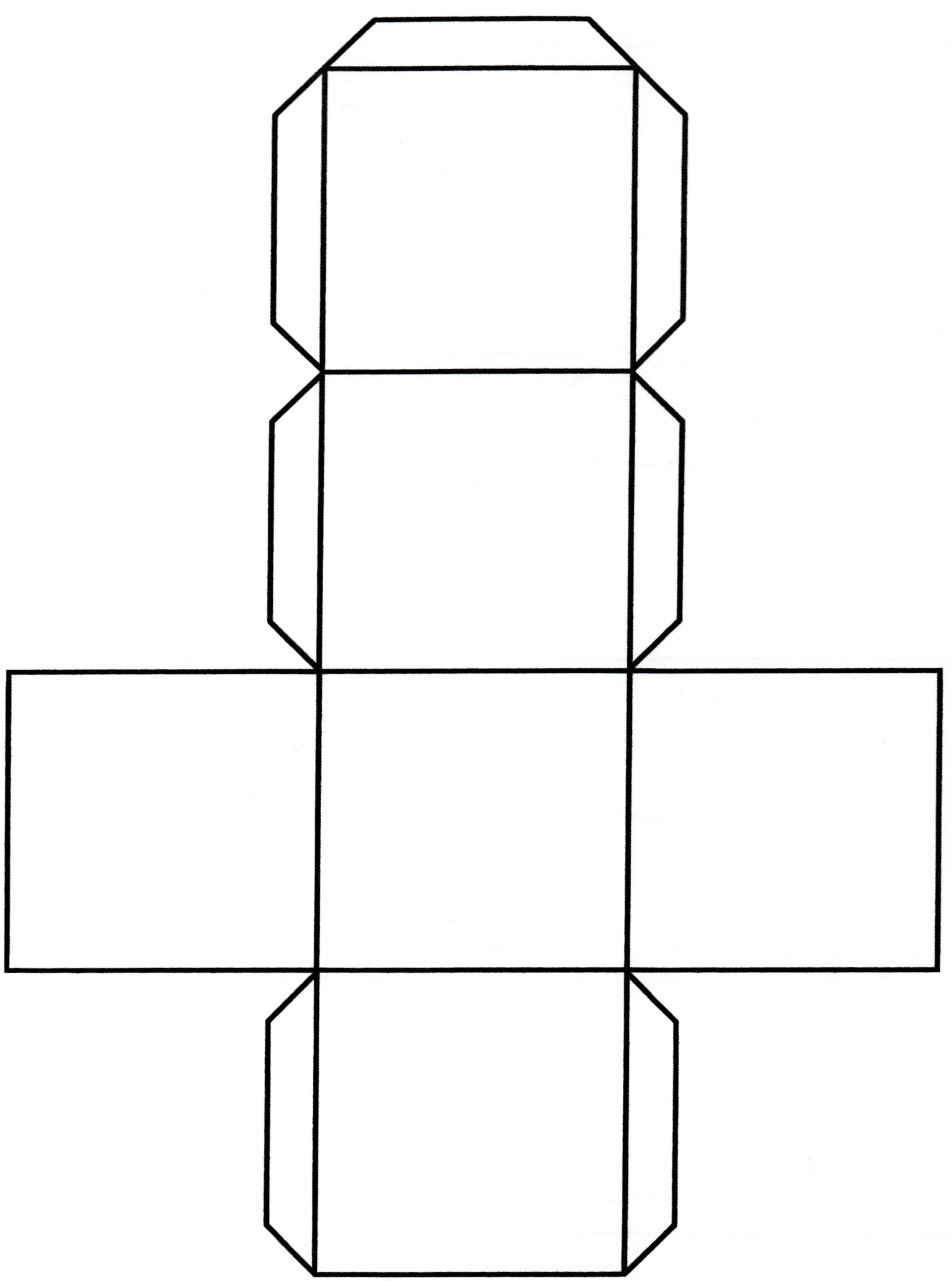

Design a State T-Shirt

Picture Graph

Title ______________________________

Storyboard

In the News

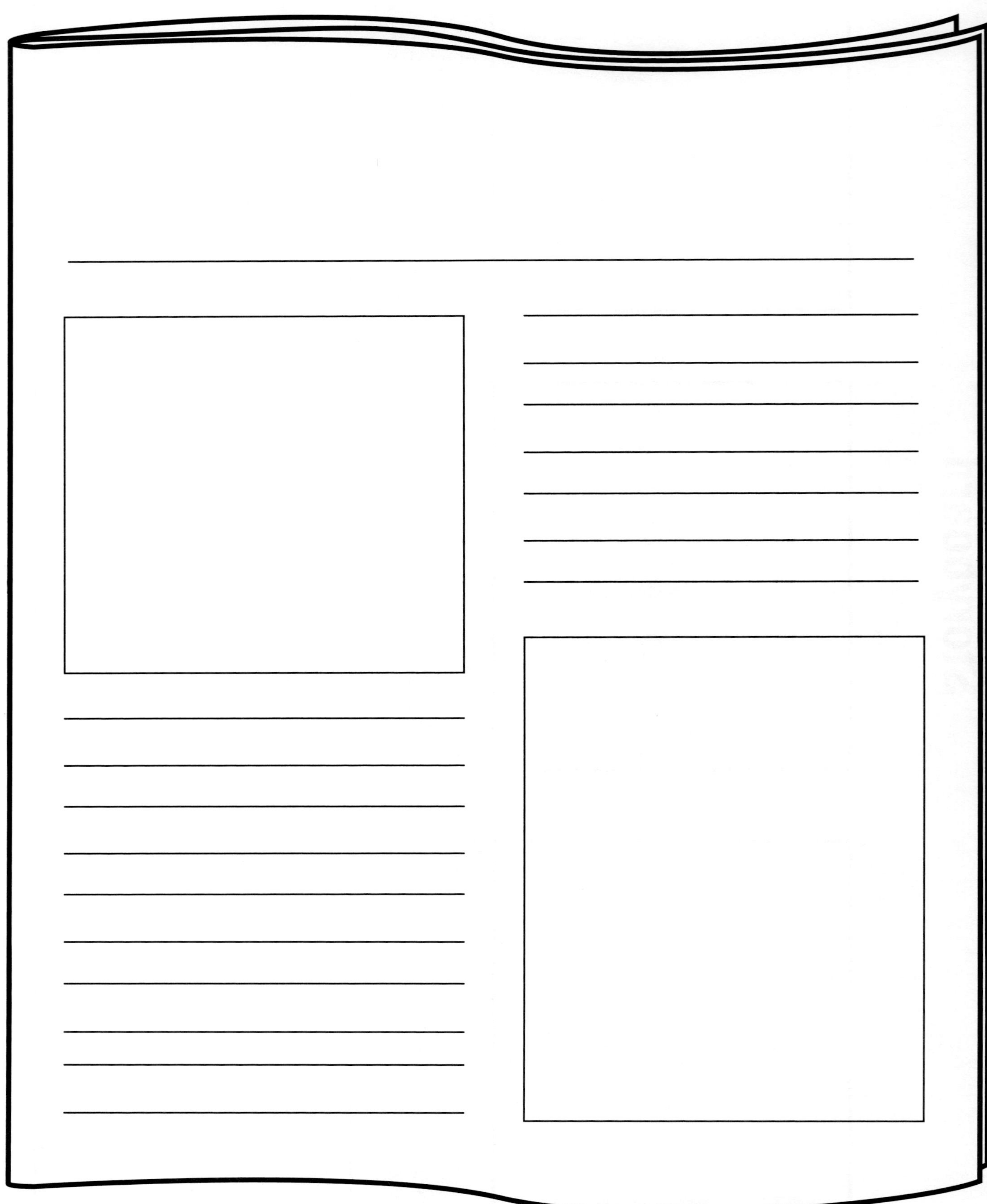

Travel Passport

Name ____________________

Date of Birth ____________________

____

Month Day Year

Place of Birth

____

____

State Country

____

Signature

PASSPORT

E PLURIBUS UNUM

United States of America

Name ____________________

Date of Birth ____________________

____

Month Day Year

Place of Birth

____

____

State Country

____

Signature

PASSPORT

E PLURIBUS UNUM

United States of America

History Filmstrip

Accordion Book

Tape

Tape

Product Table

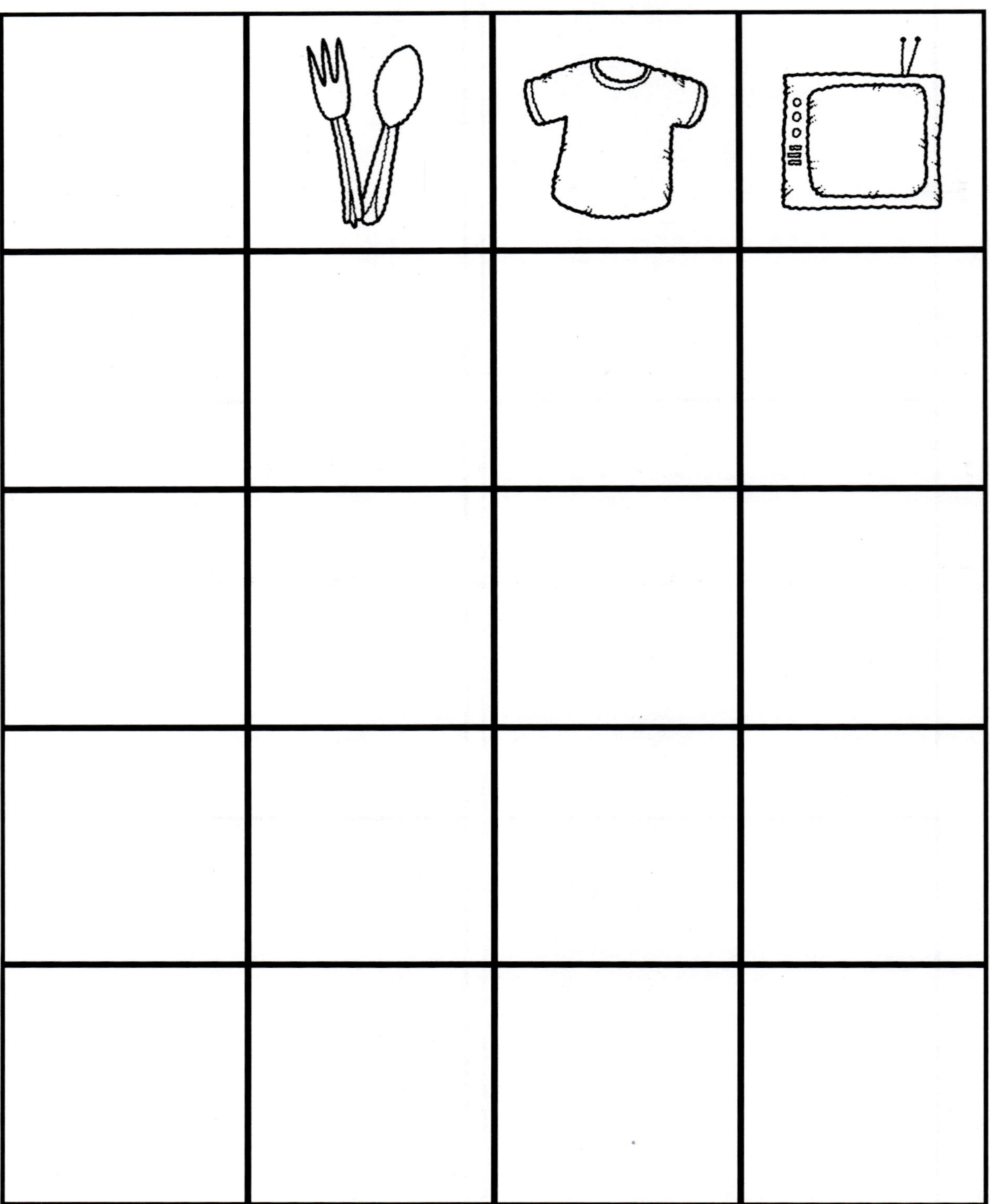

Thinking Organizers

Ideas and concepts may be organized in many different ways. The contents of the following pages are intended to act as guides for that organization. These copying masters may be used to help children organize the concepts in the lessons they have read. They may also help children complete the wide variety of activities that are assigned throughout the school year.

Contents

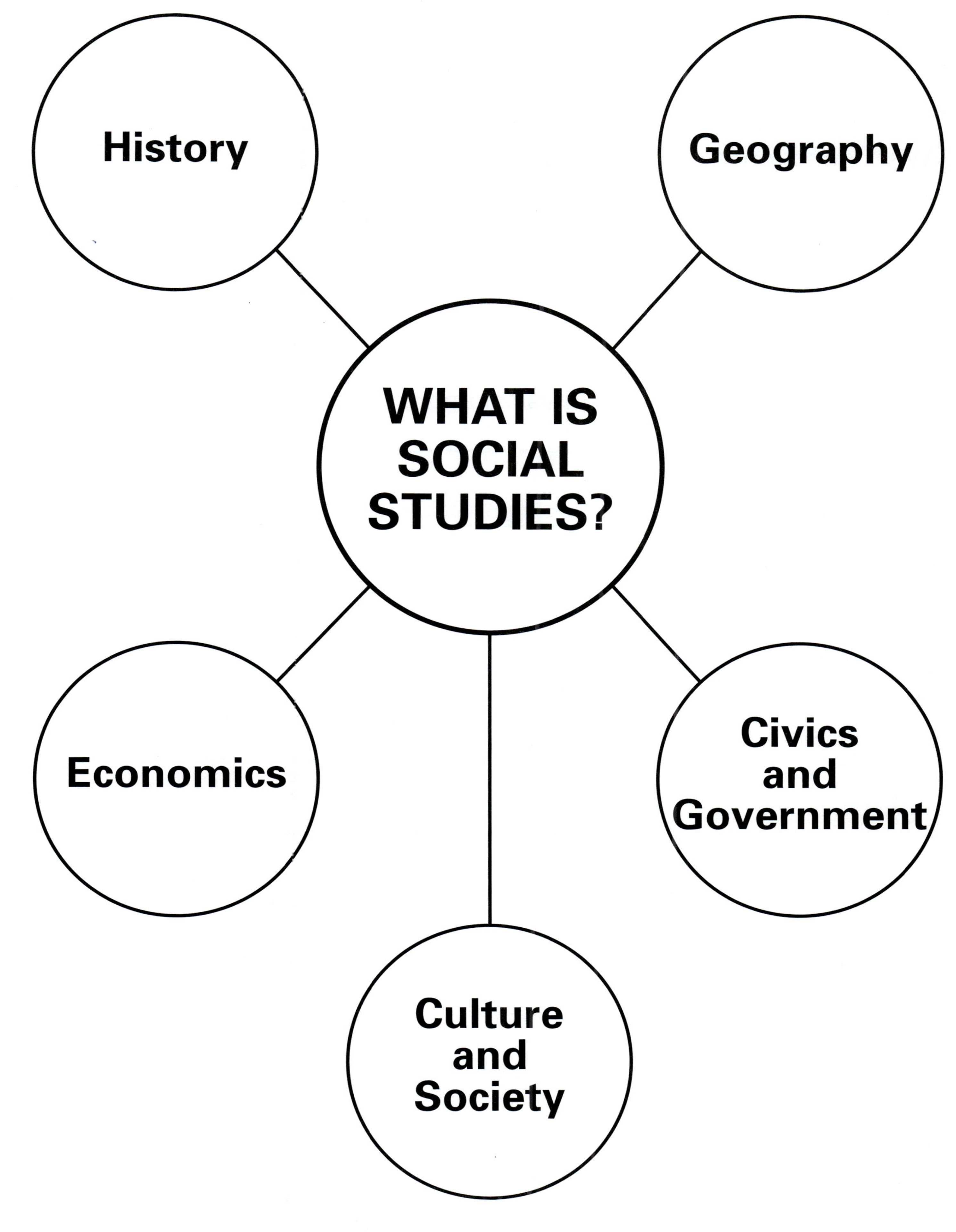
History
Geography
WHAT IS SOCIAL STUDIES?
Economics
Civics and Government
Culture and Society

Location

Where is the place located?

What is it near?

What direction is it from another place?

Why are certain features or places located where they are?

Place

What is it like there?

What physical and human features does the place have?

The Five Themes of Geography

Human-Environment Interactions

How are people's lives shaped by the place?

How has the place been shaped by people?

Regions

How is this place like other places?

What features set this place apart from other places?

Movement

How do people, products, and ideas get from one place to another?

Why do they make these movements?

Current Events

Summary of an important event:

WHO:

WHAT:

WHEN:

WHERE:

HOW:

Prediction

What do I think will happen next?

Personal Reaction

My reaction to the event:

Social Studies Journal

The most important thing I learned was . . .

Something that I did not understand was . . .

What surprised me the most was . . .

I would like to know more about . . .

Holiday Activities

At appropriate times of the year, the holiday backgrounds and activities provided in this section can be used to introduce or reinforce concepts related to important holidays. The holiday activities explore a variety of individual and community celebrations. They can prompt discussion of the similarities and differences of the traditions and cultures found in the United States.

Contents

Labor Day

Labor Day

LABOR DAY is a special day to honor workers for the contributions they have made to our community. Labor Day is celebrated on the first Monday in September. Most people do not have to work on this day. Many people watch parades, go on picnics, attend sports events, or join in recreational activities that they enjoy.

- The first Labor Day holiday was celebrated on Tuesday, September 5, 1882, in New York City.
- President Grover Cleveland signed a bill in 1894 to make Labor Day a national holiday.
- Children have a "job" to do, too—it is to go to school.
- Workers in Puerto Rico, Canada, Australia, and many parts of Europe celebrate Labor Day, too.

Career Day

On Labor Day, we celebrate the people who work hard in our community. Have children invite their parents into the classroom to have a career day. Invite guest speakers to talk about their jobs and how they help the community. Request that they bring visuals or props or wear the uniform they wear while working.

- Provide construction paper, markers, and crayons so children can make their own invitations to a parent or adult friend.
- Have children generate a list of all of the jobs they learned about from their guest speakers. Ask children to write about the job they felt was most interesting.

It's a Parade!

When Labor Day was first observed, it was proposed that there should be a parade that exhibited the labor organizations in the community, followed by a festival for workers and their families.

Have children organize a parade. First, brainstorm a list of community workers that they would like to feature in their parade, such as police officers, firefighters, teachers, construction workers, doctors, etc. Encourage children to choose a community worker that they would like to dress up as in the parade.

- Give children a variety of art materials or dress-up items to make their uniforms or work clothes.
- Supply children with classroom instruments or make instruments to use in the parade.
- Parade around the hallway. Arrange time with other teachers so children can talk about their costumes and the job they would like to do when they grow up.

Railroad Songs

Railroad builders were a group of people who worked hard in their communities. When people were making the railroad that extends across our country, they often sang songs to help them pass the time. Sing "I've Been Working on the Railroad" with children. Encourage children to make up their own verse to the song, based on a job they would like to do.

I've been working in the airport
All the livelong day;
I've been working in the airport
Just to help folks find their way.

Columbus Day

Christopher Columbus

Christopher Columbus was an Italian explorer. During his lifetime, many people thought that the world was flat, but Christopher Columbus believed that the world was round.

Columbus set sail in 1492 to prove his ideas about the world and to look for an easier route for sailors who were trading spices with Spain. He sailed on the flagship *Santa María*. He also brought two other ships with him, the *Niña* and the *Pinta*. Columbus and his crew eventually landed on an island in the Caribbean. Instead of finding a new trade route, Columbus discovered a new continent that lay between Europe and Asia. This continent was North America.

Four hundred years later, people in the United States decided to name a holiday in Columbus's honor. COLUMBUS DAY is a national holiday that is celebrated on the second Monday in October.

Ship Sculptures

Tell children that there is a monument in New York City dedicated to Christopher Columbus. If possible, show a picture of the monument. Explain that monuments are sculptures that are built to remember famous people and events. Provide modeling clay or dough so children can create their own monuments to Christopher Columbus. Suggest that children make models of the ships that Columbus sailed with—the *Niña,* the *Pinta,* and the *Santa María*. Show children pictures of the ships to use as guides.

Read a Compass

Explain that a caravel is a sailing ship like the ones used by Columbus on his first voyage. It was a wooden ship with tall masts and many sails. The shape of the boat was different from that of modern ships. But sailors on the caravels used compasses, just as crews of modern ships do, to help determine directions. Columbus and his men probably relied on a small compass.

Provide a hand-held compass and invite children to identify directions of objects in the classroom. Help them familiarize themselves with the compass first.

1. Find north, south, east, and west on the face of the compass.
2. Turn the compass in any direction, and then hold it still. The needle will always come to rest pointing north.
3. Walk south, east, and west, using the compass to identify the direction.

Track the Path

Show children a globe of Earth. Tell children that they are going to try to guess the path that Christopher Columbus took to find new land. Remind children that Columbus began in Spain and went west through the Atlantic Ocean, landing on an island in the Caribbean.

Show children Spain on the map, and then show them the Bahamas. Let volunteers show different paths Christopher Columbus could have taken.

Veterans Day

Veterans Day

VETERANS DAY is observed on November 11 to honor all veterans. This holiday began after World War I ended. Americans wanted to give thanks for peace. They also wanted to thank the veterans for their patriotism and their willingness to serve their country. The holiday was called Armistice Day.

After World War II and the Korean War, Americans realized that the name of the holiday should change to recognize all veterans from all wars. The name was then changed to Veterans Day.

On Veterans Day, Americans take time to rest and relax with their families. They also take time to think about all the veterans, living and dead, who served our country.

- A veteran is a person who served in the Army, Navy, Marines, Coast Guard, or Air Force. Not all veterans served in wartime.
- This holiday is also celebrated in France, the United Kingdom, and Canada. In Great Britain, it is called Remembrance Sunday, and in Canada it is called Remembrance Day.

Wave the Flag

The American flag has been a symbol of patriotism and love of country for most Americans. When veterans came home from war, they were greeted with people waving the American flag in celebration of peace.

Make a class American flag. Draw an outline of the flag on bulletin board paper. Ask children to paint the blue box and the red and white stripes. After the paint is dry, have children use white chalk to draw fifty stars inside the blue box.

Military Graph

Remind children that there are five branches in the military: the Army, the Navy, the Marines, the Coast Guard, and the Air Force. Talk to children about the emphasis of each branch. Explain that the Army protects the land, the Navy protects the water, the Marines protect both the land and the water, the Coast Guard patrols the coast, and the Air Force patrols the air.

Ask children whether a member of their family is a veteran or is now a member of a military branch, or whether they know someone who is. Have children write the branch of service of the person, if they know it. If not, invite children to choose one. Create a class graph of the information, writing children's names above the branch of service.

Someone Special

Explain to children that on Veterans Day, most Americans stop at 11:00 A.M. to take a moment of silence remembering those Americans who fought for peace.

Have children take a moment of silence to think about a person who they believe has done something important for the community. Then invite children to write and draw about that person. Be sure children include in their writing why that person should be recognized.

Compile children's writing to make a class book titled "Special People." As you share the book, invite each author to read his or her page.

Thanksgiving

Thanksgiving

THANKSGIVING DAY is a holiday that gives people time to give thanks, enjoy family gatherings, and join in holiday meals. Thanksgiving takes place on the fourth Thursday of each November.

In 1620, the Pilgrims sailed from England in search of a place where they could worship as they wished. They sailed from Plymouth, England, on a ship called the *Mayflower*.

Once the Pilgrims arrived near Cape Cod in Massachusetts, they started a settlement, which they named Plymouth. The settlers had to clear the land, build houses, and plant crops. It was a very difficult year, and during the first winter, half of the settlers died.

In the fall of 1621, as a gesture of thanks to God and to celebrate the first successful harvest, the Pilgrims had a feast. They invited the Wampanoag Indians to join the three-day festival.

- Turkey is the traditional Thanksgiving food. People at the 1621 Thanksgiving celebration ate wild turkey, fish, corn, fruit, and vegetables.
- President Abraham Lincoln made Thanksgiving a national holiday in 1863.

Popcorn

Explain to children that the Pilgrims did not know about corn when they landed in Plymouth. Corn was not grown in England, where they came from. The Indians introduced them to corn, showing them how to grow it and how to cook it. Tell children that the Pilgrim children may have had popcorn at the first Thanksgiving. Explain to children that corn kernels were dried out first. Then they were placed over the fire, where they began to pop.

Use a popcorn maker to pop popcorn. Have children generate a list of foods that contain corn.

Make a Scarecrow

Explain to children that farmers have been using scarecrows for many years. Scarecrows keep away crows that like to eat the vegetables in gardens. If crows and other small animals are kept to a minimum, the harvest will be better.

Make a scarecrow with children.

1. Stuff a small brown paper bag as the head of the scarecrow. Draw facial features.
2. Cut the shape of a scarecrow's body out of craft paper. Trace and cut the shape again to create the back. Ask children to decorate the body pieces.
3. Staple the body pieces together and stuff them with newspaper. Attach the scarecrow's head.
4. Attach the scarecrow to a post so it can stand.

Friendship Bracelet

The first Thanksgiving was held, not only to give thanks for a bountiful harvest, but to celebrate the help of and friendship with the neighboring Native Americans. Have children make a friendship bracelet to give to a friend who has helped them.

1. String colored beads on a piece of yarn to make a bracelet.
2. Have children exchange the bracelet with a friend in the classroom who has been helpful in some way.
3. Children may want to make other bracelets for friends not in their class.

Hanukkah

Hanukkah

Every year, between the end of November and the end of December, Jewish people celebrate HANUKKAH. Hanukkah is a celebration of the victory of the Maccabees over the Syrians.

Over 2,300 years ago, Judea, which is now called Israel, was taken over by the Syrians. The Syrians wanted all the people of the land to worship the Greek gods as they did. Judas Maccabeus and his brothers refused to worship these gods and went to war with the Syrians. After three years of fighting, the Syrians finally left Judea and the Maccabees reclaimed the Jerusalem temple.

The Maccabees cleaned the temple and lit an eternal light. They were concerned, however, that there was only enough oil to keep the lamp burning for one day. Miraculously, the oil burned for eight days, the time it took to bring in a fresh supply of oil.

Today people celebrate eight nights of Hanukkah to remember the victory and the miracle of the oil.

- A candle is lit for each of the eight nights that the oil burned.
- In America, families celebrate Hanukkah by giving and receiving gifts, decorating their houses, entertaining family and friends, eating special foods, playing a dreidel game, and lighting the menorah.

Create Gift Bags

During Hanukkah, families exchange gifts on each of the eight nights. Have children make a gift bag for a Hanukkah gift. Place a small paper bag in a shoebox. Dip a marble in paint, place it in the shoebox, and have children roll the marble on the paper bag to create a design. Allow children to dip other marbles in other colors and add to the design. When the bag is dry, encourage children to use black paint to add symbols of Hanukkah, such as the Star of David or a menorah.

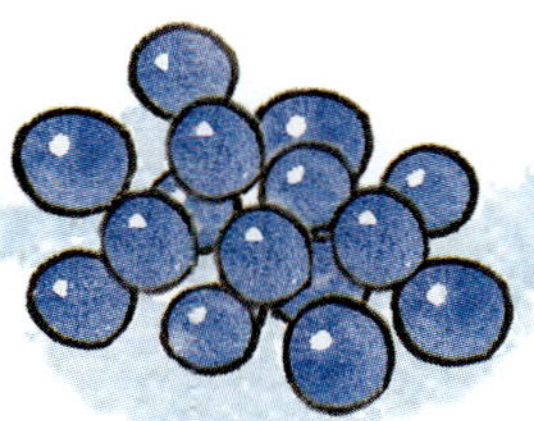

Play the Dreidel Game

You will need:
- Dreidels
- Tokens or colored cubes

Explain to children that the dreidel game is a very popular game among Jewish children. The dreidel is a four-sided top with a Hebrew letter on each side. The letters mean "A Great Miracle Happened There." In Israel the symbols are different and mean "A Great Miracle Happened Here."

Organize children in groups of three or four to play a dreidel game. Place 30 tokens in the center of each group. Direct players to take turns spinning the dreidel and following the directions indicated by the symbols. At the end of the playing period, the player with the most tokens is declared the winner.

NUN—Nothing happens and the next player spins the dreidel.

GIMEL—The player takes all of the tokens in the pot.

HEY—The player takes half of the tokens in the pot.

SHIN—The player must put one token into the pot.

Dance the Hora

Learn a traditional Hanukkah dance called the Hora. Join hands to form a circle. Follow these steps as you dance to recorded music from Israel. Each step should take two beats.

Step 1 Step to the left with left foot.

Step 2 Cross right foot behind left foot.

Step 3 Step to the left with left foot.

Step 4 Hop on left foot and kick right foot in front of you.

Step 5 Hop on right foot and kick left foot in front of you.

Repeat these steps over and over again until the music stops.

Christmas

Christmas

CHRISTMAS is probably the most celebrated holiday around the world. People in countries such as Australia, Canada, England, Finland, France, Germany, Greece, Italy, Mexico, Norway, Sweden, and Ukraine celebrate Christmas.

Christmas is a religious holiday honoring the birth of Jesus Christ. Christmas customs vary from family to family and are based on traditions of ancestors from other countries.

In the United States many Christians go to church on Christmas Eve for a special ceremony to welcome the day when Christ was born. On Christmas morning some children hurry to see if Santa Claus has left them gifts. In many homes families and friends come together for holiday meals and to exchange gifts.

- For nine days before Christmas, people in Mexico celebrate *las posadas*. They join in a search for a safe place for the infant Jesus. According to the custom, they are turned down every night except the last night, Christmas Eve.
- In France some people burn a log in the fireplace from Christmas Eve until New Year's Day. According to ancient tradition, it ensures good luck for the new year's harvest.
- Italians call Christmas *Il Natale*, which means "the birthday."

Christmas Greetings

Tell children that there are many different ways to say *Merry Christmas*. Teach children the following greetings from other countries:

Italy - *Buone Natale!*

Sweden - *God Jul!*

Mexico - *Feliz Navidad!*

France - *Joyeux Noel!*

Make Piñatas

Tell children that in Mexico, as a part of the Christmas celebration, people make piñatas for the children. *Piñatas* are papier-mâché objects filled with candy and coins. Children take turns trying to break the object using a large stick. Once the object is broken, children scramble to collect the candy and coins.

Let each child make a *piñata*.

1. Give each child a blown-up balloon.
2. Tear newspaper into strips about an inch wide.
3. Combine equal amounts of flour and water to make a paste. Place the newspaper strips in the paste. Wrap the wet strips around the balloon, completely covering the surface. Children may mold and add ears, noses, and other features to make animal faces.
4. Let the papier-mâché dry thoroughly. Then pop the balloon and have children paint the piñata.
5. Cut an opening in the bottom of the piñata and place a few pieces of candy in it. Tape the opening closed so the candy doesn't fall out.

Christmas Carols

Explain to children that Christmas caroling is a tradition that began in England. People walked around their neighborhood singing Christmas carols in hopes of a gift. Today the tradition continues in England and in the United States. Sing a variety of Christmas songs with children, such as "Jingle Bells," "Rudolph, the Red-Nosed Reindeer," and "Santa Claus Is Coming to Town." Let children sing the songs for other classrooms as if they were caroling.

Kwanzaa

Kwanzaa

KWANZAA is a nonreligious holiday that is celebrated by many African Americans. This holiday is celebrated for seven days, December 26–January 1. It was created in 1966 by Dr. Ron Karenga as a way to strengthen unity within African American families and their community. The festival was first observed to celebrate the first fruits of the winter season.

For seven nights, families gather, light a candle, and talk about one of the seven principles of Kwanzaa. Celebrations also include songs and dances, African drums, storytelling, poetry reading, and a large traditional meal.

- The seven principles celebrated during Kwanzaa are *unity, self-determination, collective work and responsibility, cooperative economics, purpose, creativity,* and *faith.*
- On the last day of Kwanzaa, many families gather for a feast called *karamu.*

Class Book

Explain to children that on the first night of Kwanzaa, African American families celebrate the principle of *umoja* (oo•MOH•jah), which means unity. Families talk about how to maintain unity in the family and in the community.

Make a class book about family traditions. *What are some things your family does together?* Ask children to draw a picture and write about a tradition that their family enjoys. Collate the pages and create a class book called "Family Traditions."

Kwanzaa Placemat

The *mkeka,* a placemat, is another symbol of Kwanzaa that represents tradition. The placemat is usually made of straw. It is placed on the table each night. The *kinara* (a seven-branched candlestick) is placed at the center of the mat, and then the mat is decorated with ears of corn (one for each child in the family) and other vegetables.

Have children make their own placemats.

1. Fold beige or yellow construction paper in half. Cut slits about 1 inch apart, starting at the folded edge and cutting up to about 2 inches from the edge of the paper.
2. Weave strips of paper into the cut construction paper. Begin each row in opposition (first one under, second over, and so on). Repeat to fill.
3. Cut fringes along the side edges. You may want to laminate the placemats for durability.
4. Have children cut out pictures of corn and other vegetables to place on the mat for decoration.

Colors of Kwanzaa

The colors of Kwanzaa are black, red, and green. Explain that many families decorate their homes with these colors during Kwanzaa. Let children decorate the classroom with black, red, and green streamers in honor of the class Kwanzaa discussion.

Storytelling Drum

Music and storytelling are important parts of Kwanzaa celebrations. Let children see and touch different types of African drums (or make drums from empty coffee cans). Have children make up stories about happiness, danger, rest, storms, or celebrations. As they tell their stories, have them experiment with different rhythms that set the mood for the events in the story.

New Year's Day

New Year's Day

NEW YEAR'S DAY is the oldest of all holidays. It is celebrated on January 1 in the United States. It is a day to remember the past and look forward to the upcoming year.

Tradition leads people to believe that what they do or eat on the first day of the year affects the luck they will have in the upcoming year.

- Many people make New Year's resolutions. Resolutions are changes people would like to make so their lives will be better in the upcoming year.
- The traditional New Year's song is "Auld Lang Syne," which means "the good old days."

The CHINESE NEW YEAR is the longest and most important festival in China. The New Year begins on the first day of the first month of the lunar year and ends with a Lantern Festival the 15th day of the lunar year. Families traditionally buy and wear new clothes, clean their homes, have family feasts, and—most importantly—pay off all debts.

- On New Year's Eve, children get to stay up as long as possible. It is believed that the longer they stay up, the longer their parents will live.
- Families decorate their homes with flowers and with eight types of sweet dried fruits.

Good-Luck Foods

On New Year's Day, many people like to eat foods that they believe give them good luck. Explain to children that many people believe that foods that are shaped like a ring will bring them good luck because they symbolize "coming full circle." Have children make a mural to show pictures of good-luck foods.

Make a Calendar

Remind children that New Year's Day marks the beginning of the year. Have children make their own calendars for the upcoming year. Provide children with twelve empty grids. Let children write the names of the months and number the days on each calendar.

Encourage children to draw pictures on the calendar for each month to symbolize the special days during that month.

Month Magic

Show children how to determine the number of days in each month. Ask each child to make a fist with his or her left hand. Beginning with the knuckle on their pointer finger, have children say the name of each month as they point to their knuckles and the space between each knuckle. Children should say *July* and *August* when touching the knuckle on their pinky finger. Then they should continue back towards their pointer finger, naming the remaining months.

Tell children that each month that they named while they pointed to a knuckle has 31 days and the other months have 30 days, except February, which has 28 or 29 days.

Chinese Envelopes

As a part of the Chinese New Year celebration, friends and relatives receive and give red envelopes. These red envelopes contain "lucky money" or other treats. Many Chinese people believe that these filled envelopes are symbols that mean the upcoming year will be prosperous.

Have children make their own red envelopes to give as gifts. Show them how to fold, glue, and decorate red paper to make an envelope. Then ask children to color play money. On the back of the bill, have children write a message of good cheer before placing it inside the envelope. Let them exchange their envelopes with a classmate.

Celebrating Heroes

Inventors

Thanks to the heroic efforts of others, we have electric lights, automobiles, telephones, computers, and a multitude of other modern conveniences. The heroes are scientists, mathematicians, and thinkers that we celebrate as famous inventors. Included in this group of heroes are such people as Thomas Edison, Benjamin Banneker, Alexander Graham Bell, and Mary Anderson.

- **Thomas Edison** is best known for inventing the electric lightbulb, the phonograph, and the kinetophone (which is a talking motion picture projector). He is credited with hundreds of other inventions that use electricity.
- **Benjamin Banneker** was a famous mathematician and inventor. Banneker is most famous for building the first accurate clock in the Americas and publishing a scientific almanac.
- **Alexander Graham Bell** is best remembered for inventing the telephone.
- **Mary Anderson** noticed that when it rained, streetcar drivers had to open the windows to see. As a solution, she invented the windshield wiper.

The Almanac

Explain to children that an almanac is a periodical, or magazine, that is still used today. Banneker's almanac included yearly weather forecasts, tide tables, lunar and solar eclipses, and sunrise tables. Share an almanac with children. Then work together to create a new page for the almanac.

The First Telephone

Tell children that Alexander Graham Bell was working with a partner when he invented the telephone. He and his partner Thomas Watson were in separate rooms when they were testing it. Bell accidentally spilled some acid on himself while working. When the accident occurred, he asked Watson for help. Bell's words were the first ever heard on a telephone. Bell was so excited that it worked, he forgot all about his spill.

Organize children in pairs so they can act out the story. Provide props for children to use while acting. Encourage them to use expression as they act like Bell getting hurt and then being excited that his invention actually worked.

The Importance of Electricity

Explain to children that Thomas Edison created many inventions that use electricity. Many people did not have electricity before Edison began introducing his inventions. Simulate what the classroom would be like if there were no electricity. Turn off the lights, computers, and television sets. Continue teaching without electricity for an hour so children can feel the difference.

Ask questions to help children think about how things were long ago, such as *What do you think people used before there were lightbulbs? What things did people do for fun before there were televisions and computers? Do you think you would have liked living long ago? Why or why not?*

Have children write about their experience with no electricity. Tell them to write why they believe Thomas Edison was such a great inventor.

Child Inventors

Research child inventors. One example is Chester Greenwood, a young boy who invented earmuffs. Then encourage children to invent a new product that could be used with a pet.

Dr. Martin Luther King, Jr., Day

Dr. Martin Luther King, Jr.

On the third Monday in January, Americans observe DR. MARTIN LUTHER KING, JR., DAY. King worked hard for freedom, equality, and dignity of all races and peoples. He helped bring about change with nonviolent actions.

While King was a minister in Montgomery, Alabama, an African American woman was arrested because she refused to give her seat on the bus to a white man. King organized the Montgomery bus boycott. He led the African Americans in Montgomery to boycott the bus system until it was fair for everyone, regardless of color. It took 382 days for a law to be passed that made the bus policy equal for all riders.

King continued to speak against the poor treatment of African American people. He organized a historic march to the White House. At the Lincoln Memorial he gave a famous speech calling for freedom for all.

- On April 4, 1968, King was assassinated. Today we celebrate his birthday by remembering his work for equal opportunity.
- Many communities celebrate Dr. Martin Luther King, Jr., Day with picnics, parades, and marches.

Handprint Rainbow

Make a handprint rainbow with children. Provide construction paper of rainbow colors. Have children choose a color, and then have them trace and cut out four handprints. Create a class rainbow using everyone's handprints.

Discuss how working together helped the class make a beautiful rainbow. Explain that Dr. Martin Luther King, Jr., felt that teamwork helped solve many problems.

Team Building

Use the following activities to develop teamwork in the classroom.

Building Structures Divide the class into teams of three or four children. Provide children with toothpicks and miniature marshmallows. Challenge them to work together to build a structure using the toothpicks and marshmallows.

Creating Silly Animals Divide children into three teams. Ask the first team to draw a picture of an animal's head on craft paper. Tell the second team to draw a picture of an animal's body. At the same time have the third team draw a picture of animal legs and feet. Explain to the teams that they should work together to decide which animal they are going to draw and that everyone in the group needs to participate. Once everyone is finished, put the head, body, and legs and feet together to see the funny animal the entire class created.

Fair Play

In 1964, Dr. Martin Luther King, Jr., won a Nobel Peace Prize for his work to get equal treatment for all people. Explain that King wanted to create a world in which everyone would be treated fairly and would obey the same rules. Ask children what they think the words *fair* and *unfair* mean.

Invite children to act out scenes that show ways of solving problems peacefully. You may want to present scenarios such as the following:

- In the middle of a game on the playground, an older boy takes your soccer ball.
- A girl you know cuts in line in front of you at lunch.
- Your classmates say you run too slowly and they don't want you on their team.

Presidents' Day

Presidents' Day

Every third Monday in February, Americans honor their Presidents, among them George Washington and Abraham Lincoln. This national holiday is called PRESIDENTS' DAY.

George Washington was born on February 22. He was the first President of the United States and he is called the Father of Our Country. George Washington is remembered as being a peacemaker and a war hero. He also defended the Constitution and the Bill of Rights.

- President Washington is the only American President after whom a state has been named. Washington, D.C., the capital of the United States, is also named after him.

Abraham Lincoln was born on February 12. He was the sixteenth President of the United States. President Lincoln is remembered for freeing the slaves when he signed the Emancipation Proclamation. He also delivered one of the nation's most famous speeches, called the Gettysburg Address.

- Americans celebrate Presidents' Day in February because both of these great Presidents were born in February.

Money Details

Share a one-dollar bill and a five-dollar bill with children. Point out George Washington's face on the one-dollar bill and Abraham Lincoln's face on the five-dollar bill. Continue discussing details on the bills.

Children can design new bills. Have them plan and then draw a bill that features the current President of the United States. The face of the bill should include a picture of the President. The back may show a monument to the President or another symbol of the country.

President for a Day

Explain to children that the President has a very important job to do. It is the President's responsibility to make sure everyone in the United States is treated fairly and is safe. It is also the President's job to keep our nation at peace with other nations.

Invite children to pretend that they have to spend the day being the President of the United States. Invite them to make a President's diary entry by drawing a picture with a caption to show something they did for the nation during the day. Encourage children to use specific examples such as *I proclaimed a new holiday. I signed a bill today. I signed a peace treaty today.* Compile the entries into a single diary, and place it in the classroom library for others to enjoy. Encourage children to compare their activities as President with those of their classmates.

Hoecakes

You will need:

2 cups self-rising cornmeal
2 eggs
1 tablespoon sugar
2 tablespoons butter
3/4 cup milk
1/3 cup water
1/4 cup vegetable oil

Explain that George Washington usually ate hoecakes for breakfast. Hoecakes are a type of bread made with cornmeal. During Washington's time they were baked in a fireplace on the blade of a hoe.

Make hoecakes with children. Let them measure and mix the ingredients. Then have an adult pour the mixture onto a griddle and cook until brown and crispy. You may want to top the hoecakes with syrup, butter, or fruit. (Note: Be sure to check for allergies before letting children taste any foods.)

Cinco de Mayo

Cinco de Mayo

CINCO DE MAYO, which means "the fifth of May" in Spanish, is a national holiday in Mexico. It is also celebrated by Mexican Americans to honor the defenders of Mexican freedom.

On May 5, 1862, French troops invaded and attacked the city of Puebla, Mexico. The Mexican troops were made up of a group of untrained commoners. The French troops were greater in number and well trained. The Mexican army fought hard and defeated the French army. This victory was very important to the Mexican people because they won against all odds; this inspired a great amount of patriotism in the people. People celebrate Cinco de Mayo with fiestas, parades, mariachi music, and piñatas.

- Each May 5 in Puebla, Mexico, a mock battle is staged to remember and celebrate the victory over the French army in the Battle of Puebla.

Flag of Mexico

Show children Mexico on the map. There are many people in the United States who are of Mexican descent. These people or their relatives were born in Mexico and moved to the United States.

Look at and talk about the colors and images on a flag of Mexico. Have children make a Mexican flag of their own design. Divide the flag into three vertical lines. Paint the first column green, the second white, and the third red. Have them paint a coat-of-arms symbol in the center of the flag.

Make Maracas

You will need:

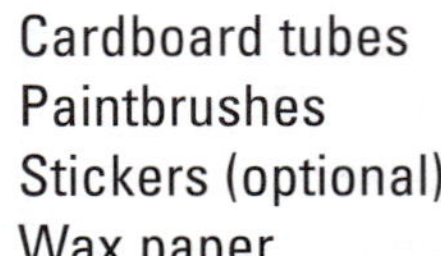

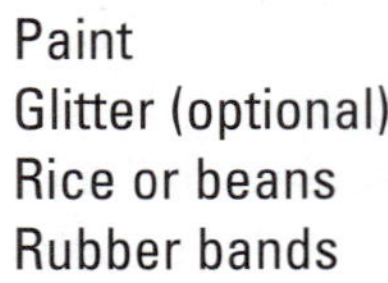

Cardboard tubes	Paint
Paintbrushes	Glitter (optional)
Stickers (optional)	Rice or beans
Wax paper	Rubber bands

Remind children that in the United States, Mexican Americans celebrate Cinco de Mayo with songs and lively dances. One instrument that is used during celebrations is the maraca.

Make maracas with children.

1. Have children decorate cardboard tubes with paint, glitter, and stickers.
2. Cover one end of the tube with wax paper and then wrap the end tightly with a rubber band. Place a handful of rice or beans inside the tube. Then cover the opposite end.
3. Play Mexican music and have children shake their maracas to the rhythm of the music.

Native American Kickball

Explain to children that this game is played by the Tarahumara Indians in Native American villages.

Organize children into two teams. Set up an obstacle course on the playground. Have children kick the ball through places such as the following: under the slide, over a chair, and through a tunnel. Ask the two teams to play as if they were in a relay. The first team to have its players kick the ball through the obstacle course wins.

Memorial Day

Memorial Day

MEMORIAL DAY is a holiday set aside to remember and honor those who gave their lives for the United States. The holiday originated during the Civil War. It was called Decoration Day because it was customary for people to decorate the graves of the war dead. In 1971 Congress declared Memorial Day to be a national holiday that is to be celebrated on the last Monday in May.

- On Memorial Day, there is a memorial service at Arlington National Cemetery. A small American flag is placed on each grave. The President or Vice President of the United States lays a wreath at the Tomb of the Unknowns and gives a speech.
- Today Americans honor those who gave their lives in battle, as well as family members and friends whom they wish to remember.

Giving Thanks

Remind children that many people died in wars. Explain to them that these people should be honored because they were fighting for our country. They wanted to make sure that this country was a place where people could live a safe and peaceful life. Ask children to name family members or friends who served in recent wars.

Ask children to make a thank-you card for one of the people who died in a war. Have them write in the cards why Memorial Day is an important holiday. If possible, send the cards to the families of the deceased.

Make a Wreath

Explain to children that the Tomb of the Unknowns is a site where people can go to grieve for loved ones who never returned from a war. For different reasons, sometimes a person is not found after a war is over.

Every year the President or the Vice President places a wreath on the tomb on Memorial Day. Make a wreath with children.

1. Provide five sheets of red, white, or blue tissue paper to each child. Ask children to place the pieces of tissue paper on top of each other. Then have them fold the paper like a fan.
2. Give each child a chenille stem to wrap tightly around the center of the folded tissue paper.
3. Pull each piece of tissue paper to the center. Mold to create a flower.
4. Attach the flowers to a cardboard ring.

Sing a Song

Tell children that soldiers often end the day with the playing of the song "Taps." It is usually played on a trumpet or bugle. Sing the song for children and ask them to draw pictures of the image the song evokes. Then sing the song together. Invite children to use horns, kazoos, and other classroom instruments to accompany the song.

Taps

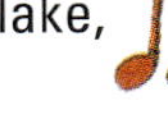

Day is done, gone the sun, from the lake,

from the hills, from the sky.

All is well, safely rest, God is nigh.

Independence Day

Independence Day

INDEPENDENCE DAY is a national holiday that commemorates the adoption of the Declaration of Independence on July 4, 1776. This holiday is the birthday of the United States of America. Once there were only 13 colonies. People in the colonies were upset because they had to pay taxes to England. However, they could not vote or have any say in the English government.

In June 1776, the people decided to write a formal declaration of independence from England. Thomas Jefferson was in charge of writing it. On July 4, the Declaration of Independence was approved and the congress began signing it.

Today Americans celebrate the nation's birthday by displaying and wearing red, white, and blue. People also have picnics, have parades with marching bands, go to the beaches, have barbecues, and watch fireworks.

- The Declaration of Independence was adopted on July 4, 1776, but it was not actually signed until August 2 of that year.
- The 56 men who signed the Declaration of Independence did not use the kind of pen we use today. They dipped a turkey feather, or quill, into an inkwell and used the tip to write on the document.

Patriotic Songs

Set out red, white, and blue streamers and American flags. Invite children to wave them to the rhythm of patriotic music such as "You're a Grand Old Flag," "America," or "Stars and Stripes Forever."

Flag Etiquette

Explain to children that there are certain rules that people should follow when waving or displaying the American flag. Model the appropriate handling of the flag with a small flag. Explain some of the flag rules.

1. The flag should not touch the ground.
2. The flag should only be displayed from sunrise to sunset unless the flag is illuminated.
3. The flag can only be displayed vertically or horizontally.
4. When the American flag is displayed with flags from cities or states, it should be higher than those flags.
5. When the American flag is displayed with flags of other countries, during peacetime, the flags should all be at the same level.

Talk about proper flag etiquette. Ask: *Why do you think there are rules about hanging the American flag?* Discuss how the flag should be treated with respect.

Give children a small flag to place on their desks for the day. Make sure children hang or display their flags appropriately.

The Stars on the Flag

Explain to children that the stars on the flag represent the number of states included in the United States. Talk about how many stars are on the present-day flag.

Tell children that Betsy Ross may have made the first American flag. She placed only 13 stars, though, because there were only 13 colonies at that time. Show children pictures of the present-day flag and the first flag so they can compare the similarities and differences.

Then provide red, white, and blue construction paper and invite children to make models of each flag.

Vocabulary Cards

This reproducible section will help you create word cards for the vocabulary found at the beginning of each lesson in your Teacher's Edition. Throughout the lesson plans, you will find suggestions for using the vocabulary cards with the children. The cards may also be used to preview the unit, build vocabulary notebooks, assist ESL children, and review vocabulary at the end of the unit. Use blank cards to add vocabulary to meet the special needs of your class.

Contents

QUIET!
SCHOOL LIBRARY

community

citizen

rule

fair

main idea
What the information you are reading is mostly about.

responsibility
Something that a citizen should take care of or do.

role
The part a person plays in a group or community.

detail
An extra piece of information about something.

cooperate

neighborhood

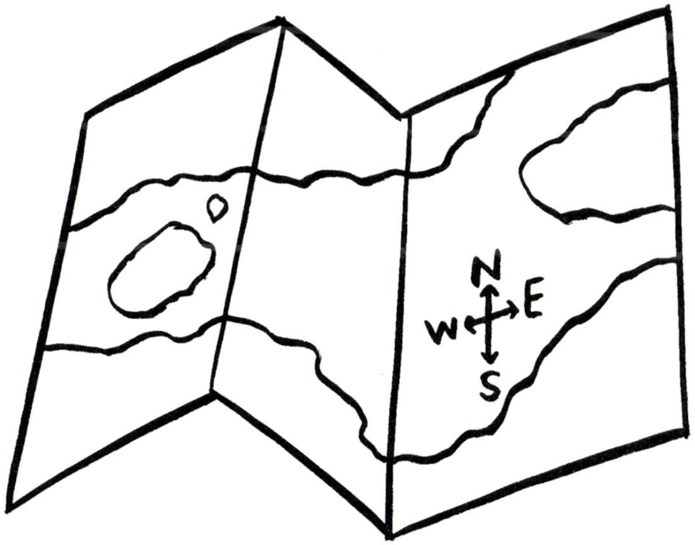

map

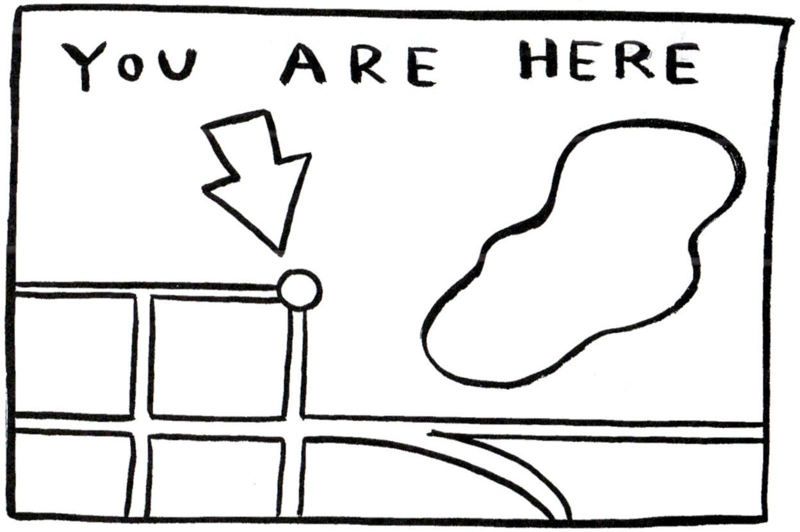

location

neighborhood
The part of a community in which a group of people lives.

cooperate
To work together.

location
The place where something is.

map
A drawing that shows where places are.

city	suburb
state	country

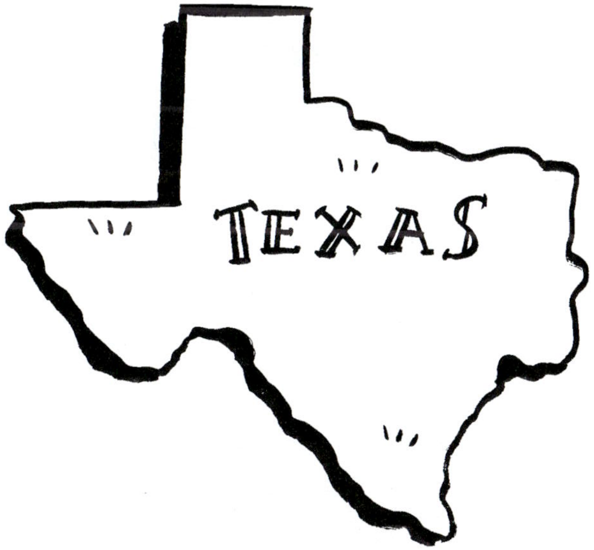

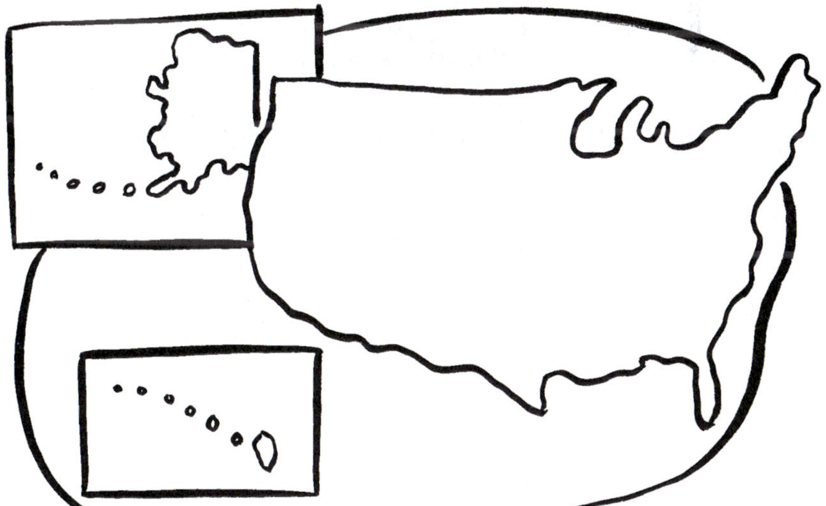

TEXAS

suburb

A community near a large city.

city

A very large town.

country

An area of land with its own people and laws.

state

A part of a country.

map key

map symbol

change

calendar

map symbol

A small picture that stands for a real thing on Earth.

map key

The part of a map that shows what the symbols mean.

calendar

A chart that shows the days, weeks, and months in a year.

change

To become different.

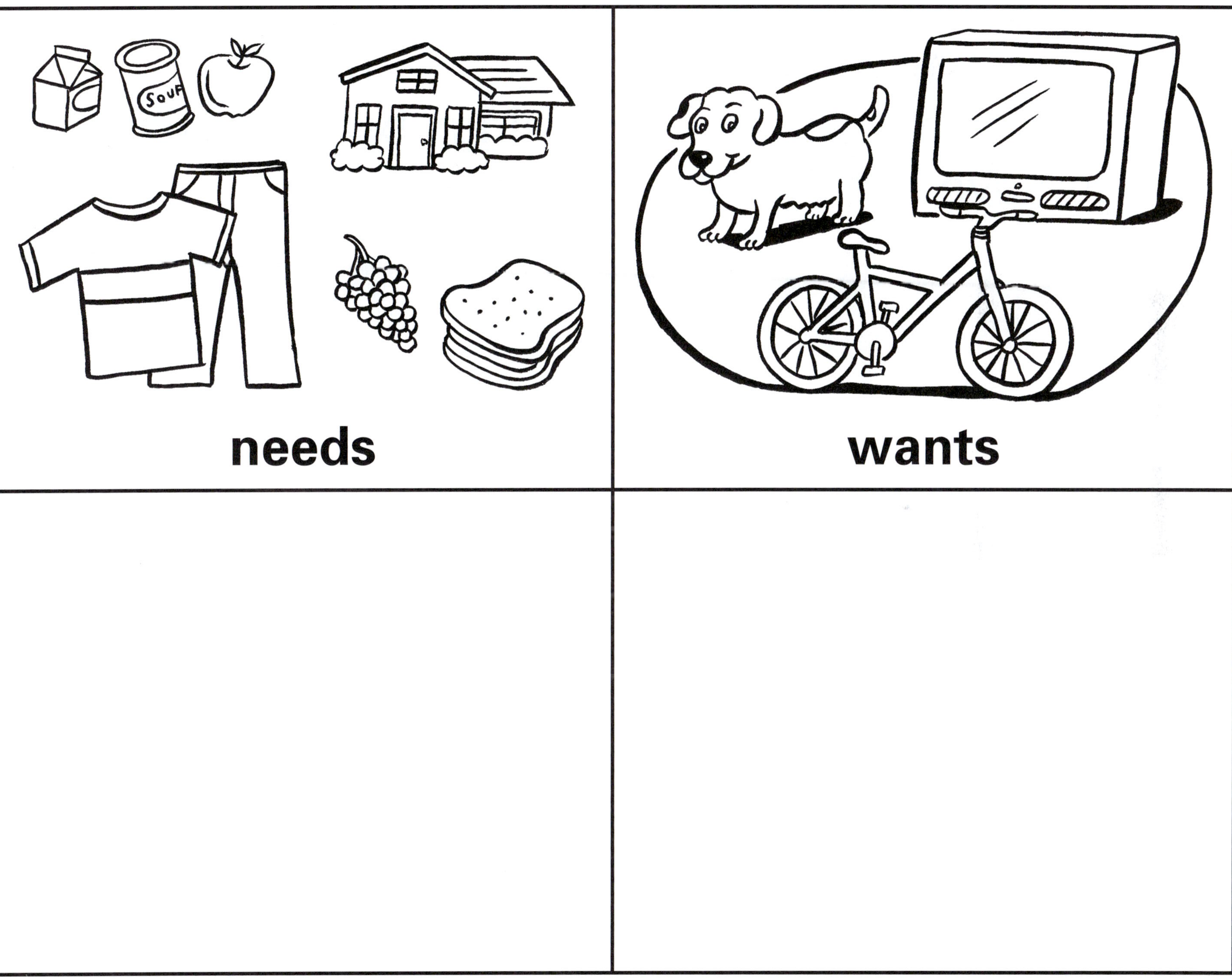
SOUP
needs
wants

wants

Things people would like to have but do not need.

needs

Things people must have to live.

government

law

consequence

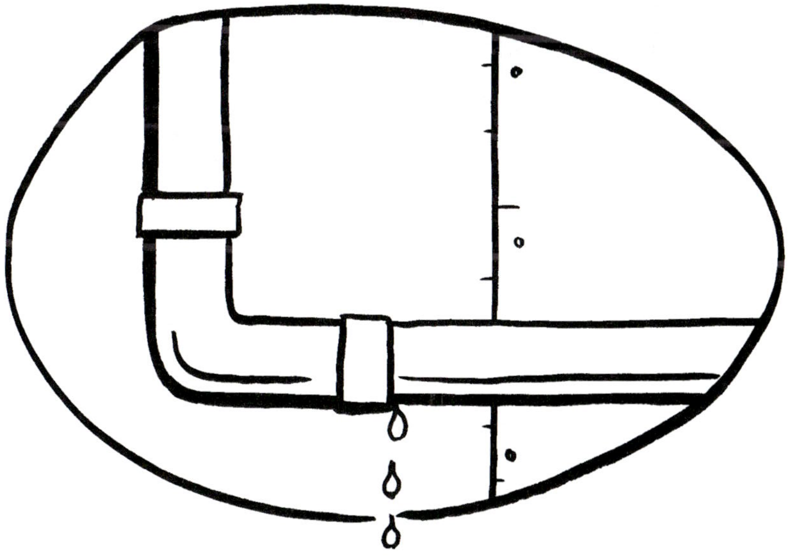

problem

mayor

The leader of a city or town government.

solution

The way people agree to solve a problem.

court

A place where a judge decides whether a person has broken the law, and if so, what the consequence should be.

council

A group of citizens chosen to make decisions for all the people.

judge

government service

tax

election

government service

A service that a government provides for citizens.

judge

The leader of a court.

election

A time when people vote for their leaders.

tax

Money paid to the government that is used to pay for services.

vote

appoint

majority rule

ballot

appoint

To name or choose for a public office or job.

vote

A choice that gets counted.

ballot

A piece of paper that shows the choices for voting.

majority rule

Rule by more than half of the people in a community.

governor

legislature

property

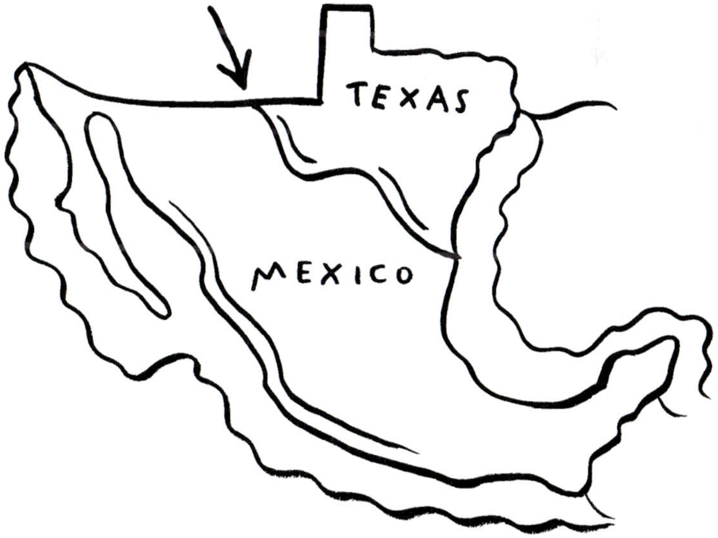

border

legislature

A group of citizens chosen to make decisions for a state.

governor

The leader of a state's government.

border

A line on a map that shows where a state or country ends.

property

Something that belongs to a person or group.

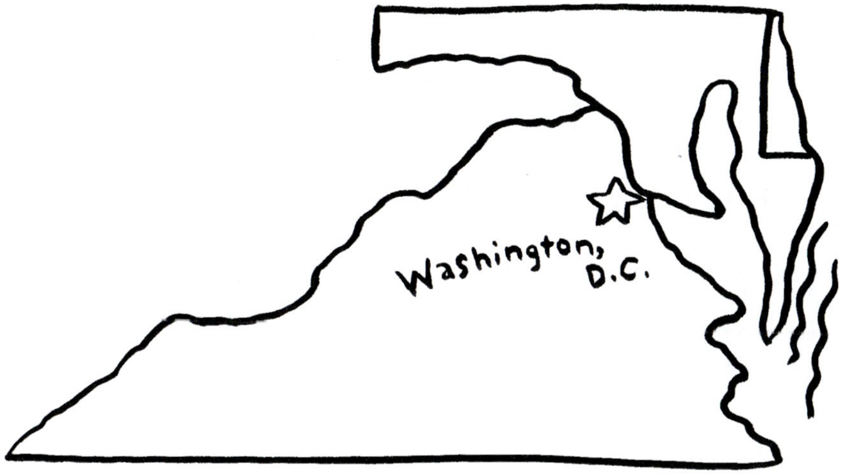

capital

Congress

President

Supreme Court

Congress

The group of citizens chosen to make decisions for the country.

capital

A city in which the government of a state or country meets and works.

Supreme Court

The highest court in the United States.

President

Leader of the United States government.

public service

fact

opinion

fact

A piece of information that is true.

public service

Work done for the good of the community.

opinion

A statement of what a person believes to be true but cannot prove.

geography
desert
ocean
landform

desert

A large, dry area of land.

geography

The study of Earth and its people.

landform

A kind of land with a special shape, such as a mountain, hill, or plain.

ocean

A very large body of salty water.

hill

plain

mountain

valley

peninsula

A landform that has water on only three sides.

island

A landform with water all around it.

lake

A body of water that has land all around it.

river

A stream of water that flows across the land.

Gulf of Mexico

gulf

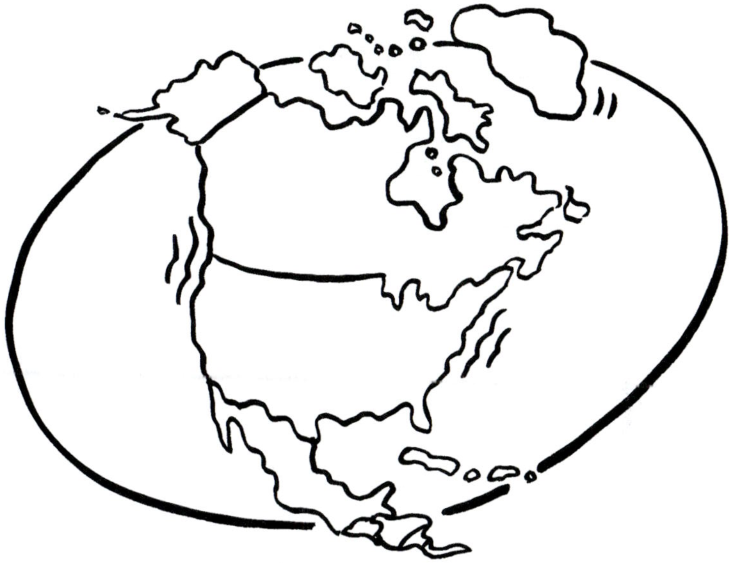

continent

W N S E

globe

cardinal directions

continent

One of seven main land areas on the Earth.

gulf

A large body of ocean water that is partly surrounded by land.

cardinal directions

The main directions of north, south, east, and west.

globe

A model of Earth.

equator	**compass rose**
natural resource	**crop**

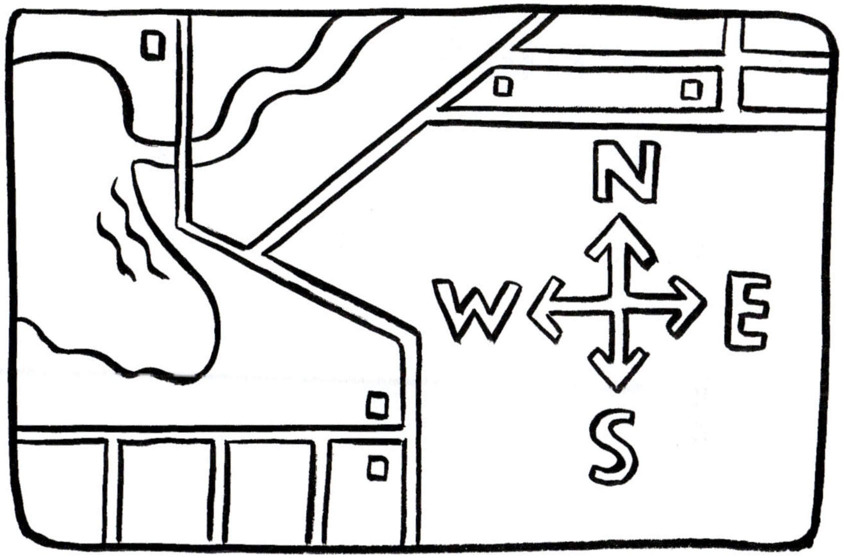

compass rose
Arrows on a map that show direction.

equator
An imaginary line that divides Earth in half between north and south.

crop
A plant people grow for food or other needs.

natural resource
Something found in nature that people can use to meet their needs.

Class Rides

	Bike	Scooter
Mike		✓
Jane	✓	
Maya		✓
Eric		✓

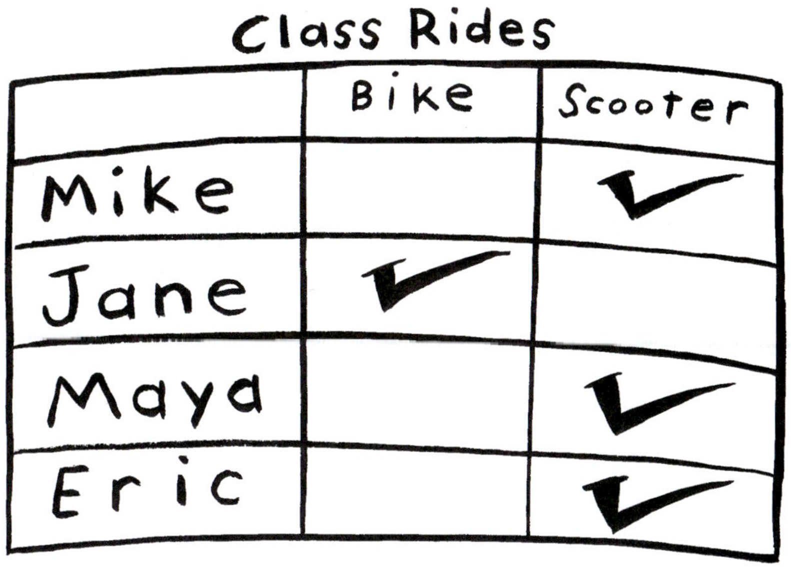

table

technology

forest

fuel

technology

The use of new inventions in everyday life.

table

A chart that shows information in rows and columns.

fuel

A resource, such as oil, that can be burned for heat or energy.

forest

A very large area of trees.

climate

tornado

blizzard

map scale

tornado

A strong, whirling wind that causes great damage to land and buildings.

climate

The kind of weather a place has over a long time.

map scale

The part of a map that helps you find distance.

blizzard

A heavy snowstorm.

conservation	recycle
pollution	decision

recycle

To use things again.

conservation

Working to save resources or make them last longer.

decision

A choice.

pollution

Anything that makes the air, land, or water dirty.

recreation	unique
culture	point of view

unique

One-of-a-kind.

recreation

The things people do in their spare time, such as playing sports or having hobbies.

point of view

A way of thinking about something.

culture

A group's way of life.

explorer	**pioneer**
immigrant	**route**

religion

A belief in a god or gods.

heritage

The culture and traditions handed down to people by their ancestors.

ancestor

A family member who lived a long time ago.

tradition

A way of doing something that is passed on from parents to children.

bar graph

holiday

custom

language

holiday
A day to celebrate or remember something.

bar graph
A graph that uses bars to show how many or how much.

language
The words or signs people use to communicate.

custom
A group's way of doing something.

communication

communication

The sharing of ideas and information.

season

ancient

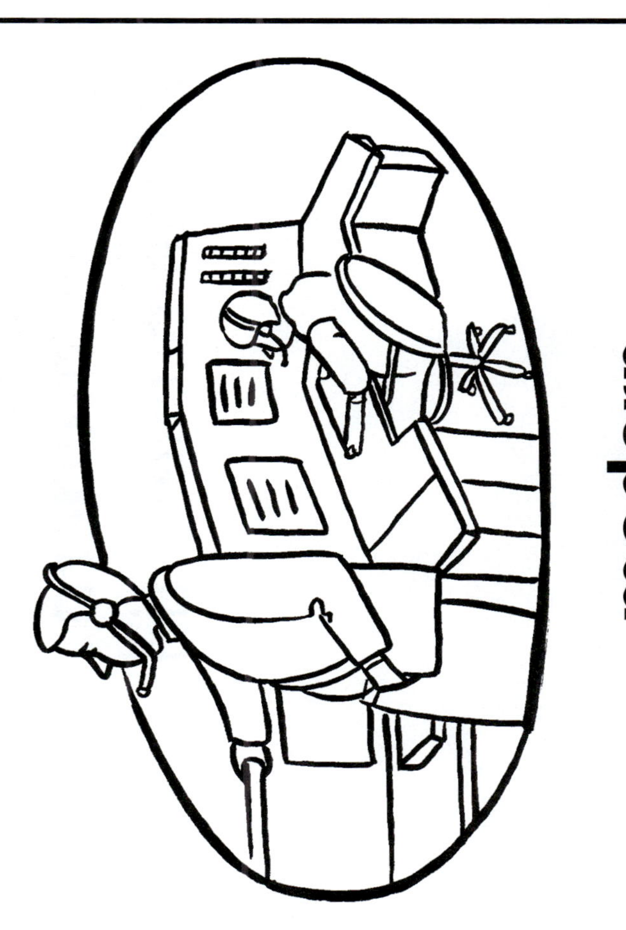

modern

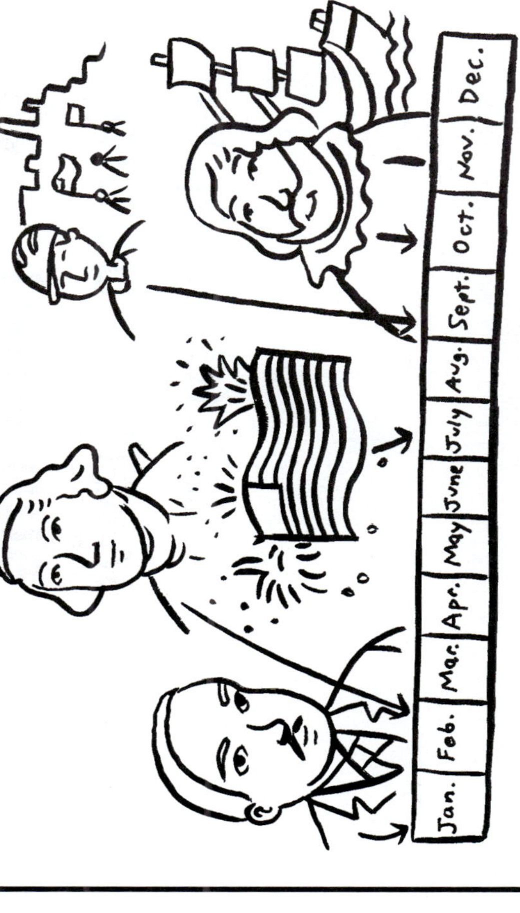

time line

ancient

Very old.

season

One of the four parts of the year that have different kinds of weather.

time line

A line that shows when events happened.

modern

Of the present time.

American History
history
ABC
ENCYCLOPEDIA
ART
Fish
NOTE BOOK
source
artifact
predict

source

The place where something comes from.

history

The study of what happened to people in the past.

predict

To say what will happen.

artifact

An object from another time or place.

museum

settler

cause

effect

settler One of the first people to make a home in a new place.	**museum** A building in which objects from other times and places are displayed.
effect What happens because of a cause.	**cause** What makes something happen.

colony

independence

freedom

landmark

independence

The freedom of people to choose their own government.

colony

A place that is ruled by another country.

landmark

A familiar object at a place.

freedom

The right of people to make their own choices.

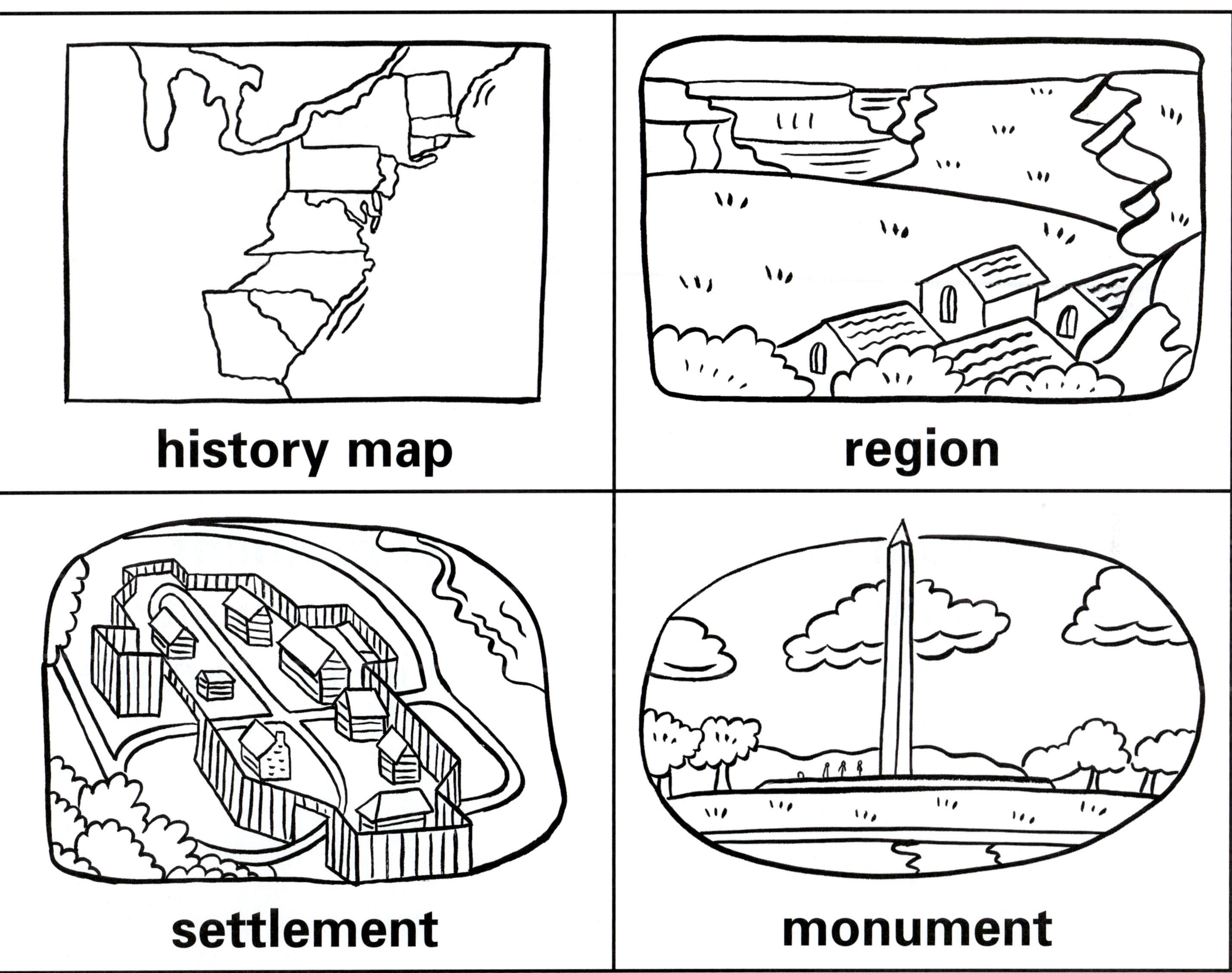
history map
region
settlement
monument

region

An area.

history map

A map that shows how a place looked in an earlier time.

monument

A statue or marker created to honor a person or an event.

settlement

A small community started in a new place.

memorial

hero

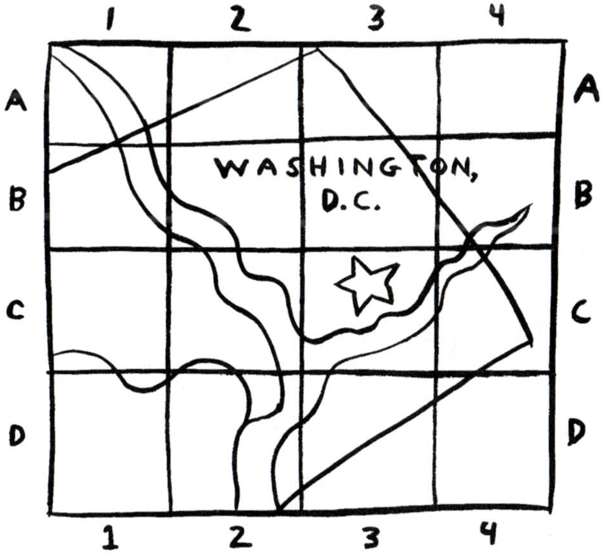

map grid

scribe

hero

A person who has done something brave or important.

memorial

A monument created to honor and remember a hero.

scribe

A person who records things in writing.

map grid

A set of columns and rows placed on a map to help people find a location.

maize

papyrus

diagram

raw material
A resource used to make a product.

consumer
A person who buys and uses goods and services.

manufacture
To make with machines.

factory
A building in which people use machines to make goods.

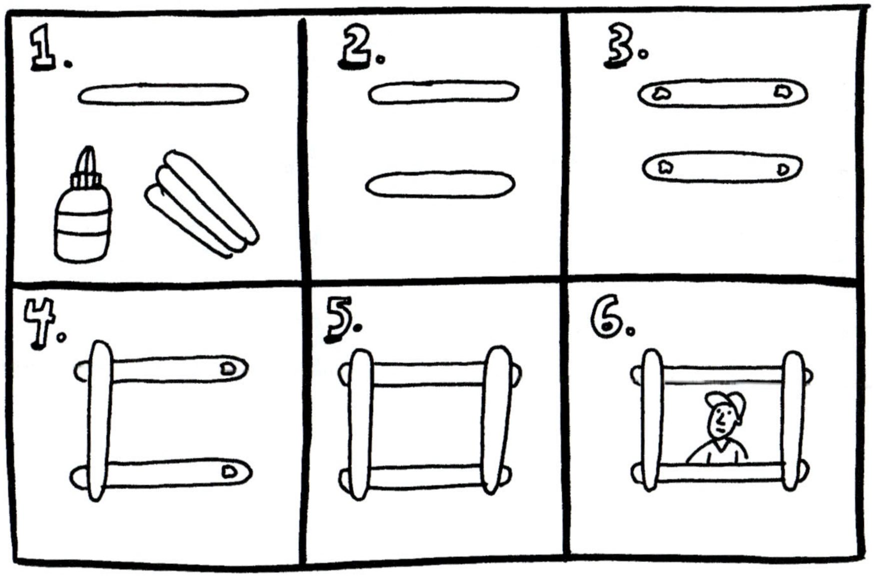

flow chart

product

income

free enterprise

product

Something that is made by nature or by people.

flow chart

A chart that shows the steps needed to make or do something.

free enterprise

The freedom to start and run any kind of business.

income

The money people earn for the work they do.

BANK

bank

Deposit $100.00
month May
interest .06

interest

scarce

barter

interest

Money that money earns in a bank.

bank

A business that looks after people's money.

barter

To trade goods and services.

scarce

Not in good supply, or hard to find.

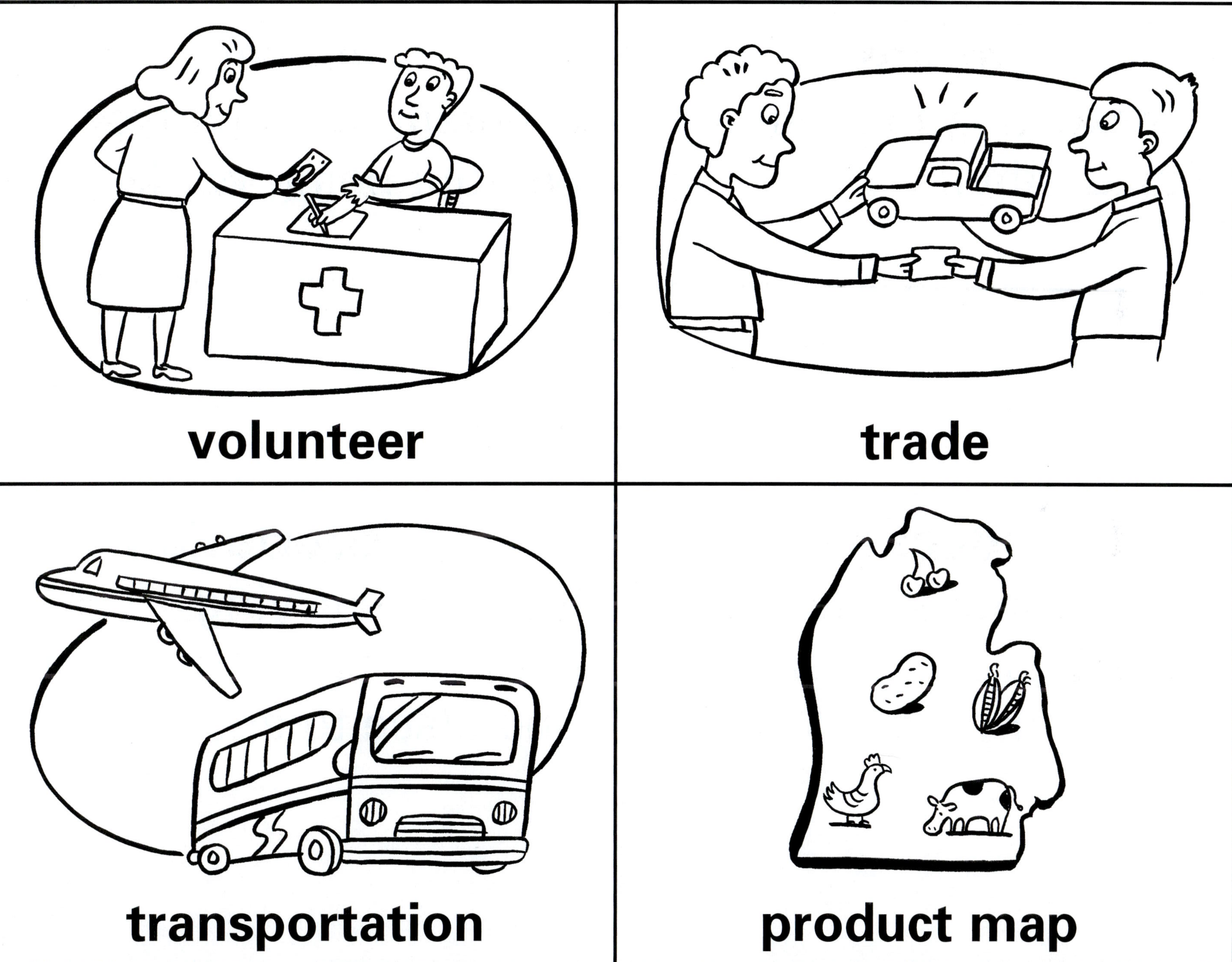
volunteer
trade
transportation
product map

trade

To exchange one thing for another.

volunteer

A person who works without being paid.

product map

A map that shows where products are found or made.

transportation

Ways of carrying people and goods from one place to another.

School to Home Newsletters

These school to home letters offer a way of linking children's study of social studies to the children's family members. There is one newsletter, available in English and Spanish, for each unit. The newsletters include family activities as well as books to read.

Contents

School to Home

Harcourt Horizons • About My Community Unit 1 *Newsletter*

Books to Read

Tangle Town by Kurt Cyrus. Farrar, Straus & Giroux, 1997.

Uptown by Bryan Collier. Henry Holt, 2000.

Under the Sunday Tree by Eloise Greenfield. HarperCollins, 1990.

Halmoni's Day by Edna Coe Bercaw. Puffin, 2000.

Betty Doll by Patricia Polacco. Penguin, 2001.

Content to Learn

Your child is about to begin learning about communities. In the first unit, Living in a Community, some of the topics that will be covered are:

- People in communities need to get along with one another.
- We belong to many groups.
- People share places in the neighborhood.
- You are a citizen of your city, state, and country.
- People and places change over time.
- Everyone has basic needs.

Activities to Try

- Take a walk with your child around your neighborhood or another part of your community. Together, list the shops and other businesses your family uses. Keep a list for a week of places in the neighborhood, such as the post office, the cleaners, or the market, that your family visits.
- Think of a family member, neighbor, or community worker who has lived in your community for a long time. Visit him or her with your child, and talk about how the neighborhood has changed over time. Encourage your child to ask questions about specific buildings, streets, or parks that he or she knows.
- Visit your community's Internet site to see what is featured there. (Your library has computers you can use.) If a Web site is not available, get a copy of a local newspaper and review it with your child. Invite him or her to circle all the articles or advertisements about people or places that he or she recognizes.

Ideas to Discuss

- How are people in our community the same? How are they different?
- What are some groups that each family member belongs to? What groups does the whole family belong to?
- What does it mean to be a citizen? What can citizens do to make our community a better place to live?

GO ONLINE Visit **The Learning Site** at www.harcourtschool.com/socialstudies for additional activities, primary sources, and other resources to use in this unit.

Carta para la casa

Harcourt Horizons • About My Community Unit 1 *Newsletter*

Libros

Tangle Town por Kurt Cyrus. Farrar, Straus & Giroux, 1997.

Uptown por Bryan Collier. Henry Holt, 2000.

Under the Sunday Tree por Eloise Greenfield. HarperCollins, 1990.

Halmoni's Day por Edna Coe Bercaw. Puffin, 2000.

Betty Doll por Patricia Polacco. Penguin, 2001.

Tema de estudio

Su hijo va a comenzar a estudiar sobre las comunidades. Éstos son algunos de los temas de la primera unidad titulada: Living in a Community, Vivimos en una comunidad:

- las personas en una comunidad necesitan llevarse bien.
- pertenecemos a muchos grupos.
- las personas comparten lugares en el barrio.
- tú eres un ciudadano de tu ciudad, estado y país.
- las personas y los lugares cambian con el tiempo.
- todos tenemos necesidades básicas.

Actividades

- Con su hijo, caminen por su barrio u otra parte de su comunidad. Juntos, listen las tiendas y otros negocios que usa su familia. Durante una semana, hagan una lista de los lugares que su familia visita en el barrio, como la oficina de correos, la tintorería o el supermercado.
- Piensen en un familiar, vecino o trabajador de la comunidad que haya vivido en su comunidad por mucho tiempo. Visítelo con su hijo y hablen de cómo ha cambiado el barrio con el tiempo. Anime a su hijo a hacer preguntas sobre edificios, calles o parques específicos que conozca.
- Visite el sitio de Internet de su comunidad para ver qué presentan allí. (Su biblioteca tiene computadoras que pueden usar.) Si no hay ningún sitio disponible en la web, busque una copia de un periódico local y revísela con su hijo. Invítelo a encerrar en un círculo todos los artículos o anuncios sobre las personas que reconozca.

Ideas para comentar

- ¿En qué se parecen las personas de nuestra comunidad? ¿En qué se diferencian?
- ¿Cuáles son algunos grupos a los que pertenece cada familiar? ¿A cuáles grupos pertenece toda la familia?
- ¿Qué significa ser un ciudadano? ¿Qué pueden hacer los ciudadanos para hacer de nuestra comunidad un mejor lugar para vivir?

APRENDE en línea

Visite **The Learning Site** en www.harcourtschool.com/socialstudies para obtener actividades adicionales, fuentes primarias y otros recursos para usar en esta unidad.

School to Home

Harcourt Horizons • About My Community Unit 2 *Newsletter*

Content to Learn

Your child is about to begin a social studies unit about how people govern themselves. In this unit, Our Government, some of the topics that will be covered are:

- People follow laws made by their governments.
- Towns and cities have their own governments.
- Americans choose their leaders.
- Every state has its own government.
- Our country's government has worked well for more than two hundred years.
- Americans show their patriotism in many ways.
- We can learn from people who have been good citizens.

Activities to Try

- Talk with your child about voting. Then make a family decision, such as what to have for dinner or what to do this weekend, by voting. Relate this experience to voting on community issues, state issues, and voting for the President of the United States.
- Make a replica of an American flag with your child. You can draw it using crayons and paper, or use construction paper, scissors, and glue. While you work, talk about the colors, shapes, and repeated patterns in the flag. Invite your child to decide where to display it. Then discuss how the flag and other symbols show patriotism.
- Invite your child to imagine that the two of you are the mayors of your community. List what you would do to make your community a better place to live. Then help your child read the list to other family members and have them vote for the idea they like best. You may even want to write a letter to the real mayor to tell him or her about your idea.

Ideas to Discuss

- Why do people need governments? What would happen if people did not obey the laws that governments make?
- What is democracy? Why do people like living in a democracy?
- What do good citizens do? What could you do to help others in your neighborhood?

Books to Read

Red, White, and Blue: The Story of the American Flag by John Herman. Grosset & Dunlap, 1998.

Amelia and Eleanor Go for a Ride by Pam Muñoz Ryan. Scholastic, 1999.

Purple Mountain Majesties: The Story of Katharine Lee Bates and "America the Beautiful" by Barbara Younger. NAL, 1998.

The Pledge of Allegiance by Francis Pledge of Allegiance to the Flag Bellamy. Scholastic, 2001.

GO ONLINE Visit **The Learning Site** at www.harcourtschool.com/socialstudies for additional activities, primary sources, and other resources to use in this unit.

Carta para la casa

Harcourt Horizons • About My Community Unit 2 *Newsletter*

Libros

Red, White, and Blue: The Story of the American Flag por John Herman. Grosset & Dunlap, 1998.

Amelia and Eleanor Go for a Ride por Pam Muñoz Ryan. Scholastic, 1999.

Purple Mountain Majesties: The Story of Katharine Lee Bates and "America the Beautiful" por Barbara Younger. NAL, 1998.

The Pledge of Allegiance por Francis Pledge of Allegiance to the Flag Bellamy. Scholastic, 2001.

Tema de estudio

Su hijo va a comenzar a estudiar una unidad de estudios sociales sobre cómo las personas se autogobiernan. Éstos son algunos de los temas de la segunda unidad titulada: Our Government, Nuestro gobierno:

- las personas siguen las leyes que hacen sus gobiernos.
- los pueblos y las ciudades tienen sus propios gobiernos.
- los americanos eligen a sus líderes.
- cada estado tiene su propio gobierno.
- el gobierno de nuestro país ha hecho un buen trabajo por más de doscientos años.
- los americanos muestran su patriotismo de muchas maneras.
- podemos aprender de las personas que han sido buenos ciudadanos.

Actividades

- Con su hijo, hablen sobre el voto. Luego voten para tomar una decisión familiar, como qué cenar o qué hacer este fin de semana. Relacione esta experiencia con la votación sobre temas de la comunidad, temas estatales y la elección del presidente de Estados Unidos.
- Con su hijo, haga una réplica de la bandera de Estados Unidos. Pueden dibujarla usando creyones y papel o usando cartulina, tijeras y pegamento. Mientras trabajan, hablen de los colores, las figuras y los patrones que se repiten en la bandera. Invite a su hijo a decidir dónde exhibirla. Luego comenten cómo la bandera y otros símbolos muestran patriotismo.
- Invite a su hijo a imaginarse que ustedes son los alcaldes de su comunidad. Listen lo que harían para hacer de su comunidad un mejor lugar para vivir. Luego ayude a su hijo a leer la lista a otros familiares y pedirles que voten por la idea que más les guste. Quizá quieran escribirle una carta al alcalde real para decirle su idea.

Ideas para comentar

- ¿Por qué las personas necesitan gobiernos? ¿Qué sucedería si las personas no obedecieran las leyes que hacen los gobiernos?
- ¿Qué es la democracia? ¿Por qué a las personas les gusta vivir en una democracia?
- ¿Qué hacen los buenos ciudadanos? ¿Qué podrían hacer para ayudar a los demás en su barrio?

Visite **The Learning Site** en www.harcourtschool.com/socialstudies para obtener actividades adicionales, fuentes primarias y otros recursos para usar en esta unidad.

School to Home

Harcourt Horizons • About My Community Unit 3 *Newsletter*

Books to Read

Mountain Town by Bonnie Geisert. Houghton Mifflin, 2000.

River Story by Meredith Hooper. Candlewick, 2000.

An Island Scrapbook by Virginia Wright-Frierson. Simon & Schuster, 1998.

Making the World by Douglas Wood. Simon & Schuster, 1998.

George Washington Carver by Andy Carter and Carol Saller. Carolrhoda, 2000.

Content to Learn

Your child is about to begin studying land, water, and natural resources. In this unit, Looking at the Earth, some of the topics that will be covered are:

- The land in our country has many shapes and sizes.
- Rivers and lakes are important to all parts of our country.
- Maps and globes help us locate places on Earth.
- People use natural resources to meet their needs.
- People affect the places they live in, and the places affect the people.
- We can conserve and protect our natural resources.

Activities to Try

- With your child, pretend that you are a river. Pantomime and talk about how the river looks, sounds, feels, and smells. Then take turns describing where your river starts, what it passes by, and where it ends. Tape-record or write about your imaginary journey, and share it with family members or your child's class at school.
- Go to a library to look at a globe or a map of Earth with your child. Together, identify the United States of America, bodies of water such as oceans, lakes, and major rivers, and at least two other countries. Make a list of everything your child finds on the globe or map.
- Have your child choose an item that can be recycled, such as a milk carton, can, or bottle. Together, turn it into something "new." For example, make a pencil holder from a can or a bird feeder from a milk jug. Invite your child to decorate the item. Then talk together about how to use recycled items to make simple gifts.

Ideas to Discuss

- How are lakes and ponds different from rivers and streams? Why are rivers important for transportation?
- In what ways are natural resources important to us?
- How can we care for our natural resources? What can we do at home?

GO ONLINE Visit **The Learning Site** at www.harcourtschool.com/socialstudies for additional activities, primary sources, and other resources to use in this unit.

Carta para la casa

Harcourt Horizons • About My Community Unit 4 *Newsletter*

Tema de estudio

Su hijo va a comenzar a estudiar los pueblos y sus culturas. Éstos son algunos de los temas de la cuarta unidad titulada: Learn About People, Aprendemos sobre las personas:

- en Estados Unidos viven muchos tipos de personas.
- muchas personas se han mudado a nuestro país trayendo consigo sus culturas e ideas.
- las familias pasan su cultura de padres a hijos.
- las comunidades festejan sus culturas.
- las personas expresan sus culturas mediante los cuentos y las artes.
- las ideas se difunden de un lugar a otro.

Actividades

- Lleve a su hijo al supermercado. Pasen un rato en el pasillo donde se exhiben los alimentos étnicos y hablen de los países donde estos alimentos son populares. Deje que su hijo elija un alimento barato para probarlo en la casa. A medida que prepara el alimento y comen juntos, hablen de las semejanzas y diferencias entre ese alimento y los alimentos que le gustan a su hijo.
- Investigue en la biblioteca o en los periódicos locales cualquier celebración que esté por realizarse en la que se honren otras culturas. Elija una y planee asistir con su hijo. Después pídale que dibuje algunas de las imágenes que recuerda de la celebración.
- Con su hijo, vea fotos y reliquias familiares para compartir la historia de su familia. Comenten costumbres, creencias y tradiciones que se han pasado de generación en generación en su familia. Visiten la biblioteca o usen Internet para investigar sobre el país o los países de donde provinieron sus antepasados.

Ideas para comentar

- ¿Qué necesidades básicas tienen las personas sin importar dónde viven?
- ¿Cuáles son algunas de las maneras en que las personas aprenden sobre su pasado?
- ¿Por qué una persona de otro país quisiera venir a América a vivir?

Libros

We All Sing with the Same Voice por Philip J. Miller. HarperCollins, 2001.

The Copper Tin Cup por Carole Lexa Schaefer. Candlewick Press, 2000.

Zora Hurston and the Chinaberry Tree por William Miller. Lee & Low Books, 1996.

Lord of the Cranes por Roberta Arenson. North-South, 2000.

An Amish Year por Richard Ammon. Atheneum, 2000.

APRENDE en línea

Visite **The Learning Site** en www.harcourtschool.com/socialstudies para obtener actividades adicionales, fuentes primarias y otros recursos para usar en esta unidad.

School to Home

Harcourt Horizons • About My Community Unit 5 *Newsletter*

Books to Read

Hog Music by Mary-Claire Helldorfer. Viking, 2000.

Laura Ingalls Wilder by Alexandra Wallner. Holiday House, 1997.

A Picture Book of Thurgood Marshall by David A. Adler. Holiday House, 1997.

Squanto's Journey: The Story of the First Thanksgiving by Joseph Bruchac. Silver Whistle, 2000.

Abe Lincoln Remembers by Anne Warren Turner. HarperCollins, 2001.

Content to Learn

Your child is about to begin a new social studies unit about history called Past and Present. Some of the topics that will be covered are:

- There are many ways to measure time.
- Every community has a history.
- We remember our country's history during holidays.
- Americans remember their heroes in many different ways.
- People from far away and long ago taught us many things.

Activities to Try

- Make a family project out of learning about and sharing the history of the place where you live. Each family member can choose a person, place, or thing to research. He or she can tell about the subject in a skit, a poem, a song, a drawing, or a short talk. After the presentations, be sure to share a favorite family snack together!
- With your child, create a timeline of historical events in your family, such as births, graduations, and holiday celebrations. Your child might like to illustrate some of the events on the timeline. Have him or her put the pictures in the correct order and then tell family members about each picture.
- Look at this month's calendar with your child. Take turns asking each other questions about the information on the calendar. For example, *Which month does the calendar show? How many days are in this month? What is today's date?*

Ideas to Discuss

- What makes a person a hero? Are heroes good citizens?
- Why do we celebrate Independence Day?
- What are some ways we can learn about our country's history? What person, place, or event would you like to know more about?

GO ONLINE Visit **The Learning Site** at www.harcourtschool.com/socialstudies for additional activities, primary sources, and other resources to use in this unit.

Carta para la casa

Harcourt Horizons • About My Community Unit 5 **Newsletter**

Libros

Hog Music por Mary-Claire Helldorfer. Viking, 2000.

Laura Ingalls Wilder por Alexandra Wallner. Holiday House, 1997.

A Picture Book of Thurgood Marshall por David A. Adler. Holiday House, 1997.

Squanto's Journey: The Story of the First Thanksgiving por Joseph Bruchac. Silver Whistle, 2000.

Abe Lincoln Remembers por Anne Warren Turner. HarperCollins, 2001.

Tema de estudio

Su hijo va a comenzar a estudiar una nueva unidad de estudios sociales sobre la historia titulada Past and Present, El pasado y el presente. Éstos son algunos de los temas de la quinta unidad:

- hay muchas formas de medir el tiempo.
- cada comunidad tiene una historia.
- recordamos la historia de nuestro país durante los días festivos.
- los americanos recuerdan a sus héroes de diferentes maneras.
- las personas del pasado y de tierras lejanas nos enseñaron muchas cosas.

Actividades

- Invente un proyecto familiar para aprender y compartir la historia del lugar donde vive. Cada familiar puede elegir una persona, un lugar o una cosa para investigar. Él o ella puede contar el tema con una sátira, un poema, una canción, un dibujo o una charla corta. Después de las presentaciones, ¡asegúrense de compartir juntos un bocadillo familiar favorito!
- Con su hijo, cree una línea cronológica de eventos históricos en su familia, como nacimientos, graduaciones y celebraciones de días festivos. Quizás su hijo quiera ilustrar algunos eventos en la línea cronológica. Pídale que coloque las ilustraciones en el orden correcto y que luego cuente a los familiares sobre cada ilustración.
- Observe con su hijo el calendario de este mes. Túrnense preguntándose información del calendario. Por ejemplo: ¿Qué mes muestra el calendario? ¿Cuántos días hay en este mes? ¿Qué fecha es hoy?

Ideas para comentar

- ¿Qué hace que una persona se considere un héroe? ¿Los héroes por lo general son buenos ciudadanos?
- ¿Por qué celebramos el Día de la Independencia?
- ¿Cuáles son algunas maneras en las que podemos aprender sobre la historia de nuestro país? ¿De qué persona, lugar o evento les gustaría aprender más?

Visite **The Learning Site** en www.harcourtschool.com/socialstudies para obtener actividades adicionales, fuentes primarias y otros recursos para usar en esta unidad.

School to Home

Harcourt Horizons • About My Community Unit 6 *Newsletter*

Books to Read

Just Like My Dad by Tricia Gardella. Boyds Mills Press, 2000.

Crackers by Becky Bloom. Orchard, 2001.

Walter the Baker by Eric Carle. Simon & Schuster, 1998.

Supermarket by Kathleen Krull. Holiday House, 2001.

Community Helpers by Bobbie Kalman. Crabtree, 1997.

Content to Learn

Your child is about to begin studying how people work and earn money. In this unit, People at Work, some of the topics that will be covered are:

- Everyone depends on people who provide goods and services.
- Businesses need both producers and consumers.
- Many kinds of resources are used to produce goods.
- People plan how to earn and spend their money.
- Volunteers help their community.
- People from different countries can exchange goods.

Activities to Try

- Help your child start saving money. The savings can be kept in a "piggy bank" or in an actual bank savings account. Suggest that your child choose something he or she wants to buy as a goal for saving.
- Choose a simple volunteer activity you and your child can do together. For example, you can help at a fund-raiser for your local animal shelter or school. Encourage your child to interview the director of the volunteer program to find out how its services help people in your community.
- Gather three or four of your child's favorite items, such as clothing, food, and a toy. Invite your child to guess where each item was made. Then check labels, boxes, and tags to find out. If possible, locate the countries of origin on a map or a globe. Have your child make a list of the different places where the goods came from.

Ideas to Discuss

- Many family members have jobs away from home. How are these jobs different from their jobs at home?
- What is the difference between goods and services?
- What are some goods that are made in countries other than the United States?

GO ONLINE Visit **The Learning Site** at www.harcourtschool.com/socialstudies for additional activities, primary sources, and other resources to use in this unit.

Carta para la casa

Harcourt Horizons • About My Community Unit 6 *Newsletter*

Libros

Just Like My Dad por Tricia Gardella. Boyds Mills Press, 2000.

Crackers por Becky Bloom. Orchard, 2001.

Walter the Baker por Eric Carle. Simon & Schuster, 1998.

Supermarket por Kathleen Krull. Holiday House, 2001.

Community Helpers por Bobbie Kalman. Crabtree, 1997.

Tema de estudio

Su hijo va a comenzar a estudiar cómo trabajan y ganan dinero las personas. Éstos son algunos de los temas de la sexta unidad titulada: People at Work, Las personas trabajan:

- todos dependemos de las personas que proveen bienes y servicios.
- las empresas necesitan tanto productores como consumidores.
- para producir bienes se usan muchos tipos de recursos.
- las personas pueden planear cómo ganar y gastar su dinero.
- los voluntarios ayudan a su comunidad.
- personas de diferentes países pueden intercambiar bienes.

Actividades

- Ayude a su hijo a comenzar a ahorrar dinero. Los ahorros se pueden guardar en una "alcancía" o en una cuenta de ahorros del banco. Sugiera a su hijo que elija algo que le gustaría comprar para tenerlo como una meta para ahorrar.
- Elija una actividad sencilla en la que usted y su hijo sirvan de voluntarios. Por ejemplo, pueden ayudar en una recolección de fondos para el refugio de animales local o para la escuela. Anime a su hijo a entrevistar al director del programa de voluntarios para descubrir cómo sus servicios ayudan a las personas de su comunidad.
- Reúna tres o cuatro de los objetos favoritos de su hijo, como ropa, alimentos y un juguete. Invite a su hijo a adivinar dónde se hace cada objeto. Luego revise los rótulos, las cajas y las etiquetas para descubrirlo. Si es posible, ubique los países de origen en un mapa o globo terráqueo. Pida a su hijo que haga una lista de los diferentes lugares de donde provienen los bienes.

Ideas para comentar

- Muchos familiares trabajan fuera de la casa. ¿En qué se diferencian esos trabajos de los que hacen en la casa?
- ¿Cuál es la diferencia entre bienes y servicios?
- ¿Cuáles son algunos bienes hechos en otros países, aparte de Estados Unidos?

APRENDE en línea

Visite **The Learning Site** en www.harcourtschool.com/socialstudies para obtener actividades adicionales, fuentes primarias y otros recursos para usar en esta unidad.

Index

T

U

V